The Lost Battalion and
the Meuse-Argonne, 1918

ALSO BY MICHEAL CLODFELTER
AND FROM MCFARLAND

*Warfare and Armed Conflicts: A Statistical
Encyclopedia of Casualty and Other
Figures, 1494–2007* (3d ed., 2008)

*The Dakota War: The United States Army Versus
the Sioux, 1862–1865* (1998; paperback 2006)

*Vietnam in Military Statistics: A History of the
Indochina Wars, 1772–1991* (1995)

*Mad Minutes and Vietnam Months:
A Soldier's Memoir* (1988; paperback 2011)

The Lost Battalion and the Meuse-Argonne, 1918

America's Deadliest Battle

MICHEAL CLODFELTER

McFarland & Company, Inc., Publishers
Jefferson, North Carolina, and London

The present work is a reprint, with corrections, of the illustrated case bound edition of The Lost Battalion and the Meuse-Argonne, 1918: America's Deadliest Battle, *first published in 2007 by McFarland.*

Maps by Philip Schwartzberg/Meridian Mapping, Minneapolis

LIBRARY OF CONGRESS CATALOGUING-IN-PUBLICATION DATA

Clodfelter, Micheal, 1946–
The Lost Battalion and the Meuse-Argonne, 1918 : America's deadliest battle / Micheal Clodfelter.
p. cm.
Includes bibliographical references and index.

ISBN 978-0-7864-6908-6
softcover : acid free paper ∞

1. Argonne, Battle of the, France, 1918.
2. United States. Army. Division, 77th—History. I. Title.
D545.A63C66 2012   940.4'36—dc22   2006031939

BRITISH LIBRARY CATALOGUING DATA ARE AVAILABLE

© 2007 Micheal Clodfelter. All rights reserved

No part of this book may be reproduced or transmitted in any form or by any means, electronic or mechanical, including photocopying or recording, or by any information storage and retrieval system, without permission in writing from the publisher.

Cover photograph: Ruins of Montfaucon;
carrier pigeon "Cher Ami"

Manufactured in the United States of America

*McFarland & Company, Inc., Publishers
Box 611, Jefferson, North Carolina 28640
www.mcfarlandpub.com*

To my father,
Corporal Lutie D. Clodfelter, USAAF 1942–1945,
and to my son,
Staff Sergeant Thomas D. Clodfelter, USAF 1999–2010,
who both, like the doughboys of the Great War,
answered their country's call to duty.

"Let all men pause before the picture of their high soldierly courage."
—German I Reserve Korps commander
General Richard Wellmann

Acknowledgments

First and foremost, I want to express my deep gratitude to my wife, Rena Katherine, for her indispensable assistance in preparing this book. Without her tireless help, this work of history and reflection would have been, quite literally, impossible.

Despite a few errors, the Rosetta Stone for any work on the Lost Battalion remains Thomas M. Johnson's and Fletcher Pratt's classic 1938 account, a gem of research and reportage, which benefited greatly from Johnson's interviews with the participants. Irving Werstein's 1966 *Lost Battalion*, based upon 77th Division Association letters, diaries and journals of the men of the Lost Battalion, is also important to anyone interested in the epic episode. A more recent study of the Lost Battalion is Truman and Meuse-Argonne scholar Robert Ferrell's brief but informative and well-researched 2005 book, *Five Days in October: The Lost Battalion of World War I*.

An essential reference, particularly in investigating and understanding the commander of the Lost Battalion, is the Charles White Whittlesey Collection at Williams College in Williamstown, Massachusetts. Special Collections Librarian Sylvia Kennick Brown and Whittlesey Collection archivist Heather Robertson were very helpful in my research at Williams.

The most invaluable single reference work about the overall Battle of the Meuse-Argonne and the AEF in general is *American Armies and Battlefields in Europe*, prepared in 1938 by the American Battle Monuments Commission. It is also essential to acknowledge the contributions of Lt. Colonel Taylor Beattie, whose research and expert's eye study of the battleground require one to take a fresh look at the events of October 2–7, 1918, and even consider a reappraisal and reevaluation of the Lost Battalion and its commander.

I am grateful, as well, to World War I scholar Edward Coffman for his advice when we met on the Apremont-Binarville road, concerning additional research tools in my quest to understand what happened there in the Argonne Forest.

I want to particularly thank Phil Schwartzberg, of Meridian Mapping, in Minneapolis, Minnesota, for the exceptional maps he produced for this book.

Thanks also to my sister and brother-in-law, Linda and Patrick Schmidt, who were my patient and helpful companions on my 2002 visit to many of the sites of the battles of the Meuse-Argonne and Verdun. I am indebted, as well, to military history scholar Robert Irving for his careful reading and perusal of the manuscript. I am also grateful to Vietnam War scholar and activist Leonard Magruder, who supplied me with several essential reference works to the battle and the era.

Finally, I want to express my appreciation to Curt Just—who contributed to two of my previous books—for alerting me to the existence of the Whittlesey Collection.

Contents

Acknowledgments vii
List of Maps x
Preface 1
Prologue 5

   1. The War and the Battle 13
   2. The Major and the Division 23
   3. The Offensive I 46
   4. The Battalion 90
   5. The Offensive II 164
   6. The Veterans 198
   7. Myth and Memory 211

Chapter Notes 231
Bibliography 235
Index 241

List of Maps

Western Front, Late 1918 41

German Defensive Lines in the Meuse–Argonne Region 51

Attack of the U.S. First Army, September 26, 1918 62

The "Lost Battalion," October 2–7, 1918 91

Attack of the U.S. First Army, October 4, 1918 124

Clearing of the Argonne, October 7–10, 1918 161

Attack of the U.S. First Army, October 14, 1918 180

U.S. First Army Operations, November 1–11, 1918 190

Sonnet

When you see millions of the mouthless dead
Across your dreams in pale battalions go,
Say not soft things as other men have said,
That you'll remember. For you need not so.
Give them not praise. For, deaf, how should they know
It is not curses heaped on each gashed head?
Nor tears. Their blind eyes see not your tears flow.
Nor honour. It is easy to be dead.
Say only this, 'They are dead.' Then add thereto,
'Yet many a better one has died before.'
Then, scanning all the o'ercrowded mass, should you
Perceive one face that you loved heretofore.
It is a spook. None wears the face you knew.
Great death has made all his for evermore.

—Charles Hamilton Sorley

Preface

The ordeal of the Lost Battalion was but a peal of thunder in an enduring storm, only a relatively minor incident in the greatest test of arms in American history. The forty-seven day Battle of the Meuse-Argonne, September 26–November 11, 1918, was without precedent in the sweep of America's story, and remains today, after the decades of the Second World War, Korea and Vietnam, unchallenged in the scope of its size and the scale of its statistics. No Civil War battle, not Antietam nor Gettysburg, no World War II battle, not Anzio nor Iwo Jima, approached the Argonne in its numbers engaged and its toll of American casualties. The Ardennes—the Battle of the Bulge—in the European Theater and Okinawa in the Pacific Theater were great consumers of American lives, but even those great factories of fatality produced less carnage for America (although Okinawa, with its enemy toll of 110,000 Japanese military and 77,000 Okinawan civilian lives, was far bloodier in total casualties for all combatants).

The month-long Battle of the Bulge, December 16, 1944–January 16, 1945, cost the U.S. 80,987 casualties, including 10,276 battle deaths. The three months required by American forces to conquer Okinawa, April 1–June 22, 1945, witnessed the battle deaths of 12,281 American servicemen and a total U.S. casualty list of 49,151. But the human cost for the Meuse Valley and the Argonne Forest exceeded any price America has had to pay for any other extended piece of real estate on the planet—over 127,000 combat casualties, including 26,277 combat deaths. Over 6,000 khaki-clad Americans died in the Argonne in the first week of October 1918 alone. Every day of the ninety-three days of the Battle of Okinawa cost an average of 132 American lives. The daily average on Iwo Jima for twenty-six days was 267. In the Bulge 321 Americans died on average for each of the thirty-two days of the battle. But in the Meuse-Argonne, doughboy deaths per day for forty-seven days averaged 558.

So many other statistical comparisons pale when placed next to the staggering toll of the Meuse-Argonne. The deadliest *year* for the United States in the Vietnam War was 1968, when 14,589 Americans died in battle, not much more than half the number of doughboys slain in less than seven weeks in the Argonne. Battle deaths in Southeast Asia from 1961–75 totaled 47,357, not even twice the toll of America's last battle—the Meuse-Argonne—in the last weeks of the Great War. Three years in the frozen hell and fearsome heat of Korea, 1950–53, took 33,686 American lives in battle. America won its independence in exchange for 6,824 battle deaths in eight years of conflict with the British Empire. The United States in 1846–48 won from Mexico one-quarter of its national territory, including California and most of the Southwest, at a cost of 1,733 battle dead. The U.S. in 1918 won (back for France) a few score square miles of tangled, thorny, shell-cratered forest, valley and hill at a cost fifteen times higher.

The magnitude of the Meuse-Argonne for the U.S. can best be statistically summarized by comparing the battle to the war in which it occurred. By Armistice Day, 29 U.S. divisions and 2,057,675 American servicemen had been deployed to France. Twenty-two of those divisions and 1,256,478 of those soldiers and Marines had passed through the Argonne and the rolling countryside fifteen miles on east to the Meuse River. In the nineteen months that America was at war—April 1917 to November 1918—53,513 American military personnel had died in battle, most of them in the five-plus months of major U.S. combat, June to November 1918. (The average death toll per day of U.S. involvement in the Great War was 195, but from June to November 1918 the daily average was 820—compared to a per-day average of 123 U.S. battle dead in World War II.) Almost half of the U.S. battle dead had fallen in forty-seven days in the fourteen-mile-deep cauldron of the Meuse-Argonne front. Nearly 100,000 of the 204,000 U.S. wounded earned their wound stripes in the Meuse-Argonne.

Though the U.S. Congress had declared war on April 6, 1917, it took the better part of a year to mobilize, train and deploy the American Expeditionary Forces to the Western Front. The first doughboys to die in France fell seven months later on November 3, 1917, and the first real battle for the AEF of any size larger than a trench raid did not come until April 20, 1918, at Seicheprey in Lorraine, where 81 Americans were killed. More than 20,000 doughboys and leathernecks died at Cantigny, Belleau Wood, St. Mihiel, Soissons and many another moonscape battlefield along the Western Front from late May to late September 1918. But if John J. Pershing and the AEF had not undertaken the Meuse-Argonne Offensive, World War I would have taken fewer American lives in combat than did either Korea or Vietnam.

Only when compared to the greatest battles of the Great War and World War II's Russian Front are the numbers of the Meuse-Argonne less likely to shock. The deadliest day in French military history, August 22, 1914, during the Battles of the Frontiers, cost the lives of 27,000 soldiers in French blue, a toll slightly higher than that for the U.S. in forty-seven days in the Argonne. The British Empire lost nearly as many dead—19,240—on the first day of the Battle of the Somme, July 1, 1916, as the U.S. did in seven weeks in the Argonne. Total causalities for the 132 days of the Somme, July 1–November 18, 1916, were 434,500 German, 415,690 British, and 202,567 French. The ten months of the Battle of Verdun in 1916 cost as many as 542,000 French and 434,000 German casualties. A million or more Soviet and Axis troops were killed, wounded or reported missing on the Stalingrad front from August 1942 to February 1943. But for the U.S., there never was and there never would be (up to this writing, at least) a greater bloodletting than the Battle of the Meuse-Argonne. And if one subtracted the 57,000 casualties of the first day of the Somme, U.S. losses in the Meuse-Argonne were proportionately more heavy than British losses were on the Somme and certainly heavier on a per day basis than were French casualties at Verdun.

And yet, despite this crushing statistical weight, this mountain that makes into molehills almost all other American battles, the Meuse-Argonne is a surprisingly obscure battle to most Americans. It is largely unheralded, uncelebrated and unmourned. But battles such as Bunker Hill, the Alamo, and the Little Bighorn, with numbers that are negligible compared to the Meuse-Argonne, are entrenched in the popular culture and imagination as martial icons.

Of course, far more than the amount of cannon fodder hurled into combat and the sheer volume of blood expended influences the degree of lasting fame or infamy achieved by any particular battle.

A battle's renown is enhanced by a quality of decisiveness, of representing a turning point—a Yorktown winning independence, a Gettysburg marking the high tide of the Confederacy, a Midway reversing the Japanese tide of conquest in the Pacific. Though the Meuse-Argonne was not one of history's decisive battles, nor the contest that broke the back of the kaiser's army, neither was it one of those profitless slaughters so common to the Western Front, in which a few square miles of mud were exchanged for tens of thousands of casualties. Indeed, it was part of the Allied general offensive from July to November 1918 that ended the war and made the "World safe for Democracy."

The legacy left by any particular battle is also influenced by the American reverence for individual heroism or celebrity. A hero or two (or an appealing villain) will always enhance a battle's reputation. We remember the Alamo as much for Davy Crockett and Jim Bowie (and Santa Ana) as for the fight to the death of 183 Texans. The Battle of the Little Bighorn is (erroneously) labeled just as often the "Custer Massacre" because the cavalier colonel who led the 7th Cavalry to disaster has become an American icon.

The more than one million American veterans of the Meuse-Argonne included more heroes and famous names than did any other battle in American history. The most famous enlisted man in U.S. military history, Sergeant Alvin York, performed his feats of daring and valor in the Argonne Forest. Eddie Rickenbacker's Spad biplane dueled with German triplanes above the Argonne treetops. Douglas MacArthur won the Distinguished Service Cross while leading a brigade of the 42nd "Rainbow" Division against the Côte de Châtillon in the Meuse-Argonne. George Patton led his tank brigade into the battle and Harry Truman his artillery battery. George C. Marshall, as an operations officer in the U.S. First Army, planned much of the offensive. Many more of the future American leaders of World War II saw their baptisms of fire in the Argonne.

Moments or incidents of high drama or, at least, high pluck, add to a battle's name recognition as well—John Paul Jones proclaiming, "I have not yet begun to fight!" as the *Bonhomme Richard* sank beneath his feet; Pickett's Charge at Gettysburg; Teddy Roosevelt leading the Rough Riders up San Juan Hill; General McAuliffe's reply of "Nuts" to the German surrender demand at Bastogne.

The Meuse-Argonne was replete with drama and incident—the carrier pigeon Cher Ami's wounded flight to save an American battalion from destruction, the whole riveting saga of the Lost Battalion, the exploits of Sgt. York, Patton's 1st Tank Brigade, the Rainbow Division at Côte de Châtillon, the tragedy and triumph of the all-African American regiments in their first major combat since the Civil War.

But for all the unequaled numbers, all the famous names and dramatic events, and the stark and overwhelming fact that more American servicemen died violently along the seventeen miles of front between the Argonne Forest and the Meuse River than at any other place on earth, Americans today are more familiar with the skirmish on Lexington Green and, for that matter, the Gunfight at the OK Corral, than with the Meuse-Argonne.

Why the Meuse-Argonne has failed to seize and hold America's imagination is puzzling. In this land where sensation and celebrity rule the realm and the media is kingmaker, maybe the Battle of the Meuse-Argonne has faded from our national memory simply because it did not receive enough media attention over the long run. Not enough memoirs and novels and histories, and, above all, movies and television treatments, have been written or produced about the battle to make it stick to memory. In a century of accelerating (and usually horrendous) events, and in a culture that lives for the moment (or the future) and lacks such reverence for the past typical of more elderly cultures, America has passed through and quickly shrugged off one experience after another, with eyes firmly locked on the newest tragedy or sensation. The newest thing is the all-consuming thing and all sense of proportion is scorned. We are a nation fascinated by current events and bored by history. In a short-attention-span culture, we are easily distracted by the latest happening, and only the largest events can cling steadfastly to our sense of remembrance. Because the largest event in human history—World War II—occurred just two decades after the Armistice, the great "distant" events we do recall are those, not of the Great War, but of the later conflict born of that war.

In the six decades since VE Day, an unending stream of World War II books continues to roll off the presses and the occasional Second World War movie continues to appear on the big screen. Though prolific in the two decades between the world wars, American books and movies about the Twentieth Century's first global conflict have, since 1945, dried to a trickle (in America). The story of the Lost Battalion was the single most celebrated episode of the war for the AEF, but, until 2001, only a single silent movie, produced in 1919, was made about the event, while, until 2005, the last major book about Major Whittlesey's command appeared in 1938.

It was not as if the great contest in the Argonne and the siege of the Lost Battalion, in particular, passed without notoriety in its time and in the two decades that followed. In the interval between the two global cataclysms, no American battle was more famous, and on the peak of that fame stood the story of the Lost Battalion. But then Pearl Harbor and Midway and Guadalcanal and Omaha Beach flamed in succession to absorb American blood and American attention. Those days endured by a doughboy battalion in the tangled scrub of a French forest a quarter of a century before faded from the nation's collective memory and remained important only to the veterans who had lain in mud and bramble beneath a shrapnel sky.

Nearly ninety years later, the Lost Battalion is "lost" once again—not, this time, in the tangles of the Argonne, but in the mists of memory. May this book aid in a second rescue to free those brave men, not from German steel, as in 1918, but from the negligence of passing time.

Prologue

None of his fellow passengers aboard the white-hulled S.S. *Toloa* suspected there was anything wrong with the most famous man aboard ship. They had not detected doom in his eyes nor despair in his demeanor. He had, in fact, been uncharacteristically voluble that evening, chatting with the captain at dinner about the Army-Navy football game and reminiscing about the war with a Puerto Rican businessman named Maloret for two hours over drinks in the ship's saloon.

Perhaps all the talk had been a final accounting. Perhaps it was a self-delivered eulogy that seemed at the time to be no more than casual conversation with his steamship companions. Perhaps he was expressing what he had been unable to express for three years, releasing himself with words from what he would shortly be releasing himself with action for all eternity.

But the only hint of his intention came when the hero rose from the saloon table to abruptly announce his retirement for the night. Then Lieutenant Colonel Charles White Whittlesey, the thirty-seven-year-old former commander of the "Lost Battalion" and Medal of Honor-winning hero of America's greatest battle, weaved his way, not to his cabin, but out onto the deserted deck, climbed over the railing, and leaped into the pale moonlight and dark water.

The weather had been wet and chilly when the *Toloa* had sailed at midnight, November 25, 1921, from its home port of New York City for a two-week Caribbean cruise. By the following evening, however, the sea was placid, the moon and stars shone brightly, and no clouds obscured the night sky as the passenger-freighter steamed at fourteen knots about 400 miles south of New York.

After dinner, Captain Farquah H. Grant, cigar in hand, had climbed to the bridge. Taking advantage of their nautical locale beyond the three-mile limit where Prohibition no longer reigned, most of the passengers were drinking and dancing to a four-piece band playing such tunes as "Peggy O'Neill," "Ain't We Got Fun," and "When Francis Dances with Me." One of the most well-received tunes of the evening was the wartime hit "Good-bye Broadway," which many of the veterans in the passenger lounge sang along to:

> Good-bye Broadway, Hello France
> We're ten million strong ...
> Good-bye Broadway, Hello France
> We're here to help you win this war.

Early in the evening, Whittlesey had avoided the gaiety, sitting alone at a small table in a corner of the lounge. He had been the center of attention at the embarkation, but now he sat undisturbed. Those who noticed him saw a man long-jawed and long-boned, with eyes behind silver-framed spectacles seeming to stare intently inward or at his hands, interlaced in a white-knuckle knot on the tabletop. Though without a companion, his lips were moving, as if carrying on an interior monologue with his memories.

Later this melancholy mood had lifted—maybe with some sort of reconciling peace he had finally negotiated with those memories—and he had joined his shipmates in conversation and conviviality. But it was to be his last worldly contact.

The day following, November 27, whipped up rough waters, and most of the 136 passengers remained in their staterooms as the four-year-old, 6,500 ton United Fruit-owned steamer plowed through the Atlantic waves toward Havana, Cuba. But on Monday the absence of the man who had been the first in the American Expeditionary Forces to be formally awarded the Medal of Honor was noted by Maloret. A search by the purser and Captain Grant of the unlocked cabin revealed an unslept-in bed, eight letters to family and friends, and a note to the captain of the *Toloa* advising him, in detail, on the disposition of the baggage left in the cabin. Though Captain Grant conducted a search for the missing hero that brought his ship twelve hours late into Havana, the sea surrendered no solution.

Though Whittlesey's body, never recovered, rested not under a stone cross along with tens of thousands of his comrades in the well-tended U.S. cemeteries in France but in some unknown league of sea between the Atlantic and the Caribbean, there is little doubt that he was a casualty—one of the last—of the Battle of the Meuse-Argonne. There is indeed some mystery in the exact motives of Whittlesey's suicide, but the source of his self-destruction almost certainly sprang from the five days spent along tiny Charlevaux Brook deep in the Argonne Forest, five days that brought him public acclaim and private agony.

The acclaim, at the time, far overshadowed that of the now much more famous Sergeant York. It arose from (then) Major Whittlesey's leadership of a mixed unit from one machine gun and two infantry battalions of the U.S. 77th Division—mislabeled by the media as the "Lost Battalion"—as it lay surrounded and under siege in the Argonne, October 2–7, 1918. The scarecrow-statured, bespectacled Whittlesey looked more like what he was before the guns had sounded—a Wall Street lawyer—than anyone's idea of a steel-willed combat commander. But, in those days trapped in what was called the Pocket, the major had proven, to nearly everyone but himself, that what he might lack in experience and tactical finesse he more than made up for with dogged determination and inspired example. General Pershing had dubbed him one of the AEF's "three outstanding heroes."[1]

The stand of the Lost Battalion was only a tiny part of a battle so vast in violence and bloodshed that it has never been surpassed in American history. It was, however, the most famous incident in the great battle, the one that fathers told their children about, the one that was small enough in scale and intimate enough in exciting detail to capture public fancy. In an Industrial Age war of assembly line butchery, romantic tales of martial glory were hard to separate from the generalized slaughter. As the commander of the fabled battalion, Whittlesey was the romantic symbol of a story that could be conceptualized and absorbed by a public traumatized by the awful totality of total war.

For the major, however, there was no romance, there was no glory. Heroic though he most certainly was, he was not a "hero" in the celebrity sense of the word. Far too introverted and introspective to luxuriate in the role of public hero, Whittlesey absorbed none of the praising words of the hero worshipers, but all of the nagging doubts of the few naysayers and the much more monumental doubts of his own conscience.

Some hint of that inner turmoil that carried him over the railing of the *Toloa* was revealed in the letters left behind and in notes and comments he wrote and rendered to friends and colleagues in the weeks leading up to his suicide. Whittlesey had so wanted to wake up from the bad dream of the war and wash away the memories of combat in the warm bath of re-emergence into his prior life and pre-war legal practice. But a hero is no longer his own man. He is a commodity to be brought forth for war bond drives, for ceremonies to honor the returning soldiers and those who would not return, to be feted and paraded. Whittlesey wanted to say no, to turn down the incessant demands on his time and temperament. But the same sense of duty that saw him through those days in the Pocket now required him to relive that ordeal again and again, even as he was being honored for it. It wore him down and, finally, it wore him out.

The letters he wrote and the actions he took in the days prior to boarding the *Toloa* verify that Whittlesey's last leap was no impulsive act. He had put his affairs in order. Having paid his landlady the next month's rent, he had told her, "You had better cash this right away."[2]

Whittlesey had tied up loose ends on pending litigation at his firm and concluded the paperwork with a cryptic note, "I shall not return."[3] He had also drafted a will. The short document left most of what he possessed, including his Medal of Honor, to his mother, and made provision for payment of his brother Melzar's debts from the $1,000 in cash he left. To his law partner and closest friend J. Bayard Pruyn, Whittlesey left his Cross of the Legion of Honor. The original copy of the German surrender demand that he had ignored while clinging to the slopes above Charlevaux Brook he passed on to his second-in-command, George McMurtry, who in turn gave it to Whittlesey's father. (The document eventually became part of the Whittlesey Collection in the Williams College archives.)

The letters left behind were addressed to Pruyn, McMurtry and two other friends, Robert Forsyth Little and Herman Livingston Jr., as well as to his parents, his brothers Melzar and Elisha, and his Uncle Granville Whittlesey. The recipients of Whittlesey's missives agreed to keep the contents confidential. The four friends issued a joint statement, printed in the *New York Times* on December 9, 1921, "The letters contain only personal farewells and in no instance attempt to explain the reason for his departure.... He was a battle casualty."[4]

The family members also closed ranks and maintained a privacy for the last written words of an intensely private man who had been deprived of his solitude since the Armistice. When pressed years later to reveal the contents of the letter he received, brother Melzar claimed to have deposited it in his safe unopened. He ended the discussion by stating, "If my brother couldn't tell me himself why he did it, I don't want to know. You must consider him to be a war casualty. I will divulge nothing further, either at this time or in the future. No, now that you have reminded me of it, I think I'll destroy it tonight."[5]

Robert Little did reveal to reporters that "He was a victim engulfed in a sea of woes. His last work as chairman of the Red Cross Roll Call this month was all based on the suffering of the wounded. He would go to two or three funerals every week, and visit the wounded in the hospitals, and try to comfort the relatives of the dead."[6]

Not until 1982 was the contents of one of the letters made available to the public. Pruyn's letter was donated to Williams College, Whittlesey's alma mater. In it, Whittlesey designated Pruyn as the executor of his estate and detailed the disposition of both that estate and his personal effects. The letter opened with, "Just a note to say good-bye. I'm a misfit by nature and by training, and there's an end to it." It concluded: "I won't try to say anything personal, Bayard, because you and I understand each other. Give my love to Edith [Pruyn's wife]."[7]

The Lost Battalion commander's spoken and written words were less reticent in his last months than those written on his last day. Comments to friends and colleagues parted the curtains concealing a deep depression in a man not given to emotional excursions in public.

Early on, Whittlesey had professed to a more positive view of his time in the Argonne. In a letter written less than a week after his battalion had been relieved at its position near Charlevaux Mill, Whittlesey wrote to Max Berking, a college friend from his Williams days:

> I appreciate your last letter; if I said it any other way I'd be trying to put into words what I cannot write.
> Because out here in the woods, Max, where the hidden things of life begin to show, one learns new things. Friendships that can reach across five thousand miles and jog your elbow becomes pretty real and fine. And believe me, I felt your cheery voice when that letter reached me, at the end of a day that had been—oh well "some digging."
> It's a great life. Finest thing in the world, and we'll never have the same small outlook on men when it's over. Some of these fellows are just finer than anyone can say.[8]

Whittlesey's view of the men he commanded and the men with whom he served lost much of its luster after demobilization and his vain attempts to regain the comforting anonymity of his previous life. He became a magnet for 77th Division veterans and other returning doughboys, his office sometimes seeming to be more a job placement center than legal chambers. Those not seeking help in finding employment came seeking solace or advice from their old CO (commanding officer) and comrade in arms. He could not deny them his time and compassion. His sense of duty did not end on November 11, nor did his devotion to these men expire with the shipboard sighting of the Statue of Liberty.

"I wish they would let me forget," Whittlesey wrote on August 12, 1921, to Major Scott, commander of the Third Battalion of the 308th Infantry Regiment (Whittlesey's regiment) in the Argonne. "Not a day goes by but I hear from some of my old outfit, usually about some sorrow or misfortune ... I cannot bear much more. I want to be left in peace."[9]

But they would not let him forget; they could not leave him in peace.

When not badgered by the personal pleas of old comrades, Whittlesey was bedeviled by official functions that he so desired to avoid but could not refuse. The iron clasp of conscience, the dictates of duty required him to make this speech or render that appearance. Though mild compared to today's media circus attending celebrityhood, the public appetite for the hero on display seemed insatiable to Whittlesey.

He turned down all requests for paid appearances from lecture bureaus and other such organizations that he saw as little better than carnival circuits presenting freak shows to hero-hungry audiences. "I am a lawyer, not a professional war hero," Whittlesey declared. "What does it all matter now? I want to forget the war."[10]

Whittlesey was more receptive, if reluctantly so, to appeals for appearances and speeches from veterans' groups, charity drives and service organizations. His speeches, however, were often disappointing to crowds anxious to hear exciting and blood-curdling details of the days in the Pocket and of feats of valor. Whittlesey was not interested in reliving the Argonne and revisiting his hours of glory. Instead he talked in general terms of the bravery and dedication of the common doughboy, and asked his audience to remember their sacrifice.

The first audience to hear praise of the anonymous foot soldier instead of self-glorification was alumni of Williams College. Whittlesey had hardly returned to the U.S., three days after the Armistice was signed, and barely had time to visit his parents before his Williams classmates began to pester him to appear at the Williams Club "War Night" in New York City on November 21, 1918. His acceptance guaranteed a packed house of over 300 Williams men. The small clubroom was too cozy for the crowd, so the event was held in the building's main hall, with people spilling into the vestibule and up onto the stairways.

The reception and dinner had the atmosphere of a football game between Williams and Amherst (according to the January 12, 1919, *Syracuse Post-Standard*). Whittlesey's fellow guest speaker, Zo Elliot of the Signal Corps, had composed the Great War song "The Long, Long Trail." With a chorus of six doughboy veterans, he sang that standard, along with the "Marseillaise," the "Star-Spangled Banner" and the Williams College fight song, "The Mountains." Club president F.T. Woods gave the introduction, during which he spoke of Whittlesey's already famous, but apocryphal, reply of "Go to Hell" to the German surrender demand. "It was a command, a malediction, and a prophecy combined."[11] This brought on a five-minute cheer, more Williams songs, and then cheering again.

Whittlesey, however, was hardly the man to play cheerleader to this patriotic pep rally. The Lost Battalion was AWOL from his ensuing speech, in which he praised the kindness of French civilians toward the doughboys and the top notch training by French military men given to American soldiers. He spoke of other Williams men at the front, and particularly of Captain Belvidere Brooks of Whittlesey's 308th Infantry, who was "our best officer—far and away the best captain we had," and who had spoken at the Williams Club, along with Whittlesey, in the spring of 1918 before shipping over and dying in battle.[12]

Most of all, Whittlesey extolled the virtues of the enlisted ranks. "You don't hear enough of the enlisted men in France. I'm afraid we didn't think much about them at first. They were just ordinary American boys when they went over, but now they've changed and the officers have adopted a different attitude towards them. I can't describe the fondness that we acquired for them as we saw them day after day doing their work without complaint. It makes you proud of America to think of these common soldiers of ours."

In his single oblique reference to his own awarded exploits, Whittlesey redirected all credit to the common doughboy. "And remember that those who have been picked out for special praise are the symbols of the men behind them. No man ever does anything alone. It's the chaps you don't hear about that makes possible the deeds you do hear about."[13]

With a melancholy look at the men who represented the placid years before his charge into the Argonne and into fame, Whittlesey concluded, "It's fine to be here and see all these friendly faces again."

As he sat down, a visitor from Cornell University raised the pom-poms again by shouting out, "But did you tell them to go to hell?"

Whittlesey, without enthusiasm, finally gave the crowd what it wanted and nodded his head in affirmation, striking his only false note of the evening. This one scrap, however, was not enough red meat. Several Williams men yelled, "But did they go?" Whittlesey's response, whatever it was, went unheard as a hundred voices thundered, "They sure did."[14]

Whittlesey's next major public appearance was before an audience more suited to his demeanor, the opening of the Union Peace Jubilee at New York's 69th Regimental Armory, attended by 6,000 members of the city's six largest Episcopalian congregations. The main speaker was Secretary of the Treasury William F. McAdoo, a future Democratic presidential candidate. Whittlesey, six foot three but slender of build and a little stoop-shouldered, attracted little attention as he sat on the speakers' platform next to McAdoo. Few in the crowd recognized the scholarly looking fellow as the foremost American military hero of the Great War. The surprise was audible when this modest-looking man was introduced as the gallant commander of the Lost Battalion, but the reception was no less overwhelming as the crowd rose to its feet for a three-minute standing ovation. Whittlesey fidgeted uncomfortably while waiting for the cheers to subside.

The chairman had described Whittlesey as a modern-day Cincinnatus "who had laid aside his sword to go back to the pursuit of peace."[15] Whittlesey struck no Roman posture, nor did he deliver a Ciceronian oration. But he did render a passionate plea for tolerance and forgiveness.

"American soldiers are not going to come back hating Germans. No man who has been out in the front line trenches is going to return with malice in his heart." He pointed out that because America and Americans had played a decisive role in ending the Great War, and because they had suffered far less grievously than the Allies, they were better able to assume a benevolent attitude toward the defeated enemy and work for a world that worshiped justice instead of power.

"I am not criticizing the foreign officers and men who suffered so terribly before we entered the war," he emphasized. "Never in any one generation have so many men suffered such keen hardships as they did. It would be a shame to sacrifice the separate immunity from hatred as our special privilege. Mind you, I do not want to let the Germans off too easily. I merely want to see justice done. Germany after the war, it must be remembered, is going to be part of our world community."[16]

Though his speech had been vigorously applauded for the most part, Whittlesey's call for justice rather than vengeance was met with silence. The assemblage had gathered to celebrate the return of peace, but for many in the crowd, a "peace with a vengeance" was obviously more to their liking than Whittlesey's call for compassion.

Whittlesey probably did not make another speech or perform another public duty that did not chip away at his composure or deepen his depression. In August 1921, after his old regiment, the 308th Infantry, became part of the Organized Reserve, Whittlesey was offered the regimental colonelcy. Once again duty issued its demands. Though he complained, "They're always after me about the war. I've got to help some soldier or make some speech or something. I used to think I was a lawyer; now I don't know what I am," he took the post and made the speech and helped the soldier—and sunk deeper into depression.[17]

After accepting yet another post as chairman of the New York Red Cross Roll Call and delivering another speech at a fund raiser later in 1921, Whittlesey told Major Francis M. Weld, "With all these distractions, how do you get through the day? Raking over the ashes like this revives all the horrible memories. I'll hear the wounded screaming again. I have nightmares about them. I can't remember when I last had a good night's sleep."[18]

On November 11, 1921, the third anniversary of the Armistice, Whittlesey was summoned to Arlington National Cemetery, where he served as one of thirty pallbearers, all Medal of Honor winners (including Sergeant York), at the entombment of the Unknown Soldier. He sat impassively beside his Lost Battalion comrades (and fellow Medal of Honor recipients) George McMurtry and Nelson Holderman, but said little and reacted minimally to the ceremonies, broadcast over the radio and featuring a speech by President Harding.

To one of the honorees, Whittlesey did confide, "I keep wondering if the Unknown

Soldier is one of my men killed in the Pocket. I should not have come. It has been too unnerving."[19]

On the 20th he shared a stage at the Hippodrome in New York with the supreme Allied commander, Marshal Ferdinand Foch, and a coterie of armless and legless veterans. Events such as these, that would have produced pride and gratification for most men, only widened the hollow place inside the colonel. To family inquiries about how he felt about these accumulating honors, Whittlesey could only respond that they had "made a deep impression."[20]

After visiting his ailing mother during the weekend, Whittlesey applied himself to a difficult legal case. On Wednesday afternoon, November 23, Whittlesey lunched with Fitzhugh McGrew of the law firm of White and Case, and they conversed about, among other topics, Egyptian funeral practices. He dictated a one-page will at his firm, then told his colleagues that he planned to revisit his parents over the Thanksgiving weekend. A friend later commented, "I think that was about the only lie Charlie ever told in his whole life."[21] Friday evening he escorted a lady friend to a Broadway show. Before midnight on November 25, without a word of farewell to anyone, he boarded the *Toloa* to put an end to his torment.

Most of Whittlesey's family and friends were perceptive enough to understand that the private and public rehashing of the five days in the forest were a drain on the colonel's emotional resources. But, apparently, no one had realized the degree of his despondency and they were, one and all, shocked by the path he took to find peace. Certainly, they knew that, three years on, a large part of Whittlesey yet remained in the mud and muck of the Argonne. Though unscarred by bullet or shrapnel, they knew that his body still bore a physical manifestation of his days in the Pocket, as evidenced by a racking cough from gas-damaged lungs that could be clearly heard by his fellow boarders through the thin walls of his bachelor quarters. But, because he remained so close-lipped and closed-off about his experiences in the Argonne, no one, it appeared, was aware of how extensive his emotional wounds from the battle were. McMurtry, who should have sensed better than anyone the depth of Whittlesey's despair, reported, in fact, that on a stopover in Atlantic City after the Washington dedication, his old friend and comrade seemed positively cheerful.

After the suicide, it seemed to family and friends that the cross of celebrity could not have been so heavy that its weight alone would have been reason enough to cast it off by such drastic action. It seemed then—and it seems now—that more had to trouble Whittlesey than just some inability to deal with his memories of the war and his—undeserved to himself—elevation to the status of an idol of American fighting manhood. To understand what may have motivated Whittlesey as he stood at the railing of the *Toloa*, one must look more closely at the man, his times, and at the great battle that made him famous and ultimately cost him his life.

1

The War and the Battle

Let us begin with a flight of fancy, an alternative Twentieth Century uncrippled by the fateful and near fatal outbreak of the Great War. It is autumn 1989 and the old kingdoms and ancient empires that have held sway and held back the future for so many centuries are finally crumbling under both the weight of their own contradictions and the power of a mighty modern wind blowing over the hollow monarchial edifices. There have been brief balance-of-power wars and sporadic uprisings by the disgruntled and the have-nots in the nine decades of the century, but the old empires have changed just enough with the times to stay ahead of modernity's gathering tides and to hold Europe and the world together in their palsied hands. The future, finally, cannot be denied, but it has been delayed long enough to be ushered in on the shoulders of a relatively benign peoples' revolution, rather than on the back of a beast of total war and genocidal tyranny. There have been minor wars, but no Great War; there have been popular uprisings, but no October Revolution; there have been riots and pogroms, but no Holocaust.

The last century of violence and tragedy has been marked by moments in which a twist or a change in a single event could have decisively turned our times away from the path of totalitarianism, genocide, global war and superpower confrontation. If only the Bolsheviks had been repulsed in their attack on the Winter Palace; if only a bullet had found Hitler during the Beer Hall Putsch in Munich in 1923; if only another bullet had missed its target in Dallas in 1963. How much of the turmoil and bloodshed that followed from those events could have been avoided? And could the whole century, the bloodiest in human history, been altered or avoided entirely if the event that effectively began it had turned out differently?

Historically, the Twentieth Century began not on January 1, 1900 (or January 1, 1901), but on June 28, 1914, when the Austrian archduke Franz Ferdinand and his wife, Sofie, were assassinated in Sarajevo, Bosnia. Ironically, the century ended with more violence in Sarajevo as a direct result of the death of European Communism and the breakup of the Soviet Empire in 1991. But what if all that had come between could have been altered for the better (it could hardly have been altered for the worse) if Gavrilo Princip had missed his target on that June day?

Because so many of the great events of the Twentieth Century up to and including the fall of Soviet Communism and the end of the Cold War can be traced back to the courses and consequences of the First World War, would not the world be greatly different had the spark that set off the explosion been snuffed. Had Franz Ferdinand survived would not the chances for a century of peace and progress—instead of war and the threat of war—been greatly increased?

Russia's disastrous defeats in the Great War led to the October Revolution and then on to Stalinism, the Gulag and, ultimately, the Cold War and its hot war offspring in Korea and Vietnam. Germany's humiliations and hardships imposed by World War I and the Peace of Versailles brought on Hitler, the Holocaust, World War II and an Iron Curtain drawn down on Eastern Europe.

The guns of August so violently twisted history and man's once hopeful view of the future that it required more than seven decades for the world to struggle free of its results. Between Waterloo and the Marne, Europe enjoyed a century without general warfare, and most people who glanced into the future saw mankind marching up a steady incline toward social and political progress that would match the scientific and technological progress so abundant in the Nineteenth Century. But a Serbian assassin sent the world skidding down a slippery slope toward a nuclear chasm.

Without the vast charnel houses of the Great War that so sickened man's collective psyche and soured his soul, maybe the world would have turned a deaf ear to the prophets of extremism who turned the century into an age of ideology that murdered millions. Man, being the fractious creature that he is, would still have had his wars and rumors of wars, but without ideology to fuel them and the madmen leaders produced by those ideologies to direct them, the wars would have more than likely remained localized and limited. Without the poisons of pessimism and fanaticism that flowed from a generation of corpses from Verdun to Gallipoli, maybe man would have pursued moderation instead of zealotry and would have employed compromise and conciliation instead of total power and total war to solve his many problems.

Of course it can be argued that the entangling alliances that ensnared Europe at the turn of the century would have eventually produced a crisis that would have touched off a general European war, even if Franz Ferdinand and his wife would have left Sarajevo in perfect health. But history, like evolution, is a series of accidents that require a unique set of circumstances to give birth to a new species or a new direction.

A thermonuclear war between NATO and the Warsaw Pact seemed inevitable for forty years, but that most mutant creature of all never appeared. A half a dozen crises from Morocco to the Balkans threatened war between the Triple Entente and the Triple Alliance, but all fizzled out until Princip fired his pistol. Without those first two killings in a century of killings, might man have fulfilled the Nineteenth Century prophecies of peace and prosperity and avoided the trenches, the ovens and the bomb? Might we have escaped the Twentieth Century?

But, of course, the fatal bullet was fired, and an Austrian archduke, as well as the German, Austro-Hungarian, Russian and Ottoman empires, all died. The Great War, and all in its wake, happened, and lives everywhere, both of the great and the small, were disrupted, disfigured or destroyed. A quirk of fate, a twist in time, and the world on June 28, 1914, was set on a seemingly inalterable and cataclysmic course. This seminal event affected man's time on earth probably more than any other in history, and would, in addition to its myriad other consequences beyond count, bring a million American soldiers into the Meuse Valley and the Argonne Forest, and Major Charles Whittlesey and 553 men of the U.S. 77th Division into a place called the Pocket on the banks of Charlevaux Creek.

The Great War gave birth to a century of great disasters unmatched in human history. The horror of the Twentieth Century can be said to have been conceived in 1870 with the Ems Telegraph and the outbreak of the Franco-Prussian War, and to have been born June 28, 1914, at Sarajevo. World War I was the formative event of the Twentieth Century. No event and certainly no war has ever had as fundamental an impact on history. We are all—individually and collectively—what the Great War wrought. The First World War was the midwife to all the mutant monsters sired by the century.

The greatest tragedy of the most tragic of all centuries—the Twentieth—was not the deaths of millions in war, revolution and genocide, not the deaths of civilizations, but the death of idealism. Idealism evolved and hardened into ideology in the Nineteenth Century and reached its apogee and abyss in the Great War and in the decades following. It breathed its last on Christmas Day 1991, when the Soviet Union, the greatest hope and the greatest failure of idealism, folded its flag. The ideological regimes that sprouted from the soil of the world war were, for many, for awhile, bright lights cutting through the fog of war. But the Great War had so brutalized the culture and conscience of Western man that what began in dream ended in nightmare.

Hitler was but the bottom of the chasm carved out by the Great War. A great many of the political and military leaders of the Second World War, starting with the Austrian corporal, were combat veterans of the First. World War II set records unmatched in human history for atrocity, war crimes, massacre and cruelty. There were a great many reasons for those hellish achievements, including ideology, technology, firepower, totalitarianism and total war. But the human decisions by heads of states and heads of armies that led to the abandonment of nearly all civilized restraints on warfare may have been primarily hatched in the horrors of the Great War. Four years of brutalization in the trenches, four years of martial madness and technological terror undoubtedly warped the senses, and severed many of the human connections that might have once tempered the Great War veterans who would incite and inflict history's worst war on their species.

World War I bred a new race of men, without souls and armed with a modern technology of mass murder and weapons of unparalleled destructiveness. Could there have been a Hitler without the Western Front? Could there have been an Auschwitz, a Babi Yar, a Dresden firebombing, a Rape of Nanking, a Hiroshima A-bomb, without Passchendaele, the Somme, Verdun and Gallipoli?

For the people of the European combatant nations (though less so for Americans), the Great War must have seemed like the end of the world, or at least of civilization—similar to the Cold War atomic apocalyptic dread typified by the movie *On the Beach*, with its soundtrack theme of "Waltzing Matilda" harking back to the Anzacs at Gallipoli. The ditty becomes a dirge—a fatalistic reflection on the hopelessness and endlessness of the slaughter, so encompassing as to even threaten extinction. With all its bloodshed and intensity, the combatant populations of World War II probably lacked a comparable paranoia (except for, understandably, the Jews and the Russians), because they had seen it all before, just twenty years in the past.

But for the people of 1914–18, nothing remotely comparable had occurred. Europe had experienced a century of relative peace; no generation since that of Napoleonic times had even experienced major continental war. And the harbingers of the Great War—the Russo-Japanese and Balkan Wars—though intense, had still been too limited in scope and time to provide a real preview of what was to come. Not until the nuclear threat arose, did people once again fear—as many did from 1914–18—that warfare could actually result in the eradication of the human race.

The bare bones of the Meuse-Argonne statistics are staggering. On a front twenty-five miles at its widest and fourteen miles at its deepest, 1,256,478 U.S. soldiers and Marines participated in the seven-week-long offensive. Of this number, 850,000 were combat troops. The rest were administrative, support or logistical personnel, not normally exposed to German machine guns and grenades, but certainly vulnerable to the kaiser's big guns. Seven French divisions, totaling 130,000 soldiers, also fought in the Meuse-Argonne.

U.S. and Allied cannoneers wheeled 2,417 howitzers and other field pieces into action during the offensive and hurled a phenomenal four million rounds of explosive ordnance against the German trenches (the greatest number of artillery rounds ever fired in support of an American battle). Aloft, supporting the grunts on the ground, were 842 aircraft, most of them manufactured by the Allies. Alongside or ahead of the attacking infantry rumbled 324 tanks, all of them turned out by Allied factories and many of them manned by Allied crews.

The AEF claimed that all or elements of forty-four German divisions were shuttled into the Meuse Valley and the Argonne Forest at one time or another during the offensive (a claim viewed with some skepticism by Allied Headquarters). The U.S. First Army counted 26,000 German POWs rounded up during the offensive (although other authorities reduced this total to 16,000). AEF HQ claimed 874 artillery pieces and over 3,000 machine guns captured by its attacking units.

For their triumph, the men of the AEF paid a price never before required and never again demanded of American military personnel—26,277 killed in action or died of wounds, 95,786 surviving wounded, and 5,000 reported missing in action or taken prisoner. Of the 470,000 enemy soldiers faced by General John J. Pershing's legions in the Meuse-Argonne Offensive, about 100,000 perished, were wounded, taken prisoner or listed as missing in action.

The AEF's last battle of the Great War was not only its greatest battle, but the dominating contest of arms for the United States in the global conflict. By every measure, by every statistic, the Meuse-Argonne was World War I for America. All before, all else prior to September 26, 1918, was a prelude. Belleau Wood, Aisne-Marne, Soissons, St. Mihiel were ghastly introductions to the abattoir of the Argonne, bloody live-fire exercises leading to the total test in the valleys and forests west of the Meuse.

No other contest in all of America's armed conflicts so defined the war's course and conduct in which the battle was waged. Twenty-two of the twenty-nine doughboy divisions in France passed through the fires of the offensive. Of 2,057,675 Americans who set foot in France prior to the Armistice, more than 60 percent endured at least one of the forty-seven days of the Meuse-Argonne. No other battle in any major war engaged more than 50 percent of the total American combatants deployed to the theater of combat. No other battle in U.S. history ever involved anywhere close to a million Americans. A total of thirty-one U.S. divisions, fielding 400,000 combatants, held or obliterated the Ardennes Bulge in World War II. But even adding one man in support for every man in action still accrues a total far short of the million-man mark. About 548,000 Americans served on land or offshore in the Battle of Okinawa.

Of 53,513 American battle deaths in World War I, nearly 50 percent died along the twenty-five murderous miles between the Meuse and the Argonne. Of 204,002 khaki-clothed Americans wounded in 1917–18, again, nearly 50 percent fell between the river and the forest from September 26–November 11, 1918. No other battle in U.S. history comes close to carrying such statistical weight. Thus, nearly two out of every three returning doughboys carried memories of the Argonne back with them, and half of those bringing back painful physical reminders of their service acquired their wounds in the great offensive. And of those who did not see America again, who would probably rest forever in French soil, half, again, saw the end of their days during the fall fury of the Meuse-Argonne.

Over about fifty miles of rolling rugged and wooden terrain in Champagne and Lorraine lay the ground over which were waged the greatest battles in both the history of France and the history of the United States. Side by side, over what was essentially one long continuous battlefield, are located the two places on the planet where the most Americans died in a single battle and the most French fell in not only their bloodiest battle, but also their longest.

The Battle of the Meuse-Argonne and the Battle of Verdun were two years apart in time, but not even a few kilometers apart in distance. In fact, a good part of the same soil soaked with French blood in 1916 was further enriched by American blood in 1918. Over the ten months of the 1916 Battle of Verdun at least 162,000 French and French Empire soldiers died. The American loss of over 26,000 dead in the 1918 Battle of the Meuse-Argonne was much less, but because those battle deaths occurred in less than seven weeks, the American battle was proportionately much more deadly than the French. And, of course, the two battles were but the most savage and spectacular of four years worth of battles and constant conflict in that relatively small span of fifty miles of French countryside. One estimate of the total sacrifice endured in the Great War in the Argonne and the Verdun salient is 420,000 dead for both sides and 800,000 wounded, making the area one of the most blood-drenched regions in all of human history.

But, though the two battles were fought over much of the same ground against the same enemy in the same war and resulted in sacrifices of similarly unprecedented scale, the historical impact on their respective societies could not be more different. To France and to Frenchmen, the arc of hills and bois (woods) on either side of the Meuse above Verdun is sacred ground, a place of veneration and homage. Save for a few Great War buffs, Americans know and care nothing about the unmatched heroism and horrible losses of their grandfathers' or great-grandfathers' generations in the forest of the Argonne and on the hills and in the valleys rolling east to the Meuse.

Although there are monuments and memorials and cemeteries, including the highest American military

Montfaucon Monument, with its 180-foot-high tower, the tallest U.S. military monument in Europe. Photograph by the author, April 2002.

monument in Europe and the largest American graveyard on the continent, they are all but empty of American tourists. Yankee visitors flock to the D-Day beaches and Bastogne and even to Waterloo, but they are ignorant or indifferent to the site of their own nation's most spectacular and most sanguinary battle. Verdun is hallowed and revered above all other battles in French history; the Argonne, in American memory, is a forgotten forest.

The crimson cataract of doughboy blood that flooded the Meuse-Argonne in the fall of 1918 did not nourish virgin soil. The Argonne was a black forest of battle and death, almost from the first firing of the "Guns of August" up to the eleventh hour of the eleventh day of the eleventh month. America's time in the woods and ravines of the Argonne was as brief as it was bloody. Frenchmen and Germans killed one another in prodigious numbers in this place of death for more than four years. Possibly only the Ardennes, barely twenty miles to the north, rivals the Argonne as the planet's most blood-soaked stretch of woods.

It is indeed arguable that the extended front of some fifty miles length—the area from the west edge of the Argonne, past the Meuse and Verdun to the Woevre and the nose of the St. Mihiel salient (and including the twenty-five miles in which America's greatest battle took place)—can claim the doleful distinction of being the world's deadliest ground. The concentrated carnage of the Great War's Western Front is without rival in body count ratio to square mile. World War II (and many of the fronts of World War I) was a war of vast fronts and wide dispersal. Millions died on the 1939–45 battlefronts, but they died more often on battlefields of much greater length and depth. The Western Front battles were fought generally on much more constricted boundaries and over ground that was contested time and time again on a front that remained static for three years. There were three great battles of Ypres, three of Champagne, three of the Aisne, two of the Somme, and near constant minor combat on the same fields in the interims between the all-out contests.

And of course, the Great War was not the first introduction to warfare for Belgium and northern France—those regions being among the most fought-over areas in world history, from Roman times to the Hundred Years War to the Thirty Years War and Marlborough's campaigns, on to the French Revolutionary and Napoleonic wars, the Franco-Prussian War and, twenty years after Versailles, the Second World War. Verdun was a battlefield in Caesar's Gallic Wars, as it was in the French Religious Civil Wars of the Sixteenth Century and the French Revolutionary Wars at the close of the Eighteenth Century. But the dead of all those centuries could not compare to the toll of the fallen in 1914–18. The calculus of the cost for the Argonne-Verdun-St. Mihiel front for the entire war totals 420,000 dead. Only the Somme, where up to 419,000 died in those four years, and Ypres, where over 400,000 were killed, can compare.

America was as unprepared for the Great War as the Aztecs were for the Conquistadors and the Poles for the Blitzkrieg. No serving American had engaged in war on a grand scale; no living American had witnessed war as anything more than a bloody adventure, small in size and brief in duration, for more than half a century. All of America's wars since independence, with the exception of the fratricide of 1861–65, had been relatively minor affairs that may have produced major consequences, but demanded only a fraction of the nation's heart and sinew. Except for Britain in the War of 1812, America's opponents had been weak, and the outcomes of the conflicts (no matter how ill-managed and clumsily waged) had been foregone conclusions. And even the War of 1812 had been fought against a Britain which was directing ninety percent of its military effort, not to the Yankee irritant in North America, but toward the Corsican conqueror in Europe.

Only during the Civil War had American armies of tens of thousands fought on battlefields that produced thousands, and often tens of thousands, of casualties. And never before had the United States fought battles involving hundreds of thousands of combatants, leading finally to the ultimate battle that engaged more than a million men for forty-seven grueling days and cost over 120,000 American casualties. America was simply unprepared, militarily, emotionally and psychologically, for combat of such stupendous scale.

There is no such thing as clockwork efficiency in a large military organization, particularly a military mass on the move and at war. Even the best organized, trained and led formations in military history, like the Germans of the Wehrmacht and the Israeli Defense Forces of 1967, blunder about in confusion and cross-purposes. Mistakes multiply and magnify, from the most minor by the private at the bottom to the most momentous by multi-starred strategists at the top. The side that wins is usually the side that makes the fewest mistakes, or has the overwhelming mass in manpower and firepower to compensate for battlefield chaos and mismanagement.

The Meuse-Argonne was no different in this respect than any other military campaign in history. The blunders were legion, the confusion was colossal. The Argonne was apocalyptic, vast in drama and daring, hugely tragic and, like all battles, hugely stupid. Only courage and determination on one side, and weakness and exhaustion on the other, were able to determine victory and defeat.

The Great War instituted the permanent division as a traditional structure, supplementing and enlarging, though certainly not supplanting, the regimental tradition of the United States Army. With the exception of the ad hoc divisions of the Civil War, the permanent division with a history and a lineage had not been part of the American military in its first century and a half. Since the Great War, the combat division has undergone many revisions and permutations—from the huge two-brigade, four-regiment square divisions of World War I to the less cumbersome triangular divisions of World War II and Korea to the ultimately impractical battle group configuration of the early Cold War and on to the Vietnam-era three-brigade structure—but it has remained the essential battlefield unit of the U.S. Army.

Five of the ten divisions that remain today (in 2005) as part of the mailed fist of American military might can boast (and weep) of their time in the Argonne—the 1st, 2nd, 3rd and 4th Infantry Divisions and the 82nd Airborne Division (which was, of course, like all divisions in 1918, an infantry division in the Argonne). The Big Red One (the 1st Infantry Division) would go on to storm Omaha Beach, scour the Iron Triangle, and join the left hook around Saddam Hussein's Republican Guard, but it would never suffer again on the scale it endured on the Meuse-Argonne front, taking 8,814 casualties in sixteen days of combat, the highest toll of any U.S. division in the battle. The 3rd Infantry Division mourned 7,873 fallen in twenty-eight days, the second highest toll among the twenty-two American divisions in the Argonne. The 82nd's 6,377 casualties ranked third highest in the dolorous listings. Of the eight U.S. divisions which accumulated casualties of at least 5,000 each in America's last and greatest Great War battle, four of them—the 1st, 3rd, 4th and 82nd—would remain as parts of the Twenty-first Century U.S. Army (the other four were the 5th, 32nd, 35th and 79th).

What this all means to the men marching in the ranks of today's Big Red One, Rock of the Marne (3rd), or All-American (82nd) Divisions is undoubtedly, in most cases, minimal. Though nominally dependent on unit pride and tradition for cohesion and combat camaraderie, the modern-day U.S. Army is reflective of American society—unaware of its history and, in all but a few superficial gestures and ornaments, neglectful of its battlefield genealogy. To be ignorant of history is to be like a leaf that is unaware that it is part of a tree, but most American soldiers—like most American citizens—remain solitary leaves. Hierarchies of pride, of course, abound. Certain divisions may boast of a superior reputation, an elite status to others. The air assault troopers of the 101st may puff with pride and flex the Screaming Eagle patch on their shoulders; the paratroopers of the 82nd Airborne may snicker with contempt at the "straight leg" soldiers of the regular infantry divisions. But for most G.I.s parading under the campaign streamer of the Meuse-Argonne, the red pennant is just one of many, and the campaign just another obscure battle in a long ago war, four or even five generations removed.

The United States Marine Corps is better at inculcating into its recruits a sense of being the latest in a long fraternal chain of warriors reaching back into the past, with comradely grasp, to the heroes who came before. But that chain has weaker links in the Army. Consequently, the men who agonized in the Argonne and earned, by their hard early deaths, the right to immortality through the fulcrum of remembrance, are little memorialized by their camouflaged-coated heirs. The footsloggers of the Indian-head, Ivy, Red Diamond and other divisions, who fought on the banks of the Meuse, up the heights of Montfaucon and Romagne, and in the green gloom of the Argonne, are as much gray ghosts to the grunts, who bear those same patches today or did in more recent wars, as they are to the rest of an America, manacled to its present day and incarcerated from its past.

One morbid measure of the extreme tardiness of the American war effort was the doughboy body count. In its first ten months of hostilities with the kaiser's war machine only 136 soldiers of the AEF or sailors of the U.S. fleet had died in combat. In none of America's major wars (with the exception of the advisory years, 1961–64, of the U.S. involvement in the Vietnam War) did the toll of the battle dead accumulate so slowly. Compared to the few fallen in America's first year of war with Wilhelmian Germany, the 385 battle deaths in the little over three months of the Spanish-American War of 1898 seemed like a cascade of casualties.

But beginning at Cantigny in May 1918, that count—sacred or sordid according to the accountant's ideological point of view—would rocket to unparalleled heights. With the exception of World War II's final year, there had never been nor would there ever be a bloodier six months in American military history. A comparative awfulness is in order. For the ninety-four months of direct American combat involvement in Vietnam, the U.S. absorbed an average of 2,250 casualties a month. For Korea's thirty-eight months, the U.S. average was 4,146. For World War II's forty-four months of American engagement, the monthly figure was 24,504. In World War I's last six months, the AEF took 35,626 casualties on average each month.

The Great War was that moment in military history when the spirit of battle finally crumbled before the technology of death. Before 1914, victory often went to that side with the greatest will to win, often regardless of numbers, weapons and terrain, After the fire of August 1914, battlefield success more often than not was gained by that side possessing the better formula of firepower.

The Great War in general and the slaughter of the Meuse-Argonne in particular changed the way the U.S. chose for the future to conduct ground warfare. Fear of massive casualties again on a Meuse-Argonne scale altered the U.S. Army, from a Civil War–World War I infantry fighting (and dying) force, to an army in which the infantry (greatly reduced in raw numbers and in ratio to total numbers) became just the point of the sword, the long cutting edge of which would now, from World War II onward, be composed of the artillery, armor, and fixed and rotary-winged tactical air. Never again would American infantrymen be sacrificed on the scale of the Meuse-Argonne.

Almost nine decades have passed since America fought its greatest battle. Very few veterans of those seven weeks of savagery remain among the living, and not many more than their number are truly aware of their sacrifices and are even moderately informed of the circumstances in which 26,000 of their comrades gave their all. Possibly a few million Americans could connect the Meuse-Argonne to World War I (although even that is doubtful) but only a relative handful could, if pressed, render any of the relevant facts of the battle.

True, the U.S. has fought another world war since 1918, as well as the Korean, Vietnam, Persian Gulf and Iraq Wars, along with more than a dozen minor military operations, from chasing Sandino's guerrillas in Nicaragua to ferreting out al-Qaeda terrorists in Afghanistan, all helping to fog and crowd our memories of doughboys in the Great War. But a significant number of Americans could reach much further back in time than 1918 to provide information and impressions of much smaller battles, such as Gettysburg and Shiloh, and of engagements, like the Alamo and the Little Big Horn, which, in comparison to the Meuse-Argonne, were mere skirmishes. How could an American battle more than twice as great in size and sacrifice as the greatest of World War II battles—Okinawa and the

Leaders of the AEF (left to right): John J. Pershing, James W. McAndrew, Billy Mitchell, John L. Hines, William M. Wright and Charles P. Summerall. Jerauld Wright Collection, U.S. Army Military History Institute.

Bulge—and many times greater than the biggest battles of the Civil War, disappear so utterly from our national memory?

It is not because of a lack of monuments, of symbols in stone and statuary. The tallest American battlefield memorial in Europe—the 234-step-high monument at Montfaucon—and the largest U.S. military cemetery in Europe—at Romagne—remain beautifully maintained by the American Battle Monuments Commission, but sadly unattended by American tourists.

Each nation has its one war which so resonates in its history and culture—World War I for Britain and France; World War II for Germany, Russia and Japan; the Civil War for the United States (with Vietnam as the second-most searing).

Although American interest in World War I may blossom or wither according to the fickle dictates of taste and time in the decades ahead, as in the decades past, one certainty endures. The Great War will never be "great" for America and Americans, not like it always has been and always will be "great" for Britain, France, Germany and Russia. The war was too brief (really only six months of U.S. combat) and too lacking in profound and lasting impact on the country's culture, history and place in the world for Americans ever to identify too intimately with the Great War. Of course, the war resulted in the U.S. emerging as a world power (and a world shaper); of course, it accelerated cultural changes that took America from the Victorian Age to the Jazz Age; of course, it murdered and mutilated American boys at unparalleled rates. But all the new turmoil and trauma, all the dead dreams and arid assumptions, left—in relative terms—shallower footprints in the sand of the American psyche than did other conflicts.

A nation measures the greatness of its wars by how much each armed conflict defines or distorts a decade or an era, by how much it divides or unites its populace, by the depth of the despair or the totality of the triumph. For the United States, only the Civil War, World War II and Vietnam climb the mountain or descend to the abyss. All other conflicts in our history are relegated to the role of historical footnotes—even the war that was for much of Europe the "greatest" great war in their history.

2

The Major and the Division

The men of the 308th Infantry called him "Galloping Charlie," first in derision, then in affection. With his long lanky form and his cantering stride through the military camps and training grounds, it seemed the perfect sobriquet for the stork-legged officer, seemingly so humorlessly methodical and so set on his purpose.

At Williams College, however, Charles Whittlesey had seemed not nearly as serious-minded and unapproachable as he later did to his largely working class enlisted men. He fit in well at the Massachusetts "society" college, nestled in the pastoral setting of the Berkshires. He was gregarious and popular, and known to his friends in Delta Psi, one of the school's most exclusive fraternities, as "Chick" or "the Count."[1]

"Chick" was not adverse to participating in the usual gambit of college pranks, and could be fun-loving, if not rowdy. But if he was not uptight, as his doughboy recruits first assumed, he was always upright. Rectitude and conscience were built into his nature and reinforced by his nurture.

His father, Frank R. Whittlesey, was the personification of the Puritan work ethic, and wore his New England piety on his sleeve, with his directorship of a YMCA chapter and other churchly duties. His mother, Annie, a photo of whom Whittlesey carried in the upper left coat pocket of his uniform throughout the war, was as equally devout toward her creator as she was devoted to her family and her rigid Yankee moral code. Frank and Annie had migrated to Florence, Wisconsin, while a young couple, and had gradually enlarged their family there, with the birth of Charles Whittlesey on January 20, 1884, followed by Russell in July 1887, Elisha in February 1892, and Melzar in July 1893.

Some time after the birth of his last son, Frank Whittlesey moved his brood back to New England. He settled in Pittsfield, Massachusetts, in the bucolic Berkshire Hills. While his father made a comfortable living working as a purchasing agent and later as a production manager for General Electric, Charles attended and excelled at Pittsfield High School.

Young Whittlesey next attended Williams College, just twenty-five miles north, at Williamstown, Massachusetts. He was described there by his classmates as an unathletic type, who "never had a ball in his hands," but was an excellent scholar.[2] Voted the third brightest man in the Class of '05, Whittlesey was honored with election to the top senior academic society, Gargoyle. He was made editor-in-chief of the college yearbook, the *Gulielmensian*, as well as editor of both the *Williams Record*, the school newspaper, and the *Williams Literary Monthly*. He wrote numerous articles for all these publications, and also contributed an essay on the "Literary Enterprises" of the Class of 1905 for the Class Book. At graduation in 1905, there seemed little doubt that Charles Whittlesey was set on a life of the mind.

Whittlesey cultivated his sensitive side at Williams. He tried his hand at poetry, and communed with nature by hiking the Berkshires and observing its feathered denizens. He was not, however, a solitary soul or a navel gazer. He enjoyed company and people enjoyed his company. He thought deeply, and those deep thoughts did not bring despair and cynicism, but optimism and a hopeful outlook for his species. Whittlesey may have had Puritan blood in his veins, but it was not prohibitionist. His late night "bull sessions" with his roommates and classmates featured plenty of hot air and cold brew.

Whittlesey's path seemed to ascend ever upward towards success and prosperity, just as did mankind's progress in general, in that deceptive decade before an assassin in Sarajevo changed everything for all time. Harvard Law School was Whittlesey's next stepping stone in his journey on toward the American success story that seemed almost preordained for him. After snagging his degree in 1908, the young attorney took up bachelor quarters on Manhattan's East 44th Street, and practiced his craft with the New York firm of Murray, Prentice and Howland until 1911.

He practiced law as he practiced life, not with an adversarial, winner-take-all philosophy, but with the attitude that the most important objective in any legal case was to arrive at the truth, no matter what side benefited. He worked hard for his clients, prepared diligently, until every "t" was crossed and every "i" dotted, and used his keen analytical powers to pick apart his opponents' arguments. But justice always seemed to take center stage in his career, not profit or prestige.

With his workaholic lifestyle, Whittlesey apparently had little time for the gals, though he did date occasionally. Whenever he did not have his nose stuck in a law book, he usually had it fixed firmly to volumes on history, philosophy, poetry and economics. He appeared perfectly content that, though he was unlikely to make a big splash in life, his time on earth would be fruitful and fulfilling and would serve some small purpose. Aspirations to greatness in any field were undoubtedly out of character for him. That he might become the primary hero in the most famous war story in the greatest conflict in human history yet, was beyond his imagining.

Then, on June 28, 1914, Charles Whittlesey's tidy little world ended, though he could not have known that the violent event in far-off Bosnia would end the life he had so assiduously acquired and impose upon him a fatal fame. The Nineteenth Century's expectations of ever greater progress in every sphere of human endeavor—moral as well as technical, social as well as scientific—would be shattered, and the Twentieth Century, history's bloodiest, with its global war, totalitarian revolutions and genocidal ideologies, would truly begin then and truly end seventy-seven years later (not one hundred), with the Christmas Day 1991 dissolution of the Soviet Union. Whittlesey would be swept up by this most violent of centuries, wrenched from his comfortable and contented life, to be initially elevated by it, and ultimately consumed by it.

Aside from his unwarlike mien and manner, Charles Whittlesey made a most unlikely candidate for military renown. Although he had taken ROTC classes in his first years at Williams, he was philosophically opposed to most wars in general and to the Great War in particular. Like many young scholars and intellects of the era, Whittlesey had become enamored with socialism while attending college. Whittlesey's socialism was a gentle ideology, picked up from books and discussions with like-minded college roommates, like Max Eastman, who went on to become one of the founding members of the American Communist Party. His was not the socialism of Bolshevik zealots, or even of working class Wobbly

(IWW—Industrial Workers of the World) activists, who picked up their Marxism in the school of hard knocks delivered by a capitalist system that had made life comparatively easy for people like Whittlesey and his family. The romantic aspects of socialism, its appeals for fraternity and egalitarianism, drew in the idealistic Whittlesey. Whittlesey had enjoyed the fruits of capitalism, but he was no Pollyanna. He was well aware that the vast majority of his countrymen were victims, rather than victors, in the rough-and-tumble contest that was the free marketplace. He hoped for a better world for all, and socialism seemed to offer the best hope for that world.

Above all, the abolition of war was socialism's most appealing tenet to the future commander of the Lost Battalion. Whittlesey was convinced that history offered few examples of the just war; that armed conflict between nations was almost always the result of greed and economic competition. War served only to make more millions for the ruling class and millions more widows and orphans for the working class.

The conflict raging in Europe in 1914 and 1915, with its wanton carnage on a scale almost beyond human comprehension, at first only reinforced Whittlesey in his anti-war and pro-socialism attitudes. The news of vast armies, composed primarily of the proletariat and the peasantry, slaughtering one another under the banners of rivaling ruling elites, sickened and appalled the New York City attorney. But gradually, his feelings about the war he detested and the creed he embraced evolved into more contradictory impulses.

If socialism was Whittlesey's song, democracy was his music. He saw the one as complementary to the other. Socialism, to Whittlesey, was a smoothing stone that could chip away the rough edges of American democracy and help make its promises whole. If the two were to ever become incompatible, Whittlesey, with his bedrock devotion to liberal democracy, would choose faith over infatuation.

The war forced that choice on him. Though he at first stood with the American Socialist Party's anti-war stance and admired the decision of Eugene V. Debs—for whom he had voted for president in 1912—to go to prison rather than renounce his anti-war agitation, Whittlesey eventually came to the conclusion that the Left's campaign to keep the U.S. out of the war undermined America's ability to defend itself against armed aggression. The war may have been a colossal calamity for mankind, but it did seem to generally align the democratic nations of Europe (with the glaring exception of Tsarist Russia) against the authoritarian and more aggressive states of the continent. Whittlesey saw Germany's invasion of Belgium, not in strategic terms, but as the action of a bullying brute against an innocent underdog. He saw the U-boat campaign, not as a legitimate naval strategy, but as a massive violation of the rules of warfare. Whittlesey fervently hoped that Wilson could keep America out of the war, but he felt that if the country should be dragged into the conflict, it had to be prepared both mentally and militarily.

His Socialist Party felt otherwise, however. When the party's efforts to promote peace went beyond verbal and written exhortations in rallies and broadsheets to the support of strikes and sabotage against the budding war economy, Whittlesey became irritated, and irritation grew eventually to estrangement. Whatever the rights or wrongs of the war, Whittlesey came to believe that America had to prepare to defend itself—its territory, its people, its dreams—and that the Left's anti-war efforts could prepare America only for submission. Whittlesey's disillusionment with the Socialist Party culminated in an angry outburst one day as he read a newspaper account of its increasingly more radical activities on behalf of non-intervention. Slamming down the paper, the taciturn Whittlesey turned temperamental and declared, "To hell with that crowd!"[3] His youthful fling with socialism was over.

Thus did Charles Whittlesey, an Athenian, not a Spartan, come to study war. Fletcher Pratt would characterize him as a conscript, not of the Selective Service Act, as was most of the doughboys in his battalion, but of conscience.[4] Though no one would demonstrate greater courage and endurance, he was not naturally outfitted for military service—not physically, mentally or emotionally—but he would serve because his code of honor and his fidelity to freedom demanded service.

Pratt compares Whittlesey to another unconventional hero—T.E. Lawrence, also a part-time socialist, a man of the mind rather than the body, an archaeologist fascinated by ancient civilizations rather than modern arms. He too saw the folly of the Great War, wanted to avoid it but could not, because, like Whittlesey, he was called to the colors by his conscience. And also like Whittlesey, Lawrence of Arabia drove himself to overcome the limitations of his physique and the inhibitions of his psyche to perform feats of intrepidity and almost super-human valor that would make him a household name and the idol of a public gluttonous for glory. Tragically, the Englishman and the New Englander were also both similarly unprepared for their fame, and the aftermath of their moments of glory would be marked by sad years of decline and early demise.[5]

So, Charles Whittlesey, a man with the soul of a poet and the mild manner of an Oxford don, took his first step in 1916 toward becoming a warrior by enlisting in the preparedness movement. Though a man of words, Whittlesey was incapable of letting words substitute for action where his principles were concerned. His action took the form of enrolling in one of the five-week-long summer training camps established by former Army chief of staff, General Leonard Wood, at Plattsburg, New York, on the shores of Lake Champlain.

Inspired by the muscular rhetoric of Theodore Roosevelt, Wood had inaugurated the camps in July 1913, recruiting 200 college boys to learn the rudiments of soldiering and pay their own expenses while doing so. The May 1915 torpedoing of the *Lusitania* had vastly accelerated interest in the preparedness camps, and by summer 1916 some 16,000 Ivy League grads, young professionals, and budding businessmen were training in twelve camps staffed by Regular Army officers and paid for now by a congressional appropriation of two million dollars. Among the bluebloods and bureaucrats running the obstacle course and scouring KP pots and pans were the mayor of New York City and his police commissioner. Though graduation from the camps did not guarantee a commission in the regular army, this "Plattsburg Movement" became an essential source of junior officers in the U.S. Army during the war.

Whittlesey applied himself to soldiering with the same focus and depth of commitment that he did to everything else in life he deemed important. His genetic tree carried not all pacifist genes, after all. His forebears had fought at Saratoga, White Plains, Vera Cruz, Chapultepec, Antietam and Gettysburg. His name stood at the top of the graduate list in August 1916. Returning to his Wall Street offices, Whittlesey resumed his legal career, while waiting for the fearsome gravity of the Great War to pull him and his country into its maw. The German resumption of unrestricted submarine warfare in early 1917 made American participation in the war inevitable. The declaration of war came on April 6, 1917, and on August 8, 1917, Whittlesey was placed on active duty and ordered to report for three months' training at Camp Upton, outside Yapshank, Long Island.

The regiment to which he was assigned was the 308th Infantry, of the newly conscripted and mobilized National Army 77th Division. Like the other regiments in the division, the

308th was seeded with a cadre core of Regular Army NCOs and OTC graduates, but most of its enlisted ranks were draftees and many of its officers were Plattsburg alumni. Whittlesey was given command of HQ Company of the 308th's 1st Battalion. He was well-liked by his fellow officers, both superiors and subordinates. They admired his meticulous attention to detail and his conscientious concern that each task handed him became a job well done. They also appreciated that he could be companionable after duty hours, could relax and ratchet down his intensity, could even unwind enough to amuse his fellow officers with an entertaining anecdote or two. But with the privates and corporals it was a different story.

Both the officers and men of the 308th (like all of the 77th Division) were largely citizens of New York City, but they might as well have come from different planets, so mismatched were they in social class and life experience. As one private pointed out, "The trouble with this outfit is that all the officers come from below Fulton Street and all the men from above it."[6]

The enlisted men were Bowery boys, lower East Side working class stiffs, and immigrants. They spoke forty-two different languages, including a variant of English that could only be called "Brooklynese." One battalion of the 308th was described as "practically a Jewish battalion."[7] The officers were professionals in civilian life, men with college degrees, either born with a silver spoon in their mouths or blessed with the luck and drive that had boosted them up from the masses. Lawrence Stallings, in his book, *The Doughboys*, described the officers of the 77th Division as "Fighting Eggheads."[8] The privates were educated in the streets, and had lived lives of calluses and constricted prospects.

To the roughnecks and street-wise kids with a stripe or two on their shoulders, Whittlesey was just another aristocratic captain, with his weak eyes and weak voice, from which spouted commands in almost another language, thick with New England cadences and Harvard accents. It was at Camp Upton that Whittlesey acquired the nickname "Galloping Charlie," as he trooped the line on his lanky legs and led the company on forced marches with his purposeful stride. "He looked like a stork on stilts," according to one lower East Side private.[9]

Whittlesey was uncomfortable with their coarse talk and crude humor, their contempt for authority, and their street-wise arrogance. Nonetheless, the privates respected their CO, recognized that he was a taskmaster, but no martinet, that he stuck close to the regulations, but did not use them to tyrannize his men. Though they might bitch about the "duty-happy Yankee so-and-so" who demanded their best, they later had to admit that Detroit Red (Whittlesey's 1st Battalion code name after he became its CO) was whipping his battalion into the best in the division, and that he "knew his oats."[10]

Corporal (later Sergeant-Major) Walter J. Baldwin pointed out that, "We knew if he was bossing the job it would be done right."[11] But their was no real affection between Whittlesey and the lower ranks. The few streets separating them in Manhattan were an unbridgeable gap—until shot and shell obliterated that distance.

If Whittlesey could not truly connect to his men, he certainly could stand up for them. He demanded that they do their duty, but was adamant in fulfilling his duty to them as well. When higher command made unreasonable demands on his troops, Captain Whittlesey became an advocate for his men, as willing to tussle with division staff over an issue of right and wrong as he had been to challenge the judicial system when his sense of justice had been offended. When, for example, Whittlesey was told to pressure his men into buying Liberty Loan bonds to help pay for the war effort, he responded, "These men are doing enough," and said no to superiors not used to hearing that word from subordinates.[12]

But Whittlesey did not use this incident or other such episodes, in which he stood as tall morally as he did metrically, to court approbation from his enlisted men. He was not seeking popularity or praise from his privates, but merely the consent of his own conscience. Thus he would remain a remote, if respected, figure to the men under his command, until deathly circumstances would change deference into devotion.

The division with which Whittlesey went to war—the 77th ("New York's Own")—was typical of the conscript National Army divisions hastily patched together to supplement the handful of Regular Army divisions and the mobilized National Guard divisions. Created on August 5, 1917, at Camp Upton (named in honor of twenty-five-year-old Civil War general Emory Upton), it was commanded, as of August 18, 1917, by Major General J. Franklin Bell. The men who wore the gold and blue Statue of Liberty division patch, would also be typical of the other draftee divisions in their lack of sufficient training and equipment. Forty thousand of those draftees, for the 77th and other divisions, would ultimately be trained at Camp Upton.

The first group of conscripts for the division arrived on September 10, but the recruits kept coming in dribs and drabs right up until divisional deployment in March 1918. The division was being put together and manned on the fly, and training was spotty and sporadic. The division never trained as a unit, and even at the company level instruction was hit or miss. In June 1918 an AEF staff survey found that up to 45 percent of the personnel in two infantry regiments of the 77th had not fired a rifle in training. On October 3, 1918, Colonel Cromwell Stacy, regimental commander of the 308th Infantry, would have to crouch in the Argonne mud to instruct a replacement soldier on how to load his rifle.

To make matters worse, a levy came down on the division in January 1918, requiring that the 77th give up 4,500 of its semi-trained personnel to fill the ranks of other newly forming divisions. Unit solidarity and cohesion, just beginning to coalesce six months after the division was created, was dealt a demoralizing blow. To compound the confusion of new faces and new problems, General Bell was ruled medically unfit for further service and relieved. Brigadier General Evan Johnson was placed in interim command of the 77th, just as its infantry regiments began embarkation, March 29–April 16, 1918, at Boston, Brooklyn and Hoboken, for the passage across the Atlantic. The artillery and divisional trains boarded Western Front-bound ships at the end of April.

The Statue of Liberty Division that began arriving in northwest France by April 15, 1918, via Liverpool, Dover and Calais, was the standard "square" U.S. division. Its roster authorized 27,124 names, including a rifle strength of 12,188 infantrymen. The 77th was, therefore, almost double the size of an average full-strength European division, and nearly as large as an Allied corps. The square division was so named because of its institutional structure of two infantry brigades, each of two regiments, plus one artillery brigade, one engineer regiment, and three machine-gun battalions.

Each infantry regiment of 3,800 men included twelve rifle companies and one machine-gun company with twelve machine guns. Each regiment also included a 4-inch Stokes mortar platoon and a 37 mm gun platoon.

The division fielded three field artillery regiments and one trench mortar battery armed with four 6-inch Stokes-Newton mortars. Two of the field artillery regiments were armed with French-made 75 mm field guns, twenty-four to a regiment. The third field artillery regiment deployed twenty-four 155 mm howitzers. Each of the 75 mm regiments was attached to an infantry brigade, while the 155 mm regiment was under the direct command of division HQ.

The division also fielded three machine-gun battalions (separate from the machine-gun company assigned to each infantry regiment). Two of the machine-gun battalions each had four companies, with each company authorized forty-eight mule-drawn machine guns. Each of those two battalions was attached to an infantry brigade. The third machine-gun battalion consisted of two motorized companies, each with twenty-four machine guns and directly under the orders of division HQ. The total weapons inventory of the square division included 13,600 rifles, 72 artillery pieces and 168 machine guns. The American standard infantry small arm was the 1903 Springfield bolt action rifle, but most of the AEF's ordnance, as well as its airplanes, came from French and British factories. Thirty-four of these square divisions, including five depot divisions used to funnel replacements to the twenty-nine on the line, made it to France before the Armistice.

The 77th's two infantry brigades were the 153rd and 154th. The 153rd mustered the 305th and 306th Infantry Regiments, supported by the firepower of the 305th Machine-Gun Battalion, armed with Allied-made Lewis, Vickers and Hotchkiss machine guns (not until the last weeks of the war would American units be equipped with American-made Brownings). The 154th Brigade fielded the 307th and 308th Infantry Regiments, backed by the 306th Machine-Gun Battalion.

The real muscle of the 77th was represented by the 152nd Field Artillery Brigade, which could fire the 75 mm guns of two battalions—the 304th and the 305th—and the "heavies" of the 155 mm-equipped 306th Field Artillery Battalion, as well as the mortars of the 302nd Trench Mortar Battery.

Besides these main combatant elements, divisional troops (those attached directly to division HQ) included the 302nd Engineer Regiment, the 302nd Field Signal Battalion, the 304th Machine-Gun Battalion, and Headquarters Troop. Division trains (the logistical troops supporting the combatant units) included the 302nd Military Police Battalion, the 302nd Ammunition, Engineer, and Supply Trains, and the 302nd Sanitary Train, consisting of the 305th, 306th, 307th and 308th Field Hospitals, each with its own ambulance company.

Once in France, the division's infantry units were attached to the British 39th Division, near St. Omar, until June 5, 1918, to learn the basics of trench warfare. Division artillery trained separately at Camp de Souge, south of Bordeaux, until July 4.

At those places and elsewhere in France, the men of the 77th (if they were not already familiar with the label) became used to their "doughboy" designation. Allied soldiers had branded the newly arriving American troops "Sammies," in sardonic honor of Uncle Sam. The term was very unpopular with the American rank and file. Within a few months, however, the term "doughboy" became affixed to the soldiers of the American republic, and would forever after remain the term of identity and endearment for the U.S. fighting man of World War I. The origin of the term was, on the other hand, obscure and would remain an item of debate.

One theory held that the tag originated with the French "poilus" (infantrymen), who compared the minimum pay of an American private of thirty dollars a month to a poilu's pay of three dollars per month, thus making the American servicemen to be seen as loaded with "dough."

According to various *Stars and Stripes* newspaper postulations, the title's origin was one of three possible alternatives. Number one was that it was invented by American cavalrymen during the 1916 Pancho Villa Campaign, in reference to the dust-covered infantrymen as "dobies," from the adobe huts they were quartered in. Number two was another contemptuous cavalry term, this time from the Philippines campaigns, to describe the dust- and sweat-swathed infantrymen after long marches as resembling doughboys. The third theory dated back to the era when infantrymen wore spherical buttons on their shirts (compared to the flat buttons on cavalry blouses) that looked like soup dumplings, called "doughboys," that were a feature of U.S. mess hall menus.

On June 21, those "doughboys" of the division's four infantry regiments were deployed to the Baccarat Defensive Sector, east of Nancy in Lorraine, and at the western foot of the Vosges Mountains. The area had been the scene of great Gallic sacrifice during the August 1914 days of the Battles of the Frontiers, but had been generally quiet since, and was now employed by both sides primarily for rest and recuperation for battered veteran divisions and training for novice divisions. It had been in the Luneville sector, northwest of Baccarat, that the U.S. 1st Division had been the first American division introduced into the line on October 23, 1917, and it had been at Bathelemont in that sector that the first three doughboys from the 1st Division had died in action during a German trench raid on November 3, 1917.

The 77th replaced the U.S. 42nd Division, a National Guard unit, called the Rainbow Division, because its chief of staff, Colonel Douglas MacArthur, had described the congregation of units from twenty-six states and the District of Columbia to Secretary of War Newton Baker as a division that "will stretch across the nation like a rainbow."[13] One of the Rainbow's regiments—the 165th Infantry (formerly the 69th New York Infantry)—was predominantly New York City Irishmen, and, as a 77th Division private from Brooklyn wrote, "Our guys came from all over New York—Flatbush, Canarsie, Richmond Hill, Yorkville, Park Avenue, the Bower," so the two units shared a common urban geography.[14]

Thus, on the moonlit night of June 21, as the men of the Metro Division passed the Micks of the Fighting 69th, headed briefly for the rear, the New Yorkers of the two divisions shouted out their respective boroughs, sections and streets. Shouted street names turned soon to song, and the summer mountain air echoed to the refrains of the "Sidewalks of New York."

The 77th established its headquarters at the city of Baccarat on the Meurthe River, and its rifle companies went into the line about seven miles northeast, with the 61st Division, of the French Eighth Army, which was to tutor them into the terrors of the Western Front. The 77th was the first conscript division to enter the line. Although designated a quiet sector, "quiet" was a relative term. To the draftees, whose military careers often had spanned no more than six months, this alternate universe of detonating "Whizz-Bang" artillery shells and night patrols into the spookscape of No Man's Land could be more appropriately termed a purgatorial prelude to the hell that awaited them.

After three weeks, their French mentors were redeployed elsewhere, and, from July 16–August 4, the New Yorkers of the 77th earned the distinction of becoming members of the first National Army division to independently hold a section of the Western Front. After suffering 375 casualties to the "quiet" of the Vosges Front, the 77th was transferred, beginning August 1, west to the Champagne Front, where the war had never been quiet. Assigned to the U.S. III Corps, which was, in turn, attached to the French Sixth Army, the 77th formally relieved the U.S. 4th "Ivy" Division on the Vesle River on August 12.

How Captain Whittlesey reacted in his heart and gut to the Vosges Front sampling of the horrors to come is unknown. He was not given to spoken or written proclamations of his apprehensions and emotions. But his physical reactions are recorded, and they were in keeping with his unwavering sense of duty and responsibility. Aware that his lack of command presence required reassurance to his skeptical soldiers, Whittlesey went to the regimental commander, Colonel Nathan K. Averill, a crusty, but kind-hearted old Regular Army man, and volunteered to lead a trench raid against the enemy. Averill was unwilling to risk his company commanders on minor missions that required no higher leadership or sacrifice than a second lieutenant and, consequently, refused permission. The divisional redeployment to the Vesle, however, gave Whittlesey another chance to show his men his moxie. There, with incoming rounds as common as sunlight and shadow, Whittlesey chose to flaunt fate and his own vulnerability by sleeping above ground, while most men sought some semblance of safety in dugouts.

As action along the Vesle heated up, Whittlesey found other opportunities to shine. Taking charge of HQ Company's one-pounder guns, he ignored heavy Hun fire to position the weapons on the most advantageous terrain, where they could give as good as they got. Impressed by his tactical finesse and taciturn courage, Averill bumped the HQ captain up to regimental operations officer, responsible for conceiving battle plans and composing those plans into orders. Whittlesey was not, however, content with simply putting plans to paper. When it was time to turn plans into action, Whittlesey transferred himself from the nib of his pen to the point of the spear to make certain that the orders were understood and carried out—if circumstance and the kaiser's boys so allowed.

The Vesle was the first real testing time for Whittlesey and the entire 77th Division. General James Harbord described the unit, also often called the Times Square Division or the Melting Pot Division, as "made up of all the racial strains that characterize the great city [New York]."[15] On the Vesle, the melting pot would prove its metal.

The Vesle Front had earned opprobrium as "Death Valley" to the Pennsylvania National Guardsmen of the 28th Division, after it had entered that part of the line on August 6. The Vesle had become a battlefield following the success of the great Allied Aisne-Marne Offensive, that had commenced on July 18, following the failure of the fifth and last of the massive German offensives of 1918 that had broken three and a half years of stalemate and had nearly won the war for the kaiser. The German Champagne-Marne Offensive, July 15–18, had penetrated beyond the Marne, but had been held in check by, among other divisions, the U.S. 3rd Division (thereafter called the Rock of the Marne Division). The Allies had suffered 45,000 casualties, including 1,485 U.S. battle deaths, but Imperial Germany had shot its bolt, had lost 50,000 men killed or wounded, and was no longer capable of general offensive action.

On July 18, eight U.S. divisions—the 1st, 2nd, 3rd, 4th, 26th, 28th, 32nd and 42nd—joined three French armies in a grand attack to eliminate the enemy's Marne salient. That objective was achieved by August 5, with the Germans driven back to the Vesle, which flowed into the Aisne River, east of Soissons. The fifty-two German divisions engaged had lost 139,000 killed or wounded, 29,367 taken prisoner, 793 artillery pieces and 3,723 machine guns. Twenty-three French divisions had taken 95,165 casualties and lost 175 tanks. Four British divisions counted 16,000 casualties, and two Italian divisions had lost 9,334 in total casualties. Pershing's AEF had absorbed 40,353 casualties, including 6,992 combat deaths—except for Gettysburg, the highest American body count of any battle up to that time in American history.

The Vesle was no great military impediment. It was a slothful stream of less than thirty feet width and six to eight feet depth, snaking its way through a one-third-mile-wide marshland, with banks snarled with brush and barbed wire. Above the river, both north and south, were 600-foot-high steep, bare ridges, composed of chalk and riddled with caves. The Germans were dug in on the northern heights, where they could clearly observe the open ground south of the river and throw down a murderous fire on any force trying to cross it.

On August 4, the U.S. 32nd Division captured Fismes on the south bank. The U.S. 4th Division and the 6th Brigade of the U.S. 3rd Division, along with the French 164th Division, then struggled for several days to secure bridgeheads on the north side of the Vesle. On August 7, the 32nd was relieved by the men of the 28th Keystone Division, after the 32nd had taken 3,753 casualties since July 30. The 6th Brigade of the 3rd Division was relieved on August 11, after losing 608 men killed or wounded from August 6–11. The Pennsylvanians of the 28th Division won a tenuous toehold on the north bank by taking Fismette, opposite Fismes, on August 10. The 4th Division, before its relief on August 12, had also won a small lodgment across the Vesle, near Bazoches and Château de Diable (Castle of the Devil), but a punishing enemy fire prevented the doughboys from laying down footbridges and forced reinforcements to either attempt a swim across or a crawl on fallen logs. By the time the 77th relieved the 4th, the Ivy Division had incurred 3,478 casualties, August 3–12. All attempts to break out of the bottomland bridgeheads or even dig in properly failed, and the beleaguered few holding them were under constant German artillery and small arms fire, as well as mustard gas attacks, as were the supporting positions in the open forward slopes south of the river. General Robert Bullard, commander of III Corps, which had assumed control of the Vesle Front on August 4, bemoaned their circumstances, "I have rarely, if ever, seen troops under more trying conditions."[16] In just two weeks, August 4–17, 623 American soldiers died on the Vesle Front.

Bullard advocated withdrawal from the perilous positions north of the river, but General Jean Degoutte, commander of the French Sixth Army, to which the U.S. III Corps was attached, insisted on maintaining the pressure on the Germans to make them think that "a vigorous attack" on the Vesle was in preparation. Degoutte ordered III Corps to both consolidate its positions south of the river and expand its bridgeheads on the opposite side. On the night of August 12–13, Bullard commenced company-size attacks from the bridgeheads, the 77th striking along a three-mile front west of Fismes, the 28th from a two-and-a-half-mile line east of Fismes. The attacks made little headway against resolute German resistance. The 77th was delayed by a storm of gas shells that killed or sickened 800 soldiers before officers could lead their panicked men out of the poisoned hollows up to the less toxic air on nearby knolls.

Starting on August 22, the Germans staged counterattacks with battalion-size units at Bazoches and Château de Diable, and on August 27 the enemy used flame throwers to blast a 150-man company of the 28th Division out of Fismette. Only a few Americans swam across the Vesle to safety; all the rest were killed or captured. Bullard had withdrawn the company from Fismette by night, one man at a time under heavy fire across the only footbridge, after it had become hopelessly pinned down by the German guns. But Degoutte, furious that Bullard had given up a bridgehead, no matter how untenable, had personally ordered them back, and four nights later they were annihilated.

The two U.S. divisions thus could neither break out from their small circles of hell north of the river, nor, because of Degoutte's stubbornness, pull back to the much more defensible high ground well south of the Vesle. The ensuing stalemate lasted until the night of September 3–4, when the west flank of the German line along the Vesle was turned as a result of the French Tenth Army's Oise-Aisne Offensive, which had begun on August 18, north of Soissons. On the morning of September 4, 77th Division patrols encountered only sporadic machine-gun fire from German rear guard positions, as the enemy pulled back toward the Aisne.

The 28th and 77th pursued the backtracking enemy across the plateau between the Vesle and the Aisne. The 77th's 153rd Brigade, on the left, advanced five miles by September 6, to Villers-en-Prayères, and pushed patrols on to the Aisne Canal. The 154th Brigade, on the right, made less progress, however, because the 28th Division, on its right, failed to keep pace and left the 154th's flank uncovered. The 77th struck again on September 14, but made little headway. After repulsing a German counterattack on September 15, the division was pulled from the line and replaced by the Italian Garibaldi Division, one of two Italian divisions on the Western Front, and commanded by the grandson of the Red Shirt liberator. The 28th had already been relieved, September 8, by a French division. The Pennsylvanians and the New Yorkers of the two U.S. divisions had paid a high price for their conquest of the Vesle River valley. The Keystone Division had lost, from August 7–September 8, 5,325 killed, wounded, missing or taken prisoner. The Statue of Liberty Division had lost in its time on the Vesle, August 12–September 16, a total of 4,755 dead, wounded, taken prisoner or unaccounted for.

In the midst of its testing time in the Vesle, the 77th again underwent a change of command. In May, soon after the division's arrival in France, Pershing had promoted George B. Duncan, a brigade commander in the 1st Division, to the top spot of the 77th hierarchy. But, like the division's original commander, General Bell, Duncan had to step down in August at the insistence of army doctors.

Picked to replace him was Robert Alexander. A mustang who had risen from the ranks, like 2nd Division commander General James Harbord, Alexander became the youngest division commander in the AEF. Alexander was rough and ready, red-faced and broad-chested. Gruff in manner, he was a hard driver, but could inspire, as well as crack the whip. His was an intimidating presence. He was even able to tame a German police dog, who lunged at him viciously when Alexander took over the ancient Château de Feré as his first headquarters north of the Vesle. With the aid of his driver, Sergeant Glass, and generous tidbits from the regimental mess, Alexander pacified the dog into mascot status. He became the headquarters pet and was Glass's constant companion, riding beside him as he drove the general's limousine. After the war, Alexander awarded custody of the dog to his faithful driver. The two retired to Flatbush, where the canine spent his remaining years chasing trolley cars and nuzzling the neighborhood kids for treats.

Born in 1863 of Scottish ancestry, Alexander had, like Whittlesey, passed the bar exams, but, unlike Whittlesey, found the life of a lawyer to be of so little satisfaction that he enlisted as a private in the U.S. 4th Infantry Regiment on April 7, 1886. His martial talents were soon recognized, and he was commissioned as a second lieutenant in 1889. By the time Alexander stepped ashore in France in 1917, he had seen a lot of action in a lot of the world. He had fought the Ghost Dancers in America's last major Indian war—the Sioux War of 1890—railroad strikers led by Whittlesey's early hero, Eugene V. Debs, in 1894, Spaniards in Puerto Rico in 1898, Aguinaldo's rebels in the Philippines in the first years of the new century, and Pancho Villa's banditos in Mexico in 1916.

Alexander had advanced steadily in rank and reputation. After attending the Army School of the Line and the Army Staff College, he was made senior inspector-instructor of the Maryland National Guard. Promoted to lieutenant colonel, he organized other National Guard units and the regular 17th Infantry Regiment for overseas duty after the declaration of war. His first assignment after arriving in France in November 1917 was as inspector of the lines of communication for the AEF. Given his first star shortly thereafter, he served briefly as commander of the National Guard 41st Division, then, early in 1918 was made commander of the 63rd Brigade of the National Guard 32nd Division.

Alexander was far from universally admired by his fellow generals, however. His reputation for poor staff work followed him from command to command. Harbord rated him as less than average as a commander, and Bullard thought his only redeeming quality was his energy. The highest praise General Hunter Liggett could convey on him was that he was "competent."[17] Both of Alexander's brigadiers requested reassignment after only three or four weeks under his command. He would rarely have anything favorable to say about his subordinates, except for Whittlesey (who would, himself, eventually seek a transfer away from the general's sway and would tell Liggett's aide that he despised his divisional commander).[18]

Morale was dragging in the Metro Division when Alexander took over in August. The division had lost too many men on the Vesle to enemy fire and too many commanders to medical unfitness reports, and the unit seemed adrift and uninspired. Alexander took hold with a vengeance, determined to turn the 77th into a reflection of his own steely and aggressive character. He weeded out the weak, transferring a regimental commander for his "defeatist attitude," and nurtured the spirited. In order to reap the advantage of the men's quarrelsome character, he issued a general order to all platoon leaders, directing them to appeal to the old "gang spirit" of their men, many of whom had been street gang members in civilian city life.[19] He promised the men two artillery shells propelled toward the foe for every incoming round, and his skeptical soldiers listened carefully to insure that the welcome crack of French 75s outnumbered the dreaded whine of German 77s (division artillery delivered over 400,000 shells to the Germans between the Vesle and the Aisne).

Not content with issuing orders from an HQ château in the rear, the major general was a frequent visitor to frontline trenches and dugouts. Although the Vesle Front was stalemated when he took command, Alexander ordered several minor operations to maintain a fighting edge and build confidence. Thus, when the German line finally broke in early September, the 77th dashed forward, toward the Aisne with so much spirit and drive that it raced ahead of the flanking divisions and amazed a number of critics, who had looked upon the 77th's performance thus far as uninspired.

Alexander was rightfully proud of the melting pot mixture of his division's enlisted ranks. As he stated, "It was currently said that there were forty-three languages and dialects in use among the men, and there were quite as many shades of religious belief and disbelief."[20]

There were Chinese boys from Mott Street, Jews from Allen Street (40 percent of the division personnel were Jewish), Italians from east of Union Square, and Germans from Yorkville and the upper East Side. Most spoke a Brooklynese English dialect (if they spoke English at all) that was captured in the popular Don Marquis ballad that included the lyrics: "Prince, when you call on a Brooklyn goil, Say Poil for Pearl, and erl for oil."[21]

The first three Distinguished Service Crosses that Alexander awarded to the men of the 77th were indicative of that wide-ranging ethnicity. Sgt. Sing Kee, who had calmly continued his Signal Corps duties as twenty-nine of his comrades fell around him to Hun fire, was from San Francisco's Chinatown. Captain Herman Stadie had been born on the Rhine River. Private Abraham Hirschkovitz had grown up in a Bessarabian ghetto.

The disparate elements of the division had been made a whole and had proved itself on the Vesle. A great deal of the credit for its success was due to the junior officers, who were also a mixed lot, culled from legal and business offices, college classrooms, and even the stage.

2. The Major and the Division

One of Alexander's college professors, a teacher of English literature at Princeton before the war, won the 77th's first Medal of Honor (by date of action) during the Vesle campaign. On September 14, Captain Wardlaw Miles, a man who the year before had been teaching students Thomas Hardy and George Eliot, now taught his soldiers a lesson in leadership and courage. His classroom was a German trench position near the Aisne Canal that had already repelled several U.S. assaults. Without any support, Miles personally led the first wave of his company through the German wire, cutting a passage through the steel entanglements, while under interlocking machine-gun fire. Maxim bullets tore into the captain's flesh five times. With both legs and an arm fractured, Miles crawled onto a stretcher, but directed the stretcher bearers not rearward to a first aid post, but forward into the enemy trench, which had been taken with heavy American casualties. There, for two hours, the machine gun-mangled professor continued to inspire and direct his company as it held against German counterattacks. Only then, and still protesting that his place was with his men, was the Princeton pedagogue carried to a medical station. In the rear area hospital, the middle-aged captain astounded doctors and nurses, as he stoically smoked with his good hand while they daily dressed his painful wounds.

Whittlesey also distinguished himself in the Vesle Valley, although, of course, his shining moment was yet to come, in a dark forest fifty miles to the east. He carried out his duties with efficiency and authority, and continued to disprove the old army adage, that to be a good leader one had to look like a leader. But the quality that came through the strongest on the Vesle for Whittlesey was his loyalty and dedication to his men, a quality that naturally magnified the respect his soldiers had for him, but one that also caused friction with the higher-ups.

It was this concern for the well-being of the soldiers in the line that caused the removal of Whittlesey's commander. Colonel Averill was the regimental commander kicked out by Alexander for insufficient aggressiveness, when, on August 17, the 308th CO requested permission for a slight withdrawal of his men from an exposed position, a position that provided no tactical advantage, but only unnecessary casualties. The never-give-an-inch division commander replaced the popular and proficient Averill with a Quartermaster Corps captain. The temporary CO proved hopelessly inept (and corrupt; he was later locked up in the Fort Leavenworth military prison), but the man who replaced him, Colonel Austin F. Prescott, though more capable, was a remote figure little concerned for what his men had to endure.

This caused frequent flare-ups between him and new 1st Battalion CO, Charles Whittlesey. The most heated exchange came when the new 308th commander ordered Whittlesey to detail twenty men from his battalion as runners. The 1st Battalion had just come off the line, spent and scarred by battle, and was in brigade reserve. Whittlesey pointed out to Colonel Prescott that, because his men were in brigade reserve status, they fell under the command of the brigade CO and that he, consequently, would not obey these orders that would further wear out already worn-out men. Prescott may have fumed and fluttered with indignation, but Whittlesey got his way, and his resting men continued to rest. Shortly thereafter, Prescott was transferred and replaced by Lt. Colonel Frederick E. Smith, a Regular, who knew how to balance his duty to orders with his responsibility toward his men.

Charles Whittlesey, Robert Alexander and the 77th Division had all passed muster on the Vesle. It had been their first real experience of Great War combat, and the nearly 5,000 casualties incurred represented nearly 20 percent of the division's strength, a very substantial toll for little more than a month's worth of battle. The battle had been real and it had been big, but it had also been only a preliminary bout before the main event, a foretaste of a feast of death and horror on an unimaginable scale.

Once pulled out of the Vesle line, the 77th was given a brief respite to refit for that next trial by fire. Just two days prior to the bloodiest battle in the 77th Division's history, it received an infusion of over 4,000 replacements, to bring division strength back up to nearly 26,000. This new blood, to replace all the blood shed on the Vesle, came by way of levies from the 40th and 41st Divisions. They were draftees, mostly from the western states, but also from Michigan, Wisconsin, Ohio and Indiana, whom the city boy veterans of the Metro Division instantly labeled as "hicks and hayseeds." Many had been conscripted as recently as July or August, and had spent most of their brief time in the Army in movement toward the front. They were dispersed among the division's infantry units, which, naturally, had taken an overwhelmingly disproportionate share of the casualties.

Many of the recruits had never trained with the most basic tools of the infantry trade— the rifle and the grenade. Some of them didn't even know how to insert the bullet clips into their rifles, and had to pay the battlewise New Yorkers—who recognized an easy mark when the opportunity rang—up to five dollars each to instruct them. But the veterans, weakened in numbers and in stamina from a month of sustained combat, welcomed the replacements' strong backs and willful eagerness to close with the enemy. To most of the veteran troops of the 77th, the fact that the green replacements were basically untrained was a plus, for their own training in the States and in the French rear had little prepared them for the reality of the Western Front. The new men could have no bad habits acquired from irrelevant or improper training. They would learn on the job the right way, or they would die.

Of the replacements, the 307th Infantry Regiment got 850 (seventy-two men to a company); the 305th was apportioned 900 new men (150 to M Company alone); Whittlesey's 308th absorbed the most—1,250 (with I Company receiving 110, after having left the Vesle line with only eighty men remaining fit for duty). In addition to the warm bodies, the 77th got new equipment, including new types of grenades and flares, both of which would subsequently prove useless in the Argonne.

A month in the active line had certainly seasoned the 77th, but it still could not be called a first-class division, on the order of the Regular Army 1st and 2nd Divisions. Among the most glaring of its remaining deficiencies was its inability to navigate by night. General Bullard later wrote that, "Until France, its soldiers had never seen a dark night ... the city boys had always had lamp posts to read street signs."[22]

The lack of country boys in the division had reinforced this proclivity to get lost, particularly after darkness fell. An example of this was the lone runner who astounded everyone by the speed by which he could reach regimental HQ, on a road north of Bazoches on the Vesle. The mystery of his rapidity was solved when it was discovered that he nightly and, totally unknowingly, crossed a half-mile of the German line on his passage to headquarters.

Bullard never knew for certain where the 77th was at the end of the day. Invariably, it would always turn out to be forward, or behind, or left, or right, of where it reported itself. The corps commander described the Metro Division as the "largest collection of babes-in-the-woods that I ever saw."[23]

Thus, though the Lost Battalion was never "lost" in the geographic sense of the term,

2. The Major and the Division

it was abundantly appropriate that Whittlesey's unit was a part of the division that had grit and spirit, but no sense of direction.

After a month in the line, the 77th deserved at least a week in the rear, but the Western Front's busy engagement calendar dictated otherwise. Within a few days, the division was headed east to take part in Pershing's great offensive between the Argonne Forest and the Meuse River. The Meuse-Argonne Offensive was to be America's big show in the Great War. In all the other battles that the AEF had fought, from Cantigny in May through the Oise-Aisne in late August and early September, Pershing's legions had served as apprentices to the experienced, if still not so skillful, craftsmen of the Allied armies. True, the elimination of the St. Mihiel Salient in mid–September had been an AEF show, with the French serving in a subordinate capacity this time, but it had turned out to be little more than a moderately contested occupation of ground that the enemy was already in the process of abandoning. The Meuse-Argonne would turn out to be the AEF's first (and last) great battle of the Great War it could truly call its own, and would also prove to be the most horrendous ordeal yet in the more than two-centuries-long history of the U.S. Army.

Before the Meuse-Argonne, Pershing's biggest battle had been waged, not against the kaiser's field marshals, but against the French and British generals of the Allied high command. Ferdinand Foch and Douglas Haig, as well as their civilian counterparts, Georges Clemenceau and David Lloyd George, wanted the disassembled Yankee divisions to be used as filler, fresh meat to replace the Allied divisions ground down by the German spring 1918 offensives. Pershing had to fight as hard as he had fought Moros and Mexicans to fend off the Allied lust for American cannon fodder, and to keep alive his vision of an American Expeditionary Forces that would make a decisive difference as an individual army, and not as a replacement depot for Haig and Foch.

If it had not been for Pershing's headstrong insistence on an independent AEF, there would have been no Battle of the Meuse-Argonne, or at least not one that was such a distinctly American battle. America's entry into the war had been for the Allies like a rescuer's lantern light to spelunkers lost hopelessly in the blackest of caves. But the Allies and the Americans differed drastically on the best route out of that cavern of horrors. Pershing was willing to plug in American divisions along the crumbling Allied line in the spring of 1918 as a stopgap measure. However, the Allied idea that the Americans would remain in a subordinate role as junior partners, contributing their divisions—like those sent to the Western Front by Portugal, Italy and Russia—to the British and French armies, whenever and wherever they were needed, was anathema to the American commander. A lifetime of hard service and harder sacrifices had not conditioned him to play second fiddle to an Allied maestro.

Pershing had arrived into the world near Laclede, Missouri, on September 13, 1860, the son of a merchant who largely scraped by and barely provided a living for his family. With his steel-beamed spine and imposing manner, Pershing seemed to have been born to be a soldier. But such a destiny was not so obvious to him, for he taught school for a few years and considered other life options before deciding on a military career just short of his twenty-second birthday. In order to more easily gain admittance to West Point, he shaved a few years off his birth date. He was no great shakes academically at West Point, but he excelled in every aspect of leadership, becoming president of his class and first captain, the highest military rank of the Cadet Corps. He graduated in 1886, thirteenth overall in standing in a class of seventy-seven.

Pershing's thirty-eight-year military career straddled sawlegs of time that enabled him to serve from the post–Civil War frontier army, fighting the last of the Indian outbreaks, to the modern Twentieth Century army of mass numbers and even more massive firepower. His first five years of active duty was with the 6th Cavalry in New Mexico, culminating with service in the last of the major Indian wars—the Ghost Dance War of 1890. Appointed professor of military science and tactics at the University of Nebraska in 1891, Pershing capitalized on the opportunity by earning a law degree in his spare time. In the minimal Army of the era of minimal military action in the decades between the Civil War and the Great War, Pershing saw little chance of gaining glory and garnering rank. Thus he seriously considered leaving the Army, changing his venue from cantonment to courtroom. He chose, however, to remain a soldier, and returned to the place that made him one—West Point—as an instructor in 1897.

Pershing's choice was largely motivated by "successive assignments that offered chances for active duty and adventure."[24] Those "chances" came in rapid order in the next two decades. The sinking of the battleship *Maine* brought the thirty-seven-year old lieutenant to Cuba as a troop commander in the 10th (Negro) Cavalry Regiment. There, he shined on San Juan Hill and caught the eye of Teddy Roosevelt. After a tour in the Philippines fighting the "Flips" and the Moros, he attended the Army War College from 1904–05, and then was dispatched to Manchuria to observe modern warfare and firepower in all their premonitory horrors, as the Russo-Japanese War wound down.

Promoted by fellow Republican and now President Theodore Roosevelt—who had attended his wedding to the daughter of a prominent Republican senator—over the heads of 862 senior officers, to the rank of brigadier general in 1906, Pershing returned to America's newest and most fractious colony in the Pacific. He spent the next eight years in the Philippines, climaxing a series of successful campaigns against the Moro rebels by leading a joint U.S.–Filipino force that killed 500 Moros at a volcanic crater named Bud Bagsak, on June 12–15, 1913. Returning to the states, he was eventually given a command on the volatile Rio Grande frontier, where the chaotic carnage of the ongoing Mexican Revolution frequently lapped across the border to moisten the desert dirt with the blood of American innocents.

It was while stationed with his 8th Brigade at Fort Bliss, near El Paso, Texas, that Pershing's personal life took a tragic turn, from which he probably never fully recovered. Before dawn on August 27, 1915, the telephone rang in Pershing's quarters. The news it brought caused the general's square jaw to sag in horror, as he loudly lamented, "Oh God! My God! My God! Can it be true?"[25]

Anxious to shelter his family from the heat and hardships of a Texas summer, Pershing had left his wife and four children comfortably quartered in San Francisco's Presidio, where he had been previously stationed before his assignment to the bloody border. Comfort had turned to conflagration when a hot coal popped out of the fireplace one fatal night, and his thirty-five-year-old wife and three daughters had perished in the flames. Only his six-year-old son, Warren, away on an excursion, remained of all those Pershing held most dear.

Pershing had adored his wife, twenty years his junior. Though not a ravishing beauty, Helen Francis Warren was charming and vivacious. She was also wealthy and well-connected, which surely added to her appeal to an officer anxious to advance. They had met in Washington, where her father, Francis Warren—the richest man in Wyoming—was chairman of the Senate Military Affairs Committee. Their marriage, celebrated by a wedding ceremony in the Washington Cathedral in 1905, was pronounced by T.R. as a "bully match."[26]

Pershing obviously agreed to Teddy's valediction. During one of their separations caused by his military service, Pershing wrote his "Frankie," "I cannot live without you. And I shall not try. It is only half a life. It's so incomplete, so aimless."[27]

The pain of his loss had to be all the more piercing when he found out that the incendiary coal had combusted on the wooden floor recently coated with a thick wax, at the insistence of the spit-and-polish Pershing.

His had always been an aloof and taciturn personality. The fire burned away what little softness remained of a rigid exterior and further hardened his inner steel. It did not entirely extinguish his ardor for the softer sex, however, Though he seemed a broken man on the train trip to San Francisco to bury his family, Pershing, just seven months later, turned his attentions on George Patton's twenty-nine-year-old sister, Nita, and later, in France, he entered into a long-term relationship with a Parisian mistress. But, although he lived another thirty-three years, he remarried only in his very last years.

Pershing was all soldier and all business, at least in his relationships with the men under his command. He was almost universally admired, but rarely adored, by his troops. His attitude toward discipline was rigid and by the book, and he was rarely susceptible to sympathy. His frosty and unbending nature helped earn him the sobriquet of "Nigger Jack," derived from his time with the 10th Cavalry Buffalo Soldiers in Cuba. That tawdry tag was later softened to "Black Jack," and it stuck through the rest of Pershing's career, though the racist origin of the appellation faded. But though the recipient of both curses and commendations, the man demanded and received respect.

Pershing was three inches shy of six feet, but his manner and energy made him seem of commanding height. His self-confidence often tipped over into arrogance. Charles Dawes once remarked of him, "Jack Pershing, like Lincoln, recognized no superior on the face of the earth."[28]

Though not a man of great intellect or an obvious master of the art of war, Pershing always stood out and consistently won command positions of both peril and promise over those more senior or more experienced than him. In 1916, Woodrow Wilson picked Pershing to lead the retaliatory expedition into Mexico to chase down Pancho Villa, after the revolutionary's raid on Columbus, New Mexico. Though the wily desperado escaped the columns of the Punitive Expedition, Pershing garnered more acclaim and appreciation for his handling of a difficult campaign that lessened the number of potential predators on the border by 251, at a cost to the U.S. Army of fifteen killed and thirty-one wounded.

Black Jack's next assignment elevated him from commanding 6,675 troopers chasing mounted guerrillas through the Sonoran Desert, to the helm of the largest field force yet deployed by the U.S. Army—one that eventually would grow to twenty-nine rifle divisions deploying 1,981,701 officers and men, including 32,385 Marines and 1,078,222 combat soldiers. The force of events—five all-out German offensives between March 21 and July 17, 1918, that pried the fossilized fingers of stalemate and slaughter from the trenchline throat of the Western Front—had forced Pershing to postpone his plans for a great and sovereign American army. His best divisions had helped plug the gaps on the bludgeoned Allied lines and served to spark a revival in Allied fortunes, with the first British and French counteroffensives of July and August. But after Aisne-Marne and Amiens, the AEF's leader was at last given the opportunity to put on an American-sponsored show. That first U.S. production came at St. Mihiel.

Pershing's vision of the American Expeditionary Forces had been from the first monumental. The U.S. commander had initially advocated a 100-division AEF (equivalent to 200

Allied divisions and equal to the total German force deployed on the Western Front). The U.S. War Department whittled this Xerxesian host down to eighty divisions in a 3,335,000-man AEF and Pershing acquiesced, with the proviso that the eighty divisions would not include a planned twenty training and replacement divisions. Secretary of War Newton Baker adamantly held to a total eighty-division force, however, and Black Jack had to accept this diminution of his dream. Of course, Pershing's grand concept had been most threatened by the almost constant blandishments of the Allies, begging for U.S. combat troops to help staunch the bleeding all along the severed Western Front between March and June 1918. Pershing had insisted on his course of continuing to build up an infrastructure for a Yankee Grand Army by shipping in support and logistical personnel in proportionally much greater numbers than combat soldiers.

Thus, Pershing's 2nd and 3rd Divisions had helped hold the line against the Germans' Aisne Offensive of May 27–June 4; then the 2nd (and its attached Marine Brigade) had cleared Belleau Wood and Vaux, June 6–July 1, at a cost of 1,811 killed and 7,966 wounded. Another 1,485 doughboys had died in the Second Battle of the Marne, July 15–17, and 6,992 more had made the supreme sacrifice in the Allied Aisne-Marne Offensive. But while doing what was necessary to prevent a German victory, Pershing maintained the momentum of a U.S. buildup, that he saw as a process that would carry America from the position of a junior partner in the war effort to the status of the decisive actor in bringing about a German defeat by the spring of 1919. St. Mihiel would be the place where that process would truly begin.

The target of the American attack—the triangular St. Mihiel salient—began a little over six miles southeast of Verdun, and was shaped like a hound's head, with the snout thrusting across the Meuse just above the city of St. Mihiel. This Boche dog extended sixteen miles into the Allied lines and was twenty-five miles across at the base. Seized in the war's first months, it had retained its original boundaries and shape for almost four years. The 300 square miles of the salient, between the Heights of the Meuse and the Moselle River, were dotted with woods and ponds, and wrinkled with small streams that turned to swamps in wet weather and made the attacking infantry's job that much more difficult.

This hernia in the Heine line had special value for Germany, because it buffered the railroad hub of Metz and the iron ore digs at Briey. It also cut the railroad line leading north into the now sacred symbol of French resolve at Verdun, and made anticipated Allied offensives east towards Metz or north from Verdun and into the Argonne toward Sedan doubly dangerous, with this salient threatening the east flank of all such attacks. Two German defense lines—the lightly fortified Wilhelm and Schwetter Lines—(with a third, the more heavily defended Michel Line across the salient's twenty-five-mile-long base) made the St. Mihiel bulge a thicket of elaborately prepared positions, whose bunkers, barbed wire, and machine-gun battlements had repelled a number of French attacks over the preceding three years. Defending the salient and manning those emplacements were Lt. General Klaus Fuchs and about 23,000 German troops in Army Detachment C, composed of six second-rate trench divisions and two independent brigades, with two more divisions in reserve. The Hun divisions contained only nine battalions each (compared to the twelve battalions in a U.S. division). Two of the divisions were Saxon, one was Landwehr (reserve militia), and one was Austrian.

The salient had been for months the planned primary target of the American First Army, which cranked into operation on August 10, with AEF commander J. J. Pershing donning a second hat as CO of this first of several anticipated American armies. Preparations

2. The Major and the Division

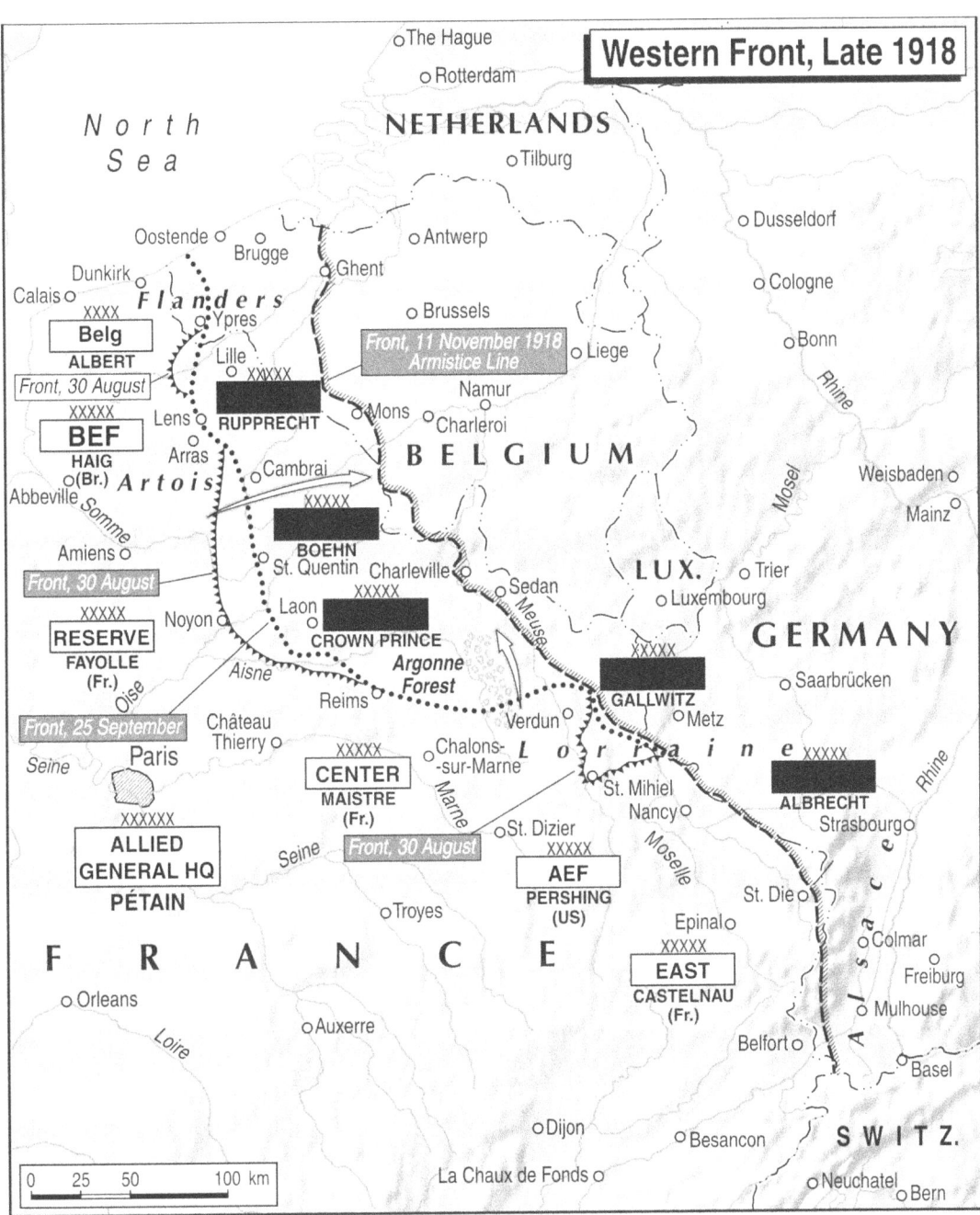

for the offensive were well along, when—also on August 10—Allied Commander-in-Chief Foch upset the apple carts of both Pershing and his primary operations planner, Colonel George C. Marshall, by proposing that the St. Mihiel Offensive be reduced to a sideshow, so that the majority of the doughboy divisions might be employed in a grand attack north between Verdun and Reims, under the control of the French baton.

Thus ensued the greatest contretemps yet between the competing visions of the Allied and American high commands on the proper employment of the incoming Yankee millions.

In a series of conferences that frequently degenerated into shouting matches, Pershing held the high ground against the hero of the Marne, insisting that St. Mihiel would go forward generally as originally planned, and that in the future American divisions would fight only as part of an independent American command.

On August 30, Foch, in exasperation at Pershing's intransigence, threw down the gauntlet. "Do you wish to take part in the battle?" Pershing certainly did, but only on his own terms. He replied to what amounted to a Foch ultimatum, "Most assuredly, but as an American army and in no other way."[29]

On September 2, Foch agreed that the seizure of the salient would go ahead, but Pershing conceded, in turn, that the attacking forces would limit their objectives, stop in their tracks wherever those tracks might be by September 20, and shift forty miles to the northwest to launch a much more massive attack between the Meuse and the Argonne, in order to sweep the eastern wing of Foch's grand double envelopment around the German side of the Western Front. To carry out two major offensives just two weeks—but many miles—apart, was truly a monumental endeavor for a novice U.S. First Army that had not yet carried out a single military operation of any scale. That such a mighty task was even undertaken demonstrated an almost uniquely American combination of high hopes and hubris. That it was a success, though clumsily carried out at a colossal cost, displayed American drive and determination at its most profound level.

Fortunately, for American pride and morale, the opening act of this two-part extravaganza was performed with ease. German commander in chief Erich Ludendorff had long considered the salient a convenient, but hardly vital, buffer zone. Now that intelligence reported the U.S. buildup on the salient's south face, Ludendorff felt that clinging to the zone was counterproductive, particularly in view of the British victory at Amiens in August. The Germans were running out of reserves, and a shortening of their lines was a paramount concern. Thus, on September 8, Ludendorff and local commander General Max von Gallwitz ordered a pullout from the Wilhelm Line and a withdrawal to the Michel position. Two divisions were already in the process of withdrawal when the American blow fell. The U.S. First Army, consequently, was prepared in those early September days for a great battle for ground the Germans no longer thought was worth defending. By the hellish standards of the Western Front, St. Mihiel turned out to be a walk in the park.

The "walkover" was conducted by one French and three American corps. Delivering the main blow on the south leg of the St. Mihiel triangle were the U.S. I Corps on the east flank, with the 82nd, 90th, 5th and 2nd Divisions in line from right to left, and the U.S. IV Corps extending the attack on west, with the 89th, 42nd and 1st in line. The French II Colonial Corps of three French divisions supported the main American assault by holding the enemy at the jaws and snout of the salient dog. The U.S. V Corps, composed of the U.S. 26th and 4th Divisions and the French 15th Colonial Division, carried out a secondary attack in the salient's forehead and ear. Of the three American corps and nine American divisions initially carrying out the offensive, two of the corps and three of the divisions had not yet been bloodied in offensive combat. The nine U.S. divisions carried 216,000 men on their rolls; the four French divisions counted 48,000. Including three reserve divisions and support and logistical troops, some 476,000 Americans, as well as 110,000 French, participated in the St. Mihiel Offensive. In the course of the battle, elements of nine more second-rate German divisions were committed, making a total of 75,000 enemy soldiers against nearly 600,000 Allied personnel.

Supporting the ground-pounders were 3,020 guns, 1,329 of them French-manned—including huge French railroad guns—stocked with 3,300,000 shells (40,000 tons of ordnance). Also in support was Colonel Billy Mitchell's air corps of 1,481 planes, mostly Spad 13s, the largest concentration of air power on any battlefield yet in the relatively short history of aerial warfare. Also backing up the infantry columns were 419 tanks, including 168 in Lt. Colonel George Patton's 1st Tank Brigade and 251 in Lt. Colonel Daniel T. Pullen's 3rd Tank Brigade. Most of the tanks were light, French-made Renaults, but 59 were the heavier St. Chaumonts and Schneiders, also of French manufacture.

The bombardment of the Boche positions began at 0100 on September 12, not long after a nightlong drizzle matured into a deluge. The Allied fires were so intense that German artillery was, in general, unable to respond with counter-battery fire. The U.S. 1st Gas Regiment laid down for the south face attacking divisions a forty-minute smoke screen. The shelling lifted at 0500, as the American and French infantry headed through the chilling mist for the German wire. Though most of the tanks slated to take part in the attack were late in arriving on the battlefield, or broke down before they could reach the Wilhelm Line, the infantry easily broke through the enemy wire, rusty and weakened from three years of weather and wear. Where artillery fire had not cut lanes in the sagging loops, rolls of chicken wire laid over the German barbs provided a pathway. General George Cameron's V Corps on the left, driving from Le Esparges on the Heights of the Meuse, and General Joseph Dickman's IV Corps on the right, debouching from Seicheprey, made rapid progress against German troops, who withdrew in good order and resisted with professionalism, if not with passion.

By the late morning of September 13, V Corps' 26th Division had linked with IV Corps' 1st Division at Vigneulles in the center of the salient. By evening, Pershing could celebrate his fifty-eighth birthday by proclaiming victory in his first battle as the commander of a great army. He could even begin redeploying units from the salient toward the next big push in the Meuse-Argonne, days ahead of schedule. Though a few pockets of resistance remained to be cleaned up, that job was accomplished by September 16, and the St. Mihiel Offensive went into the books as a spectacular American success, even if it was against an enemy who had decided to surrender the ground days before the first shot was fired.

The American victory was easy—particularly in comparison to what lay ahead of them forty miles west. About the most difficult chore during the battle was managing the vast numbers of doughboys operating in so comparatively small a space. On the south leg of the salient, as many as five infantrymen packed every yard; troop density there was a nearly unmanageable 800 per square mile. If the Germans had been determined to sti· y resist, losses to the tightly packed American regiments might have been astronomical. As it was, losses in this battle, which was really a race between one side trying to occupy ground before the other side could evacuate it, were minimal—about 7,000 in total, including 1,799 U.S. battle deaths. Casualties were about one-third the most optimistic predictions of the U.S. Medical Corps, which had assembled sixty hospital trains and prepared 15,000 beds for south face casualties alone. The 82nd, 89th and 90th Divisions all had an easy baptism of fire for offensive operations. The veteran and very bloodied 1st, 2nd and 42nd Divisions had fought their only battle in France that they would escape from with "light casualties." In winning the salient, U.S. and French forces had killed or wounded 2,300 Germans and had swept up 13,251 POWs and 466 mortars or artillery pieces. They had also liberated over 200 square miles of France occupied by the invaders for nearly four years.

The victory was confirmation to the U.S. high command of their confidence in American arms. The fact that the victory had been achieved against an enemy who basically chose not to fight was ignored or obscured in the flurry of self-congratulatory huzzahs bandied about by the American brass. Wilson sent a cable to Pershing congratulating him "on the brilliant achievement of the Army under your command."[30]

It was, of course, on Pershing that St. Mihiel had its most important impact. The easy triumph seemed to confirm the AEF commander's fondest fantasy—that American confidence and cold steel could easily overcome an entrenched foe who had defeated all the best efforts of the French and British for three-plus years. Pershing proclaimed to a member of his staff that, "the reason for the American triumph lay in the superior nature of the American character" and that "Americans had the willpower and spirit that Europeans lacked." Given training equal to that of a European soldier, the doughboy, he boasted, "was superior to his Old World counterpart."[31]

Pershing must have endured numerous moments in the weeks ahead when he had to wince in memory of that arrogant aria, as his officers and men indeed showed willpower and spirit, but also demonstrated sorely deficient tactical proficiency and serious leadership liabilities, while they slogged through the mangled slough of the Argonne. The AEF would prevail in the end, but not by any innate superiority. To gain victory, the Americans, in the words of Colonel William Griffiths, would have, "to play their trump—inexperienced but willing manpower.... They would succeed by manpower and enthusiasm"—and the exhaustion of an outnumbered and outgunned enemy.[32]

Other observers of the battle, particularly the French, were less exultant of the American performance than was the official line. In staff officer Lt. Colonel Fox Conner's official report: "The greatest result of the operation was the development of the First Army as an efficient offensive weapon for more vital fighting."[33] But French staff officers, jaded by more than three years of "runaway successes" which turned out to be but bloody steps forward that left the attacking units with crippled ankles, were less impressed. They conceded that American troops were enthusiastic and ready to rip, but their dynamism was not matched with efficiency.

The Americans, according to French staff analysis, had not defeated the Germans, but had merely "relieved them." The U.S. victory was due solely to "favorable conditions ... a debilitated enemy, a withdrawal in progress, the larger part of the artillery already withdrawn."[34]

Their list of U.S. deficiencies was long and lashing—command and staff was lacking in foresight and decision; the troops were poorly trained and their officers often lacked such basic skills as map reading; the artillery (the true master of the battlefield in the war) was poorly deployed with too many guns brought forward with too little ammo; liaison between units was lackadaisical, with coordination between infantry and air nearly non-existent; and traffic control was abysmal, with titanic road jams that the MPs seemed helpless to unsnarl.[35]

Still, St. Mihiel, as an American success story, cannot be gainsaid in the final analysis. Hailed as a great victory and a display of American military prowess at the time, and relegated by many since as little more than a vast tactical training exercise with a heavy volume of live fire, St. Mihiel, on close examination, has every right to claim pride of place as a full-fledged battle of weight and significance.

It is incontrovertible that the operation coincided with the timing of the pre-planned German withdrawal from the salient, thus making the offensive, in one sense, unnecessary and redundant. But the attack did provide combat experience and build confidence for a half a million doughboys, including those of three divisions which had not previously gone over the top. Of course, compared to what the Yanks would face two weeks later on the heights of Montfaucon and in the tangles of the Argonne, the salient-busting of St. Mihiel was like enduring a playground tussle before taking on the most vicious street gang in the inner city.

But it was not simply a walk in a pummeled park either, not just a mopping up promenade against demoralized conscripts anxious to surrender—like the white flag-fluttering Iraqis of Operation Desert Storm in the last days of February 1991. Second-rate trench troops though they might have been, the equivalent of eleven German divisions committed to the salient knew how to fight, particularly from defensive positions, and even staged several counterattacks.

Seven thousand Allied fallen in five days seems insignificant set against the massive casualties of so many Western Front battles of 1914–18, but such losses are not the trivial toll of light skirmishing. The 1,799 American battle deaths belie the characterization of St. Mihiel as little more than an exchange of real estate ownership, accompanied by a great deal of noise and cordite. In the sad arithmetic of combat, the 360 U.S. battle deaths per day of the St. Mihiel Offensive can compete in grimness and gore with the 558 dead per day of the Meuse-Argonne Offensive. The 13,000 German POWs taken and the nearly 500 guns and mortars captured for the five-day operation were indicators of major success, certainly on a par with the 26,000 (or, as some counts claim, only 16,000) German POWs and 874 artillery pieces gathered up in the Meuse-Argonne.

To belittle the sacrifices of St. Mihiel is to diminish the human cost of much of American military history. Only the greatest battles of the Civil War and the world wars cost more American lives. In no single battle of the Revolutionary War, the War of 1812, the Mexican War, the Spanish-American War, the Korean War, the Vietnam War, and the two wars with Iraq did as many men in American uniform die as the number lost in retaking the salient. The twelve divisions of doughboys were not occupation troops, and, though the Germans were already intent on surrendering that ground, they did so only with a resolute and deadly reluctance.

3

The Offensive I

Even before the guns fell silent in the salient, the prodigious task began of moving 600,000 troops—428,000 of them by truck (20,000 at a time)—more or less secretly, from the St. Mihiel area and elsewhere, forty to sixty miles (forty-eight miles on average) into the Meuse-Argonne zone. At the same time, some 220,000 French and Italian troops in eleven divisions were being redeployed from positions in the Meuse-Argonne sector, most of them being sent farther west into Champagne. Planned largely by First Army Operations G-3, Lt. Colonel George C. Marshall, this vast repositioning displaced forward three corps HQs, fifteen divisions, 3,980 artillery pieces, 93,000 horses, and 900,000 tons of ammunition and supplies.

Because of Foch's last minute changes (at Haig's insistence) in the overall Allied offensive plan, this shift to America's most massive military effort had an air of improvisation about it. Prior planning had focused on expanding the St. Mihiel Offensive. When the change was made to the Meuse-Argonne, what should have taken months of careful planning was reduced to two weeks. Thus, an American staff, whose attention was devoted to one project for many weeks, had to suddenly shift gears and literally move a mountain in a matter of days.

This anabasis to America's greatest battlefield was, in many ways, as difficult (if far less bloody) an ordeal as the battle itself. Just to transport the personnel of one of the big-shouldered American square divisions required 900 trucks. All traffic, motorized and horse-drawn, had to weave a passage to the operational zone along only three narrow roads, rapidly turning into mud slaloms as the fall rains commenced. These same arteries, blocked with the plaque of massive traffic jams, were, at the same time, the primary routes used by tens of thousands of French troops, redeploying from the Vosges Mountains across the rear of the U.S. First Army to take part in the simultaneous French Fourth Army offensive, planned in Champagne to supplement and support the western wing of the American attack in the Meuse Valley. To further complicate this mass military migration, this narrow-banked Nile of humanity and materiel could flow only at night, to conceal this great sluggish stream from the eyes of the enemy.

Pershing and Marshall realized that switching the St. Mihiel divisions to the Argonne front in time for the jump-off hour was akin to relocating the pyramids to Poughkeepsie, but the artillery from those divisions was indispensable if the offensive was to achieve the hoped-for initial breakthrough. Consequently, over 2,000 guns and 600,000 tons of artillery ammunition and supplies had to make the move, most of it from the more distant south face of the St. Mihiel salient, where the preponderance of American power had been concentrated. The seventy-two guns in each U.S. division's order of battle jammed up ten miles of road, and the total would require 300 miles of roadway. Marshall also had to move non-divisional artillery from St. Mihiel to the new sector—a total of three artillery brigades and sixty-eight separate artillery regiments, mostly French, to be somehow squeezed through the clogged capillaries of the French road system. Once in place, this armada of artillery would require fourteen trainloads of shells each day, drawn from twenty-four ammo depots positioned at nineteen railheads.

In addition to the ammo depots, the Quartermaster Corps would need nine depots to funnel rations and supplies to the battlefield. The Engineer Corps required twelve depots for their equipment and tools and eight more for water. The Chemical Corps would set up six depots, and the Medical Corps erected thirty-four evacuation hospitals. The engineers had one of the most titanic tasks assigned them—the rebuilding of 164 miles of small gauge railway, out of a total of 215 miles in the area of operations, along with reconstructing sixty-five miles of track and twelve miles of standard gauge railway.

Marshall, who many would consider as the architect of victory over the Axis powers in the next great war, may have carried out his most amazing feat of logistical legerdemain in the Meuse-Argonne troop movement. But he was greatly aided by Major Doumenc, the super-competent chief of the French Military Auto Service. In a duet of cooperation and coordination, the two carried out their mission superbly. It was, in fact, aboard the vehicles of the French Military Auto Service that—along with French ground troops—the majority of the U.S. forces, ammunition and guns were transported into and out of the sector.

Lt. Colonel George C. Marshall (left), First Army G-3 Operations Officer, with Maj. General Henry T. Allen. National Archives, 111-SC-49024.

Marshall's planning on paper may have been a masterpiece of orchestration, but the implementation on the ground—in the mud—was a sixty-mile nightmare. This netherworld of the night could be consigned to the realm of dreams by the hundreds of thousands of doughboys as they napped in laagered concealment during the day, the lucky ones in village cottages, hay lofts, barns and other outbuildings, the less fortunate majority in the wringing wet woods. But at nightfall, the marches resumed and the nightmare returned.

Marshall had carefully calculated the varying rates of speed of mechanical conveyance versus that of four-legged and two-legged transport. Thus, he had directed all motor vehicles onto the best (southernmost) route, and men and horses on the other two roads, until all streams converged northwards at Bar-le-Duc. But his precisely programmed movements broke down into a muddle of Brobdingnagian proportions once the movement on paper congealed with the movement in the mud.

The worst traffic jams in the young history of motorized transport ensued. Breakdowns were frequent, both mechanical and temperamental. Artillery tractors, plowing along three abreast, often careened off the road to stick fast in the ocher-colored sludge. Horse-powered traffic fared hardly better. Thousands of horses succumbed to their exertions, dying in harness, to further frustrate forward progress. Engineers labored round the clock to patch syrupy conduits with rocks, gravel and logs.

Commanders lost control of their units, as parts of their commands made progress, while other segments found themselves locked in logjams. With French and American units moving at the same time and often in different directions, language problems threw up additional barricades across the narrow roads. Marshall was tethered to the telephone for days on end, sorting out the confusion and unknotting the kinks in this human pipeline. When he was not office-bound by his Olympian tasks, he was roaming the roads, often accompanied by a fulminating Pershing.

Many of the poor foot soldiers in that pipeline thought that the forthcoming battle could not possibly be as difficult an endeavor as the nocturnal agony of the approach to the battlefield. In this assumption they would be monumentally mistaken, but in the chaos of those cold nights on the road to Armageddon, they certainly ingested a foretaste of hell. Whether on foot or in vehicles, the anguish was for many just short of unendurable. After hours of slogging through the mud, under the icy assault of the rain, and being splattered by the sludge of staff officers' automobiles, exhausted infantrymen would welcome the arrival of trucks to carry them onward. After a few hours of spine-pounding, stop-and-go torture in the beds of springless trucks driven by poorly trained Vietnamese from French Indochina, the doughboys were often more than ready to hop off and resume their stagger through the soup under which the roads had disappeared.

The miracle of the Meuse-Argonne campaign may have been not that victory was finally achieved in the face of defenses rarely encountered on such a scale in modern warfare, but that all the units that commenced the forty-seven-day slog to that ultimate victory arrived in position at the designated time.

The night march magnified the difficulty of the redeployment, but did not blind it to the watchful eyes of the enemy. The movement was simply too massive, no matter how deep the darkness and how secretive the plans, to conceal it from any but the most negligent of foes, let alone the experienced and professional force that was the kaiser's army. German units along the target area were certainly aware that something of major importance was afoot, even if their command staff still generally had their attention fixed on the St. Mihiel area. German intelligence reported on September 24: "The circulation in hitherto quiet sectors points to the possibility of an attack along the whole front from Reims to Verdun.... At night great activity reigned along our front. The noise of narrow gauge railroads, the unloading of heavy material, loud cries, sirens and klaxons could be heard through the whole night."[1]

The French continued to man the trenches and outposts west of the Meuse up to the last moment to screen Pershing's buildup, and American reconnaissance units scouting the routes of the forthcoming offensive donned French helmets, blue overcoats and battle dress to dupe German observers, but such ruses were less than totally successful. German intelligence noted that, "Brown uniforms having been observed along our front on September 23, it would appear ... that the presence of American troops must be taken into consideration."[2]

French deserters may have alerted the Germans to an American attack in the Meuse-Argonne, and German patrols captured a private from the U.S. 79th Division and another from the U.S. 4th Division in sectors supposedly manned by poilus. German staff officers may have even ascertained the precise day the offensive was to kick off, as evidenced by the testimony of POWs from the German 5th Guards Division, who fixed the date correctly at September 26. But, although some German reinforcements seemed to have been ordered to move to the Meuse-Argonne sector before the offensive began, and American intelligence indicated that the enemy "appears to be extending his policy of echeloning in greater depth" in the projected area of operations, the overall preponderance of evidence seemed not to be enough to convince the German commander in the sector, General Max von Gallwitz, that a major Allied offensive west of the Meuse was in the offing.[3]

Pershing and his staff had endeavored diligently to distract and deceive the enemy high command as to the true location where the anticipated win-the-war blow would fall. The AEF high command tried to keep German eyes fixed east, on the St. Mihiel front. The ruse was primarily conducted by radio waves and tank treads. Orders were given on September 18 to the Signal Corps Radio Detachment to erect five or six radio stations on ground visible to the enemy between the Moselle and Luneville, both to create the impression of a concentration of considerable force and to relay messages, in a meaningless code but of obvious American origin, to simulate the heavy radio traffic of an impending operation. A fifteen-tank task force from the 1st Tank Brigade rumbled through the wire near Liverdun on the night of September 19–20, and again near Sivry on the night of September 22–23, to plow the darkness of No-Man's Land.

The sleight of hand worked some magic on von Gallwitz's strategic senses. Combined with the fact that the AEF's tested veteran divisions were still committed to the St. Mihiel sector, the German commander was convinced, as late as September 21, that the next American offensive would simply be a continuation of the St. Mihiel Offensive east of the Meuse, with the railroad hub of Metz as the ultimate objective. The civilian population of Metz was sent packing, and reinforcing artillery batteries were installed as late as the day prior to the real American attack, far to the west. Additional reserve units were sent in motion to buck up the lines from the Woevre Plain to Switzerland, but none were dispatched to spice the reserve recipe behind the Argonne line.

That line was supremely strong as it was, even without further reserves to bolster it. The true target of the grand AEF offensive presented a challenge more difficult, both in the shape of its terrain and the soundness of its defenses, than any faced by American soldiers in their combat history. Douglas MacArthur, George Patton, George Marshall and many other American officers had expressed intense regret that the success of the St. Mihiel Offensive had not been further exploited by rolling on to Metz. I Corps commander (and later First Army CO) General Hunter Liggett had demurred, worried that the gallop through the salient would have been slowed to a sticky stagger in the mud of the Woevre plain, and then would come to a jarring halt before the vast fortified complexes defending the vital city of Metz. The weeks that Liggett foresaw as necessary to reduce the ramparts of the German city could hardly have been more than those required to conquer the ground between the river and the forest west of the Meuse, but the argument was academic anyway. Foch had assented to the St. Mihiel Offensive only on the condition it be limited, so that the Americans could render the right hook to his sweeping series of attacks from Flanders to Champagne that would pound Germany to the mat.

Thus, America, with the freshest but least experienced officers and men, had been fitted by Foch into his strategic scheme along the segment of the enemy line where the defenses thrown up by both nature and man were the most formidable. The natural fortress that the terrain presented had been refined and expanded by three years of labor by the masters of mayhem from across the Rhine. The front embraced about twenty-five miles of a landscape pastoral and serene in peacetime, but now savaged and surreal in this fiftieth month of the Great War.

This ground that would absorb the American blow started just northwest of Verdun. There had certainly been disagreement and discord within the alliance between the heirs of Gaul and the sons of liberty, particularly, among the men who wore the stars. But by entrusting the sacred soil of Verdun to their new American allies, Foch and the French had acknowledged a great magnum of faith in the AEF. Confirmation of this confidence came on September 21, when Pershing was allowed to establish his new headquarters in the same building in Souilly in which Marshal Henri Pétain had directed the defense of Verdun.

No location in French military history, before or since, has carried such near religious evocation as has the fifteen miles of rolling woods arcing across both sides of the Meuse above the provincial city of Verdun. For ten months in 1916—February 21–December 18—sixty-six French divisions fought to preserve General Robert Nivelle's promise of "They shall not pass" against the crown prince of Germany's forty-two divisions. In history's longest sustained battle, and its third bloodiest (after Stalingrad and the Somme), nearly a quarter of a million soldiers were reported killed or missing—162,308 Frenchmen and 71,504 Germans—and total casualties (by the most accepted count) exceeded 700,000—377,231 French and 336,831 German. Just in the battle's first five months, close to 4,000 artillery pieces had pulverized the Lorraine countryside around Verdun with some thirty-seven million shells.

Now the soldiers of France, whose comrades had fought to the death for every foot of this smitten ground, had voluntarily surrendered this place, already a shrine to the passing

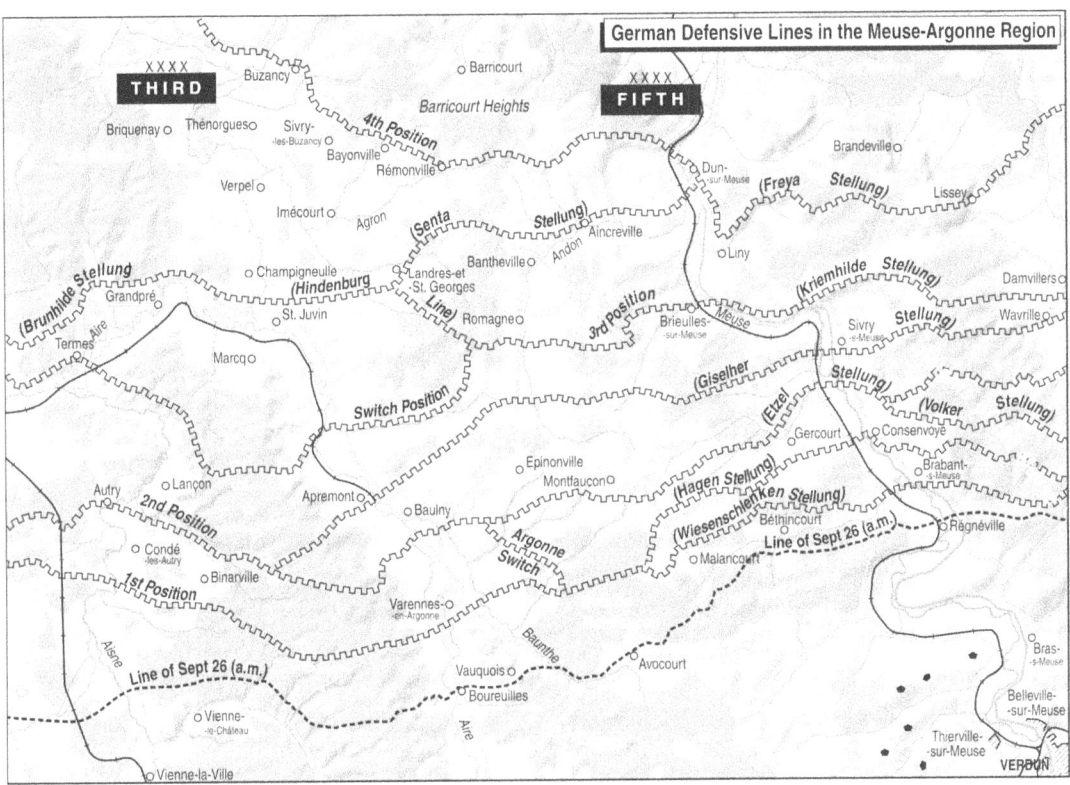

of a French generation, into the safekeeping of an army of Yanks, whose ardor was matched only by their inexperience.

On September 22, Pershing formally took over the sector previously protected by the French Second Army, and now his command extended from the Moselle River west to the right flank of the French Fourth Army, on the western side of the Argonne Forest. There were still French soldiers protecting the sacred site of Gallic sacrifice on the east bank of the Meuse and on to the Moselle—the French II Colonial and the XVII Corps—but they were under the operational leadership of a Yankee general from Missouri.

Pershing could hardly have been assigned more difficult terrain to tackle on the Western Front. General Hugh Drum concluded that, "This was the most ideal defensive terrain I have ever seen or read about. Nature had provided for flank and crossfire to the utmost in addition to concealment."[4]

This seventeen deadliest miles in American history was bordered by heights on the east and woods on the west, and featured a trio of topographical challenges that had to be conquered at any cost. Two of those features anchored the line, east and west, and the third stood in the middle as a natural bulwark, like a god-given watchtower over the land. Running north and northwest along the east bank of the unfordable Meuse River, and parallel to the Argonne Forest twenty miles to the west, were the Heights of the Meuse. Those wooded hills rose to an elevation of 600 feet, and provided a plethora of concealed positions from which the enemy could observe the eastern half of the zone and call down the thunder of Odin (or Krupp), or sweep with a Maxim scythe any column attempting to advance from south to north. Any effort to conquer those heights would first have to find a way across the river, then negotiate a passage through the low-lying brush at the foot of the hills, that turned soupy or even flooded in the downpours of autumn. And those fall rains were as solid in their certainty as were the area's trees and hills. The locals had a saying. "No snow, always rain, rain, rain," and they were as firm in that belief as in the sun's western setting.[5]

On the western wing of what was to become a seven-week trial by combat, sprawled the prickly promenade with which the forthcoming battle would be most closely identified. Though the proper and official title of the AEF's great battle was designated as the "Meuse-Argonne Offensive," or the "Battle of the Meuse-Argonne," it would, in the looming decades, be simplified and popularized as the "Battle of the Argonne." For those woods, deep and dark, and the most deadly dangerous in American history, would, in the trauma of memory and the testament of fate, overawe and overwhelm the hills and villes to the east, well removed from the forest, but just as furiously contested.

The Argonne was (and is) a forest more reminiscent of the muscular thickets of Africa or the Americas than of the usually well-ordered, almost park-like, woods common to western Europe. Its pines and ancient broadleafs beginning twenty-three miles west of Verdun, the Argonne straddled the French earth on a southeast-to-northwest angle for nineteen miles, and stretched its leafy sprawl for seven and a half miles at its widest east-west reach. The south half of that nineteen-mile-long tessellation was in American hands at the commencement of the offensive. The 140 square miles of the forest constituted the largest wooded area in Europe west of the Rhine River. The forest crowned a ridgeline that ran forty-four miles in length and reached an average height of 1,150 feet. The Argonne forms a natural boundary between Champagne and Lorraine, and is hemmed between the Aire River on the east and the Aisne River on the west. Both the rivers and the woods run an almost parallel course to the Meuse, twenty miles across the valley.

The forest and the ridge are razored by ravines and hills, rising to 300 feet or more over the surrounding terrain. One natural obstacle gives way to another even more formidable. Draws and gullies are choked with undergrowth and brush. The deep ravines, boggy at the bottom, emerge to the challenge of looming heights, with crests concealed with more briar and thicket. To many of the native New Yorkers of the 77th Division, it seemed like the spooky Adirondacks transplanted to the Old World.

In the middle of this 420 square mile zone of conflict between the river and the woods rose a third cluster of heights and hills that gave the defenders all they could hope for in the lay of the land, and the attackers everything that they might dread. The shape and direction of the Argonne Forest and the Heights of the Meuse on the flanks gave the terrain between the aspect of a funnel, under the eye and the fire of those elevated wings, all leading to a cauldron dominated by natural strongpoints that rose one after another, like iron fists to the faces of the doomed attackers. The terrain would dictate the tactics. As General Drum observed, "There was no elbow room, we had to drive straight through."[6]

The most dominating feature in the center was Montfaucon (Falcon Mountain), 342 meters (1,250 feet) high, six miles west of the Meuse, and about four miles from the offensive's start line. It was defended by several battalions of the German 11th Grenadier Regiment. Because the general area is about 1,000 feet above sea level, Montfaucon did not appear so forbidding to the naked eye. But the hill did indeed provide a falcon's view of the battle zone, giving the Germans a panoramic scan south to Verdun. The land seemed to flow from Montfaucon in succeeding ridge lines, and the twenty-three German artillery observation posts peppering it allowed direct observation over 80 percent of the battlefield. After four years of experience and improved technology, artillery had attained a deadly accuracy, and the view from Falcon Mountain gave the greedy guns of the German artillery a marvelous opportunity to feast upon the open targets of both attacking troops and their rear support. The German observers surveyed the surrounding countryside from the ruins of a once quaint Lorraine village and an ancient church atop the knoll, all pummeled by Hun guns before their regiments swarmed over the hill in September 1914. Futile French counterattacks in 1915 further pulverized the rubble, and French counterfire against the German crown prince's positions during the 1916 Battle of Verdun tore yet more tufts from the hill's pounded pate.

Beyond Montfaucon, still in the shadow and the crossfire from the Heights of the Meuse and the bluffs of the Argonne, some ten miles north of the start line, lay more leafy logjams to any advance—the heights and woods of Romagne and Cunel, the Côte de Châtillon and the Côte Dame Marie—one obstacle after another, devised by nature and made even more devilish by man, all the way to the Barricourt Heights, some fifteen miles from where the doughboys would rise from their trenches on September 26.

Those doughboys would be treading on ground already enriched with the blood of their French allies. Almost since the day—September 23, 1914—that the Germans had swept over the area, the French had been attempting to reclaim the forest and its attendant heights. From January 15–March 31, 1915, the French First Army had lost 27,026 men, including 10,340 killed in action and missing, futilely flailing at the German-occupied sections of the Argonne and at the nearby butte of Vauquois (one thousand tons of explosives were detonated in 520 mines by both sides on the butte in the course of the war, to practically level the promontory). General Maurice Sarrail's French Third Army counted 83,200 casualties, from January 8–September 27, 1915, contesting the Argonne with General Bruno von Mudra's German XVI Corps, all to no avail. (On January 29, 1915, a German lieutenant named Erwin Rommel had won the Iron Cross, First Class, while leading a platoon in the capture of four French blockhouses. After his exploits in the Argonne, it was common to hear in the regiment, "Where Rommel is, there is the front.")[7] Now the defenses that had rolled back every French attempt to reconquer the woods, had been further refined and improved by almost three years of vigorous Teutonic industry.

Those sorcerer's apprentices in feld grau (field gray) had fashioned five successive stellungen (belts of fortifications) across the monstrous maw awaiting Pershing's regiments. As in a demon dream, the paralleling rows of pillboxes and bunkers would pull their victims from one bloody horror to the next.

These spiked collars, the last three bearing the names of Wagnerian witches in the Ring Cycle, offered up an opera of Sturm und Drang every five kilometers or so. The first entrenchment, near the line of departure for the attacking Americans, was only lightly fortified and lightly held, mostly by machine gunners. But, once through that tripwire, into the rolling countryside that resembled the Shenandoah to many Americans, the doughboy columns would face immediate challenges before even reaching the first of the witches' rings. The Germans had devised a defense in depth, dealing out punishment with each step forward, never abating but only growing in intensity the further the penetration.

In the woods below Montfaucon, the Americans would encounter an outpost zone replete with interlocking fire from machine-gun nests, mazes of barbed wire, and sniper stalls that channeled the attackers into killing zones before running up against a line of resistance just beyond Bethincourt. Having penetrated this line, the attackers would encounter, five kilometers north, the biggest barrier yet, in the Etzel-Giselher Stellungen, the Etzel portion of the line anchored on Montfaucon itself and the Giselher dominating the ground north of the hill. This swath of fortifications and camouflaged pillboxes, many of concrete that only a direct hit from heavy artillery could knock out, were more densely clustered and laced together by trenches. The barbed wire was thicker, in places hundreds of yards across, trench mortars proliferated, and the stone houses in the hamlets had been renovated into miniature forts. Recent additions to this panoply of defenses included minefields and tank traps. And of course, the whole area was under the guns from 600 artillery emplacements west of the Meuse and 500 on the Heights of the Meuse, with barrages registered in defiladed zones, so that there was no place safe from the slash of shrapnel.

Six kilometers north of Montfaucon, lay the strongest line of all—the Kriemhilde Stellung, strung among the pines along the rocky ridges running west from the Meuse at Brieulles, across the Romagne Heights and the Côte de Châtillon, and on into the Argonne. German engineers had started digging and tunneling the Kriemhilde in October 1917, and it was part of the Western Front-long extended line called the Hindenburg by the Allies. Its mutually supporting and stoutly constructed network of defensive positions, many of them sited on reverse slopes, lay beyond the range of all but the biggest of Allied howitzers.

Behind the Kriemhilde were local and area reserve forces, primed to counterattack the inevitably disorganized American units that had managed to get this far. German tactical doctrine adhered almost religiously to the dogma of counterattack in dealing with enemy offensives. Their long experience of mostly defensive warfare on the Western Front had convinced the Germans that a sure way of stopping Allied attacks was to vigorously counterattack their troops as they were trying to consolidate their gains. The Germans believed that no matter what the odds, they could "hold out until the enemy's will to fight is drained."[8]

Some eight kilometers north of the Kriemhilde, stretched the last-ditch defenses of the Germans—the Freya Stellung, extending from Dun-sur-Meuse west across the Barricourt Heights and on into the Bois de Bourgogne, the forest north of the Aire River and the Argonne. This final fallback position was lightly manned, because the Germans assumed that very few surviving attackers would make it through the first four lines. The stellungen would burn themselves into the memories of the men who would have to face them. As one Yank participating in the battle observed, "If I live to one hundred, I'll never forget Giselher, Kriemhilde and Freya. They were real witches."[9]

All these lines flowed on east and west of the target area, but they were compressed tightly in this American sector to act as an impenetrable buffer between the Allies and the strategic railroad line from Sedan to Metz. The Allied high command had diagnosed the German defenses as impregnable. Pershing had determined that "no Allied troops had the morale or aggressive spirit to overcome the difficulties in that sector."[10] Pétain estimated that winter would arrive before the Americans reached the top of Montfaucon. But Pershing, nonetheless, planned on taking the falcon's mount on the first day of his offensive, breaching the Hindenburg Line in two days, and pushing on toward the ultimate target—the Sedan-Metz Railroad.

The American commander's seemingly pie-in-the-sky optimism was based not only on his overblown confidence in American grit and gumption, but on German deficiencies as well. The stellungs might have, at first glance, looked invincible, but the kaiser's shield here was less sturdy than it appeared. German construction teams and engineers had erected bunkers and observation posts with both comfort and security in mind. Five miles north of the front line in the Argonne was the epitome of German defensive engineering, at the Alris der Kronprinz (the crown prince's HQ during the 1916 Battle of Verdun). The concrete bunker featured marble floors and crystal chandeliers. To maintain the defenders in comfort (and even splendor for the aristocratic officer corps), the Germans had laid narrow-gauge railroad tracks to supply dumps within hailing distance of the front.

But such was the resulting confidence in these defensive arrays, that, in the last year, complacency had crept in, and neglect had even nudged its way into the German mindset. A good number of the artillery emplacements were without guns, transferred elsewhere on the Western Front during this season of great offensives. In places, the wire entanglements had been allowed to rust away (as they had at St. Mihiel). The Etzel Line, zig-zagging across Montfaucon, was incomplete. The wire in front was sharp and sturdy and the earthworks expertly sited, but the connecting trenchline was only the depth of a single spade. Gaps existed in the Kriemhilde, as well. The barbed bulwark in front sat in sinister contemplation of the flesh it would flay, but the trenches here too were shallow, and the German infantry lacked sufficient dugouts with the thick overhead cover needed to protect against Allied artillery.

The primary German debility, however, and by far the most significant factor in Pershing's calculus of confidence, was the simple fact that the Germans were spread too thin within all those magnificent defenses. The terrain may have been splendid and the fortifications, in general, superb, but the number and quality of the men manning the defenses were subpar. In early September, only five German divisions, totaling about 61,500 men, guarded the territory between the Meuse and the Argonne. The German divisions, in line and reserve, each deployed only nine infantry battalions, in contrast to the twelve in a U.S. division, and most of the personnel were either second-line Saxon or Austro-Hungarian reserve troops of maximum age and minimum training, or worn-out veterans, like those of the 1st Guards Division, hoping for rest in a quiet sector after enduring the trauma of the spring 1918 offensives. Some of the divisions were of only one-third authorized strength. Of eighteen Central Powers divisions between the Aisne and Verdun, only three were rated first class.

It was because of this resulting eight-to-one superiority in front-line troops and a three-to-one advantage in artillery that Pershing felt confident that his doughboys could punch a salient ten miles deep in a single day. Though this faith in his army's ability flew in the face of three years of Western Front experience—that measured progress at yards attained in weeks of bloody futility against defenses and terrain far less imposing than that of the Meuse-Argonne—Pershing believed that, with the right spirit and right determination, St. Mihiel could be repeated and on a vaster and more decisive scale. But speed was of the essence and even more so was secrecy. For beyond the five feeble front-line German divisions were huge numbers of enemy reinforcements only a short railroad ride away.

Total German strength on the extended front, from Verdun to the Argonne, was eighteen divisions, all of them assigned to the Third and Fifth Armies of Army Group von Gallwitz, with twelve more in reserve, most of which were arrayed around Metz. Pershing's staff estimated that four German divisions could be added to the fray within a day after H-Hour, two more in forty-eight hours, and as many as nine additional divisions by the end of the third day. With twenty enemy divisions on the Meuse-Argonne battlefield, even understrength or of less than top-notch quality, the defenses would become virtually unbreakable. American success, consequently, even with all their vaunted vigor and verve, depended absolutely on striking without warning and striking with unprecedented rapidity.

The AEF staff went to great lengths to shield both their paper plans and their plans put into motion from the inquisitive eyes of the enemy. Pershing stressed that, "Absolute secrecy must be maintained until the last moment."[11] In addition to restricting all troop movement to nighttime, the First Army changed its communication codes from those employed in the St. Mihiel Offensive only days before. The AEF also attempted to deceive the enemy into thinking that the Allied assault would occur east of the Meuse. To that end, decoy radio stations were set up, a dummy force assembled to simulate a strike on that opposite side of the river, and American tanks and air squadrons increased their activity in and over the zone of distraction. Though a good number of local German commanders remained undeceived by these measures, the Hun high command seems to have been taken in by the Yankee trickery.

Army group commander von Gallwitz was convinced that Pershing's First Army would undertake an important and independent mission against his armies, but he continued to assume that the AEF would roll out from its newly won ground in the St. Mihiel Salient, across the Woevre plain toward Metz. He imparted that assumption to Fifth Army commander Georg der von Marwitz on September 16, and increased the number of reserves east of the Meuse.

Still, even with German eyes (or at least the most important of enemy eyes) focused east of the Meuse for the onrush of the khakied columns, Pershing's plan, nonetheless, represented a roll of the dice, probably the riskiest offensive gamble any American commander has ever undertaken. Black Jack's hopes rode on the unbloodied elan of a quarter of a million doughboys, half of whom were draftees, swamping the few tired troops of the German Empire, driving to the Kriemhilde Line by the end of the offensive's first day, and punching on through on the second. St. Mihiel was the inspiration for his hopes, but Pershing was tasking the First Army with an advance of ten miles in less than two days, a rate of progress twice that achieved at St. Mihiel across easier terrain and against an enemy already in full retreat.

Prospects for such speedy success were dimmed further by the fact that none of the best Yankee divisions—the 1st, 2nd, 3rd and 42nd—had yet redeployed from St. Mihiel or the Aisne-Marne. The offensive would also be without the veteran 27th and 30th Divisions, sent to help the British at St. Quentin, the rookie 76th, serving with the French in Champagne, and, later, the 37th and 91st in Flanders. Four of the nine divisions launching the attack had not been "kissed" (Army slang for having seen no combat), not even in "quiet" sectors. As Private Vernon Nicholls, one of the green soldiers in those untested divisions, related, "going over the top" was "still but a figure of speech."[12] He and his comrades in arms had neither the training nor the discipline for any kind of tactical finesse. They could only charge straight up the gut with an enthusiasm born of youth and ignorance—an enthusiasm that would probably shatter with the first burst of the Maxims.

Pershing was well aware that, aside from the heavy metal of his massed artillery, success rested almost entirely on his soldiers' innocent savagery, and on the sheer numbers of those young men carrying that aggressive spirit into battle. That spirit would inevitably shrink before the blast of German firepower and in the hard hump up all those rocky ridges, but Black Jack was betting that the American dynamo would have energy enough to force a passage before the arrival of enemy reserves and reinforcements drained it of all power. Pershing insisted that, "The attack must be pushed with the greatest vigor.... Division commanders will deploy their infantry in sufficient depth to give fresh impulses to the attack when necessary."[13]

The minuet of advance would be at a pace of 100 meters every four minutes, in step with the rolling artillery barrage and regardless of all the waiting wire and crazy quilt of defenses. His foot soldiers would maintain this extraordinary pace by "utilizing lanes of least resistance, outflanking, etc."—a tactical two-step that Ludendorff's storm troops had performed with expertise in the spring 1918 offensives, after months of special training, years of front-line experience, and lifetimes of ingrained discipline, but totally beyond the capabilities of untrained and untested American city boys and hayseeds.[14]

To a good number of observers, however, this very inexperience was an asset. American troops, hitherto untainted by the toxic stalemate of the Western Front, might seek, regardless of losses, the keys to an unattainable kingdom, up to now locked securely against the wiser and sadder veterans of the Allied armies. German morale might be undermined by all those headstrong hordes of fresh troops insistent on glory no matter what the price. After all, hadn't the American victory at St. Mihiel, following the German debacle at Amiens on that "Black Day" just a month before, turned Ludendorff from the architect of victory into "a completely broken man?"[15]

Such optimism was not shared by all, particularly not by gloomy French observers, who maintained memories of Joseph Joffre's confidence in 1915 and Nivelle's ebullience in 1917, both wrecked disastrously on the plains of Picardy and the ridges of the Chemin des Dames. A French liaison officer with the 77th Division predicted to General Alexander, on the eve of the offensive: "I have no doubt that your men are brave and that you have made every preparation that will give them a chance of victory tomorrow, but permit me to say that, in my opinion, the line in your front will not move. It has been in place for four years, is solidly established, well wired in, and the Boche is a good soldier. I fear that you will not be able to make the advance you hope for."[16] Alexander, undaunted by this foreboding forecast, assured his French adviser that the street scrappers of his 77th would prevail.

Pershing's operational plan envisioned a first wave of 100,000 infantrymen rolling over the enemy line at H-Hour, followed closely by the commitment of the rest of the 250,000 men in the three U.S. corps. Eight divisions would surge across the land between the river and the woods, while one division—the 77th—would storm into the Argonne Forest itself. The might and power of a young America would carry all before it. It was to be the single greatest attack yet in U.S. military history.

The ultimate aim of that attack was in the eye of the beholder. For Foch, the American mission was just part of a flurry of body blows to the increasingly brittle spine of the Boche lifeline, specifically a movement in support of the French Fourth Army, deployed west of the Aisne, that would outflank the German line on the east. Foch's September orders directed the U.S. First Army to breach the Kriemhilde position, continue toward Buzancy, and on north to Stonne. Pershing concurred with those limited ambitions, as far as they went, but foresaw a far grander sweep beyond, to the vital railroad links at Mézières and Sedan (the site at which Napoleon III's empire had died in 1870), where the Meuse curved west some twenty miles beyond the Aisne, and twenty-seven miles north of the First Army's line of departure. The doughboys' supreme commander projected his khakied conquerors unhinging the whole Hun line, becoming an unstoppable force that would not abate, even at the banks of the Rhine.

The city slickers of the 77th, tasked with conquering the toughest terrain on the front, served as the westernmost division of three in the offensive's left wing corps—General Hunter Liggett's I Corps. Liggett's other two divisions, from left to right, were the 28th (Pennsylvania National Guard) and the 35th (Kansas and Missouri National Guard).

Making the main effort against Montfaucon in the center was George Cameron's V Corps of three divisions—from left to right, the 91st, 37th and 79th. Unlike the experienced Liggett and his 28th and 77th Divisions, Cameron had no combat experience at corps level and all his divisions were unblooded. Arriving in France only in July 1918, the 79th had not even completed the minimal training other AEF divisions had received before being moved up to the line, 50 percent of its personnel had joined the division only since May 1918, and many of its experienced NCOs had been levied to other divisions as replacements. And yet, the 79th was assigned the Falcon Mountain itself as its first day objective. To compound the challenge, because of the rugged nature of the terrain, the division would undertake this mission with only minimal tank support.

The right wing corps—General Robert Bullard's III Corps—faced less daunting demands, and its leftmost division—the 4th—was a Regular outfit that had fought at Soissons. To the right of the 4th were the 80th and 33rd Divisions, with the right flank of the 33rd (and of the whole U.S. First Army) resting on the Meuse.

Across the Meuse, facing the heights east of the river, was the French XVII Corps of three divisions—from left to right, the 18th, 10th Colonial and 15th Colonial. This French corps, charged with protecting the right flank of the American offensive, was under the operational command of the U.S. First Army.

Beyond the Argonne, west of the Aisne, stood the French Fourth Army, which was to advance into Champagne, in conjunction with Pershing's offensive, to clear the Bois de Bourgogne, the vast forest north of the Argonne. A brigade, under French tactical command, consisting of a French infantry regiment and the all–African American 368th Infantry Regiment of the U.S. 92nd Division, was charged with maintaining contact between the flanks of the U.S. First Army and the French Fourth Army.

Much depended upon the might and muscle of the artillery. The guns of the III Corps had a particularly vital mission in suppressing the German howitzers atop the looming heights east of the Meuse. The batteries of I Corps also had a primary part to play in whatever success was in the offing; those guns had to silence the enemy artillery hidden in the Argonne depths.

Though the campaign took its official title from the terrain features on its flanks—the Meuse River and the Argonne Forest—the focus of the offensive, in its first phase, was on Falcon Mountain. The First Army staff knew full well what a formidable chore capturing Montfaucon would be. Rather than take on the position directly, the staff planned to seize deep salients in the enemy lines on both sides of the stronghold. From that captured ground, American units would then sally toward the rear of Montfaucon's garrison. Pressed in front by the 79th Division troops arrayed directly south of the hill and harassed from the rear by the flanking regiments, the strongest enemy position on the front would, hopefully, fall without too severe a struggle. The V Corps would then, without waiting for the adjacent corps to keep pace, vigorously maintain its momentum, surging to the northwest of Montfaucon to pierce the next Boche line, near Romagne.

Such was the theory, at least. On the morning of September 26 the paper plans would be held up to the fire, and god-awful reality would have its sway. The human instruments of the staff's dreams were—by way of Marshall's logistical miracle—in their jump-off positions on the evening of September 25, wet, weary and tremulous with anticipation. The old French positions and the tracks leading to them, now occupied by the Yanks, were a muddy malediction, a gray soup stirred by years of German shellfire and French autumn rains. Senses nearly benumbed and nerves rubbed raw by days of ceaseless movement were granted no reprieve to rest and revive in the French rifle pits before the massed batteries commenced a long-range harassing fire on the Hun rear areas at 2330 on the eve of the offensive.

The men of the Metro Division hunched expectantly, at that hour, in their trenches north and east of the village of La Harazeé, swallowing hard with the anticipatory lumps in their throats, waiting for the word and the whistle to propel them into the northern half of the forest, held by the enemy since 1914. The ground they would have to cross had been thoroughly investigated and analyzed by corps commander Hunter Liggett and his divisional COs—Robert Alexander of the 77th, Charles H. Muir of the 28th, and Peter E. Traub of the 35th—in collaboration with General Hirschauer of the French Second Army, which, up until just a few days ago, had held the sector.

Liggett was keenly aware of the obstacle the Argonne presented to Allied ambitions. He described the forest as similar in geographical terms to Manhattan Island, but a Manhattan of malign intent. Its Hudson and East Rivers equivalents were the Aisne on the west and the Aire on the east. The Aire is a secondary stream, flowing northwest to curve beyond the north border of the Argonne and join the Aisne at Grandpré.

No man more acutely delineated the treacherous contours of the devil's den into which his soldiers had to descend on that September morn: "The region was a natural forest besides which the Virginia Wilderness in which Grant and Lee fought was a park. It was masked and tortuous before the enemy strung his first wire and dug his first trench.... The underbrush had grown up through the German barbed and rabbit wire, interlacing it and concealing it, and machine guns lurked like copperheads in the ambush of shell-fallen trees. Other machine guns were strewn in concrete pillboxes and in defiles. On the offensive, tanks could not follow, nor artillery see what it was shooting, while the enemy guns, on the defensive, could fire by map.... Patently it would be suicidal to attack such a labyrinth directly; it must be pinched out by attacks on either side."[17]

The I Corps commander was one of the Army's most respected leaders, a soldier who had won the admiration and, just as often, affection, of superiors and subordinates alike. Loyalty was one of his sterling qualities, both to the men he commanded and to the men who commanded him. When those respective loyalties came in conflict, as they inevitably do in the milieu of the military, Liggett's moral integrity took over as the final arbiter.

Born on March 21, 1857, in Reading, Pennsylvania, Liggett was the son of a tailor and part-time politician. Graduating from West Point in 1879, it took him eighteen years to make captain in the peacetime Army, serving in Texas, Georgia and Florida. His first real exposure to combat came against Aguinaldo's guerrillas in the Philippines in 1899–1901. He attended the Army War College from 1909–10, and two years later, after making colonel, he served as president of the same institution.

The expansion of the Army in the months before the U.S. entry into the Great War enabled Liggett to sew two stars onto his lapels. He disembarked in France in October 1917 as commander of the 41st Sunset Division. In January 1918, Liggett's manifest qualities of character and competence overcame his primary physical shortcoming—his excessive weight— to win him command of the AEF's I Corps. Pershing, with his firm belief that a well-defined body was indicative of a disciplined mind, was generally contemptuous of senior officers with supersize waistlines. Liggett's answer to his fat-conscious critics was that weight was "the more serious if the fat is above the collar."[18]

Liggett's I Corps first saw action at Château Thierry, during the Second Battle of the Marne, while attached to the French Sixth Army during Germany's Champagne-Marne Offensive. The ensuing Allied counteroffensive (the Aisne-Marne) witnessed Liggett's corps driving the expended enemy divisions across the Ourq and Vesle Rivers.

On August 10, 1918, the I Corps became part of Pershing's First Army, and four of its divisions made up the right wing of the offensive that eliminated the St. Mihiel Salient, September 12–16. In the Argonne Forest and the Aire Valley, the men of the I Corps would face their paramount challenge. The corps commander was one of their greatest assets in this the greatest of their endeavors. Guided by principles of fair-mindedness, this taciturn man of simple tastes and subdued self-regard was a master at analyzing both a tactical situation and a man's heart. He was an expert at separating the wheat from the overabundance of martial chaff. Liggett once commented that, "War provokes more muddled thinking than any human activity I know of."[19] Liddell Hart judged him "the soundest reasoner and the strongest realist in the American Army."[20]

Other than faith in their corps commander, the only lantern lighting the hopes of the 77th's soldiers as they faced the dark display ahead of them was the overconfidence of the enemy. The Germans had consigned the defense of the Argonne to the middle-aged reservists of a single Württemburg second-line division—the 2nd Landwehr—so certain were they that the forest was impenetrable. Nevertheless, it was recognized by all that the treacherous traceries of the Argonne made rapid progress improbable, if not impossible. Consequently, the 77th's assignment was not penetration, but containment. The mission of the boys from the big city was to fix the foe in place to prevent them from interfering, by way of either artillery fire or infantry counterattack, with the 28th Division, to the right of the 77th. The 28th Division's objective, in turn, was to screen the east side of the forest and the Aire River, in order to protect the flank of the V Corps, undertaking the main breakthrough assault in the center.

Alexander's New York division faced the opposing German division along a four-mile front, the longest divisional front of the American offensive. The commanding general had all four of his infantry regiments on line for the big push—from west to east, the 308th,

307th, 306th and 305th—with each battalion column in each regiment arrayed in a two-company front.

The preliminary cannonade, meant to vex the enemy, but nearly as onerous a harassment to the doughboys in the forward trenches, ended at 0230 on September 26. At that moment, the darkness disappeared in a blinding flash, and heaven collapsed in a resounding crash. The lightning of cannon flashed across the sky like great yellow snakes. Gunners, simultaneously or in quick succession, had tugged the lanyards of 2,417 artillery pieces—one gun per eight meters of front—ranging in size from 75 mm field guns to 14-inch U.S.-made railroad guns (later five American 15-inch naval guns, mounted on trains, would add the weight and twenty-five-mile range of their 1,400-pound projectiles to the pummeling power of the Allied artillery.)

Both because he had lacked the time to build up a huge artillery ammunition supply, and because he had opted for surprise to overwhelm the enemy, Pershing had decided on a relatively

Maj. General Hunter Liggett, C.O. I Corps. National Archives, 111-SC-73140.

brief three-hour-long bombardment. But while it lasted the shelling was stupendous—1,000 rounds per battery, six rounds per gun per minute, 2,600,000 rounds in total. There had certainly never been anything like it in American military history. With the aid of the observers in thirteen balloons tethered over the front, the Allied cannoneers blasted the enemy's trenches, wire, rear and roads with 40,000 tons of explosives, more ordnance than was expended by both sides in all the artillery duels of the American Civil War. Included among those hundreds of thousands of impacting artillery rounds were 800 phosgene and mustard gas shells that killed 278 Germans and sickened up to 10,000 more.

The troops in the trenches called it the "million dollar barrage" as they huddled against the quaking ground. Veterans of the Second Marne were astounded at the power unleashed, and the soldiers of the green divisions were nearly untethered from their senses by the reverberating roar of the tubed terror obliterating the night sky.

General Alexander witnessed the bombardment atop a knoll near his HQ dugout. Captain Eddie Rickenbacker, flying with his Hat-in-the-Ring squadron against German observation balloons, reported that, "Through the darkness the whole western horizon was illumined with one mass of jagged flashes," as if a switch had been thrown on a giant switchboard.[21]

III Corps commander General Bullard watched this mind-numbing display from his

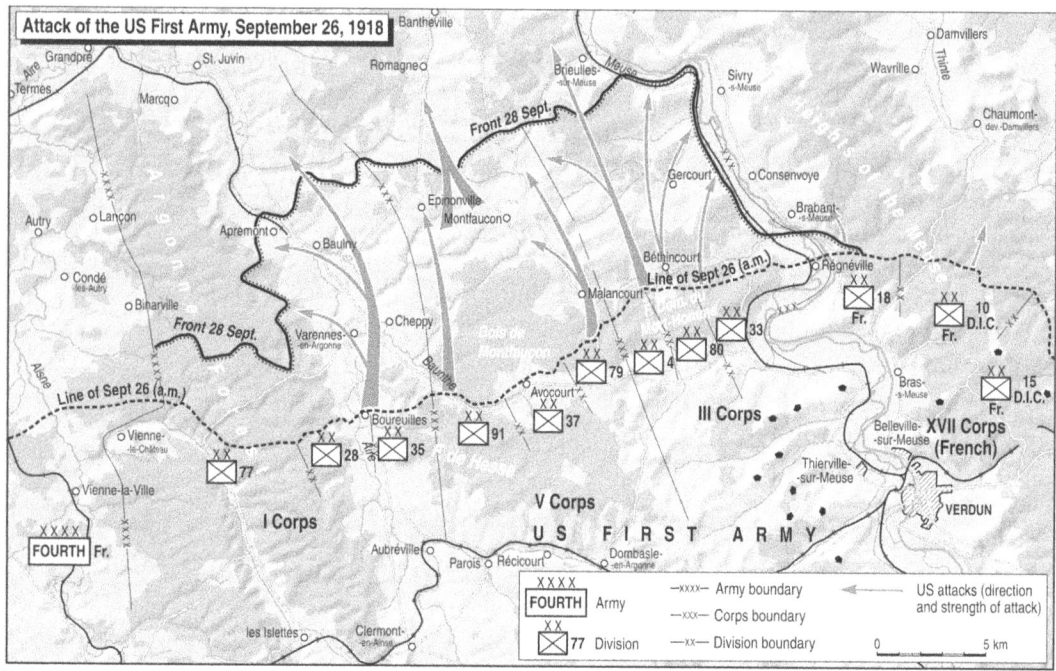

infantrymen's forward positions and recalled, "Silent blackness gave way to what one vivid imagination described as the sound of a million express trains. Besides the noise there was the feel of concussion, quivering ground, livid skies."[22]

On the other side, where the targets of all this tempest lay, General von Gallwitz watched his windows rattle in his headquarters at Montmedy, twenty-five miles distant from the Allied batteries. Most of the Germans under the falling fury burrowed down in their bunkers and survived this shrapnel-slide, but the men of the 5th Bavarian Reserve Division, ordered across from the east bank of the Meuse to reinforce the 7th and 117th Reserve Divisions, were caught in midstride by Pershing's barrage and suffered mightily. Overall, however, the light French 75 mm field guns, which made up much of the Allied artillery, were unable to penetrate the heavily fortified German defenses.

At 0530 the Allied artillery shifted gears and the prepatory fires were reforged as rolling barrages, which were to lay down a carpet of cordite 100 meters beyond the bayonets of the advancing infantry. It was time for the troops to go over the top. As George Marshall observed: "The troops were tired when they went into the fight. They had been held in the woods in wet clothes and wet feet for a week or more, made a long march the night before going in, without any sleep."[23] Even worse, a good number of the men making the attack were debilitated further by the flu, making its first inroads into an army that would suffer cataclysmically from its scourge in the coming months. Now their bodies and minds had incurred further stress from the thunder and awe of a three-hour shellstorm, and it was time to step foot into the inferno.

The infantry, indeed, had endured much travail in simply deploying from their assembly areas to the formerly French front-line positions the evening before. As the redlegs of the artillery opened up fields of fire in front of their gun pits—by severing the cable holding up the concealing trees (already sawed through to save time)—the foot soldiers had gathered their gear and started the trudge up the approach roads. Those narrow lanes were clogged with ammunition wagons and supply trucks headed toward the front and with last-minute poilus, who had, moments before, manned the forward trenches and were now making their way toward the rear. Though the evening was free of rain, the roads were still swampy from prior downpours, and the poor grunts of the infantry often had to help free the vehicles, animal-borne and motorized alike, from the muddy tracks. Nonetheless, with all the congestion and all the delays, the infantrymen were in place and ready when the whistles blew.

Though those infantrymen and their indomitable will would have to carry the main load of the offensive, Pershing's planners had tried to supplement that fighting spirit with as much firepower as possible. The rifle battalions themselves carried Stokes mortars, two-man-operated 37 mm field guns, and rifle grenades, as well as two 75 mm field guns for each battalion. In addition to all the conventional artillery, the Allied batteries were amply supplied with poison gas shells. On the front's right wing, the French XVII Corps artillery would be spiraling mustard gas rounds onto the parapets atop the Meuse Heights. The mustard gas would cling to and contaminate the landscape, but would not be a danger to Allied forces, since no attack was scheduled there in the battle's early stages. However, on the American length of the front, only non-persistent poison would be laid down, so that the deadly fumes would dissipate by the time the doughboy regiments rolled forward.

Rolling along with those doughboys were 189 French-made light tanks, only 47 of them in support of the V Corps in the center. Lt. Colonel George Patton's brigade of 142 tanks accompanied Liggett's I Corps in the Aire Valley, where the terrain was more an undulating plain and not so broken by copse and stream. Twenty-five percent of those tanks carried French crews. Aloft were 842 aircraft, commanded by Colonel Billy Mitchell, 600 of which were piloted by Americans. Pershing had hoped for more planes—he had been able to send nearly 1,500 into the sky over St. Mihiel—but the need for air support was Western Front-wide, as the British attacked at Cambrai and across the Lys River and the French Fourth Army prepared to attack in Champagne, on Pershing's left. Nevertheless, the air resources available to the U.S. First Army still outnumbered the enemy in the Meuse-Argonne by three to one.

Fog and cordite smoke drew heavy drapes across the landscape, but the Allied gunners went ahead with the preplanned smoke barrage to further conceal the attacking infantry. With the order of "Fix bayonets!" relayed up and down the trenchline, officers took one last orienting glance at their maps, checked their watches, and then whistled their largely untested troops up the ladders and over the top. For more than fifteen miles, from La Harazeé to Brabant, from the Argonne to the Meuse, the helmeted infantrymen, burdened by backpacks and gas masks, advanced, nearly shoulder to shoulder, at a solemn pace into the morning mist and into history. The only light in the gray gloom was the occasional glint from a bayoneted rifle. The men remaining in the trenches lost sight of the first wave of American infantrymen as they disappeared into the wooly atmosphere, though their cordite-coarsened cheers could still be heard.

For a minute or two, once the last cheers had died away and the rolling barrage had momentarily lifted—as it did every four minutes to adjust fires forward another 100 meters in front of the advancing troops—the noise of battle abated. The saturated shroud of gray seemed to smother all in silence. The men paraded forward in perfect order, across ground turned, "as if by a giant's plow," for perhaps fifty yards, before the impediment of their own wire and the broken furniture of war and nature began to sow confusion.[24] The smoke laid down by the American artillery caused some of the initial disarray, when a good many of the green doughboys mistook the screening haze for German poison gas. In their frenzied haste to don gas masks, soldiers lost contact with their comrades and their units. Most men did manage to cling closely to their platoon commanders, but some of those officers themselves led men astray, as they followed the assigned azimuth on compasses crazed by the distorted polarity of this four-year-old battlefield, replete with the embedded steel of constant combat.

The barbed billows of wire, both friendly and foreign, further disrupted the tidy formations and stately procession before a single enemy gun had sounded. The old wire laid down by the French first confounded them. The 79th Division, chaste before Mars, but given the day's most vital mission in the center of the line, was allotted twenty-five minutes to cut through those tangles, while Allied 75 mm guns and trench mortars attempted to slash gaps in the German wire up ahead. Designated details laid chicken wire bridges over the wire, while engineers out in front of the infantry were already trying to blast passages through the steel web with Bangalore torpedoes. As wiggle room opened, soldiers started bunching up at the gaps, further degrading unit integrity. Their ears still ringing from the rolling barrage, the boys in khaki finally cleared the first wire to meld into a miasma of fog, shell craters and old trench networks. The original parade-ground formations were rapidly turning into a jumble of disoriented men. The chaos accelerated when supporting battalions, trailing the first wave by 1,000 yards, caught up and merged their befuddlement with the original bewilderment.

Nevertheless, the doughboys' momentum and the fog's obscurity carried them forward toward the enemy wire and emplacements. The attackers had encountered many obstacles already, but, except for the isolated machine-gun burst, enemy fire was not among them. Reaching the German wire, soldiers hacked away at the strands to scurry and squirm ahead to within a few yards of where their own artillery was impacting on the German trenches.

Now, shaking off the concussive punches of the Allied bombardment, the enemy outpost zone started sputtering to life. Counter-battery fire sent shrapnel slashing, and machine-gun nests—both tripod-mounted Maxim 08s and the lighter bipod-mounted Maxim 08/15s—cranked into action. The Pennsylvanians and Marylanders of Maj. General Joseph E. Kuhn's 79th Division tasted the toxic flavor of battle for the first time as they approached Montfaucon butte. A brigadier general of this Liberty Division was soon relaying rearward to his division CO a message of distress: "Fields are covered with barbed wire and 'cheveaux de frise'. Men cannot get through. The men are disorganized and are under heavy shrapnel fire. As soon as the sun raises fog, men will be cut to pieces by machine-gun fire."[25]

That fog began to lift about 0930. Evaporating with the mist was the 79th's hopes for a quick success. The division was in no way prepared for what was to come. Everything that had been lacking about American training, preparation and deployment was accented and epitomized by the Liberty Division. Its deficiencies started at the top, with a commanding officer, General Kuhn, who, though a fine and experienced officer overall, had served most of his career as an engineer and was poorly cast as a leader of warriors. The division, while still in training, had been gutted several times to provide filler for other newly formed divisions—60 percent of the infantry and 50 percent of the artillery were composed of personnel who had sewn its Maltese Cross-on-a-blue-shield patch to their uniforms only after May

25, 1918. Many of its senior officers had been transferred shortly after the division arrived in France in July 1918. The two infantry brigades of the division were going into battle without the organic division artillery regiment, which had been kept behind the lines for further training. The 79th's training at Camp Meade, Maryland, had been so minimal that a War Department inspector had recommended that the unit be retained for further instruction just before it was to embark for France. Now the 79th, ticketed with the toughest assignment, with the fewest resources of any of the nine attacking divisions, was to suffer for its shortcomings and endure the only major setback on a day of otherwise nearly unbroken American success.

Kuhn sent 12,000 men of his division into the uphill attack in a column of brigades, one behind the other, even though his assigned division front was a much-too-wide 3,000 yards long. The fog of war and the real fog, the clamor and confusion, conspired to disrupt communication both between the attacking units and back to 79th Division HQ. Kuhn and his staff heard little of what was transpiring. Kuhn optimistically translated this absence of information into a picture of progress. Acting on this assumption that no news was good news, Kuhn at 1040 advised Cameron's V Corps HQ that the division had reached a line running north of the Bois de Montfaucon to northeast of Montfaucon butte itself. Cameron passed the joyful news of the capture of the butte on to First Army HQ at Souilly. But Montfaucon had not fallen; the Liberty Division's regiments were not yet even close to their objective.

The lead regiments did indeed make it through the wire and the first enemy trenchline, as the sun broke through to warm the morning air. But once into the open, they began to encounter the wrath of the aroused enemy. Caught in the fire-swept ground, the troops demonstrated their lack of training, poor small-unit leadership, and inexperience, by milling around and bunching up, confused and disoriented, and by failing to take action against the ratcheting machine guns. Unable to pick out direct rifle-fire targets among the well-concealed enemy, the rookie riflemen generally did not think to use their grenades or call for indirect fire from supporting trench mortars. The few tanks in support got hung up in ditches and presented easy targets for German artillery. Battalion commanders, obsessed about their flanks, held up their units until sister units could move up and restore proper alignment.

The 314th Infantry Regiment did seize the ruins of the village of Malancourt, southeast of Montfaucon, but the sister regiment, the 313th, got scattered in the Bois de Cusy to the west as the day lengthened and enemy resistance stiffened. By the time the regimental commander put his battalions back together for an assault on the butte, it was too late. Without Stokes mortars, and with their machine guns and 37 mm guns unable to keep up with the advancing infantry, the 313th, as dusk set in, threw a battalion, meagerly supported by French tanks, across the valley two kilometers in front of the Montfaucon heights. Six of the tanks were quickly destroyed by German batteries. The doughboys attacked straight into the fire lanes of the expertly sited Hun machine guns. They had no chance, and after forty-five minutes of bloody futility, the regimental commander conceded failure. As darkness fell on the offensive's first day, the 79th could claim an advance of three miles—a vast distance by Western Front offensive standards—but the key to the whole German line remained beyond their grasp, another one and a half miles away.

The essential element in Pershing's breakout strategy was thus in question, but success that first day on both flanks of the butte position provided hope that the setback was only a delay, not a disaster. Deep salients were dredged into the Boche line, east and west of the butte, to render the position vulnerable. On the right, Maj. General John Hines and the Regulars of the 4th Division, from Bullard's III Corps, stepped off smartly, took Septsarges, seven miles from the line of departure, and advanced a mile beyond Montfaucon on the low-lying ground east of the butte. They fought off three German counterattacks by the 5th Bavarian Reserve and 7th Divisions during the afternoon. Unfortunately, in its sweep, the Ivy Division left a line of German machine guns intact on the 79th's extreme flank. This, plus fears of crossing corps boundaries in apprehension of friendly fire incidents and entangled units, prevented the success of the 4th Division from carrying over much to the benefit of the beleaguered 79th. Two companies of the 4th, for example, were in position for five hours to storm Montfaucon, but waited in vain for the 79th to come up.

To the left (west) of Kuhn's division, Maj. General Charles Farnsworth's 37th Buckeye Division (National Guard troops from Ohio and West Virginia) punched into the Bois de Montfaucon, and even made a brief, but unsuccessful, swing at the butte itself, before digging in for the night to the south of Ivoiry. Further west, Maj. General William Johnston's 91st Wild West Division moved forward with alacrity four miles through Cheppy Wood to secure, late in the morning, Epinonville on the Giselher Line. Though enemy artillery and infantry counterattacks pushed the 91st out of the town in short order, the division swerved left to extend its salient to the town of Very.

Bullard's other two divisions also had a successful day. Maj. General Adelbert Cronkhite's 80th Blue Ridge Division, to the right of the 4th, swept past Bethincourt and forged its way forward four miles to a line just north of Dannevoux, where the division dug in under heavy machine-gun fire from Brieulles Wood and continual shelling, directed by observers on the Borne de Cornouiller (Hill 378), east of the Meuse. The furthest right of all the U.S. divisions—Maj. General George Bell's 33rd Prairie Division (National Guard troops from Illinois)—represented the hinge of the whole American offensive. With supporting fire from Morte Homme (an infamous landmark of the Battle of Verdun), the division banged through the Forges Wood and moved up along the Meuse, on the First Army's eastern border and the pivot point with the French XVII Corps, east of the river. Division and corps engineers led the way into the marshland cuffing the Meuse, as, under steady fire, they used fascines and wooden planks to build foot bridges for the infantry coming up behind them. The 33rd overran an enemy engineer depot and a light railway, and captured thirty cannon, as well as dozens of machine guns. Three men of the division, all from the 132nd Infantry Regiment, won the Medal of Honor that first day in Forges Wood.

The three flanking divisions of I Corps, on the opposite (west) wing of the offensive, also fared well on September 26. Liggett's rightmost division, astride the corps boundary with V Corps, was the 35th Santa Fe Division (National Guard troops from Kansas and Missouri), commanded by Maj. General Peter Traub. The frowning obstacle before the Midwesterners was the Butte de Vauquois, threaded with tunnels and pillboxes. Vauquois, two miles east of the Argonne, had been contested for years, and the top of the butte had been obliterated by 520 French and German underground detonations, as the rivals tried to blow each other off the escarpment with almost 1,000 tons of explosives. (It is to this day only a series of overlapping craters.) All those explosions and 4,000 dead Frenchmen had not removed the Hun from the butte. General Traub wisely chose to bypass the position on both sides and leave follow-up units to convince the cut-off German garrison to surrender. Pushing on to Cheppy, the men of the 35th battled through barbed wire and concrete pillboxes to a line south of Charpentry, with their left flank anchored on the Aire River, four miles beyond the trenches they had left at dawn.

Among the redlegs seeding a shrapnel screen ahead of the 35th's infantry was Captain Harry S. Truman, commander of D Battery, 2nd Battalion, 129th Field Artillery, made up mostly of Irish Catholics from Kansas City, Missouri, and Truman's own home town of Independence, Missouri. Truman had awakened at 0400 to take charge of his battery, just moments before a German barrage landed in the woods where he and his men had been sleeping. His four-gun, 194-man battery had pumped out rounds rapidly during the rolling barrage—3,000 rounds from 0400 to 0800—making the guns so hot, according to Truman, "that they would boil the wet gunnysacks we put on them to keep them cool."[26]

To maintain cover for the swiftly advancing foot soldiers, the 75 mm guns of the 129th were directed to "march order" from their original battery positions to a new deployment, one and a half miles across No Man's Land. The cannoneers' objective was a grove north of the Vauquois Butte that offered plenty of concealment, but the terrain in between was a misery of mutilated earth and pretzeled wire utterly open to the "screaming mimies" of the enemy incoming. Truman preceded his battery to reconnoiter the way forward, but soon found himself cradling the ground to duck a vicious stream of machine-gun bullets. To the redlegs, it seemed that, "every goddam German there who didn't have a machine gun had a cannon."[27]

Captain Harry Truman's 35th Division identity card. Harry S Truman Library.

Returning to his batterymates, the bespectacled Missourian rallied the gunners and led them into the kill zone. It took every ounce of strength from both men and horses, and twelve hours under almost constant artillery fire, to cross the 2,500 yards to the new position. Even friendly artillery presented a danger. A French 155 mm battery fired right over the heads of Truman's gunners as they slogged forward under an embankment. Sixty years later, the man who became a U.S. president still had hearing problems as a result.

By the end of this endless day, Harry Truman's men were nearly asleep on their feet, regardless of all the metaled thunder and screeching shrapnel.

To the west of the 35th and in the center of Liggett's corps, was Maj. General Charles Muir's 28th Keystone Division. The Pennsylvanians' progress was less spectacular than that of the 35th's, as it fought its way up the meandering Aire River, bordered by steep spurs, like Le Chêne Tondu (the Twisted Oak), projecting out from the east slopes of the Argonne ridge. This extension of the Argonne slowed down the leading left-wing regiment of the division near Champ Mahaut, but the right-hand regiment took the ruins of Varennes (where Louis XVI and Marie Antoinette were captured in 1791 while trying to flee the rages of the French Revolution), and slashed forward three miles into the more open country of the Aire Valley.

Providing an armored amphetamine to the 35th and 28th Divisions was most of the tank strength of the First Army. In practical command (if not nominal command) of the tank brigade was the flamboyant George S. Patton, a man blessed with the black arts magic of a natural born military leader, and cursed with an almost mystical sense of himself and his place in posterity.

Born and bred in high society—in fact, the Army's wealthiest officer—Patton could be both a social gadfly and a filthy-mouthed rabble rouser. Omar Bradley pointed out that Patton spouted his "earthily profane" verbiage to counter the rodent tone of a voice that was, "almost comically squeaky and high pitched, altogether lacking in command authority."[28]

The thirty-two-year-old veteran of Pershing's Mexican Expedition had, by quite natural selection, evolved from a saber-wielding cavalry officer to a passionate proponent of armored warfare. Having been scolded by tank commander Brig. General Samuel Rockenbach for leaving his command post to gallivant with the spearheading tanks at St. Mihiel, Patton, at his forward HQ, tried to rein himself in this time, as his 1st Tank Brigade of 142 six-ton French Renaults and a few heavier French Schneiders lumbered up the valley of the Aire. His impulsiveness got the better of him by 0630, and America's ultimately most famous armored officer gathered a dozen signal officers and runners with field phones and pigeons to traipse along the path of the tread tracks of the tanks that had preceded him in the direction of Boureuilles and Varennes, east of the Aire.

Gathering up infantry stragglers separated from their units in the fog, Patton's less-than-merry band soon grew to over 100 men. Advancing to a point between Cheppy and Varennes, Patton's party found itself pinned down by machine-gun fire. Scurrying back to bring up tanks to break the deadlock, Patton discovered a big French Schneider tank stuck in the muck between two wide ditches and blocking passage for all the tanks behind. Instead of digging their way out, the French crew was cowering in the trench under a swath of artillery and machine-gun fire.

Patton took charge, ignored the bullet swarm, and roused out the French crew and

American tankers to pick and shovel a passage. He parried any reluctance by the tankers to expose themselves to the heavy enemy fire with threats, imprecations, and, finally, a shovel to the skull of one malingerer. Proclaiming, "To hell with them. They can't hit me," Patton got the tanks through the mire and moving again. Waving his walking stick like a bandleader's baton, he rallied his followers with, "Let's go get them. Who's with me?" to lead them on foot toward the foe.[29]

His invulnerability ended minutes later. Cresting a rise, Patton's ad hoc platoon was raked by Maxim volleys. Flattened across the charred French earth, Patton experienced an epiphany that he described to his father in a letter nine years later: "Once in the Argonne just before I was wounded I felt a great desire to run, I was trembling with fear when suddenly I thought of my progenitors and seemed to see them in a cloud over the German lines looking at me. I became calm at once."[30]

The vision propelled Patton forward. Only six men followed, five were rapidly slain, and Patton went down with a leg wound. The only man untouched, Private Joseph Angelo, dragged his commander to a crater and applied a dressing, as Patton insisted for some time on remaining on the field to direct his tanks.* The Battle of the Meuse-Argonne lasted just one day for George S. Patton. His days in Great War combat, including St. Mihiel, totaled five. He had spent not one moment inside a tank on September 26, but he had seen his vision of armored warfare—as a concentrated strike force, not as a dispersed supporting force to supplement the infantry attack—at least partially validated. His 1st Tank Brigade made substantial gains that first day in the Aire Valley against the middle-aged Swabians of the 2nd Landwehr (Württemberg) Division, though enemy fire, particularly from Austrian 77 mm trench mortars, and mechanical malfunction swiftly sapped its strength to the point that the tank's role in the continuing offensive sputtered to insignificance as the battle ground on. Two-thirds of the 189 tanks actually engaged in the battle broke down or were destroyed. Infantry-armor cooperation and coordination had been minimal. They had not trained much together as a combined arms force and, consequently, they had not fought together effectively. Patton's tanks, for example, clanked into Varennes by 0930 on September 26, but then had to wait—while momentum slipped away—nearly four hours for the infantry to reach them. Because of the lack of spare parts, more than half of the intact tanks remaining were out of action by mid–October. Maintenance crews were scavenging the wrecked hulks of the armored vehicles in the Aire Valley, cannibalizing parts to revitalize tanks sitting idle because of mechanical breakdown. When Patton took a leave from the hospital on October 28, his inspection of the abysmal condition of his men and machines left him in a rage.

George Patton, by all accounts, carried with him from his single day in America's greatest battle no remorse for the five men he had personally led forward to their deaths, but only confirmation in his conviction of a golden destiny for himself and his iron chariots.

The westernmost U.S. division in the American offensive on September 26, and the only division fully engaged in the forest which provided the popular name for the great

---

*Fifteen years later, Private Angelo and Colonel Patton, as well as many other veterans of the Argonne, would again be locked in combat—but this time against one another. With MacArthur commanding, Patton would be one of the regimental commanders who led their troops to the violent dispersal of the Bonus Army camp in Washington, D.C. Among the Depression-devastated veterans who had come to Washington to ask for early payment of their $500 bonus promised them in recognition of their service in the Great War was the man who had saved Patton's life. Two of the veterans and two of their children died in the shameful melee in July 1932.

Doughboys of the 307th Infantry Regiment, 77th Division, in the Argonne Forest, September 26, 1918. National Archives, 111-SC-24445.

battle, was the 77th. The primary mission of the "Melting Pot" men of General Alexander's division was to fix in place the enemy in the Argonne—the 1st Prussian Guards Division, deployed from La Harazeé to Vauquois—to prevent them from impeding the sweep of the 28th Division up the west side of the Aire. A secondary mission for the division was to maintain contact and liaison with the French Fourth Army on the western edges of the forest, by way of linkage with the "sable doughboys" of the African American 368th Infantry Regiment of the 92nd Division.

Every advantage in the Argonne seemed to rest with the enemy. The 77th was wearing out before taking a first step or firing a first shot into the forest, having spent the last nine days on the march from the Vesle to get into position for the opening hour of the offensive. At almost five miles, the forested frontage that the 77th was assigned was twice that of most of the other American divisions. Artillery support for Alexander's men was limited by the poor visibility afforded the forward observers. Units, quickly confused about their exact locations, would become targets for their own artillery by calling in incorrect coordinates. Conversely, the enemy artillery had their guns and trench mortars already carefully registered, and were ready to pound the Americans as they attempted to cross each clearing. Treetop bursts would double the volume and violence of every shrapnel round.

In the green entrails of the Argonne, the leadership of junior officers and NCOs would be vitally important, but such experienced leadership was as sadly lacking in the 77th as it was in most of the AEF. And once deep into the forest, resupply for the scattered units, along the few primitive tracks, seemed a pipe dream.

The German defenses the 77th faced seemed particularly formidable. Girding the pillboxes, bunkers and machine-gun nests were several massive "pavilions," tunneled underground and prickly with weapons, as well as creature comforts that even included wine cellars. Their ground level coverings were constructed of concrete twenty feet thick and almost impervious to all but the heaviest cannon.

Alexander knew his men had the "toughest nut" to crack on the front. Trying to inject his own steel-spine drive into his men, the division commander's order of the day for September 26, read: "I want you to go in determined not to yield an inch.... Fight hard, keep your spirits high and your bayonets bright!"[31]

The fog that eventually cleared for the other American divisions on the line on September 26 lasted all day for the 77th. For when the white morning mist dissipated, the green obscurity of the forest replaced it to

Maj. General Robert Alexander, C.O. 77th Division. National Archives, 111-SC-53485.

blind Alexander's men to the peril into which they stumbled. Maintaining unit formations was nearly impossible, as the men staggered and tripped over the detritus of combat, the usual obstructions of an untamed wilderness multiplied multifold by the scything and smashing implements of war. Company commanders, even platoon commanders, lost contact with their subordinates. The ground and the gloom seemed to swallow whole squads. Senior officers, including General Alexander, left their command posts to help sort out the crazy quilt that a few German snipers and a wealth of undergrowth had created. Unit coordination dissolved, but progress was achieved in spurts by individuals and small group initiative.

Initially, the barbed wire was the most vexatious enemy encountered by the 77th. Captain Kerr Rainsford of the 307th recalled that, "everywhere [were] the piles of rusted wire. It looked as though it had taken root there among the iron chevaux-de-frise and had grown; and it was so heavy that only the longest handled cutters would bite through it."[32]

The 77th infantrymen found most enemy front-line positions abandoned, and several pavilions fell with hardly a shot fired, but as the day wore on German resistance stiffened. Machine-gun nests on the crests of such strongholds as the Bagatelle Pavilion and St. Hubert's Pavilion opened up, the barrels traversing side-to-side to send a steel stitchery against doughboys as they groped their way across gullies and ravines. Thirty-seven millimeter cannon and Stokes mortars were hauled forward to silence bunkers, and individual infantrymen wiggled within range to hurl grenades into the narrow firing slits of camouflaged machine-gun posts. But more effective in slowing the 77th's advance was the forest itself and all its frustrating profundity. The regiment on the right—the 305th—somehow moved the line ahead two and a half miles from its starting point. The left-flank regiment—the 308th—on the other hand, could manage only one mile of forward progress. As dusk descended on the grueling first day of the offensive, the 77th reported less ground conquered than any of the other American divisions (but it could console itself that the division had penetrated deeper into the northern Argonne than the French had in three years of sporadic effort). The division had reached a line flanked by the cliffs of Le Chêne Tondu on the right and La Palette Hill on the left.

The 305th and the 308th had captured several of the steel and concrete pavilions. Some of the conquests, such as Bagatelle, had been built and refined over a period of three-plus years, providing heated accommodations for up to fifty soldiers, bathrooms with hot and cold running water, larders stocked with ham, bacon, wursts and sausages cured in smokehouses, billiard tables, even flower gardens and arbors to soothe the soldiers' souls and a soccer field and grandstand to keep them athletically fit. Even the outlaying outposts of the pavilions were furnished like officers' clubrooms.

Other needs were accommodated as well. A wine cellar was discovered stocked from floor to ceiling with schnapps, champagne, fancy wines, and liqueurs. Discarded feminine apparel indicated another source of solace for the pavilion garrisons.

Luxurious they may have been, but the pavilions were powerful strongholds that, had the Germans not given them up almost without a fight for fear of being outflanked, would have caused the 77th a world of grief. The Statue of Liberty Division had trouble enough just with the rear guard units. If the pavilions had been properly defended, the New Yorkers might have barely made it beyond the start line.

Though the 77th had made only a limited lunge into the Argonne, and the Montfaucon keystone to the arch of the enemy defenses remained intact, the U.S. First Army could congratulate itself, as rain and darkness closed out September 26, in achieving progress as substantial as any made by Allied pushes over the last three years. Pershing's divisions had certainly gained more ground than the French Second Army had on the right and the French Fourth on the left. At least 950 Germany POWs had been snagged (although the official First Army records claim 5,000 POWs and 50 guns taken). The Germans had obviously been surprised, their gaze still fixed on the Aisne to the west because of the extended French artillery prep. Pershing, by first day's end, had some 140,000 men fighting or supporting the fight in a seventy-square-mile area. His doughboys, green as most of them were, had shown that they could contend—independently of their Allied big brothers—with the fearsome Hun.

Those Huns, however, were far from the precipice of panic as the second day of battle dawned. Erich Ludendorff, the supreme German commander, at his headquarters at Spa, Belgium, was, indeed, in despair as one Allied offensive after another unfolded. On September 30, he confided to General Hermann von Kuhl, "We cannot fight against the whole world."[33]

His primary hope for salvation now rested, not with his tired troops, but with the deus ex machina of the great flu epidemic ravaging Allied ranks. But otherwise, the kaiser's commanders were not unduly pessimistic about the situation twixt the Meuse and the Argonne. Gallwitz, aware that Pershing's best divisions were yet to be deployed from the St. Mihiel area, counted on American inexperience to give him time to plug the holes on the Meuse-Argonne front with reserve divisions. Four additional German divisions had trucked or tramped into the Meuse-Argonne valley by the first day's demise, and six more would arrive by nightfall of September 30. Gallwitz was not yet, in fact, even completely convinced that the Meuse-Argonne attack was the main event, but only instead, a grand diversion from the real effort further west. The German general showed his lack of worry by recording on the evening of September 26 his observation that, "On the 27th and 28th, we have no more worries."[34]

Pershing, on the other hand, spent a night suffused with worry. His troops had indeed broken through the first stretch of enemy positions against stiff resistance from three German divisions—from left to right, the 1st Guards, 117th and 7th Reserve—and had, in places, overrun the second line—the Giselher. But the enemy front-line forces had already been reinforced by elements of two more divisions, with an additional two deploying as night fell. Half of the First Army tanks were already out of action, and German artillery fire was intensifying on the American units from three sides—the Kriemhilde Line in front to the north, the Argonne ridge on the west flank, and the Meuse Heights on the east flank. Communications among and between units, as well as between artillery and infantry, was breaking down or already broken. Worst of all, the supply situation for the nine divisions immersed in the fiery furnace of combat was ominous. The terrain taken, beyond the conquered first line of German defenses, was a wilderness of shell craters over which replenishing ammunition, rations and reinforcements had to struggle. The roads and paths north from the rear into No Man's Land were almost impassable, with roadbeds collapsed and vehicles so jammed that it required twenty-four hours for a truck to inch forward ten kilometers. Pioneer troops

Traffic jam at Esne during the Meuse-Argonne Offensive. National Archives, 111-SC-24644.

and engineers were working frantically to reconstruct the ruined roads, manhandling boulders from nearby fields to resurface the avenues of approach. Staff personnel were shanghaied to moonlight as traffic control officers. But most worrisome of all was the distressing fact that Montfaucon, the fulcrum and focus of Pershing's hopes for a quick victory, yet remained in enemy hands.

This central failure, this profound miscarriage that aborted the chance for a lightning victory—possibly a knockout win-the-war blow on the eastern wing of the Allied front—and resulted in seven weeks of stalemate and deadly statistics unsurpassed in American history, has to be, to a large extent, placed on the shoulders of Black Jack Pershing. His corps commanders certainly seemed to concur with this judgment, according to their later statements. Aside from Pershing's cardinal blunder of assigning the offensive's most important objective to probably the least capable division, Liggett and Bullard agreed that their commander's rigid adherence to unit boundaries and corps objectives short-circuited several opportunities, particularly on the wings, to broaden the breakthrough and possibly win the war on a single day.

The corps commanders argued later that Pershing made a fundamental mistake when he ordered the flanking corps to hold up their advance until the center V Corps could come up abreast. Liggett's and Bullard's boys had reached, with varying degrees of difficulty, their goal lines for the day. Instead of being required to rest on their laurels and conform to a pre-programmed schedule—at least until V Corps could come up even with them—I and III Corps should have been allowed to expand on their success. But countering this craving for the icing on the cake was the AEF commander's apprehension that his overextended wings would be vulnerable to the Germans on their flanks and rear in the Montfaucon salient, as well as to the enemy reserve divisions pouring into the valley. The haunting fear that one or both of his flanking corps might become isolated and defeated in detail kept Pershing from further unleashing the dogs.

Other critics would later complain that Black Jack could have committed a reserve division to garrote the exposed neck of the Montfaucon position. But there were already 140,000 Americans milling around in confused and jumbled disarray in the valley as the day waned, and the prospect of adding more to the mix would as likely intensify the chaos as it would complete the conquest. Command and control on this dizzying day was minimal most of the time and non-existent for a good part of it. Bullard would record: "At HQ, all dumb, blind, deaf. Even I, a corps commander, was told nothing."[35]

Perhaps a more dashing and dynamic leader—a Patton or a Rommel—would have tossed the dice and trusted that his inalterable destiny would have guided him to victory. But Pershing was solid and stolid, not a dynamo of decisiveness. He was not about to risk his creation—an independent American field army—in a clouded environment in which, as author Hubert Essame observed, "The fog of war had come down like a blanket."[36] Thus Pershing held back his horses and waited for the picture to clear, and the sudden storm—that could have brought triumph or disaster within days—turned into a savage season of stagnated combat.

As the second day of the offensive dawned, Pershing was desperate to take Falcon Mountain. He had come so close that first day, closer than he could have imagined. After the Armistice, he would find out that the 11th Grenadier Regiment had decided to pull out from its positions there that first night. But when the American effort slackened and the pressure decreased as darkness deepened, the Germans decided instead to hunker down and summon reinforcements.

After a full day of battle and a night of repositioning and relocating, Pershing's soldiers were exhausted. The rain that had resumed with the darkness intensified with the dawn. Artillery support for this second day would diminish, both because the gunners were unclear of the locations of so many friendly units and because the rain and the terrain blocked the big guns' ability to move forward, regardless of all the back-breaking labor by the pioneer companies to shape roads across the shell-torn shapelessness of the valley.

Fully aware that Pershing would brook no further delay and that his job was on the line, the 79th division commander, General Kuhn, relieved the CO of one of his stalled brigades and ordered the attack on Montfaucon renewed. The driving rain pouring down on Montfaucon became a slashing and poisonous rain as U.S. artillery pounded the mount with HE (high explosive) and gas shells. All four of the 79th's regiments struck in the wake of the artillery, but the initial assault was checked by 0730. Finally, after another massive shelling, Kuhn's infantry swarmed the hill and at last could report, "Montfaucon captured, 11H (hour) 45." Some twenty-four hours behind schedule and 3,000 casualties poorer, the 79th had conquered the Falcon's butte.

That triumph, however, was about all that day two of the battle had to offer the Americans. The Germans may have been caught flat-footed on the offensive's opening day, but they had rapidly recovered their balance and were now displaying a rabid resolve to defend every inch of territory. Their shells fell thicker and faster on the Americans; 65,000 rounds fell on III Corps alone, compared to just 5,000 the day before. German reserves poured into the valley to fix whatever fissures might appear in the foundations of their defenses. Where the men of Liggett's I Corps had faced little more than one enemy division the day

Ruins of Montfaucon. National Archives, 111-SC-23669.

before, they now flailed and faltered against the might of four. The semi-spectacular gains of September 26 were without a second act on September 27. What limited progress occurred was, more often than not, reversed by German counterattacks. The esprit and ardor of the first day was gone; the men were wet, cold and beyond exhaustion. In two days, 23,000 of their comrades had toppled dead or wounded, had fallen into captivity, or were lost in the woods and ravines.

Worse yet, they were becoming hungry, thirsty and low on ammo. Already, on just this second day of the offensive, the logistical situation was passing from unacceptable to intolerable. The rain seemed never to stop, just alternate in its magnitude. The ground, a malignancy of shell craters before the attack began, was, by midday of September 27, a swamp of desperation. Supply and artillery trains sank into the soup. Roadbeds dissolved as soon as they were built. Very little could get forward and not much more back. Many of the wounded lay in the toxic slop for hours without medical attention. Pleas for artillery support went unanswered, as gun teams, rigged to either horses or trucks, bogged down hundreds of meters short of effective range of the front lines. There was not enough of anything—Liggett's corps alone reported a shortage of 7,000 horses and mules—but yet too much of everything, as the fragile roads sank under the weight of impacted traffic. Eddie Rickenbacker, observing from above like an angel peering down into a cesspool, described the appalling panorama: "As far as the eye could reach, the shell holes covered the landscape.... The soil was yellow clay. Since the rainfall, the country resembled a desolate fever-stricken swamp."[37] In the pre-dawn

Captain Eddie Rickenbacker, C.O. 94th "Hat-in-the-Ring" Squadron. National Archives, 111-SC-50126.

darkness when he had first taken off, the scene below his wingtips had been spectacular, with horizon-wide arcs of fire from the opposing sides illuminating the black vastness of the battlefield. Now the sight under his slipstream was only sickening.

As it was for most of the American divisions, the 27th was a day of physical misery and miserly gains for the 77th. The division was now facing the first major German defensive position—the one already overrun by the other divisions on September 26—and its job on this second day was to reconnect its own fragmented line and, through the arduous process of trial and error by way of fire and maneuver, find, fix and destroy the enemy earthworks so cleverly concealed and so cunningly sited in the green gut of the Argonne.

The men of the Statue of Liberty Division tried to fight their way through a section of the Argonne called the Bois de la Grurie. Though the rumble on the wings told them they were part of a much greater battle, the soldiers of the 77th could see, at most, only twenty yards in all directions, intensifying the feeling that they were fighting the war utterly alone. Liaison with flanking units—the XXXVIII Corps of the French Fourth Army on the Aisne to their left, and the Keystone Guardsmen of the 28th Division across the Aire escarpments on their right—was often less than minimal. Even contact with regimental and battalion HQs was broken more often than it was intact, requiring inexperienced platoon and company commanders to find a way around or through an undergrowth sodden with rain and toxic gas and studded with enemy strongpoints. The New Yorkers did not often even have the consolation of outgoing artillery fire to make them feel less isolated. Though the 77th had not outdistanced its supporting artillery like other divisions had on September 26, the treetops of the Argonne's towering pines often blocked the angles of sight and elevation for the Allied field guns. The only artillery, in most cases, was incoming, as German howitzers emplaced on the edges of the ridge laid down barrage after barrage. The fall of 1918 was an autumn of iron in the Argonne. Artillery slew the trees as it murdered the men, and its fragmenting foliage left a scarlet mulch of mayhem. In many places, the shrapnel stripped the forest of what foliage the autumn had not already deposed. The men of the 77th could only endure it. Other than their integral machine guns and 37 mm guns, the division would have to conquer the Argonne with only their Springfields and grenades.

Early on the morning of day three—September 28—the 77th was able to plant its banner on a bit more of the woods, as the Germans fell back one mile to the Etzel Stellung, the second belt of defensive fortifications. The men of the Times Square Division followed this receding tide of gray and made murderous contact with this next stellung as evening closed. The next day, September 29, the right-hand brigade—the 153rd—struggled mightily to make any headway. The 154th Brigade on the left wing, on the other hand, moved the American line forward nearly two miles. Within this newly captured territory, the Americans secured an old Boche railroad area near Abri de Crochet and Champ Mahaut, featuring deep concrete shelters to protect the kaiser's conscripts as they relaxed, and amenities that included a bowling alley, a theater, and a library.

It was during these last days of September that the Lost Battalion got "lost" for the first time, not on October 2 when, cut off and isolated, it won its fame and title (though it was never lost in the conventional sense of the term). "Detroit Red" (Charles Whittlesey's communications handle), his poker face revealing no nervousness or apprehension as his battalion was whistled over the top in the glare of three signal rockets on the morning of

September 26, had shouted a laconic, "Let's go," as he boosted one of his lieutenants above the trench berm, who then turned to lend a hand to his battalion commander. Whittlesey had then led his boys into the brush, their bayonets fixed, looking, to a British observer like "boy scouts on a picnic."[38]

That first day had not been too trying for the 1/308th (1st Battalion, 308th Infantry), the elements being a more formidable foe than the enemy. But the 27th, when German resistance had intensified all along the line, had been a tougher day in the Argonne, and the 1/308th, designated as the brigade's assault battalion for the day, had seen some of the worst of it. The new major of the battalion placed himself at the point of the morning attack, brandishing a pair of wire cutters, like a Celtic king waving his claymore, and inspiring his men with an outfront display of leadership.

Whittlesey pushed and pulled his city boys into this alien landscape, a green complexity the size, not of Central Park, but of all Manhattan Island, and so utterly unlike anything most of them had ever seen or could conceive. It wasn't supposed to be this hard. The French on the left and the U.S. 28th Division on the right were, according to plans, to have outflanked the enemy defenses in the forest. Their failure to do so meant that the polyglot regiments from New York City had to push straight up the gullet of the Argonne and take out the German machine guns and artillery batteries directly. Otherwise, Pershing's left would be in peril and, according to his staff, "it may be necessary to draw back the lines of resistance south of Montfaucon and eventually to our old positions."[39]

The men of the 308th inched forward under the canopy of the forest, its branches twisted together like the crooked fingers of an arthritic green god, shutting out the sky and allowing only a subdued, sickly light to penetrate. Mulches of mud and leafy debris, slashed prematurely from their branches by this early autumn of artillery fire, hid shellholes and thorny bushes to fall into and exposed roots and trailing vines to trip over. The lacery of trails, the only "streets" the street hustlers of the 77th could find on this malign isle, turned out to be not paths to progress, but highways to hell, as every avenue seemed to lead to a machine-gun nest. The undergrowth was so thick that the advance companies had to proceed in single file, following the navigation of their officers' compasses. Rifle fire from snipers and the scimitar sweep of traversing Maxims continually staggered the forlorn files, unable to effectively return fire into thickets that concealed the muzzle flashes of the enemy weapons. Along one particularly intertwined ridge line, the Americans encountered a German emplacement every fifteen yards. The enemy employed every advantage, adding deceit to their deadly arts. Boche riflemen would appear to concede, holding their hands skyward and pleading "Kamerad," only to dip those same hands into bushels of grenades as the Americans came forward to accept their phony surrender.

Communication between units and between the men in each unit, difficult enough in the trees to begin with, was further complicated by the melting pot mixture of Poles, Italians, Greeks, Jews, Irishmen and Armenians in the 77th, with a very broken English being the lingua franca in the Argonne. Thinly spread through the forest, split apart by gullies and washes, and with a limited ability to understand what words and phrases could be heard through the racket, the division lacked not only the communication, but also the weight and punch to knock down the enemy, let alone knock him out.

The Germans craftily used the same labyrinth of radiating ravines that scattered the 77th into small units to infiltrate behind the New Yorkers and cut off platoons, companies and, finally, whole battalions. Isolated in tiny pockets through the woods though they may be, the division and brigade commanders allowed these separated salients no options of retreat or surrender. To Brig. General Evan Johnson, this peppering of American positions about the woods was the division's only hope for a base to build on for future advances. He demanded, "The troops holding it must be supported. If I find anybody ordering a withdrawal from ground once held, I will see that he leaves the service."[40]

It was in the midst of this blistering maelstrom that Major Whittlesey, on September 28, led his brave but bewildered battalion into the first of two encirclements by the enemy within a week's time—the second of which would win him international fame. Cognizant of the impossibility of maintaining a battalion line in the bramble, Whittlesey sifted his 600 men forward in platoon-size groups of skirmishers, working their way across a Heine cemetery to a point about one kilometer south of Binarville by 1715. Whittlesey established his command post on the reverse slope of Moulin de l'Homme Mort (Dead Man's Mill), bearing a similar ominous appellation to the infamous hill further east—Mort Homme—where some of the fiercest fighting of the Battle of Verdun had taken place. This mill in the Argonne had supposedly earned its moniker by becoming the final resting place for a German lieutenant general. In the next seventy-two hours the site would acquire further credence to its title.

Whittlesey knew already that his flanks were in the air, but, as his men dug their funk holes (foxholes) for the night, he learned, by way of runners and recon patrols, that he was cut off. Too dark to fly pigeons and the tactical situation too confused to dispatch combat patrols to reestablish contact with the rear, Whittlesey settled his men down for another soggy and chilly night.

By morning, Whittlesey confirmed that his chain of runner posts had been broken by German infiltrators, and that the African American regiment connecting his left flank to the French had retired under heavy enemy pressure. As the day broke, so did the rain. This first light brought also the first rather startling appearance of a Heine officer and noncom at the opposite side of the glen on which Whittlesey had sited his battalion CP. While Whittlesey hastily fumbled with his disassembled pistol, being cleaned by his aide, Corporal Walter Baldwin, the rest of the battalion HQ staff opened fire on the interlopers. The German officer was fatally wounded, but, before he gasped his last, he informed Whittlesey that his company of seventy men was in the 1/308th's rear and much larger forces were waiting for the Americans just ahead.

The major sent rearward a message by pigeon express calmly detailing his situation: "Our line of communication with rear still cut at 1230 by machine guns.... We can of course clean up this country to the rear by working our companies over the ground we charged. But we understand our mission is to advance, and to maintain our strength here." He asked that the line of communication be reopened from the rear and urgently requested rations and ammunition.[41]

The regimental commander, Lt. Colonel Frederick E. Smith, responded to Whittlesey's "sitrep" (situation report) by issuing orders to consolidate all the separated detachments in the woods, in order to prepare for a further advance, and by organizing a small relief party to remedy Whittlesey's immediate difficulties. Until that relief could be effected, Whittlesey's four companies had to stay glued to their gooey holes, arranged in a ragged square, fighting off sporadic enemy feints and probes throughout the day. As the black doughboys to the west continued to cave in to German muscle and scramble further rearward, more "Kraut" units filtered in behind the 1/308th and the attacks intensified. By late afternoon, the battalion was suffering from heavy casualties, no food, only gunky rainwater to drink, little ammunition, and no response to their calls for aid via pigeongram.

Whittlesey had dispatched two patrols at noon to reconnoiter and to try to reconnect with the rear. The first, led by Sgt. Major Ben Gaedeke, did manage to bring back the corpse of a German lieutenant bearing maps of the Argonne, but the second, directed by Sgt. Herman Anderson of Company A, made it only two miles southwest before running into too many Germans to deal with. The major then organized a stronger patrol, officered by his battalion adjutant, Lt. Arthur McKeogh, to pass back through the Boche cemetery to try to reacquire the rear. McKeogh got no further than the Heine boneyard before encountering the enemy in strong numbers and stronger positions. The adjutant sent his runner, Private Quinn, back to battalion HQ to inform Whittlesey of the situation, but the message was never delivered. The runner's body was located four months later, along with the remains of three enemy soldiers he had killed before he went down. McKeogh, along with Private Joseph Monson of A Company and Private Jack Herschkowitz of C Company, succeeded, after some time, in wiggling away from their pinned-down positions to scoot through the German lines. Though wounded, the adjutant finally found the American rear to inform the assembling relief force of Whittlesey's posture and position. For his bravery and his exploits, McKeogh was awarded the DSC (Distinguished Service Cross).

Meanwhile, Lt. Colonel Smith guided his own tiny relief party of two other officers and ten men up the trail, everyone weighted with extra ammunition for the isolated force. Running into machine-gun fire from a range of just fifty yards, Smith had his men take cover while he, though immediately wounded in the leg, single-handedly took on the Maxim position armed only with his .45 semi-automatic pistol. Another machine-gun bullet slammed into his side, but the gallant colonel continued to blast away at the German gun until his men had found relative safety. Still not willing to call it quits, Smith gathered grenades to go after the machine gunners, but his heroics were then culminated by a third and this time fatal round. The regimental commander would posthumously receive the Medal of Honor on February 19, 1919.

A sister battalion of the 1/308th finally came abreast of the unit's position late that night, though it was late afternoon on September 30 before the enemy pressure on Whittlesey's men finally abated as more 77th Division units reached his line. This was, however, not a relief, only a reinforcement. There would be no steps backward for pause and rest. Marooned for more than two days on a soggy island in the Argonne sea, the men of the 1/308th, diminished by heavy casualties and depleted by the arduous labor of fighting for their lives, would move forward again, with but the briefest of interruptions between the harshest of ordeals.

Whittlesey found out there would be no rest for his almost terminally weary troops, when he was ordered to report back personally to regimental advance headquarters on the night of September 30, the day his battalion was "relieved." As he noted, his journey to the HQ was through, "The blackest night I've ever seen, and I had to pass on from reserve post to post holding the hand of each successive guide. Then back to the battalion again, which I found with great difficulty in the darkness. Orders were to advance at daybreak."[42]

Those orders were not relayed on to his battalion without protest by the bearer of the bad news. Whittlesey complained—to regiment, to brigade, and on up the chain to General Alexander himself—that too much was being asked of a battalion reduced to half-strength from the mortal exertions of the past several days. But the order of the day, so familiar now in syntax and intent, was "to advance independently without regard for exposed flanks or contact with adjacent units. Upon reaching the objective of the day, dig in and hold out for the rest of the Division to catch up."[43]

The 77th, at the hinge of fate for the whole American offensive, was to continue the attack, even though the rest of the First Army had effectively suspended offensive operations two days before. Pershing was adamant about maintaining the pressure on the enemy in the Argonne, and Alexander was just as adamant about keeping his command. Black Jack's desires could not be defied, and Whittlesey would have to press on.

The New Yorkers (and their Midwestern replacements) had basically been waging the Battle of the Meuse-Argonne on their own since September 29, the fourth day of the offensive. The U.S. First Army had suffered 45,000 killed, wounded, missing or taken prisoner in four days September 26–29. Never had an American army suffered so many casualties in so short a time; not Lee at Gettysburg (though the two opposing American armies, Union and Confederate, did take a combined 50,000 casualties), not Hooker at Chancellorsville, not Grant in the Wilderness. The losses represented almost 25 percent of the some 200,000 combatants committed to the seventeen-mile front.

Though far short of the hoped-for twenty-mile or more penetration, the offensive's first phase had moved the Western Front eight miles farther north, a far larger gain than any French or British offensive in the three meatgrinder years of 1915–17. And though losses were high—in American terms and in any terms—they were far short of the colossal casualties suffered by the British Empire on the Somme in 1916 or at Passchendaele in 1917. They were also far fewer than those mutiny-motivating piles of dead and wounded Frenchmen fallen in Artois and Champagne during the 1917 Nivelle Offensive.

It was not so much the casualties, horrendous as they were, that forced Pershing to temporarily stay his hand against the "whaleback"—the central, rolling hills section of the front. Rather it was the utter disorganization that characterized the American army by the evening of the fourth day—along the front and even more so to the rear—that required a suspension of offensive operations until this skein of confusion run riot could be rectified.

Fortunately, the enemy lacked the resources to take advantage of the American disarray. The Germans had certainly been hurt, too. Whole battalions on the forward stellungs had been all but annihilated. The 7th and 117th Reserve Divisions had lost a combined 6,700 killed, wounded, missing or captured by September 29. Several of the German divisions first engaged had lost all but a dozen or so of the machine guns that provided the muscle in the arm of the Boche defenses. The divisions rushed into the fray from reserve status were mostly dangerously understrength, and they had to be fed into the fight piecemeal, by regiment or even by battalion. There were now nine German divisions on the front, with elements of three others, but most were of no more than brigade strength. Fortunately for the Germans, their artillery, though lacking in numbers compared to that of the Allies, had ammunition stocks remaining sufficient to continue a heavy interdiction of the American front and supply lines. The Germans needed the respite provided by Pershing's pause as much as the Americans did.

Some of the U.S. divisions were as sorely spent by day four of the offensive as the

German front-line units. The Kansans and Missourians of the 35th Division had seen, by late morning of October 1, 6,006 of their comrades fall, 1,126 of them fatally, to enemy fire, in trying to fight their way through Charpentry and Baulny, out on the fringes of the Montrebeau Wood—six miles north of the jump-off trenches—and into the ravine and the town of Exermont. The division's survivors were under intense fire from machine guns and artillery firing HE and gas, as well as from strafing German biplanes. Men untouched by German steel were being knocked out of action by the rapidly spreading flu; dysentery was rife because the primary water supply came from the scum lapped up from shell holes.

The links in the chain of command were nearly all broken; what few company and field grade officers who had not fallen often got separated from their units. The division commander, General Traub, went sleepless for four nights trying to reestablish contact between his units, and at one point wandered lost in the woods, sick with gas fumes and almost straying into enemy lines. The division had almost stopped functioning as an organized force and was rendered combat ineffective. As one 35th Division sergeant noted, his men, "looked terrible ... exhausted, sleepy, hungry, worn down and sick. Worse—they didn't feel lucky anymore. They'd lost the soldier's bullet-proof ego, that feeling of 'others might get hit, but never I'.... Not even the clowns were wisecracking anymore."[44]

The Midwesterners were trapped in a kill zone and helpless before the threat of counterattack. That inevitable German counterattack came on September 29 and erased what limited gains the 35th had won around Exermont. Superbly supported by mobile infantry cannon, the Germans rolled over the 35th. Traub had to allow his ravaged regiments to fall back to prepared positions manned by 1,200 men of the 110th Engineer Regiment on a ridgeline fronting Montrebeau Wood, giving up all the ground they had won since the morning of the second day. The broken division was relieved by the Regular Army 1st Division on September 30. Sent to a quiet sector to rebuild, the war was over for the 35th Division.

Probably no American division on the Meuse-Argonne front was more ill-used and brought closer to disintegration than the 35th. To add to the cornucopia of challenges that faced all the doughboy divisions, the 35th had also to deal with a particularly unstable and poorly functioning level of leadership, intensified by rivalry and resentment between the Regular Army officers assigned to the division and the National Guard ninety-day wonders who filled most of the junior officer ranks. Hardly more than a week before the offensive, the commanders of both brigades, three of the four regiments, and the artillery regiment, as well as the chief of staff, had been replaced by Regulars. Given no chance to bond with their units and their subordinates, and no opportunity to prepare for what lay ahead by way of large scale maneuvers, the new commanders and their units were destined for disaster. City boys from Kansas City and St. Louis, prairie pups from the Kansas wheatfields, and farming lads from the hard-scrabble hollows of the Ozarks may have fought bravely and well in pairs and packets, but unit cohesion and competent command performance for the 35th lasted hardly beyond the echoes of the whistles that propelled the division into the valley on day one. The 35th would lose 1,298 men dead in battle and 5,998 wounded; of those losses, 82 percent fell in the Aire Valley from September 26–October 1, 1918.

Other divisions of the U.S. First Army, if not knocked out of the ring like the 35th, were down on the canvas for a mandatory eight-count. General Farnsworth's 37th Division butted its tin-hatted head against Cierges Ridge, east of the Exermont Ravine, only to be checked by the appalling accuracy of the German howitzers. The left flank regiment was shattered, a broken-winged blackbird flapping helplessly and exposing the right flank of the neighboring 91st Division.

To the right of the 37th, Kuhn's 79th Division was barely able to survive its success, for after finally taking Montfaucon, it could make no further headway and was nearly cut off by the accelerating rush of German reinforcements. All forward momentum ceased, as did supplies to the front. Rations were minimal for three days and the water was shellhole Chardonnay, vintage 1918. The signs of demoralization became obvious by Sunday morning, when the 315th Infantry of the 79th listlessly tried to storm the fortified farmhouse called Ferme de la Madaleine. After the almost inevitable failure of the attack, the regiment, instead of falling back to its pre-attack position, started drifting en masse back toward the spurious safety of the rear. As a later 79th Division report concluded, German artillery "came nearer than anything else to destroying the morale of the units. Troops with three months service will stand the ordeal but a short time, as was proved."[45]

The sputtering offensive, that was now frozen in place, that had actually lost a considerable part of the ground conquered in its first two days, was not, however, due to a failure of nerve or a lack of effort by the troops on the firing line. The failure came at the top, from the command leadership and staff of the First Army, and from an almost complete logistical breakdown. As a French staff officer noted, "Once the attack commenced the army behaved as if it had been struck by paralysis.... It was just one more demonstration of the old truth that an army cannot improvise."[46]

Georges Clemenceau, the "Tiger of France," ever restless in his Parisian cage, habitually broke free on Sunday afternoons to prowl, via motor car, his domain. Wishing to visit the German crown prince's command post at Montfaucon and see first-hand the luxurious accommodations he had long heard of, the Tiger chose to pop into Pershing's HQ at Souilly on the last Sunday in September. Black Jack, desperate to kick-start his stalled offensive, was in no mood to nursemaid the premier of France. Pershing diplomatically tried to point out that the clogged crumbling roads to the front could hardly accommodate one more man, let alone the limousine of the French head of state. But Clemenceau was insistent, and Pershing grudgingly agreed to guide him into the morass.

What Clemenceau saw as his vehicle idled along at far less than the speed of a marching soldier, appalled him and convinced him that Pershing and his staff were not up to the task of independent command. The impossible roads were, on this drizzling day of September 29, even more congested than normal, as elements of the U.S. 1st Division tramped from St. Mihiel to the Aire River to relieve the malfunctioning 35th Division. Banging and bouncing with almost every rotation of the wheels, Clemenceau's car often came close to high-centering onto the ridges of the deep ruts left by the massive weight of 155 mm guns trying to move forward on a spongy roadbed that could barely sustain the weight of a soldier with his rifle and pack. The road was a mire of men, mules and every form of conveyance, all seemingly fixed in place for all eternity in the epoxy of the Meuse Valley mud. Noncoms and officers were bellowing mightily to move this congealed mass along, but all to no avail.

Pershing may have missed the contempt curling Clemenceau's lips beneath the premier's brushy mustache, but he could not fail to have seen the fury in the Tiger's eye at the sight of so much chaos in khaki. Clemenceau never came close to sampling the crown prince's wine cellar at Montfaucon, as the afternoon and the impossibility of reaching their goal wore on. Certain now that the Americans were fit for nothing greater than to serve as cannon fodder for the understrength Allied armies, the French premier diagnosed the AEF as gripped with the fever of "complete chaos."

Disregarding the fact that the Americans, for all their amateurism, had fought their way forward farther than the French forces on their flanks, Clemenceau called on Foch to relieve Pershing of his command. "These Americans will lose us our chance of a big victory before winter" he complained. Urging Foch to go over Pershing's head, he declaimed, "They are all tangled up with themselves. You have tried to make Pershing see. Now let's put it up to President Wilson."[47]

Foch, however, was more tolerant of and patient with his New World allies. Though he did try, unsuccessfully, to shanghai the U.S. I Corps for service with the French Second Army, the French marshal defended Pershing and his Yankees. "The Americans have got to learn sometime. They are learning now, rapidly."[48]

Pershing did not need Clemenceau to inform him of his army's deficiencies. They were by now glaringly obvious. Clemenceau may have seen the logistical derangement at its worst—because of the 1st Division's movement to the front—but the difference was only in degree. From the second day, the jumble in the rear had become as much an impediment to the offensive's momentum as was the enemy's stiffening resistance. The squalor seemed to only get worse with each succeeding dawn. Twenty-five hundred tons of ammunition and supplies were required each day to feed the appetite of the offensive. At times, vehicles were lined up for miles, waiting for a parade that never commenced. Vehicles in route often did not turn a wheel for up to thirty hours. The average speed along the three roads, those first four days, was one mile per hour.

The arteries clogged with confusion, the beating heart of the offensive was weakening. Rations, ammunition, communication, medical support, fire support, everything ran into and got bogged down in the viscosity of logistical breakdown. Also breaking down was the morale of the attacking soldiers, as every support system began to fail them.

Although some 75 mm guns were able to keep up with the infantry, the big stuff was stuck in the rear, with hardly a heavy caliber weapon moved forward for an entire week. Roads everywhere were blocked by the nine-foot-wide tracks of the 155 mm howitzers, unable to go forward or backward.

Communication to the front was laggard at best. Orders got lost or fatally delayed. Directions from the top drizzled to the bottom hours or even days late. At 2330 on September 27, Pershing dispatched orders to V Corps for an attack to commence at 0700 on the 28th. The message finally reached corps HQ four hours after the directed jump-off time. Units were shu· ed hither and yon, often in direct contradiction to the current tactical situation because of the receipt of long-delayed orders that were outdated and bore little relation to the reality on the ground.

Food delivery had broken down, and the hungry infantrymen were beginning to react. Rolling kitchens and food trucks were looted by men who had left their positions to prowl the rear for rations. Military policemen had to be sent to the edge of the battle lines to prevent men from leaving their funk holes to conduct rear area raids on YMCA carts carrying cigarettes and coffee.

Most damaging of all to the sinking spirit of the fighting men was the collapse of the medical system. The Army Medical Corps was grossly overburdened by the scale of the offensive to begin with, and the massive logistical snarls only made a bad situation worse. The First Army had only enough personnel, medicine and equipment for a static campaign of trench warfare. Plans were in the pipeline for a medical organization able to handle the demands of a full-scale offensive, but they were distant from fruition on September 26. The situation was at its worst in the center V Corps, burdened with the most vital role in the offensive. The corps' TO&E (tables of organization and equipment) strength chart called for a sanitary train of four ambulance companies, four field hospitals, forty-four cargo trucks, eight motor cars, twenty motorcycles, fifty officers and 800 enlisted men, but the corps' actual medical staff and equipment on day one of the offensive did not even approach those fantasy figures. Hugely short of equipment, medical personnel had scrambled to borrow from the Allies everything from buses to bandages.

As a result, a doughboy seriously wounded in the Argonne or in the Meuse Valley faced long odds in surviving his injuries. A fallen soldier, after being collected by a stretcher party and carried to a first aid station, then had to endure a harrowing journey of up to twenty-four hours along the traffic-jammed roads to reach the rear. If major surgery was required, it might take another forty-eight hours for the casualty to be transported to a field hospital. Some wounded men lay where they had fallen for days before help arrived; for others, in the green Gehenna of the Argonne, that help never came.

The casualties of V Corps had a particularly long road to medical salvation, because no roads led directly south out of the corps zone. All sick and wounded personnel had to stagger, limp or be lugged across to I or III Corps areas before they could head south to succor.

The logistical logjam was, however, just the worst of a whole catalogue of First Army failures. Pershing's four-day pause between offensive surges was hardly adequate to do more than give his worn-out warriors an opportunity to gasp for breath. The list of American shortcomings was long, and the little that could be accomplished in four days could not noticeably shorten it.

The AEF headquarters staff summarized that lengthy list into a triad of tribulation—incompetent tactics, undermined further by an impossible resupply situation, encountering unexpectedly and increasingly fierce German resistance. Colonel Willey Howell, the G-2 assistant chief of staff, concluded: "I believe that the Germans were overwhelmed by our original advance, but that the advance has been so dilatory as to enable them to recover from their first surprise to readjust and establish themselves."[49]

The inspector general's report of First Army defects ranged from inadequate artillery support, to poor use of carrier pigeons, down to pessimistic talk among the officers and men about their staggering losses. The IG bill of particulars basically expressed profound disappointment with almost every phase and facet of the First Army's offensive effort.

The one area that the IG had few complaints about was in the demonstrated valor of the individual doughboy. Tarnishing even this glitter amongst all the grime, however, was the sad spectacle of the thousands of stragglers wandering the woods and ravines behind the front lines. Estimates of the numbers of these stragglers, adding to the chaos in the rear and drastically weakening the front line units, went as high as 100,000 (or 40 percent of the approximately 250,000 men committed by now to the battle). Many were physically lost; many were psychologically lost (if, hopefully, only temporarily), their sensory systems knocked haywire by shell shock. And a good number were malingerers, men shirking their duty, staining the honor of those who stood and fought. Sickness was rife among the stragglers, as it was among the men still manning the trenches and fighting holes. A week of chilling rain had accelerated the flu outbreak. By October 15 over 16,000 men were down with the disease.

But sickness, stragglers, and all other strains and stresses on his army could not compel Pershing to further delay the resumption of the offensive. The AEF chief could not bear the onus of commanding the one Allied offensive of late summer and early autumn 1918 that had stalled out. Haig's Anglo-Belgian offensive in Flanders demanded constant pressure on the opposite end of the Western Front. Haig, Clemenceau and many other Allied leaders were, in effect, calling for Pershing's head. Even had that pressure been absent, the American general's character would not have tolerated treading water much longer. Foch was now demanding six U.S. divisions pulled from the overcrowded and inactive Meuse-Argonne front to the support of his French armies. Pershing resisted the marshal's demand, but, with Foch insisting on, at the very least, immediate action, the commander of the AEF and of the First Army marked 0525 on October 4 as H-hour for phase two of the Meuse-Argonne Offensive.

Pershing was adamant in his ambition. "All objectives are to be gained without regard of losses and without regard to the exposed conditions of the flanks.... The word is forward! I will tolerate no excuses ... every objective must be taken!"[50]

His order of battle for this second assault included eight divisions this time, not nine as in the first attack. Three of the divisions—Maj. General Beaumont Buck's 3rd, Maj. General William Haan's 32nd, and Maj. General Charles Summerall's 1st—were experienced, but fresh to the Meuse-Argonne. On the right (east wing), Bullard's III Corps, less battered than the other two corps from the September 26–29 rhapsody of arms, kept its original divisions in place on the assault line—the 33rd, 80th and 4th—with no reserve. In the center, Cameron's V Corps had all three of its September 26 assault divisions pulled out of the line. The 79th, victor and victim of Montfaucon, was replaced by the 3rd; the 37th by the 32nd. The 91st, which had incurred 4,699 casualties from September 26 to October 4, was relegated to corps reserve, along with the veteran and newly arrived to the area 42nd Rainbow Division. Liggett's I Corps on the left (west wing), would continue the attack with the 28th and 77th, but with the 1st taking up the standard of the debilitated 35th. Corps reserve for Liggett would consist of the 82nd Division, commanded by Maj. General George Duncan, and of the French 5th Cavalry Division.

The AEF would be going up against (along most of the front) the Kriemhilde Stellung this time, aiming for the high ground to the north of the line, ground that Pershing had optimistically planned to conquer on the first day of the offensive—September 26. Bullard's boys were assigned the chore of capturing the Cunel Heights. Cameron's corps, less weighted with responsibility for phase two, was ordered only to take the Bois de Chauvignon and support the I Corps in securing the Romagne Heights. The really hard work was farmed out to Liggett—in particular, his 1st Division. Along with continuing the clearing of the Argonne, the I Corps was directed to seize the most important elevations of the Romagne Heights—the Côte Dame Marie and the Côte de Châtillon.

The 77th Division had, of course, continued to tumble over the natural and unnatural tripwires of the Argonne without a break to refresh and refit. The companion offensive by the French Fourth Army, to the west of General Alexander's forest dwellers, had also rolled (or rather, crept) on. The 92nd Buffalo Division's 368th Infantry had been the regiment linking the U.S. First Army with the French Fourth Army's XXXVIII Corps, south of Binarville. Poorly trained, scorned and belittled by their racist white officers, the African American enlisted men of the regiment had performed down to expectations, bugging out (to use the terminology of a later war—the Korean) at practically the first shot fired. Their failure forced the 77th to extend its left flank to make contact with the French and diluted their spearpoint strength in the push through the forest. The 368th's insipid effort and poor performance could be gauged by their light losses—only 266 casualties in six days. The all-black regiments of the 93rd Division—the 369th, 371st and 372nd—better trained and led, and attached to the more racially tolerant divisions of the French Fourth Army, demonstrated courage and competence equal to any Allied unit during comparable stretches of the Fourth Army Champagne Offensive. The 369th lost 785 killed, wounded or missing, September 26–October 1; the 371st suffered 882 casualties, September 28–October 1; the 372nd counted 579 casualties, September 28–October 7. And all three African American regiments captured substantial ground in the Sechault, Ardeuil and Monthois areas west of Binarville. Freddie Stowers of the 371st earned the Medal of Honor while fighting to the death on Hill 188 on September 28, though it would require seventy years before a more tolerant America awarded the medal to his heirs.

Another U.S. division—the 2nd, with the U.S. Marine 4th Brigade attached—joined in General Henri Gourard's 240,000-man Fourth Army offensive in Champagne. The French had made minimal progress in their offensive between Reims and the Argonne, penetrating in the center to just north of Sommepy by September 30, an advance of just three and a half miles, compared to the six miles ground out by the Americans in the more difficult terrain of the Argonne to the east. The main German position north of Sommepy was Blanc Mont Ridge, the last natural defensive line south of the Aisne, sixteen miles farther north. An urgent plea by Foch for American assistance brought the 2nd and 36th Divisions to the front.

The 2nd took over the line near Sommepy from the French XXI Corps on October 2. The next day, the 2nd and its attached Marines stormed the heavily fortified Blanc Mont and Hill 210. Outracing the French divisions on either flank, the 2nd Division and the 4th USMC Brigade mastered Blanc Mont and resisted brutal enemy counterattacks on October 4–5. After the lagging French on the wings finally forced their way forward, the advance, on October 8, punched on to take St. Etienne-a-Arnes and hold the village in the face of intense counterattacks. The 2nd was relieved by the 36th on October 10, after breaking the German lines to a depth of four miles and rounding up over 2,000 Hun POWs. The soldiers and Marines of Brig. General John Lejeune's 2nd Division had provided the pike thrust that would enable the French Fourth Army's Champagne Offensive to drive to the Aisne by October 13. The 2nd Division had lost—from October 2–10—726 killed, 3,662 wounded, 585 missing. Of those numbers, the Marines of the 4th Brigade counted 494 killed and 1,864 wounded. The Devil Dogs of the USMC 5th Regiment—the heroes of Belleau Wood—had absorbed 1,120 casualties alone, representing 60 percent of its original strength.

In the Argonne, the cicada choir of the gunfire had surged and subsided, but never entirely ceased in those first days of October. By October 1, the men of the 77th Division were muddied, bloodied and in desperate need of respite from their murderous toil. As noted, when Major Whittlesey reported on that Tuesday evening to the new regimental commander, Colonel Cromwell Stacey (code-named Detroit One), he had been stunned to hear that instead of the anticipated relay to the rear for his mangled battalion, he would be required to lead it back into battle at 0630 the following morning.

The orders had filtered down from the 154th Brigade commander, Brig. General Evan M. Johnson (code-named Delaware One), a slender and snap-tempered twenty-five-year Regular Army veteran. "You will proceed north straight ahead, then bear westward up the ravine from the valley of Charlevaux Brook. On the crest above lies the Giselher Stellung. Take it; push on to the road on the opposite slope above Charlevaux Valley. There dig in, establish liaison left and right, and await further orders."[51]

Whittlesey's 1/308th was to be the tip of the brigade lance, a point considerably dulled and dented, but still deadly. The battalion would advance one and a half kilometers and anchor the left flank of the 154th Brigade. To the east, the 153rd Brigade, led by Brig. General Edmund C. Wittenmeyer, would attack in unison; to the west, dismounted French cavalrymen from Gouraud's Fourth Army would try to keep up.

Acting Major (his formal promotion was snarled in red tape) George McMurtry would lead his 2/308th in direct support of Whittlesey. Several sections of the 306th Machine-Gun Battalion would accompany the two attacking infantry battalions. The 308th Infantry Regiment's 3rd Battalion hung back in brigade reserve. The 308th would go into action without their supporting 37 mm guns or Stokes six-inch mortars. The ground to be crossed was far too rugged to convey the carts necessary to carry the heavy weapons (the Stokes, for example, weighed up to 829 pounds and the Hotchkiss, with its tripod, weighed almost 120 pounds).

Whittlesey was not one to comfortably question authority, but his first loyalty was to his men, and he had laid out to Colonel Stacey a long litany of objections to the go-for-broke orders. He pointed out that both attack battalions were down to 50 percent authorized strength—from 800 to about 400 each. The men remaining were drained, in body and spirit, from six days of hard-core combat. The broth of the battalions had been rethickened somewhat by replacements, but they were as green as the youngest saplings in the secondary growth of the Argonne. Only 10 percent of the replacements, for example, could be trusted to handle a grenade properly.

Whittlesey complained that the terrain ahead was no less difficult than that behind, traversed with so much difficulty through an unendurable week. Boche determination and resistance was hardening and intensifying daily. Support from both man and machine, left, right and overhead, would continue to be as problematic as it had been since the first day's first hour. The French were making minimal progress into the Aisne Valley; the 77th's left flank still flapped freely in the trees. Liaison with the 28th Division on the right was little better and maintaining contact with sister battalions and regiments was hit and miss, with the misses far more prevalent. The close-order columns of the Argonne trees masked targets from the eyes of the artillery FOs (forward observers), and deflected the shells in their trajectory once those targets were finally detected. Finally, the foot soldiers of the 308th were being ordered back into battle lacking even the rudiments of survival, let alone the sureties of success. They lacked sufficient blankets and raincoats to deal with the persistent rain and declining temperatures, and enough coffee, rum and rations to sustain a diminishing energy.

Stacey sympathized with his 1st Battalion commander. Southern-born, but Army-bred, having been weaned as a drummer boy twenty-four years ago, the colonel was as worn out as any man in his regiment. He, rather forlornly, had passed Whittlesey's demurrals on up the chain of command to the brigade CO, General Johnson. The 154th Brigade's leader concurred. Johnson, frazzled and sunken-eyed from sleepless nights (and a medical condition that would end his life soon after the Armistice), had already expressed to General Alexander his concerns that the Germans might once again infiltrate around the unsupported wings of an American advance, as they had three days before. Alexander had merely scoffed at Johnson's worries, claiming that a heavy French cannonade and infantry attack at Autry, to the west of the Argonne, had diverted the Germans away from the 308th's open flank. Then, when Johnson rang up division HQ to request a postponement of the operation, Alexander's response set the landline sizzling between division and brigade. The brigadier was flailed with the starkest of options: either attack on schedule or be relieved on the spot by "somebody with guts."

The heat, if not the fury, of the division commander's refusal leaped on down the line to punch into the gut of the man whose blood and muscle, as well as that of his men, would have to render the real work of fulfilling Alexander's rhetorical resolve.

When Stacey pronounced the weighted words, "You will attack, Major!" Whittlesey, his silver-framed spectacles emphasizing eyes leaden with dread and resignation, intoned, "Very well, sir. But I doubt you'll ever hear from me or my battalion again!"[52]

4

The Battalion

Wednesday, October 2. On the west fringe of the forest, the men from the big city boroughs and the flat plains burgs awoke early to a chilling wind from the east and low-slung clouds that leaked a slow drizzle on their sleeping and fighting holes, already mud-caked from the previous day's downpour. The promised hot breakfast, like so much else, never made the leap over the logistical moat separating the soldiers from their supplies. Hardtack and the unpalatable canned beef, unfondly called "Willy," was the fare for the day.

At 0600 the artillery cranked up, commencing a thirty-minute preparatory bombardment from mostly French 75 mm field guns. Ten minutes into the fusillade, noncoms scurried down the line to ready the men for action in twenty minutes. At 0630 a signal rocket sent a crayon smear of light into the gray vault arcing above the trees. Whistles shrilled and the soldiers of the 308th arose to walk deeper into the woods. Whittlesey, armed with his usual .45 pistol and his wire cutters, moved just behind the skirmishers and scouts—much farther forward than the typical battalion commander, but indicative of his concern that his soldiers might easily veer astray among the puzzle pieces of the Argonne.

On their left, far out of sight beyond the trees and within the mist, the French division of dismounted cuirassiers advanced with exaggerated care in countryside open but still rugged. With each German bunker or machine-gun nest encountered, the Gallic cavalry would wait for their 75 mm guns to be dragged forward to blast a path forward. The days of elan and gleaming bayonet assaults were long gone for the French army by this final quarter of 1918. The French now fought carefully and methodically; the ardor of the attack was left to the little tested Americans, who had not yet lost much of a generation in the No Man's Land of the Western Front.

On the right of Whittlesey's battalion, units of the 307th, the 306th, and the 305th advanced, but each regiment quickly lost the struggle to maintain contact as they climbed over a hill, traversed a draw, then mounted a second hill, before they could link with the 308th as it neared the Giselher Stellung.

The 1/308th faced to its immediate front a deep ravine, 600 to 800 yards wide, dividing its front with a diagonal slash. On its east side, Companies A, B and C struggled through the brush, while Company D advanced on its own on the ravine's west side. Closely behind Whittlesey's battalion moved McMurtry's battalion, with E, G and H Companies of the 2/308th following on the east side of the draw and Company F of the 2/308th moving up behind D/1/308th on the west. The dense tree line limited visibility to no more than ten yards. The squads of each platoon struggled to stay together, but for awhile the advance continued without meeting resistance. Though there are varying estimates for the number of

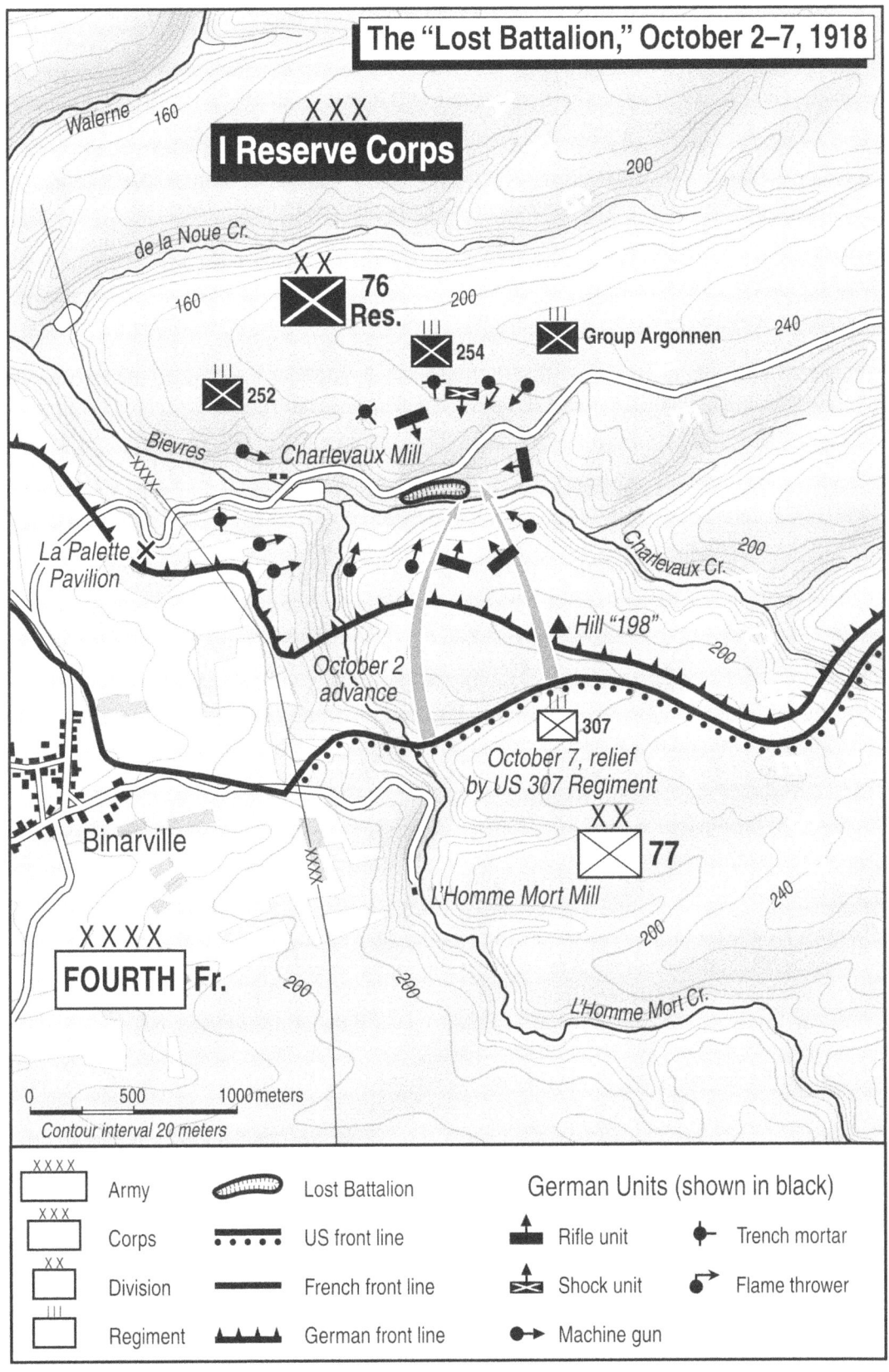

men that Major Whittlesey led into the ravine on October 2, a total of 456 seems most likely. Though authorized company strength was 250, the companies led by Whittlesey were nowhere near that strong. An April 1919 accounting lists: Company A with 18 men; B with 54, C—85; E—21; G—56; H—101; Battalion HQs—65; two sections from the 306th Machine-Gun Battalion—53; plus 3 medics. Including the later reinforcement of K/3/307th's 98 men, the total number who fought their way into the Pocket would have been 554.

When snipers finally opened up, their fire came from the Mausers of the 76th Reserve Division. These Germans were mostly middle-aged men considered second-rate troops best fit for "quiet" sectors or easily defensible zones. Because the Boche high command considered the Argonne as all but unconquerable, given the difficult terrain and the dominating defensive positions, it deemed the deployment there of shock troops or first-rate infantry a waste of a dwindling resource. After all, leaders who would send and spend their infantry against such impossible odds had to be either incompetent or insane!

The commander of the 76th Division was General Freiherr Quadt-Wykradt-Hüchtenbruck, a Prussian of the old school, but admired by his men for his energy and efficiency. At the first word of the American advance, he rushed reinforcements to Major Manfred Hünicken's 254th Regiment, which held the Charlevaux Mill and the ridges that were the objectives of the 1/308th. The 76th's commander also ordered additional sniper squads into the woods, as well as dispatching machine-gun sections to man prepared positions that covered the approaches with interlocking fields of fire.

Higher up the German chain, General Richard Wellmann, commander of the I Reserve Korps, of which the 76th Division was a part, felt little trepidation at the news of the new American attack. From his headquarters at a château outside the village of Briquenay, Wellmann declaimed, "The Yankees have traveled a long way to get killed."[1]

The very model of a modern German general, a man of action and intellect, Wellmann was confident that his lines would hold and that the American attack would falter. The only flaw in the diamond of his defenses that he could detect was on his left—eastern—flank, where Wellmann's corps tied into General Heinrich von Kleist's Group Argonnen at Hill 198, an elevated confluence of limestone rock, caves and coulees. A September 30 probe by General Johnston's 91st Pacific Coast Division had caused von Kleist to shift his focus to the east to contain the 91st. Consequently, von Kleist manned the trenches atop Hill 198 with relatively few and inexperienced troops—the elderly home guards of the 2nd Landwehr Division's 122nd Regiment—assuming that the rugged approaches to the hill and the ever dependable German artillery would deter the Americans from this obviously weak link. He also depended on Wellmann for rapid reinforcement if the position came under significant attack.

At the receiving end of the German defensive fires, Whittlesey and his HQ section continued to lead the vanguard of the American advance. Just steps behind the battalion guides, Major Whittlesey scouted the course to his objective, one mile away, sniper fire be damned. His battalion shu· ed down a steep slope, their forward movement in rapid rushes from cover to cover. There were no enemy soldiers to be seen, but howitzer shells and machine-gun volleys slowly revved up to impede the charging doughboys and thin their ranks. The major called a halt to this wavering charge at the rim of a musky ravine and had his battalion go to ground. The ravine led straight north to Charlevaux Brook, and its contours would keep the battalion concentrated and minimize straggling. But it would also funnel the attacking companies into a killing zone crisscrossed with machine-gun fire from the brush-lush slopes on either side. Any hope that the French on the left or the 307th on the right might eliminate that deadly machine-gun threat by striking the Maxim crews from the rear went aglimmering, as the French failed to keep up, as usual, and the 307th ran up against a wired and entrenched incline where machine-gun barrels were sighted down every approach.

To the west of the 1/308th, beyond the ravine in which the battalion was now huddled, sprawled the hill of La Palette, relatively treeless, but thick with sited-in machine guns and a twisting network of trenches, peppered with pillboxes. It was to have been taken by the French, but, weakened by the removal of the African American regiment, which had collapsed the week before, and slowed by their overcautious tactics, the French had gotten no ways near the hill. Whittlesey decided, consequently, to veer left toward La Palette to take out the machine-gun interdiction on his flank. From there, he could turn north again to win the day's objectives—the paralleling road and railway running across the north slope of Charlevaux Valley, behind the Giselher Stellung line.

With the casualty count still relatively low, Whittlesey moved his men to the left toward the caves at the foot of La Palette. Soon heavy fusillades of enemy fire were sleeting the air with limestone chips. Hit from both front and flanks, the battalion had to break off its climb up La Palette and seek cover. While his soldiers returned fire, Whittlesey, at around 1000, sent a runner back to Stacey, informing the regimental CO that his advance both north and west was blocked without increased artillery support and help from flanking units. Stacey, as far forward as he could get without being under direct German fire himself (and as far forward as the telephone line thus far reached), in turn informed brigade HQ that both the 308th and the 307th were checked. The brigade commander, General Johnson then had the unpleasant task of advising General Alexander that, in effect, his attack was a failure.

Commanders on the other side were also busy messaging their superiors about the escalating situation. Wellmann's attention had been pulled west early by the French artillery and infantry diversionary attacks, begun October 1 around Autry. By 0800, however, reports of U.S. shelling and infantry movement cleared the murky situation for Wellmann and convinced him that the French efforts had been launched to attract his reserves west away from a weakened line in the Argonne. The local French attacks were obviously less serious than those of the Americans, whose combat naiveté made them easier to kill but more difficult to defeat. In the five months that German commanders had been facing Americans in major combat, they had learned that these Yankees fought with a stubborn valor that had been bled from the French in 1914 and 1915. In comparable situations, a French unit, isolated or outflanked, would withdraw or surrender; an American unit would dig in and fight nearly to the last man. Wellmann and his fellow German generals also knew that discipline and organization were very transitory qualities among the Americans, and that the best method of handling an American attack was to counterattack as soon as the Yankees had won their initial objective, at the moment when they were most prone to disorganization and disorientation.

When Wellmann was alerted that the 254th Regiment was under attack, he ordered his corps reserve and their artillery pulled from the French Fourth Army front and redeployed to deal with the new American offensive in the forest. The German corps commander also phoned Hüchtenbruck, commander of the 76th Reserve Division, directing him to use his division reserves to hold the line until the corps reserve could reach the woods. The French, seeing this development, tried to do their part for their American allies by resuming the assault on Autry. Though this effort sucked back in a small part of the German corps reserve, most of that force continued with its redeployment into the Argonne. The pressure on all the attacking American units in the forest swiftly escalated, most particularly on Whittlesey's 1/308th at the point of the attack.

When General Alexander received General Johnson's unwelcome report at around 1100, he reacted with predictably volcanic displeasure. He had not scaled the mountain, from enlisted private to two-star general and the youngest division commander in the U.S. Army, by mildly accepting failure and compassionately empathizing with the difficulties faced by subordinates. The reservoir of his patience already drained by the floundering of the first Argonne offensive, the tough Scotsman, red of face and black in disposition, was unwilling to brook any further failure. Pershing, with reprimands and even demotions, had made it clear that, since the German defenses in the Argonne apparently could not be flanked and folded in, they would have to be assaulted directly by the units facing those fearsome positions. Losses, no matter what their scale, were irrelevant; the task would be completed or the 77th would come under new management.

Alexander, consequently, complained to Johnson that the languid pace of his 154th Brigade was derailing both the French on the left and the 153rd Brigade on the right, and he demanded that Johnson's boys must complete their mission today. "By must, I mean must, and by today, I mean today and not next week."[2] Because the casualties Johnson reported thus far were light, Alexander discounted his claims of relentless machine-gun fire blocking the way ahead.

After the war, in an inquiry into why the Lost Battalion became "lost," Alexander admitted that he had lied to Johnson about the progress of the French. The division CO had assured his brigade CO that the French were well up on Johnson's left and thus in position to protect his flank, even though he knew the French had hardly moved. Concurring with corps HQ and army HQ that the Germans were in general retreat and that secure flanks were not, given the circumstances, so very vital, Alexander felt that a little deception to underlings was justified when so much could be won. Now was the time and opportunity to batter the Boche into surrender, before winter interrupted the victory parade. "Audacity and perseverance" were the essentials at this critical moment in the war, not honesty and loyalty to the pawns that might have to be sacrificed in order to checkmate the opponent. Alexander's outlook was certainly in tune with the current philosophy of the Allied war leaders. Pershing was adamant in his advocation of unrelenting attack and, if his aggressiveness ever flagged, he had the prodding missives of Marshal Foch to urge him on, such as, "Troops, thrown into the attack have only to know their direction of attack. In this direction they go as far as they can, without any thought of alignment."[3]

When Johnson continued to fret about the closed curtains of the German defenses, the lava flowed again. The attack would go forward, open flanks and running wounds be damned. If Johnson could not perform, there were other brigadiers waiting in the wings.

Johnson whiplashed the Alexandrian demands on down the line to Stacey at 1120. "The advance of the infantry will continue at twelve-thirty.... The General says you are to advance behind the barrage regardless of losses."[4]

Ten minutes later, Detroit One (Stacey) sent a runner to Whittlesey advising him that a one hour barrage would be followed by resumption of the infantry attack. "You will press on to your objectives at all costs."[5] Stacey did, at least, concede that the bald summit of La Palette was too hard to handle and granted Whittlesey the option of advancing on the other side of the ravine—the east side—to break the enemy line at Hill 198.

Whittlesey was still worried about his Frenchless flank. He prophesized, "It will be the same thing all over again. We'll be cut off."

Stacey was unbending now. "You're getting panicky."

Resigned to the seemingly inevitable, Whittlesey bowed to his fate and agreed to attack.[6]

Whittlesey shared his misgivings with a staff officer, expressing his fear that they would be cut off as they had been the week before. The staff officer agreed, certain that at that very moment the "Krauts" were maneuvering to pinch off the battalion.

Whittlesey was just as pessimistic, but was resigned to the inevitable. He and his men were helpless beneath the cataract of Pershing's blind ambition. "You can't argue with the Brass. Black Jack wants victory and he'll have it."[7]

The artillery preparation began arcing in at 1230, pounding the woods and ridge line ahead of the 308th. The shelling was generally inaccurate, but the sound and fury did mask the arrival of the 2/308th, led by Detroit White (Captain McMurtry), to join Whittlesey's battalion in the march up Hill 198.

George G. McMurtry would afterwards always be associated with Whittlesey and their joint leadership in the cauldron of the Argonne. The friendship forged in those harrowing October days would become unbreakable and last to the last of their days (which, in Whittlesey's case, was not that far into the future). But on the surface, there seemed to be little that would have bonded them, if the special circumstances of combat had not worked its fusion. McMurtry, a native of Pittsburg, was, in most respects, the opposite personality type from the quiet, studious, introverted and introspective Whittlesey. Like Whittlesey, McMurtry was a college man, of Harvard pedigree rather than of the Williams College creed, and worked the Wall Street beat as well, though as a stockbroker rather than a lawyer. But he was stumpy where Whittlesey was stork-like, gregarious where Whittlesey could seem standoffish. McMurtry witnessed the world in vivid color, while Whittlesey saw largely shades of gray.

McMurtry was a natural-born leader, commanding respect with his fearless appetite for the fight, and affection for his egalitarian embrace of his men. Attracted to hearty men and headstrong action, McMurtry had cut short his college career to enlist in Theodore Roosevelt's Rough Riders and fight his way to the top of San Juan Hill. In 1917, he tossed off Wall Street just as easily as he had Harvard to again answer the call to action, accepting a commission as second lieutenant in the assembling AEF. Now on the afternoon of October 2, 1918, the old Rough Rider was about to storm another hill and embark on his greatest adventure.

Companies E, G and H of McMurtry's battalion swiveled into line alongside Companies A, B and C of Whittlesey's battalion on the east side of the ravine, while Company F, 2/308th linked with Company D, 1/308th on the draw's west side. At 1330, once the artillery barrage had lifted, the two battalions moved off toward Hill 198. The German position on the hill, rising above Charlevaux Brook, zigzagged some 500 yards east along the crest to abut up against a pox of brush and boulders, concealing a honeycomb of limestone caves.

On to the east was deployed von Kleist's Group Argonnen. It was where the two German corps touched that the 307th's morning attack had hammered the Boche line sufficiently for the enemy to shift his attention to the east, while the 308th was making its lodgment near La Palette, one mile to the west. Garrisoning Hill 198 when the morning attack by the Americans fell was a mixed unit of Hessians from the 254th Reserve Regiment (from Wellmann's corps) and the home guards from the 122nd Landwehr Regiment (from von Kleist's group). Low on ammunition, unfed for two days, senses scrambled from more days of artillery pounding, no one on the hill knew who was in charge, and no one knew exactly what was expected of them. Confusion, distraction and unusually abysmal German staff work left the men on 198 in a muddle.

When the 307th struck that morning, many of the Hessians and Landwehr took to their heels. At around 1000, the 307th's Company L, led by Captain Kerr Rainsford, smashed through the German wire and into the trenchline, just at the point along the crest where the corps boundary ran. L Company had won a signal victory. If the company had consolidated or exploited its success, it most likely would have prevented Whittlesey's battalion, approaching 198 from the other side, from being cut off and becoming the "Lost Battalion." But the L Company commander allowed victory to slip from his weakened grasp, an understandably lost opportunity, given the circumstances.

A sense of triumph was not what Captain Rainsford felt. Unaware that he had actually penetrated the main German line, the L Company CO was immediately a·icted with doubts. He was a sensitive soul, of artistic bent, not a natural-born soldier. With no idea that Whittlesey's battalion was working its way toward his position, the captain feared for his flanks. Scouts sent out on either wing reported no supporting units nearby. The usual Argonne attrition had sapped his company's strength, and his men were flummoxed with fatigue. When Acting Major Crawford Blagden, dispatched by the 307th regimental commander to scope out the situation, arrived on scene, he agreed with Rainsford that their position was untenable. Fearing the inevitable German counterattack, the two officers decided to pull out. "We can't fight the war alone" was their evaluation.[8]

Their original orders were to break through the enemy lines, then reform for the counterattack the Germans always launched when they had lost ground. Blagden and Rainsford spun those orders into a two-step of rapid breakthrough, followed by a quick withdrawal to the position they had held prior to the attack, in order to repel the enemy's counter-thrust. Company L, consequently, retraced its exacting steps to their jump-off line. Thus the gap ripped open was abandoned and would soon rapidly reclose. A German officer observed, "In a moment that had called for audacity, the Americans acted with timidity."[9]

About one hour later, around 1600, Whittlesey's men would reach the top of Hill 198. His patrols, right and left, found no friendly units with which to combine. If Company L had maintained its rapidly won ground, Whittlesey's recon would have located the unit and a solid line—the 308th linked to the 307th—could have been forged, lengthened and reinforced. Because of this lost opportunity, the 308th would suffer isolation and besiegement for the better part of five days. (It would be a decade later, in a New York City bar, before the commander of the 307th would learn that a company of his regiment had pierced the enemy line, then precipitously withdrew, to put the 308th in peril.)

The two battalions of the 308th had gained the summit of 198 without, by the sanguinary standards of the Argonne, too great a struggle. Whittlesey had sighted a forested finger pointing east up the ridge, with a configuration that would shield his men from the enemy guns on La Palette. While automatic riflemen armed with French Chauchats and Hotchkiss machine gunners from the 306th Machine-Gun Battalion triggered volleys into the flanking woods to suppress sniper fire, the men of the 308th leapfrogged by ones and twos from cover to cover up the ridge. Bracketing rounds plunged into the woods from German 77 mm guns, but the artillery was blindly fired and inflicted no casualties. Long-range machine-gun ripples stuttered across the valley from La Palette to the left rear, but the ridge banks absorbed the abuse. As the Americans maneuvered through the wire, red from the rust of five autumns, sniper rounds from the flanks and sporadic fire from 198 in front did rip through the entwining undergrowth to tear into the flesh of more than fifty doughboys.

After stymieing the advance for some time, the sniper teams were suppressed when Whittlesey's scouts located their nucleus off to the right and Lt. Harry Rogers's Company B was detailed to shut down their operation. Behind a base of fire, Rogers, at about 1400, led his company around the enemy riflemen and their supporting machine-gun nest. Catapulting grenades, the American infantrymen forced the surrender of an enemy dugout, manned by two officers and twenty-eight enlisted men, armed with six automatic rifles. Local reserves from the 76th Reserve Division, the "Kamerad"-shouting soldiers had been promised rest in a quiet sector, not spiraling 75 mm artillery shells and hard-charging Yankee infantry.

This one significant locus of resistance eliminated, Whittlesey led his task force on up the ridge, encountering only a few more sputters of rifle fire and harmless machine-gun bursts from La Palette to the west. Hill 198 was claimed with so little opposition, that Whittlesey suspected he was being enticed into the jaws of a smothering counterattack—the tactical specialty of the kaiser's army. He wisely ordered out recon patrols.

At approximately 1600, those scouts reported back with a surprising discovery. The major and his staff followed the recon team through barbed wire obstacles to their find— heavily camouflaged permanent positions, of vintage age, but complete with elaborate earthworks, dugouts, firing platforms and revetments, all served by a sophisticated drainage system

Walking wounded of the 308th Infantry, 77th Division, in the Argonne, October 2, 1918. U.S. Army Military History Institute.

and living accommodations. Manned by determined defenders, the position could have held out for days or even weeks, but not a single soldier in field gray was in sight. Whittlesey realized he was standing within the Haupt-Widerstands-Linie, a castle keep of the Giselher Stellung, which the German command had ordered held to the death of the last defender. Major Whittlesey and the men of the 308th Infantry had broken the steel band of the Giselher Stellung as if it had been made of paper.

As evening approached, Whittlesey was both pleased and perplexed about his situation. His unit had captured an important enemy position, but because that capture had come so easy—a stronghold untouched by artillery bombardment, yet abandoned basically without a fight—Whittlesey feared he might be leading his men into a trap. Equally troubling was the apparent fact that the 1st and 2nd Battalions of the 308th were way out front of everybody, without a friend on either flank—no French cuirassiers on the left, no fellow Metro Division soldiers on the right. A repeat of the September 28 encirclement loomed large in the major's mind, and the odds of escaping disaster a second time within a week must have seemed unlikely to the careful and cautious Whittlesey. The major was not a risk-taker, but he was a loyal and obedient soldier. He had his orders and he would follow them, even though he had registered his doubts about them. Downhill from 198 was tree-choked Charlevaux Valley, and above those woods ran the old Roman road that was his assigned objective. He would lead his men there, lay out a perimeter for the night, and send out further patrols on the long chance that allies could at last be located on each or either flank.

This fateful decision, one that resulted in isolation and near-annihilation for his 554 men, requires examination. As Lt. Colonel Taylor Beattie observed, after numerous visits to the site of the Lost Battalion (while conducting research for his *Military History* magazine article about the Lost Battalion), Major Whittlesey had three options open to him in the twilight of October 2. He could have dug in on the "military" crest of Hill 198 where he and his men stood. Alternately, he could have secured equally defensible terrain on the high ground north of the road. But he chose the third option, which was really no choice at all, but rather a strict adherence to orders—advance to the road and set up a perimeter there. Instead of remaining short of his objective or advancing slightly beyond it—with either choice resulting in the placement of his unit on dominating high ground—Whittlesey elected to move up to the reverse slope of the hill, just short of the targeted road, and hope for the arrival of supporting flank units.[10] Surely the choice Whittlesey made that evening led irrevocably three years later to the final decision of his life, as he stood at the railing of the *Toloa*.

The choice made—the decision rendered that would bring him unwanted and, ultimately, unbearable fame—Whittlesey, at 1715, led his men down the north slope of 198 into the thickets of Charlevaux Valley. With the sun setting behind both the day's last rainclouds and the darkening headland of La Palette to the west, the greens and browns of the brook and opposite inclines faded to gray. The major led the battalion with his HQ element, runners at his side, followed by Private James Larney, bearing signal panels, and Privates Omer Richards and Theodore Tollefson, lugging pigeon cages. Five hundred yards across the valley, on the road-bearing ridge, two figures in "coal scuttle" helmets and German gray emerged from the greater gray of the Roman road. A rifleman in Whittlesey's advance party snapped off two rounds at the enemy soldiers, but the bullets missed and the targets took flight into the trees. The doughboy's apology for missing his marks was shrugged off by Whittlesey, never one to scoff at honest effort. "That's all right, son. You can't expect to get a hit in this bad light."[11]

Assuming further enemy contact, Whittlesey assembled his officers: Lt. Henry Williamson, leading the remaining eighteen men still standing from Company A; Lt. Rogers of B Company; Captain Leo Stromee, just into the second night in command of his C Company (the most intact company remaining in the battalion); along with platoon leaders, Lieutenants Gordon Schenck and Leo Trainor. Also present were the officers of McMurtry's battalion: Wilhelm, Leak and Harrington of E Company; Buhler and Eager of G Company; Cullen and Griffin of H Company; along with Peabody, Revnes and Noon of the 306th Machine-Gun Battalion. Whittlesey's instructions were simple and clear cut: "Take your men forward."[12]

And so they did, sliding down the hill and into destiny. Coming off the tree-studded slope, the Yanks lumbered across a cleared arena of grass, where dress-right-dress lines of bootprints gave evidence of a former Boche drillfield. With long-range crackles of machine-gun fire from La Palette to the west warning them to zig as well as zag, the infantrymen of the 308th and the machine gunners of the 306th bounded single file over a creaky wooden bridge spanning the marshy green of Charlevaux Brook. Though the dash across the bridge was made with proper intervals between men, a few soldiers were still struck by enemy fire. But most of Whittlesey's men made it to the opposite north side of the stream and headed up the wooded slope below which the brook meandered.

With the dusk deepening in the shadowy woods, Whittlesey was anxious to get his force defensively deployed and his men settled for the night. In what was to be famously called "the Pocket" (although for its residents, it would have more appropriately been labeled "the Noose"), the major delineated a perimeter some 300 to 350 yards long and sixty to seventy yards deep. He sited in the nine machine guns first, most of them along his west flank and pointed toward the nuisance of La Palette. The twenty automatic riflemen, with their 8 mm, twenty-round-clip, French Chauchats, were positioned to cover the flanks. Sentry posts were tabbed and the rest of the men were directed to scratch funk holes out of the flint-flecked ground. While Whittlesey inspected his perimeter, a water detail lugged coveys of canteens back to the brook, and a famished formation of infantry soldiers broke out their iron rations—two-pound cans of beans and tomatoes or the barfable "Willy" beef (also called "monkey meat") and hardtack.

The perimeter checked by Whittlesey constituted, in Taylor Beattie's reckoning, the major's second significant misstep that day. When added to the initial error of leaving defensible ground at the shank of the day in a bulldog focus on carrying out orders, this faulty deployment of his battalion may have added another ball and chain that would one day drag the major down to the Atlantic depths.

Charles Whittlesey was indeed a sterling example of the citizen-soldier—the bedrock of the American Expeditionary Force. He was brave, dedicated, determined, resourceful. But he was not a professional soldier. Beattie, a Special Forces lieutenant colonel, with the trained eye of a professional, came to realize, after repeated inspections of the site of the Pocket, that Whittlesey, in his eagerness to accomplish his mission and maintain personal control of all the men under his command, had committed the mistake so common to inexperienced and amateur officers—he had allowed his men and his unit to bunch up.[13]

Simply put, Whittlesey deployed too many men in too small an area to conduct an effective defense. The 554 men of the composite battalion were crowded in a rectangle three football fields long and some sixty yards deep. The funk holes were dug in a seemingly haphazard pattern on the hillside just yards away from the road. The seventy-five yards of the hillside were steep, with poorly anchored soil replete with rocks. The men on this sliding slope would have been largely protected from the plunging fire of German artillery and mortars from the enemy positions above, but were little protected from machine-gun fire from Hill 198, south across the ravine and quickly reoccupied by the Germans.

As Beattie (and the author in an April 2002 trip to the site) observed, the U.S. fighting positions seemed to have been dug without particular design, wherever weary warriors found a halfway suitable site to dig. Although the flanks offered clear fields of fire for sixty to ninety yards, the view from most of the length of the perimeter north to the German positions was restricted to the road. Only by rising from their holes and presenting a clear target to German small arms fire from the cliff-top positions above the road could Whittlesey's men observe anything beyond the road. The 308th infantrymen were tightly grouped, so constricted in their acne of fighting holes, that only those on the rim of the perimeter could fire effectively at enemy probes on the line. The limited fields of fire for so much of the battalion meant that its firepower was reduced by as much as two-thirds on any particular stretch of the perimeter, with the exception of the flanks.[14] Anxious to carry out his mission and keep his men in a cohesive formation, Whittlesey had made his whole command more vulnerable. The enemy Whittlesey faced that October evening was outnumbered and outgunned by his hodge-podge command, but, in sewing his battalion tightly into the Pocket, he surrendered the initiative to the Germans, who were given the time and opportunity to find, fix and surround the American unit.

After the Argonne, Charles Whittlesey would be honored and praised for his courage and leadership displayed on the thickety slope above Charlevaux Brook. He would deserve

Debris-laden funk holes in the Pocket. Photograph by the author, April 2002.

Steep hillside below the Roman Road in the Pocket. Photograph by the author, April 2002.

The author stands beside the American Battle Monuments Commission marker on the Apremont-Binarville road, pointing to the site of the Lost Battalion and the Pocket. Photograph by the author, April 2002.

every token of appreciation and every word of praise. But all the medals were pinned to a bleeding heart, and all the cheers sounded like accusations. Whittlesey was not a professional soldier, but he was an intelligent man and a perceptive man. He must surely have realized, soon after the fact, that his errors in judgment put the more than 500 men he commanded in mortal peril and brought on the very event for which he garnered such overwhelming approbation.

Sensitive he was, by all accounts, but not so sensitive that the deaths and injuries suffered by his battalion would have alone driven him to his self-ordained demise. He had been at war long enough, had seen men die under his orders and his command, knew that combat commanded a price. Every moment of leadership, every order given or carried out could and often did carry a cost in flesh and blood. He could live with that reality, but he could not live with what he apparently believed was a fraudulent construct.

Above all, Whittlesey was a man of integrity. That honesty of character and intellect would surely have shortly revealed to him the same fatal errors of command judgment that Taylor Beattie uncovered. That he was seemingly "condemned" to a life of iconic stature, of being the object of a hero-worshiping public, for miscalculations that nearly resulted in the annihilation of his battalion was beyond Whittlesey's capacity for self-delusion. He would probably have been more reconciled with the reality of those five days in the Pocket had he been court-martialed for his actions there instead of being awarded the Medal of Honor. It is easy to believe that during the final moments of Whittlesey's life, he was not standing on the deck of a tramp steamer but in the muck of a French forest, and that he made the last and the most heroic of many decisions of his Argonne argosy as he climbed the railing. He would pay final recompense to the fallen of the Lost Battalion, for whom he felt responsible, by joining them.

It is unknown exactly when the awful insight fell on Whittlesey that he had inserted his men into the jaws of the jackal. Maybe there was no sudden thunderclap of revelation, but a gradual tightening of a mental vise of dread, as runner posts to the rear got picked off, and patrols in all directions returned to report contact with or at least a sighting of the enemy.

At first, however, the noose was loose and remained hidden in the hills. The leader of the 1/308th seemed to have little reason to worry, beyond the world of worries that was the common lot of the combat commander. Having set his men to digging in, Whittlesey wrote out a message to Colonel Stacey, advising him that the 1/308th had secured its goal for the day. Corporal Baldwin started the message on its relayed way through the chain of two-man runner (called "cossack") posts established every 100 to 200 yards as the battalion had made its way up Hill 198, past the enemy trenchline, down the slope and across the valley. Should the khakied links in the chain be broken, Whittlesey would have to rely on his pigeons to communicate with the rear. The birds had been trained to wing it back to their base loft at division HQ, with messages scribbled on rice paper and rolled into thimbles hooked to their legs. The bird handlers of the battalion claimed their cooing couriers were superior to every other form of communication, including runners, wireless and land lines, but Whittlesey was skeptical of this avian express and relied more commonly on runners.

As darkness deepened the gloom of the woods, Whittlesey put out patrols. He sent one up the hill to cross the road and the parallel-running railroad to check on what lurked beyond his positions. A second reinforced patrol was detailed to the east (on the right flank) to attempt liaison with the 307th. McMurtry threw out a recon from G Company to the west (on the left flank) in hopes of finding the French.

The rest of the battalion, unaware that they were soon to become unofficially "lost" to the world, settled into what, ironically, seemed to portend a night of relative ease in an environment where misery and mortal danger were the usual accommodations. A few shells impacted off to the east, but they fell far from the perimeter. The stars appeared as night fell, instead of the usual rain, and the sky was clear and crisp with a slight wind stirring the treetops.

While Whittlesey and McMurtry conferred at the battalion CP, the enlisted men pulled out their meager rations. They bitched about their growling stomachs, but celebrated the relative ease of their victory for the day. Compared with far harder days on the Vesle and in the Argonne itself, October 2 had not been a particularly harsh twenty-four hours. Casualties were minor—eight men killed and eighty with minor or serious wounds—and the enemy seemed to be conceding his ground. For the replacements from the West and Midwest, who had seen little action yet, the day hardly seemed the walk in the park claimed by the veterans of the Vesle and of the offensive's earlier days, but to avoid the scorn of the

New York City soldiers who had been tussling with the Germans since July, they too put on a jaded nonchalance toward the day's events.

The "old-timers," though, were, indeed, as relaxed as they could be. With time and tenure in battle, the omnipresent fear fades from the forefront. It doesn't go away, but becomes a common companion, disagreeable and unwelcome, but one that nags from a distance and is kept in its place. Fear no longer immobilizes the typical combat soldier or threatens emotional and mental paralysis; it just drags at the heart and pricks at the gut.

The attitude on the opposing side, on the other hand, was one more of alarm than complacency. The American lodgment within their lines was a matter of grave concern to the German command. The I Reserve Korps commander, General Wellmann, got the news at around 1830 that the American enemy had crossed Charlevaux Brook, one mile east of Charlevaux Mill. Although intelligence claimed this was the only breach of the Haupt-Widerstands-Linie, Wellmann fully understood that this Yank advance constituted an immediate danger to the Giselher Stellung and the German possession of the northern Argonne Forest. Nothing less than the total elimination of the *Amerikanernest* (the American nest) would suffice. Finding sufficient units and personnel from his undermanned Argonne garrison to carry out this task was, however, no easy task.

The most serious problem with the Yankee puncture of the stellung hull was that it endangered liaison between Wellmann's corps and Group Argonnen to the east. Wellmann had expressed concern about the weak link between the German commands with Group Argonnen leader von Kleist, but his colleague in *feld grau* had shown his indifference to any American threat by stating, "The Yankee buffoons will never reach that point."¹⁵ When Wellmann phoned von Kleist to discuss the American breakthrough, von Kleist changed his tune. He assured Wellmann, with whom he had served in the same brigade in the 1914 march to the Marne, that he would round up every man in his sector not holding down a direct front-line position and truck them to the Charlevaux Mill area.

Closer to the cusp of the crisis, Hauptmann von Sybel, chief of staff of General Quadt-Wyckradt-Hüchtenbruck's 76th Reserve Division, was desperately trying to rush reinforcements to the point of rupture. Earlier that afternoon, most of the 76th Division reserve had been siphoned off by Wellmann to bolster the corps reserve, which had been sent to contain the French attack at Autry, west beyond the Argonne. This left only a battalion of the 254th Regiment in the division's reserve pool. Bombarded by bad news—the 253rd Regiment losing ground west of La Palette, the Yanks severing the connection to Group Argonnen, even the division bakery under threat from the American advance—von Sybel decided to employ his last reserve battalion to aid the 253rd beyond La Palette, pulled a machine-gun company from its rest area to slow down the Yankees at Charlevaux, and scoured corps logistical units for personnel to launch a counterattack. Pioneer battalions repairing roads near the bakery were recruited by von Sybel, as were cooks and clerks, mechanics and members of the band, hastily supplied with grenades and boxes of machine-gun ammunition, and sent forward to apply a patchwork tourniquet to the hemorrhaging lines.

The German leaders fully expected that the Americans would exploit their success, push beyond the Charlevaux road, and widen the breach, both left and right. They had no intelligence that the enemy breakthrough was achieved by just one composite American battalion. Wellmann breathed easier when he was advised that the Americans had apparently suspended their attack for the night. The situation brightened even more for him when he learned that the French thrust at Autry was contained, and that the 252nd Regiment had beaten back the other French attack west of La Palette. With the French stymied again, the corps reserve was ordered redeployed to the east to check the American advance.

The crisis then, though no longer white-hot, was still burning bright for Wellmann and his staff. Recently analyzed aerial photos revealed that the Americans had repositioned numerous artillery batteries on the far left flank of their forces in the forest, indicative of an all-out effort in the Argonne. The Charlevaux breach was thus, to the German command, not simply a probe, but a significant threat to the whole Haupt-Widerstands-Linie. Without a quick counterattack, the Americans would surely reinforce their success and expand their bridgehead left, right and straight ahead, attempt to flank the linchpin of La Palette, and possibly unhinge the entire German line in the Argonne. The tear in the line must be patched over.

I Reserve Korps staff labored half the night to coordinate movements and redeployments. German artillery was assigned the primary task of deterring the French at Autry, the 252nd was ordered to counterattack the French cuirassiers west of La Palette, and the 254th was handed the responsibility of hurling the Yankees back across Charlevaux Brook.

As the German units threaded their way east through the woesome woods, the men who had set them to their stumbling progress chipped away above Charlevaux Brook with bayonets and spades at the limestone ledges of the reverse slope. McMurtry and Whittlesey knew their enemy by now and thus also knew a counterattack was inevitable. They were both anxious to get their men dug in and deployed before the dark claimed total dominion.

General Quadt-Wyckradt-Hüchtenbruck indeed had patrols from the 254th filtering around the flank to the left of the breach. One of those patrols, a corporal and nine privates, encountered a two-man American recon on the masonry blocks of the Roman road, 600 yards from the Pocket. One of the doughboys was captured*; the second escaped back to the battalion. The bad news that the left flank was festering with the foe was seconded by the American patrol sent east, which had weaved its way 1,000 yards in unsuccessful search for the 307th. Whittlesey now knew that the enemy was infiltrating around his left flank, that his right was unprotected by the 307th, and that it would be only a matter of time before Heines started harassing him from the east. Northwards—straight up the hill and beyond—was no better. Scouts returned from the immediate front to report, "The Krauts are thicker'n flies around a dung heap."[16]

The October 2 events along Charlevaux Brook riveted the attention of the star-shouldered commanders on the American side as much as they did on the German side. Hopes and fears at brigade and division HQs competed in a cascade of blind ignorance of events and information that ranged from ironclad to hogwash. General Alexander at division headquarters had received little cheerful news as the day devolved. Progress had been minimal along most of the forest front, and what units were moving forward were doing so with open and inviting flanks. The division commander's temper bubbled hot, constantly

---

*The American apprehended on the Roman road, Private Hutt, would remain a POW for five weeks, until the Armistice liberated him. After release, he staggered back to U.S. lines, a khakied ragman covered with cootie bites. When he pleaded with the YMCA section for sweets to celebrate his regained freedom, the keepers of the candy had no qualms at turning away this doughboy who had endured enemy captivity, but was short of change. Hutt, apparently, would not be deterred. That night the candy cart's chocolate ration fell victim to a "midnight requisitioning."

in danger of boiling over. He pestered General Johnson at 154th Brigade HQ without mercy, and fumed in a fury when the advance of Colonel Eugene Houghton's 307th Regiment petered out. Whittlesey's messenger arrived at the brigade HQ at about 2000, and the news that the 308th had opened a gap in the enemy front and had actually attained the day's objective gave Johnson his first real moment of brightness just as the day grew darker. At last he had good news for Alexander, and the telephone to division HQ, briefly at least, became less an instrument of dread.

And for the first time this day, Alexander had praise instead of criticism for Johnson and his units. Confident that Whittlesey could unlock the gates to the whole Giselher Stellung position if properly reinforced, Alexander ordered Johnson to bolster the bridgehead with additional battalions.

Johnson set about his assignment of reinforcement and exploitation. He directed Houghton to send the 3rd Battalion of his 307th Regiment across Charlevaux Brook to secure Whittlesey's right, ordered the brigade's reserve battalion—the 3/308th—to find the French at Binarville on the left and restart their offensive engines, and readied the rest of the 307th for a daybreak frontal attack, to be coordinated with flank and rear assaults on the Germans by Companies D and F of the 308th. Johnson envisioned Whittlesey's rupture of the German line being expanded battalion by battalion, until the Giselher Stellung was torn asunder. Whittlesey would "rip up the German line with the crowbar" of his battalion, the 307th would extend the fissure, then the 306th and so on eastwards, until the whole enemy edifice collapsed.[17]

It all looked good on the paper orders. But on the ground, in the frightful forest, where precise plans often deteriorated into debacle, the view of the situation was as muddied as the ground. These woods were truly deep and dark, and moving the non-nocturnal infantrymen of the 77th Division through them was a guarantee of straying soldiers and lost units. And this black forest was thick not just with thorns and tripwire, but with ever increasing numbers of German infiltrators, armed with sniper rifles and machine guns.

Part of the plan did work. "Detroit Blue" (the 3/308th)—the regiment's reserve battalion, held back because of its decimating losses in the first week of the offensive—hacked its way to Binarville that night of October 2 to reforge liaison between the French right wing and the U.S. left. Promptly at sunrise, the battalion was to swing east to secure the left flank of Whittlesey's position. The 3/308th was unaware, however, that German forces were already ensconced between Binarville and the west curve of the Pocket.

Johnson's operational plans started unraveling with the movement of the 3/307th to the opposite flank. The 3rd Battalion (Companies I, K, L and M) was understrength, totaling about 500, but the men had enjoyed the twin treats of an extended rest and a hot meal. Roused from their sleep at 2100, the battalion, with Captain Nelson Holderman's Company K in the lead, followed guides along a twisting trail. Clouds had moved in to deepen the darkness, and the only stars were those of German illumination rounds around La Palette. As a 3rd Battalion private later recounted, "You couldn't see a thing. Every man hung on to the belt of the man ahead. We were like blind men groping our way."[18]

The battalion proceeded in single file, companies M, L and I in ragged order behind Holderman's Company K. The hours grew longer and the path more difficult. The column stutter-stepped along as midnight meandered past and doughboys slipped and slid. The halts to reorient and rearrange the buckling chain of encumbered men grew more frequent and frustrating. An ebb tide of exhaustion rolled over the men, and soldiers started nodding off along the trail as the guides, with increasing frequency, interrupted the march to try to match their maps with the maze in which they stumbled.

Some time after midnight, the exhausted commander of Company M fell out of the march for a brief rest, lost sight of the column ahead, and subsequently, took a wrong turn that separated his men from the leading Company K. After trying to reorient himself for some time, the lieutenant in charge gave up, set up a perimeter, and waited for daybreak to resume his wanderings in search of his objective. Companies L and I, behind M, followed that company on its wrong track, but when M gave up for the night, the trailing two companies kept on the move. L and I eventually reached a prominent ridge, which they calculated to be near Whittlesey's position. Climbing into old enemy dugouts they had discovered, the two companies planned to link with the 1/308th at dawn's light. That light revealed them far from Whittlesey's men, close to La Palette, and effectively out of the loop. Reoriented, the companies backtracked to re-form with the rest of their regiment.

Company K, in the meantime, without realizing that the other three companies of the battalion no longer walked in their wake, continued along the proper course toward the Pocket. Captain Holderman, a robust young Californian who had taken up soldiering with a cheery zeal, was determined to complete his mission. He had been ill that day, but refused to absent himself from the mission for fear of losing face with his men. Scoffing at a rumor passed up the column from the rear that the mission had been scrubbed, Holderman insisted on holding course. At around 0400 he reached the first of Baldwin's three-man runner posts.

Closing in on his objective, Holderman had one of the runners guide his ninety-eight-man company to the next station, on the other side of the abandoned German trenchline. The men there pointed out the landmarks ahead—the drill field, the bridge over the brook, and the final messenger post before the 308th bivouac. Aware now that the other three companies of the 3/307th had disappeared into the darkness, Holderman cautiously maneuvered his men down the precipitous slope. Once on level ground, the captain made a head count. All were present and accounted for, if many were a bit battered from tumbles taken and weariness accumulated.

Holderman sent his XO (executive officer), Lt. Thomas Pool, ahead to locate the next runner outpost. The Texas-born Pool found it vacant and reported back to his CO an enveloping blackness that utterly obscured the sloping terrain and invited wrong turns. Convinced by Pool's warning that, "It's darker than the insides of a cow's belly," and that further stumbling around might invite disaster, Holderman decided to settle in and wait out the remaining hours of the night.[19] Posting guards, Company K's captain allowed the rest of his men the luxury of sleep, however brief. His company was only 200 yards short of the Pocket.

The perimeter of the Pocket was shaped like a crescent and 300 yards long. The star of that crescent, the battalion CP, lay at its center, just under the rim of the road. Downhill from the CP and just yards from the stream were the rifle pits of Company A, the most worn-down of the units of the composite battalion and consequently placed in the more secure middle of the Pocket. Company A's primary responsibility was to secure the center of the position and provide runners for the battalion commander.

Off to the right, Lt. Karl Wilhelm was put in charge of the 2/308th's Companies E and G, buttressed with three Hotchkiss machine guns from the 306th Machine-Gun Battalion. Off to the west, on the left flank, where the French were supposed to be but were not, and where the Pocket and the battalion was most vulnerable, Whittlesey had positioned the preponderance of his firepower. A machine-gun moat of the command's six remaining Hotchkisses provided enfilading fire from any direction against a German assault. Interspersed among the machine guns were Companies B and C from the First Battalion and Company H from the Second Battalion. McMurtry was in charge of this dangerous flank. Company H's Lt. William Cullen, with his flaming head of hair and a flaming self-confidence to match, was second-in-command.

While Company K, 3/307th had struggled along its reinforcing route, and while the men of the 308th had settled in for the night, McMurtry and Whittlesey had huddled at their CP in the center of the position to hash over today and anticipate tomorrow. Both felt the position they had chosen for the night was fairly secure against artillery fire from La Palette and raking fire from long-range machine guns, but both were uneasy about the supply situation. The men had no coffee and no blankets to warm themselves against the chilly October night, little tobacco to help settle their nerves and palliate their hunger, and only limited iron rations to sustain them. Two of the infantry companies had gone into battle with no rations issued at all.

These insufficiencies were indicative to Whittlesey and McMurtry of what seemed to them the slap-dash nature of the American offensive. The attack of October 2 appeared to the major and the captain to have been mounted by the high command with the same set of presumptions as that of the original attack of September 26, even though circumstances had changed drastically. The 77th had gone lightweight into the Argonne on September 26, carrying no blankets, overcoats or tents, and no heavy supporting arms like mobile guns, trench mortars and tanks (Holderman would subsequently, in a monograph he wrote for the Army about the Lost Battalion, recommend that a battalion-size force never be sent into action without its supporting Stokes mortars and 37 mm guns)[20]. The plan had been to contain the enemy in the forest, while the divisions on either flank did the real work of pinching out the Germans with their wide sweeping attacks on the wings.

Those surging regiments had gained disappointingly little ground and the Argonne had remained impervious as ever. Now the 77th was expected to do the job those units on the flanks had failed to do, and to do it frontally with little more than they had been given for the initial assault. The bruising toe-to-toe fight that nobody had anticipated in this most rugged section of the front had materialized, and the only extra help given the 77th Division had been artillery preparatory fire that had fallen far short of enough.

Whittlesey's pessimistic musings were interrupted by the approach to his funk hole of the battalion sergeant-major. While German star-shells gave off their sputtering light above the trees, the sergeant-major reported that Private William Powers had overheard German voices near his position. Whittlesey was skeptical. "Private Powers is having nightmares. Tell him to go back to sleep."[21]

Whittlesey was wrong; the private was right. The Germans were scurrying past his rifle pits and, in increasing numbers, violating both flanks of 308th's bivouac as the night wore on. As many as 180 Germans had infiltrated behind the Pocket by morning. Slowly this composite battalion from the Metro Division was being surrounded and cut off from the rest of the U.S. First Army.

A full-scale enemy reaction to Whittlesey's breakthrough was, indeed, rapidly developing. As a gray dawn gave way to a sunny and cloudless day over the forest for the first time in over a week, Wellmann and von Kleist were organizing counterattacks that they were confident would reverse the situation. From their long experience on the Western Front, the Germans had come to prefer dawn counterattacks, when weather, visibility and troop morale, fortified by a good breakfast and a shot of schnapps, was most favorable for the attackers. Conversely, the Allied troops, having most likely outrun their supply lines with the progress of their assault, would usually be both hungry and haggard from a nervous night of sentry duty.

And so, with the new dawn and the new day of October 3, German infantry started swarming toward the American perimeter, left, right, to the front and to the rear, like white blood cells marshaling to fight an infection. Chief of staff von Sybel of the 76th Reserve Division had sent troop- and ammo-bearing trucks driving through the night to the Charlevaux area. In the general shift of forces east, away from the contained French and toward the American eruption, von Sybel had directed the 252nd Regiment to take over the area west of La Palette, and the 253rd to secure La Palette itself and the draw leading to Hill 198. The 254th would undertake the counterattack along the Hill 198 front, with that regiment's reserve battalion of foot-uhlans, Pioneer Battalion 376, and two detached pioneer companies, earmarked for the elimination of the two U.S. battalions that had penetrated the lines.

Though long familiar with the Argonne, the deep night, the confusion of the situation, and the narrow tracks that served as roads all combined to slow down the German concentration—though nothing on the order of the American snafu in their reinforcing attempts that same evening. Thus the counterattacks were slower in developing than the German staff had hoped. Overall, however, corps commander Wellmann was encouraged by the reports brought to him with his morning coffee at corps HQ near Briquenay. The French incursion near Autry was closed, with the last eighty French soldiers there capitulating. One breach was thus eliminated and the second—that achieved by the Americans—would hopefully also soon be closed.

Tromping east into the rising sun in the first hours of daybreak were Major Hünicken's Hessians from the 76th Division's 254th Regiment. They were headed down the valley behind La Palette and toward the ridge that ran up to those trenches of the Haupt-Widerstands-Linie lost the day before to the Americans. The foot sloggers of the 254th advanced with care. They had a clearer picture of the overall situation than their Yankee adversaries, but did not know the enemy's exact positions nor their exact strength. They had been told that two battalions of Americans had burst through (not elements of two battalions, which was actually the case), and two battalions of U.S. troops—even allowing for normal combat wastage (a full-strength U.S. battalion numbered about 900)—would equal some 1,500, about the same strength of a full German infantry regiment. Hünicken's men were, consequently, surprised as they ascended the spur opposite La Palette to encounter no heavy opposition. Steep-sided and scrub-shrouded, the spur was expected to be rife with American Hotchkiss and Chauchat teams. Hünicken had even attached a heavy 170 mm, 900-meter range *Minenwerfer* ("mine thrower") section to his assault groups to blast the auto-rifle nests he assumed his men would encounter.

This lack of resistance worried Hünicken as much as it pleased him. Fearing he was being lured into a trap, Hünicken had his men advance along the Haupt-Widerstands-Linie in small clusters, each grouped around a light machine-gun team and preceded by vanguard patrols fanning across a wide front, in conformity to the tactical system laid down long ago by Ludendorff.

With the early morning light still wan under the forest canopy, the stalking Germans probably did not spot across the valley the Americans to the north, dug in along the Roman road. The Huns were in approximately the same location on Hill 198, from which Whittlesey had the day before spotted the two German soldiers. But if the Germans did not immediately zero in on the Pocket, one of their flank patrols did discover a Yankee runner post and killed the three Americans there. Notified of this development, Hünicken detailed more three and four-man patrols to seek out and destroy the U.S. messenger chain. While Whittlesey's runners were being picked off one by one, other German sections slithered east to seed light machine-gun teams on both sides of the American perimeter below the road. Meanwhile, the main body of the German battle group was reoccupying the trenches of the Haupt-Widerstands-Linie, with riflemen and machine gunners plopped down into posts facing alternately north and south. By 0600, a German cordon was being drawn behind Whittlesey's Pocket, and the isolation of the 308th was nearly complete.

Major Whittlesey was not yet aware of the impending isolation of his unit. The first events of the day, in fact, seemed to indicate otherwise. Not long after first light, Holderman, still fueled by "bounce and ginger" that few of his weary troops seemed to share, walked into the perimeter. He informed the major that three more companies were somewhere behind him and would surely soon arrive. Whittlesey cheerfully responded, "Well, we're in pretty good shape then."[22]

Whittlesey had felt fairly confident the night before that the enemy would not launch a nocturnal attack. There had been no illumination or artillery prep, the tactical prerequisites of a German night assault, and the terrain was too unforgiving to permit a blind thrust. With his doubled-up runner posts to keep regiment, brigade and division up to snuff on his situation, Whittlesey expected his higher-ups to maintain communication, secure the rear, and protect his left flank, regardless of what the French did or did not do. Surely after the near disaster of September 28, his superior commanders would not grant the Germans a second chance at cutting off and crushing his battalion!

The first indication that all this confidence might be unwarranted came when a sentry from the farthest left outpost, over near the mill, escorted a forlorn-looking German soldier to the CP funk hole. Taken prisoner as he grunted his way through the brush, the German was quite forthcoming to his American captors after they set him at ease with a pipeful of Bull Durham. Through the battalion interpreter, the POW identified his regiment—the 254th—and predicted, "You will be wiped out."[23]

While the privates who had snagged the POW admired the Luger pistol they had taken off him and Whittlesey and McMurtry pumped him for more information, further intelligence from patrols and outposts came in to confirm the sinister image of a woods crawling with enemy infiltrators in all directions.

Danger lurked from all points of the compass, but it was obvious that the biggest dragons were gathering on the western flank. Whittlesey and McMurtry concurred that it was time to bring up Companies D and F, led by Lt. Paul Knight. They had been positioned west of Charlevaux Valley on October 2 to guard the 1/308th's left rear. Because of Whittlesey's right oblique maneuver across Hill 198 and the merger of the 1st and 2nd Battalions of the 308th, the gap between Knight's companies and Whittlesey's force had lengthened, and that gap was now turning gray with German soldiers. The left flank was fast becoming an open invitation to disaster, and Whittlesey wanted to withdraw that invitation. He therefore decided to move Knight closer and link with Companies D and F. Determined to employ Lt. Karl Wilhelm's Company E to achieve this linkage, he ordered the lieutenant to report to him.

Wilhelm, a German-American from Buffalo, N.Y., led his command past the CP, while, thirty minutes later, Holderman's Company K filed over the brook bridge and echeloned right to fill the gap on the Pocket's eastern curve left by Company E. While these two companies were redeploying, most of the rest of the men labored to deepen their funk holes, and others hacked away at the limestone to excavate those other always necessary holes—latrine pits.

Those early reports of German dialogue that Whittlesey had initially shrugged off could now no longer be denied. Other German-rendered sounds also chimed in, as the swoosh and thunder of impacting artillery rounds spiraled around the Pocket at 0830. On their sharp-angled hillside positions, the men of Whittlesey's force felt little threatened by the enemy artillery punching blind at their perimeter. Most of the shells screamed in on the opposite side of the stream, some splattered up ocher eruptions from the brook itself, a few barreled into the far fringe of the road. None fell within the oblong of the Pocket itself.

After Wilhelm's departure from the perimeter, a message from Colonel Stacey had arrived by runner, timed from 1900 of the previous day. The fact that the message was twelve hours old alerted Whittlesey to the vulnerability of his runner-chain. The regimental commander offered Whittlesey rations, blankets, overcoats and slickers, but required a detail sent back from the Pocket to acquire them. Stacey also ordered Whittlesey to prepare for a renewed advance after 0700.

Whittlesey's reply message pointed out the lack of spare bodies to ferry supplies back and forth, particularly if a renewed advance was to be attempted, and informed regiment of his casualties from the October 2 combat—eight killed and eighty wounded from Companies B, C, E, G and H.

Rations and raincoats were important, but of more immediate concern was the enemy artillery. The incoming rounds were still stray and sporadic, but, given the Germans' usual energy and efficiency, it would only be a matter of time before they either tightened their aim from the north or trundled guns over behind La Palette to the west to place the hillside battalion under better sighted and more direct fire. With the runner relay system in obvious trouble, Major Whittlesey turned to his other communications option—the pigeons cooing in their cages. At 0850 the major had Private Omer Richards, a York Street French-Canadian who was in charge of the seven battalion birds, dispatch in a metal capsule tied to the pigeon's right leg this message: "We are being shelled by German artillery. Can we not have artillery support? Fire is coming from northwest."[24]

A second pigeon was released with a plea for howitzer support from Lt. J. Teichmoeller, the artillery liaison officer attached to the 1/308th. Teichmoeller asked for counter-battery fire from the 305th Field Artillery, in support of the 308th Infantry, and noted that one shell per minute from either *Minenwerfers* or 77 mm guns was arcing into or around the Charlevaux Brook position. The first bird failed to home into the 77th Division HQ loft, but the pigeon with Teichmoeller's note was discovered there at 1055, and the information and instructions were telephoned to the 154th Brigade field artillery CP. For the men along Charlevaux Brook, the vital infantry-artillery partnership, the most basic of war-fighting alliances, would seem to have been back in play. But the inherent mischance of martial events and the fog of war—that tragically truest of clichés—would soon align to turn this fraternity of arms into fratricide.

The men of the 308th, however, would face a more immediate threat before artillery would circle around from a harassing hazard to a saving grace and back to a deadly menace.

While the pigeons were winging their courses over the battlefield, the soldiers in the Pocket were receiving confirmation of their fears—the enemy was all around them. Added to the fiery brown blossoms of the artillery shells came fusillades of machine-gun fire from Hill 198. Bullets zipped into the creek and raked the bank, while 77 mm shells threw up plumes of muddy water as high as the trees.

A higher crescendo of fire from the direction that Wilhelm's company had taken alerted Whittlesey to the near certainty that Company E had found, not Lt. Knight and Companies D and F, but the enemy in strength. Corroboration came at 0930, when Lt. James Leak of E Company, sporting a blood-soaked battle dressing on his head instead of a steel pot, signaled the OP on the left flank that he was coming in with the survivors of Wilhelm's unit. Behind him trailed another officer, Lt. Victor Harrington, propping up two wounded privates. Of the fifty-one men who had walked west out of the perimeter two hours before, only eighteen, most of them hobbled with wounds, staggered back to the Pocket.

Leak reported to Whittlesey the sad details of E Company's encounter. After wading Charlevaux Brook, Wilhelm's men had started up Hill 198. Twenty yards from the crest, a voice from the verdancy called out in accented English for the unit identity of the column. After the Americans responded, the subterfuge was dropped and an order rang out in German. Private Max Probst, a German-American with a brother in the kaiser's army, warned, "He's giving them our range!"[25] Then the lightning struck.

Maxims laid down a deadly drumbeat along the length of the column, potato masher hand grenades twirled into the troops. Snagged in a shallow draw, E Company took fifteen casualties in fewer seconds. The rest of the men, rattled by a volume of fire heavier than most of them had ever experienced, hunted for cover and a way to fight back. Enemy snipers popped up along the length of the American file to plink their rounds into many of the 308th infantrymen. A Mauser bullet drilled through Lt. Leak's helmet to plow a path across his scalp. Lt. Harrington got nipped in the arm, but kept pulling the trigger of a Chauchat he had picked up from a gunner dropped by the first volley. A few other Americans fought back effectively. Private Henry Miller kept his combat composure, and serpentined his way through the scrub brush to take a German sniper in flank and dispatch him with his Lee-Enfield rifle. Turning to his comrades to proclaim his kill, Miller was struck by Maxim rounds and killed. He would receive a posthumous Distinguished Service Cross.

A quarter of an hour into the firefight, Wilhelm ordered his two wounded lieutenants to work their way back to the battalion with the rest of the injured, while he attempted, with the ten men still fit to fight, to complete the link-up with Knight. There was no fighting their way through the German ambush position, however. Wilhelm had to give up on his mission and try to squirm back to the regiment. The lieutenant finally made it to regimental HQ a day later, badly wounded and accompanied by only four other survivors.

Lt. Leak was adding the last doleful details to his report to Whittlesey, when a rolling-car rumble and a "woof woof" whine sirened a warning to the men in the Pocket that a *Minenwerfer* round was on its way. The warhead greeted the ground explosively, and the consulting party in the CP hole was layered in the Argonne earth. Two more drum-shaped rounds powered in, one only to raise the water, but the other to bury the living and the dead. Private Tomasso Cavello was killed and his death surely eventually invoked sympathy among his comrades, but the first reaction was indicative of the ruthless world now inhabited by these men. The voice of a desperate soldier sounded soon after the *Minenwerfer* explosion. "The wog got whacked that time. Do you suppose he's got anything to eat? I saw him with something this morning."[26]

The detonations had also buried alive Private Harvey Farncomb. The Californian had been brought into the perimeter not long before by a morning patrol, after he had spent the night lying in the open with a broken ankle inflicted by German bullets as he was crossing the bridge. A final fate seemed in deadly pursuit of Farncomb, as the funk hole in which he lay collapsed in on him when the mortar shell impacted. Once again, however, his comrades came to the rescue, disinterring him, his eyes and mouth packed with dirt, but otherwise unharmed.

Whittlesey, while the *Minenwerfer* shells were still spiraling in, had risen from his hole to determine the direction of the mortar fire. Quickly gathering a platoon-size patrol from C Company, Whittlesey appointed Lt. Gordon Schenck its leader and sent him on his way northwest to take out the mortar. As the *Minenwerfer* "flying pigs" (as the British Tommies called them) continued to plummet into the perimeter, Private Shano Collins, one of Baldwin's runners, brought more bad news. He was the sole survivor from his station, having bent down, for some purpose, just as a machine-gun swath sickled down his two colleagues. Collins also reported that the next station down the line was likely lost as well. Collins was bereft. "The Krauts got all my buddies! Oh, this rotten war!"[27]

Deadly evidence of increasing encirclement piled up. The overlapping streams of fire from machine guns above the road and on the spurs of Hill 198 sounded like the chirping of "a flock of canaries," according to one 77th Division grunt. Patrols left and right were running into Germans. A five-man scout sent 300 yards to the west before dawn was unaccounted for and probably by now the victim of an enemy ambush. The detachment sent east returned with the report of a half dozen Germans greeting them with grenades and machine-gun fire. Schenck's combat patrol had also encountered machine-gun nests about 600 yards out from the Pocket and was not close to putting the *Minenwerfer* out of action. Those spark-tailed shells continued to punish the perimeter, though, fortunately, a good percentage (as many as 85 percent during the entire siege) of the rounds were duds.

All this, combined with the racket of Wilhelm's platoon in obvious distress, convinced Whittlesey that the enemy was all around and was particularly clustered about his left flank. When the din encircling him diminished briefly, the major could discern the cacophony of combat far west in the Aisne Valley, indicating that the French Fourth Army was still fighting there. But those audible indicators were no closer to his position than they had been the day before, so hope for French succor went awry. Pressed hard from all directions, the commanders of the 1st and 2nd Battalions of the 308th agreed that they had to take action before their position became hopeless.

Most imperiled was the 308th's rear. The German machine guns on Hill 198 had the Pocket zeroed in. They had to be silenced. Just as important, the severed lines of communication to regiment and brigade had to be patched back together.

Whittlesey summoned Captain Holderman and his XO, Lt. Pool, to his CP and gave Company K of the 307th the job of retracing the steps of its odyssey of the night before, to eliminate the Boche Maxims on 198, restore the relay posts, and reopen the route of supplies so that rations and ammunition could reach the Pocket.

This was asking a lot of a weary band of men, only ninety-eight in number, but the hard-charging Holderman was typically enthusiastic, though many of Holderman's men were less gung-ho. Lt. Pool, himself, was pessimistic. "We haven't men enough for such an operation." But Whittlesey was firm. "You have your orders. Proceed."[28]

Within minutes K company had gathered its gear and was recrossing the brook and heading into the trees cloaking the slope of Hill 198. Heading upslope for 200 yards, Holderman's men got snagged on two new weaves of barbed wire strung by the Germans during the night. The irrepressible captain shrugged off the escalating machine-gun fire from the terraces of 198, and scooted up to the snaring strands with his wire cutters to snip a tunnel through the steel thorns. His men wiggled through to take out two of the Hun guns with catapulting grenades. But as soon as the machine guns in front were knocked out, others on the flanks opened up and snipers slithered behind the company to turn every compass point into deadly angles of fire.

Pool, dragging a wounded sergeant to cover, registered the imminent danger confronting the company, and even Holderman had to admit that the mission had gotten too messy. Detailing thirty men to serve as a rear guard, he ordered the rest of his men to pull back to the brook. Most of them made it, but Private Arthur Fein was riddled with three bullets. His first sergeant, Jim Carroll (who not too many months before had been selling drapes in New York) bobbed and weaved his way through intense fire to pull his trooper to safety, while encouraging the hemorrhaging Fein with, "You gotta keep going. You can't let go!"[29]

By 1330, Company K had crossed Charlevaux Brook for the third time in seven hours, slightly reduced in numbers and severely reduced in confidence. While medics tried to rejuvenate the wounded, the rest of the men shambled back to their funk holes on the perimeter's eastern arm.

Schenck's platoon had also staggered back to the perimeter by noon, minus a couple of men lost to machine-gun fire. Downcast, the lieutenant reported his failure. Whittlesey commiserated. "I know you did [your best], lieutenant. Don't worry. We're not licked yet."[30]

Whittlesey now called a council of war to decide what to do next. It was alarmingly clear by now that the Germans had his unit encircled. A further advance seemed out of the question and, for many reasons, a retreat was an unlikely option. Whittlesey's inclination, governed by his superiors' orders and his own natural instinct, was to hang tough and cling to his position until reinforced or relieved. After all, his little force and the small lodgment they had effected in the German lines was the only success the 77th Division had to show for their October 2 offensive, and it should not be given up without a fight.

A withdrawal, even a partial withdrawal to reestablish communication with division, would be a near-run thing at best. An all-out effort by the whole command against the enemy on Hill 198 might succeed, where Holderman's understrength company had not. But there were practical problems that would render such an effort tactically difficult or unwise. Every soldier in the Pocket was hungry and exhausted, and many of them were wounded. Evacuating the wounded would consume much of their remaining physical strength and combat strength. Holderman still maintained that the rest of his 307th might very well push its way through, like his company had, to reinforce the 308th on its right. The redlegs presumably had the coordinates of their position now and might soon wrap the 308th in a comforting cocoon of defensive artillery fires. The French might even conquer La Palette and roll up the Germans on the left! And most pertinent to Whittlesey in his disinclination to take one step rearward was that, to his eye, the place his men now occupied was more defensible than any he had seen in yesterday's sweep to Charlevaux Brook.

There were also powerful psychological motives for hanging tough in place. The Allies had taken the offensive bit between their teeth since mid–July. The direction all along the front had been forward and any retreat, even on the small scale of this mired battalion, had to be, in the firm opinions of the command leadership, avoided at all costs. Progress had been too long delayed to allow a setback to sour the victory-in-sight mood of the Allied soldiers.

Whittlesey was fully aware of the morale-plummeting effects of the withdrawals under fire by the 35th and 79th Divisions in the offensive's first phase. He felt a moral obligation to avoid damaging the morale of his own men, as well as that of the whole division and of all the soldiers serving in the democratic armies. After their retreat, the 35th and 79th had been removed from the front line, their reputations clouded by failure and their honor stained by shame. Whittlesey's background and character made him an unlikely catalyst for any similar fall from grace for his 77th Division.

Quite beside his own strength of purpose and gritty determination, Whittlesey was further held true to his course by the clear and uncomplicated orders from above. He had been instructed to advance to his objective without regard to his flanks and he had done so. It was now incumbent upon those on up the chain of command—Stacey, Johnson, Alexander—to secure and enlarge upon his success. Things looked threatening now, but things could change. Were Whittlesey to step back from success now, the whole operation might become unharnessed and the hard-earned credit the battalion had compiled could be wasted and reversed.

To Whittlesey's mind and ear the orders were explicit. Alexander had issued a general order to all officers, captain and above: "Ground once captured must under no circumstances be given up in absence of direct, positive, and formal orders to do so emanating from these HQs. Troops occupying ground must be supported against counterattack, and all gains held."[31] The order went on to warn against the common ruse of the enemy to sow confusion by calling out "Retire" or "Fall back!" Alexander fumed that anyone giving orders to fall back was committing treason and should be shot on the spot. (This from a man who had earned the sobriquet of "the Private's General," because of his expressed concern while the commander of a depot at Saint-Aignan that every man headed for the front carry a mess tin full of ham sandwiches and a canteen brimming with hot coffee.) "We are not going Back, but Forward!" he proclaimed.[32]

Not all 77th Division officers took such draconian orders totally to heart. Major Blagden and Captain Rainsford of the 307th, for example, had retreated on October 2 (and thus, in part, setting up the circumstances for the isolation of the 308th). But Whittlesey had accepted the literalness of the orders and, combined with specific attack directives that emphasized holding their ground and preparing for a further advance, he could discern, with his New England moral code, no wiggle room for an alternative interpretation. At Charlevaux Mill, he may have been far from Alexander and 77th Division HQ, but the fierceness and implacability of the order's wording seemed to leave no gray area open to revision or individual initiative.

Likewise, the officers under Whittlesey's command were no more ready to challenge higher authority than the major was. McMurtry may have been a rugged individualist, but he was no military maverick. Asked fifteen years later why the battalion stayed put on October 3 right in the path of a speeding express train painted field gray, McMurtry responded to what was to him a ridiculous question, "Why, what else was there to do? Those were our orders."[33]

The other officers in the Pocket either felt similarly bound by orders or were too new to the battalion, too inexperienced, or too timid to raise objections. The rambunctious Holderman, of course, felt blessed to be in this perilous position; Cullen assumed his leaders could do no wrong; Wilhelm, who might have had the pluck to protest, was, at that moment, trying to find his way back to American lines. There was, in short, no one to suggest that it might be time to call it a day.

And so, the consultation with the battalion officers was really only a confirmation of Whittlesey's determination to hold fast. Addressing his second-in-command, the major directed McMurtry to take over if he should fall and to never give up the position. McMurtry agreed and managed to find a silver lining. "Maybe the Krauts have us in a bind—but we're pinning them down too. The longer we stick, the easier it becomes for the rest of our guys. They'll get us out of here if we just hang on."[34]

Making it official, Whittlesey scrawled out the order of the day to his officers on a field message pad and had the runners distribute it. It read: "Our mission is to hold at all costs. No falling back. Have this understood by every man in your command."[35] Then he joined McMurtry in a tour of the perimeter to more directly and personally inform the enlisted ranks of his decision.

While Whittlesey was deciding the fate—or at least the location of the fate—of his men, the commanders on the opposing sides were drafting plans to shape that fortune. Thus, while the German leaders were trying to fashion a fate of destruction for Whittlesey's force, the American generals worked to devise a rescue scenario for the men trapped in the Pocket.

Both General Johnson of the 154th Brigade and 77th Division commander General Alexander were fairly confident that the relief mission could be accomplished before dusk. The French cuirassiers were still stuck around La Palette, 1,500 yards to the left rear of the Pocket, and the 306th Regiment had taken so many casualties from the belching belts of German machine guns on the right during the past day and night that it had to be withdrawn briefly from the line. But Alexander intended to renew the push on both wings. The main effort would be mounted on the right, where the 153rd Brigade's 305th Regiment would strike at dawn. Alexander calculated that the enemy line there on the right would have been weakened as the Germans pulled troops away to sandbag the break in their dyke at Charlevaux Mill. At the same time, the 77th Division CO ordered renewed efforts by rear elements of the 308th on the left flank. The attack battalions were to "go all out" to break the isolation of the 1st and 2nd Battalions of the 308th at Charlevaux Brook.

Operations Officer von Sybel, of the 76th Reserve Division, planned for quite a different outcome to the confrontation along the creek. The *Amerikanernest* north of Charlevaux Brook could not be allowed to fester and further erupt. The picture seemed fairly clear to von Sybel by mid-morning of October 3. He knew that approximately two U.S. battalions—which he estimated totaled about 1,500 troops, almost triple their actual strength—had breached the Haupt-Widerstands-Linie on the afternoon of October 2, and had dug in on the reverse slope beyond the Charlevaux Brook, not far from the mill. He understood that the U.S. force constituted a bubble floating free from the American wave that had generally receded. Von Sybel determined to exploit the Americans' open flanks and their severed communication to the rear, and "gobble up the morsel the Americans had bitten off" from the Haupt-Widerstands-Linie.[36]

The 76th had eliminated breaches west of La Palette on October 2 and around Autry on October 1. This time the breach seemed more serious, but von Sybel was convinced he could marshal the resources to contain it and then eliminate it. Major Hünicken had reported that his 254th Regiment had relinked with the 122nd Landwehr Regiment from von Kleist's group, and that the length and layout of the *Amerikanernest* had been gauged by the 254th on the left and the pioneer troops on the right. Hauptmann von Sybel understood that his forces had to prevent the Americans from either breaking out from their perimeter or being relieved by their main body. He was also aware that an American company had already tried this morning to reestablish contact with their rear lines, but a German patrol had spotted the Yanks and had successfully ambushed them in the shadow of La Palette.

The operations chief ordered his pioneers to string extra wire. He also had more machine-gun sections detached to the crisis sector of the Haupt-Widerstands-Linie, so that every ten meters of front featured a machine gun facing alternately north and south against both the Americans in the Pocket and those to the south who might attempt to relieve them. The artillery on La Palette, still unable to pound directly the *Amerikanernest* because of the U.S. reverse slope position, was to maintain its containment fire along the brook to keep the Americans pinned to the perimeter.

Once Major Hünicken had secured the old line on Hill 198, his 254th Regiment was to pump up the pressure on the Americans—*verpflaster* them, in German argot—with intensified sniper and machine-gun fire, as well as increased *Minenwerfer* rounds. The soldiers of the 254th were to employ the usual Argonne tactics that had been refined and revised in these woods over the last three years—constant probes, constant activity (real and simulated), constant fire. Ideally, the doughboys would imagine, because of all this ruse and stratagem, that there were far more German soldiers surrounding them than a single understrength regiment. In such a state of alarm, they might waste their strength on forlorn-hope assaults against the besiegers, or, better yet, wave the white flag.

From all reports that morning, von Sybel's strategy seemed to be working. The machine-gun phalanx around the *Minenwerfer* had broken up a platoon-size American effort (that led by Lt. Schenck) to end the mortar's rain of fire. The *Minenwerfer* was still verpflastering the Pocket. The German line across Hill 198 was reestablished and secure, and a rather bumbling blow by the Americans from the south against La Palette had been repulsed. The U.S. thrust at around 1100 from the Pocket back through the Haupt-Widerstands-Linie toward Hill 198 to reopen communication with their brigade and division HQs had been stopped in the wire, savaged by snipers on the flanks, and forced back across the creek by noontime.

Still, time was not an ally of the Germans. With all the fire and noise and effort, the Yanks were hardly acting as if they were getting ready to throw in the towel. The Americans may have been deceived into thinking the woods were crawling with Huns, but if they were doomed, they were obviously determined to take as many Germans down with them as they could. Every probe, every maneuver was met with spirited volleys of American rifle and auto-rifle fire. Casualties for the 254th were accumulating, and the understrength German regiment had little manpower to spare. The longer the *Amerikanernest* held out, the more likely the American battalions to the south and the French regiments to the west would burst through to relieve it. Every hour the Pocket remained intact further endangered the sanctity of the Giselher Stellung line and the entirety of the German position in the north Argonne woods. Von Sybel deduced that nothing short of a full-scale assault by the 254th—which he planned for the afternoon—would suffice to decide the issue.

While the Germans were closing the ring and hatching their plans for a major effort against the Pocket, Alexander's plans and hopes for a mid-morning relief of Whittlesey's warriors fizzled out. Lt. Paul Knight and the 100 men in Companies D and F of the 308th tried their best to reach Whittlesey's left, but quickly got snagged in the new wire laid down by Boche pioneers during the night and got shot up by interlocking strobes of machine-gun fire from Hill 198 and La Palette. Knight's valiant attempt went for naught and cost the two companies heavily. Everybody else either made only half-hearted efforts or no effort at all.

The 3/308th (Detroit Blue), in brigade reserve along the Binarville road, stood pat and spent the morning only digging deeper holes, while the Germans completed their closing of the door into their line that Whittlesey had opened the day before. The 307th, on the right, put out a few probing patrols, but failed to mount a significant attack.

General Alexander did not accept these limp-wristed slaps at the enemy in good grace. An aide recalled his tantrum: "I never saw the Old Man get so mad before. He cursed, hollered, shook his fists, kicked up a storm. Then he got on the phone and chewed out those brigade commanders something fierce."[37]

At mid-afternoon, the volatile Celt boarded his staff car for the jarring ten-mile ride over the cratered road to Hunter Liggett's I Corps HQ for a conference of divisional commanders. Alexander had earlier assumed that he would be able to paint a picture of progress to his corps CO, but he could now offer only a rough sketch of escalating crisis, if not impending disaster.

While Alexander's motor vehicle was bouncing down the rutted road to share more sad tidings with Hunter Liggett, Major Hünicken was preparing to launch his first large-scale assault on the Pocket. The men there had enjoyed a few hours of relative calm before the inevitable next storm. The tempests and tensions of the morning had receded to a deceptive lull. As the day warmed, the racket waned. The *Minenwerfer* ceased its harsh hacking, the stuttering of the Maxims abated. The almost ceaseless sounds of combat had dwindled to the remote mumbling of distant artillery and the low moans of the wounded. The respite allowed a ration of relaxation, as men nibbled on crackers and sucked at the butts of their last cigarettes. The welcome break in the action even allowed Whittlesey time to detail an unlucky few to widen and deepen the latrine trenches.

These peaceful pursuits were instantly ended at around 1500, when a drumroll of grenade blasts announced the curtain rise of the 254th's attack. The ringing detonation of the potato mashers was followed by the renewed coughing of the *Minenwerfer* and the jackhammering rumble of machine-gun fire all along the perimeter. The first nexus of the assault came on the right, where Holderman's Company K held the line. The German assault troops were hidden in a stratum of brush and trees beneath a twenty-foot high limestone cliff projecting from the hillside. Holderman's men opened up on the bluff with their Springfields, Brownings and Chauchats, but the enemy was well concealed and took few casualties.

German return volleys hit not only Company K on the right, but B and C in the middle and Lt. "Red" Cullen's Company H on the left as well. When their guns briefly quieted, a Hun officer took the opportunity to sound roll call of his unit. A Company H sergeant later recalled, "It sure was spooky hearing them out there as though on parade. The roll call took a long time. Maybe Fritzie was trying to outfox us by having the same guy answer two or three times so we'd think they had lots of men. If that was their game, we didn't bite. Pretty soon our guys were yelling 'Yo!' or 'Absent!' after each name. Some of the boys added nasty cracks as well." Following the roll call, a Boche officer shouted, "Jetzt, alle zusammen (Now, all together!)"[38]

McMurtry and Cullen on the left readied their men for the infantry attack they knew nearly always followed a German grenade barrage. They reassured their troops that the enemy confidence in their grenading tactics was unjustified in these woods, where tree trunks and undergrowth would deflect many of the mashers—which had relatively low explosive charges, anyway. A second, then a third round of arcing grenades and pummeling machine gun-fire hit the American line, the German grenadiers raising up in an erect position to catapult their stick grenades from maximum distance in a full-body motion—unlike the Americans who often more effectively flicked their grenades from short range with a snap of the wrist from a prone position. After each volley, the assault troops maneuvered through the brush closer to the American line. Their fire began to tell on the American defenders. Captain Leo Stromee of Company C had his shoulder ripped open by *Minenwerfer* fragments. Lt. Maurice Griffin, who the night before had sat with Whittlesey fondly reminiscing about his wife, grimaced in pain but maintained his composure, as he staggered to the aid station with a bullet in his shoulder.

As a fourth volley tore into the U.S. line, the men of Companies C and H could make out the gray forms, fixed bayonets and distinctive helmets of the attacking enemy soldiers. Doughboys opened a heavy fire all along the loop of the perimeter as the Germans erupted out of the screening trees. Whipping grenades and triggering their small arms, the American infantrymen sent many of the attackers tumbling to the ground with abbreviated shrieks. The 254th's "knock-out" blow failed abysmally, and the survivors backtracked into the bushes.

As the light faded on October 3, Major Hünicken lamented his losses and his failure to extinguish the *Amerikanernest*, but he did not dwell long on those lamentations. Having gained little with grenades and bayonets, he tried firepower in place of infantry assault as evening approached. The *Minenwerfer* cranked into full gear; a 77 mm artillery battery pumped in "Whizz-Bang" high explosive shells. Every machine gun framing the American position opened up in a simultaneous scream. Snipers plinked Mauser rounds into the Pocket with every flicker of movement by the bedeviled doughboys.

The khakied recipients of this trial by fire clung to their slopeside sanctuaries and waited for death to pass on by. The machine-gun soldiers on the west flank of the American redoubt took the brunt of the barrage. A *Minenwerfer* round barreled into a Browning position, destroying the gun and slaying Sgt. Robert Graham and the other two members of the machine-gun crew. Lt. Marshall Peabody, a platoon commander in the 306th Machine-Gun Battalion and in charge here, took a machine-gun burst that ripped open his leg from knee to ankle. Lt. Maurice Revnes took charge of the platoon while a tourniquet was applied to Peabody's wound, and the lieutenant immediately sent a runner over the heaving ground to beg Whittlesey for reinforcements. The major scraped together a handful of soldiers from Companies H and A, but half of them were hit or pinned down trying to reach the embattled flank. Even before this meager help could arrive, Lt. Revnes was knocked out of action by a bullet striking his ankle and he had to pass command on down to a junior NCO.

The attack by fire, direct and indirect, persisted for an hour, then the full-blast volume faded to static. Whittlesey took advantage of the lull to fly off another pigeon through the diminishing hail of metal fragments, carrying this message to Delaware One (General Johnson):

> Germans on cliff north of us in small numbers and have tried to envelop both flanks. Situation on left flank very serious.
> Broke through two of our runner-posts today.... We have not been able to reestablish posts today. Need 8,000 rounds rifle ammo, 7,500 Chauchat, 25 boxes MG, 250 grenades.
> Casualties yesterday in companies here (A,B,C,E,G,H), 8 killed, 80 wounded.
> In same companies today, 1 killed, 60 wounded.
> Present effective strength of companies here, 245.
> Situation serious.[39]

The pigeon had hardly lifted off when another ratcheting of small arms fire announced that the lull in the action was not a cessation. Then came the doleful report up the line that Pvt. Roland Judd had been fatally struck by that fire, while attempting to fill canteens for the many wounded from the sluggish stream at the foot of the slope.

The water-gathering details were the top targets for the Boche snipers, who popped off rounds at any movement by the Yanks in the Pocket. The brook was directly exposed to their fire from most directions, unlike many of the funk holes on the hillside, but the murky liquid there, now thickened with American blood, was the only source of water. Volunteering for the dangerous mission—that had already taken the lives of two soldiers—was an Italian-American private from New York City named Philip "Zip" Cepeglia. Wiry and athletic, "he could move like a shadow, silently and swiftly."[40] Carrying up to a dozen canteens tied together, Zip hardly seemed to notice the bullets splattering around him as he wiggled streamwards.

Never one to slight the valor of his men, Major Whittlesey told his staff that should they ever make it out of the Pocket, he was "going to make certain that boy gets a medal."[41] Whittlesey made good on his word. Cepeglia would be awarded a DSC for his water-fetching feats.

After the second assault of the day was checked, snipers continued to pick out their targets of opportunity as the darkness deepened, but the machine-gun and mortar harassment trailed off. Artillery fire lessened but did not entirely cease, with brief bouquets, of three shells each, falling ever so often. The bursting blooms would come with an initial starshell, followed by two HE rounds. The starshells illuminated burial parties of 308th infantrymen, hungry and droopy-eyed, further weakening themselves as they scraped at the dark ground to spade out shallow graves for their dead comrades (and for a few slain Germans at the edge of the American perimeter, as well).

The grave diggers attracted random sniper fire, but as one of them later observed, "We couldn't leave our buddies uncovered."[42]

The interred did not always remain buried, however. Occasionally, one of the artillery or trench mortar rounds would violently disinter the dead, hurling the broken bodies into the funk holes of their still living comrades.

Other men were put to work moving the wounded to better cover, either near the CP or in a small cave on the slope. The battalion's three medics were doing their best, but the supply of field dressings was exhausted by 1800, and now only the bandages in individual first aid packets remained. Wounded officers were trying to comfort their injured men and keep their moans to a minimum. The ruthless enemy seemed to hone in on each and every groan from the wounded Yanks. Lt. Peabody, the pain from his mangled leg preventing any sleep, tried to buck up the spirits of the wounded with jokes and assurances that this too shall pass. McMurtry, a knee wound limiting his mobility, gimped his way to the aid station by hooded flashlight to encourage the suffering soldiers into stoic silence.

"We don't want Fritzie wasting lead on us. It isn't good economics," he joked. A soldier with a hemorrhaging stomach wound did his duty to the last, gripping McMurtry's hand and promising, "It pains like hell, captain. But I'll keep as quiet as I can."[43] He kept the pain private for another half hour and then passed beyond all pain.

Whittlesey had set up sentry pickets for the night, and sent out recon patrols to see if the 307th had come any closer to relieving them during this long day. The rest of the men, cold and hungry, ground down further by at least fifty-six casualties twixt sunup and

The water hole in the Pocket. Williams College Archives and Special Collections.

sundown, tried to find what rest and comfort they could, with rations all but gone, little ammunition remaining, and no blankets or coats to warm them on this second night on the hillside above Charlevaux Brook.

The trapped troops along the stream hoped and prayed for relief, but they could not have known that their planned rescue on October 4 was conceived as just one element in a grand overall resumption of the Meuse-Argonne Offensive by the U.S. First Army. General Alexander had motored to I Corps HQ that afternoon of October 3, deeply disgruntled by the reports of his brigadiers about the progress, or the lack thereof, of the units of his division. The right brigade—the 153rd—was stymied. Its 305th Regiment had sacrificed five officers and 200 enlisted men killed or wounded before the aprons of enemy wire and the crossbelts of German machine guns. The 306th Regiment was too shot up already to do anything but play a supporting role, and what they managed to support was only bloody stalemate.

Johnson's report for the 154th Brigade was particularly disturbing. Fully half of his brigade appeared lost in the woods, wandering about trying to locate either the enemy or their isolated comrades in the Pocket. The regimental commanders seemed to have lost control of their units. Colonel Stacey of the 308th was a leader with two citations for his leadership and valor, but was also a man whose nerves were shot and who seemed to be unable to prevent rampant straggling in his regiment. Colonel Houghton, of the 307th, a Minnesota lumberman in civilian life, was a top notch commander, one of the best officers in the division, and a veteran of seventeen Great War battles already, most of them while serving in Canadian units prior to the U.S. entry into the conflict. But his battalions were scattered and disorganized, and one of his company commanders was already under arrest for gross incompetence. The 154th Brigade as a whole had suffered 1,600 casualties in the first two days of the renewed push in the Argonne, October 2–3.

Alexander's mood was not improved when Hunter Liggett informed his division commanders at the I Corps conference that the Allied high command was pointing fingers at Pershing for the lackluster performance of his army, and Pershing was wagging his own imprecating digit at I Corps for its failure to expand on Whittlesey's breakthrough or at least to relieve him. Liggett then announced that the stalled-out offensive would resume all along the seventeen-mile front at 0530 the next morning. The 1st Division had moved into the line east of the Argonne to replace the kayoed 35th Division, and the 82nd Division had deployed to back up the beat-up 28th.

The main emphasis of the attack would fall on the right of the 77th, from the east edge of the Argonne to the Aire Valley. On the left of the 77th—where the French cuirassiers had been checked, October 1–3—a reinforcement push by the French Fourth Army was to flank La Palette and sweep beyond the west rim of the woods to link, beyond the Argonne, with the I Corps divisions sweeping up the Aire. This linkage would entrap the Germans facing the 77th in a double envelopment. Pershing had ordered his commanders to "Shoot the works!" in an all-out effort to show Foch, Haig, Clemenceau and all the other critics and doubters that his Yankees could pull their weight and pull down the Germans.

Wounded by Pershing's and Liggett's criticisms of his division, but wound up by the opportunity the renewed push offered the 77th to reburnish its reputation, Alexander motored back to his headquarters with all his fires restoked. He resolved to commit every ounce of the 77th's lethal force into the Argonne. Rear area elements would be rounded up and transformed into front-line fighters. Division artillery would belch out enough shells to "shake the teeth out of the Boche."[44]

Alexander gave Johnson's 154th Brigade the primary task of relieving Whittlesey. Employing both brigade and division reserves, Johnson was to use the 3/308th, the 3/307th, headquarters and logistic elements, all of the 306th Machine-Gun Battalion not already pinned down in the Pocket, and the bulk of the 77th's big guns to reach and rescue Whittlesey by way of the same Argonne avenue that the 1/308th had humped on October 2. To the 153rd Brigade—the 305th and 306th Regiments—Alexander assigned the duty of holding the Germans on the right of the Pocket in position and incapable of reinforcing those enemy units between Whittlesey and his rescuers.

Johnson brandished the same cudgel of fire-and-brimstone resolution over the heads of his subordinates. "We're hitting the Boches and won't stop until he's smashed. Whittlesey will be rescued or, by God, I'll make heads roll.[45]

The new day—October 4—had a difficult time awakening, as pewter skies pregnant with rain discouraged the sun. The darkness was still dueling with the daylight, when the encircled men in the American perimeter received a sudden injection of hope into their sodden spirits. At 0530, discharging artillery echoed from east, west and south in a growing barrage of such intensity that no soldier, no matter how new to the regiment and to the war, could miss the message. Help was on the way!

There had already gleamed a glimmer of light for Whittlesey and his men even before dawn had struggled for dominance. A detachment sent rearward across the stream and up Hill 198 to try to reestablish communication with the regiment had run into a German patrol and could not get through. However, two patrols sent out from the east side of the perimeter, where Holderman's men held the line, reported back that the German ring around the Pocket was missing a link—no enemy soldiers occupied a narrow gulch there, by which the men along Charlevaux Brook might possibly be able to regain contact with the 307th on the right.

Here was an option for men who, for more than a day, seemed to lack any viable alternative to standing in place until they were either destroyed or rescued from destruction. Whittlesey conferred with McMurtry, but only to confirm what they both understood was their duty. Their orders had not changed. They were to: "Organize along this line, establish liaison to left and right and wait for orders for a further advance."[46]

If the rest of the division had not fulfilled those original orders for October 2, and had left Whittlesey and McMurtry and their battalions exposed and isolated out front with no possibility of liaison left or right—or now, even to the rear—it was not their prerogative to withdraw back to the division, but the duty of the rest of the division to close up on them. Even if orders could be put aside or superseded by the press of events—and they could not be in the world and mindset of Major Whittlesey—the wounded would have to be abandoned if they chose to retreat from this position. There were too many of them and the terrain was too unforgiving to carry out an evacuation. Leaving behind the wounded was even less of a possibility for Whittlesey than ignoring orders.

And so they would stay, even though morale was starting to diminish as fast as the ammunition and food, even though the trench mortar kept pounding away and they could not stop it, even though the Germans were tightening the cordon and seemed intent on eliminating this lodgment in their lines. McMurtry and Whittlesey were aware of the grumbling among the ranks, increasing with their hunger pains and the ever more desperate–

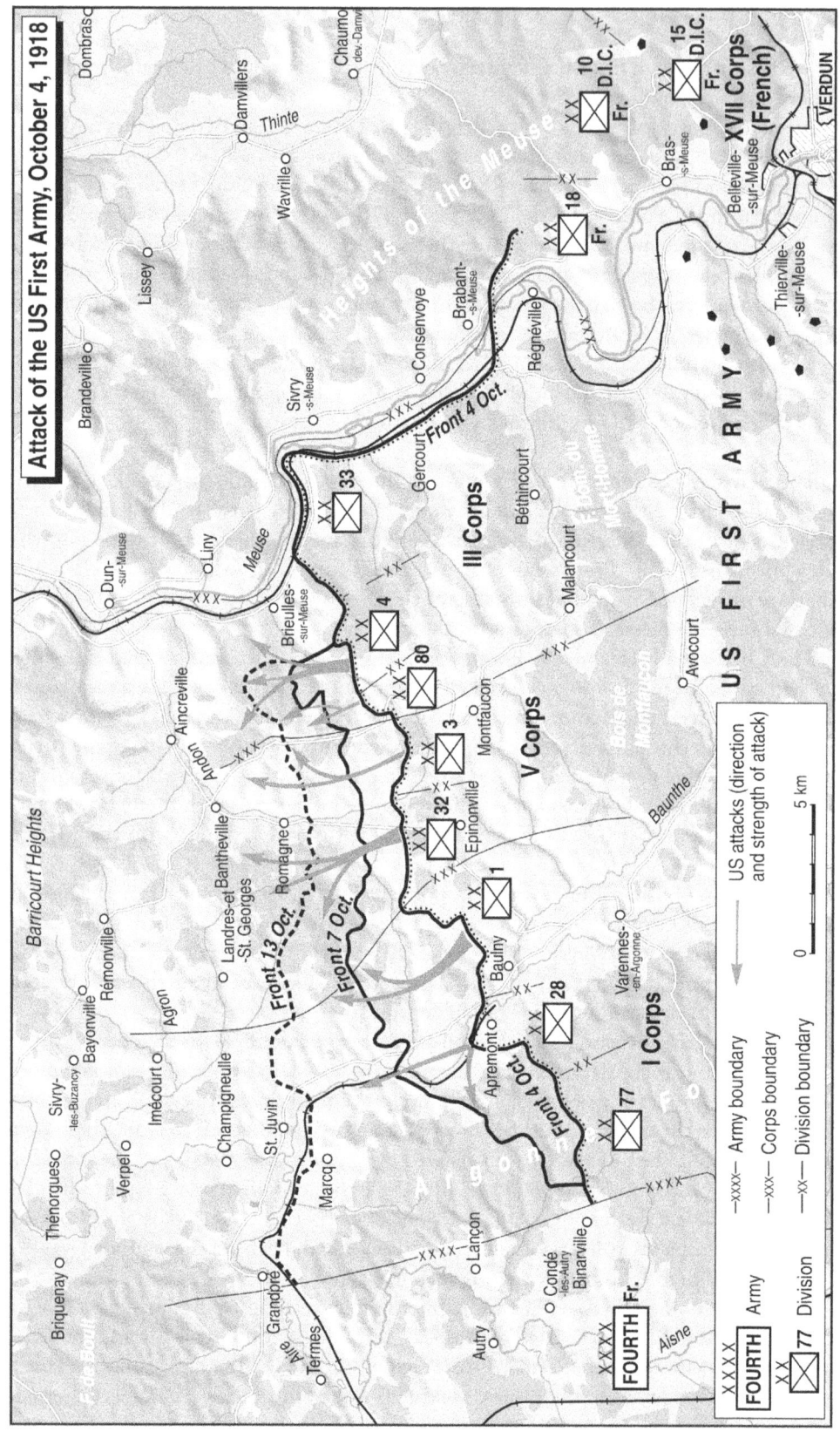

sounding moans of the wounded, for whom there was no surcease in their suffering. The junior officer ranks in the 1st and 2nd Battalions of the 308th were thinning. Wilhelm was gone; Buhler, Peabody, Griffin, Stromee and Revnes were down with serious wounds, and Leak and Harrington nursed minor wounds. Holderman, Cullen and Schenck were all still up and running, both in body and spirit. But Whittlesey could not quiet a qualm or two about his men's steadiness should he or McMurtry go down.

To compound his worries about his men's sinking spirits, Whittlesey strongly suspected that neither regiment nor brigade headquarters fully appreciated the danger that was closing in on the Pocket position. He had received no reply to any of the numerous messages he had sent by runner and had to assume that none had gotten through. The pigeons may have reached their coops in the rear, but the information conveyed in their tiny capsules could hardly compare in volume and in value to the details of desperation that a runner's report could communicate.

Whittlesey had already sent three messages via birdwing, but at 0725 he employed one of Private Richards' last four pigeons to flap an appeal to Delaware One for rations and for help. He complained about the condition of the wounded, the lack of any word from Companies D and F, and about an early morning shower of six friendly-fire shells that had impacted within the Pocket. Whittlesey probably assumed that these errant rounds were just shells falling short, and did not suspect that because of wrong coordinates his men were zeroed in under the guns of their own army. That assumption would soon be shattered.

There were doubts and worries too, as day dawned, on the other side, up and down the chain of command. At I Reserve Korps HQ at Briquenay, General Wellmann set at breakfast satisfied that the Yankee breakthrough seemed contained. Given the fact that the German units engaged were probably still weaker in numbers than the two U.S. battalions at Charlevaux, he was not overly disturbed that the tiny American salient had not yet been erased.

The distant thunder of artillery and the jangle of phones at around 0530 alerted corps HQ that preparatory fires were pounding across the whole front. Within minutes, von Kleist called to report that his Group Argonnen was under heavy attack in the Aire Valley. Wellmann soon deduced that his corps was the object of a double-envelopment assault from the wings, and correctly assumed that the 77th in the center would be moving forward to pin the Germans there in the forest and fight its way through to the units in the Pocket.

The corps commander knew it was imperative to hold up the French on his right and the Americans on the opposite horn of the envelopment, and hold firm against the 77th coming up the middle. To stand tight against the French, Wellmann marshaled his remaining reserves to secure La Palette and the ground from there to Autry. Turning to army group command for further aid, he was promised an infantry regiment and two artillery batteries from the 45th Reserve Division as reinforcements. These expedients worked on the west wing. By 0800, the French advance once again ground to a halt, and their further efforts during the day were relegated to harassing artillery fire.

Because of the Franco-American attack, no more men could be spared to deter and destroy the two U.S. battalions along the creek. Division commander General Quadt-Wyckradt-Hüchenbruck had ordered the extermination of the *Amerikanernest* by day's end, but that mission had to be accomplished with the troops already at hand. To Major Hünicken's requests for reinforcements, particularly *Stosstruppen* (shock troops), to replace the pioneer soldiers that made up a large part of his manpower, Quadt-Wyckradt-Hüchenbruck could only provide cheerleading. He pointed out that the Yankees must be short of everything and demanded that Hünicken "Snuff them out!"[47]

Quadt-Wyckradt-Hüchtenbruck's staff suggested the tactics of attrition by fire, employing machine guns, mortars and snipers to diminish American numbers and U.S. morale until they either surrendered or were swamped in a later all-out attack. Hünicken took his CO's orders and advise with the phlegmatic and unblinking acceptance of the traditional Prussian officer, of which he seemed a paragon. With his stocky frame outfitted in a starch-stiff uniform and high-gloss boots, his shaven head tattooed with dueling scars, and his severe gaze given a Junker emphasis with a monocle, Hünicken seemed to fit the prototypical picture of Wilhelmian arrogance.

But behind the imperious veneer, he was riven with doubts that day of October 4. He had assumed that the Yankee hordes would be nothing better than armed mobs, and that even the second-rate German troops he now commanded would handle them as easily as if they were the Hottentot or Bushmen insurgents in Southwest Africa he had fought a decade ago. That contempt had been modified by the events of the past few days into a grudging respect. Now Hünicken feared that the two American battalions he faced in the Pocket might number as many as 1,500, while his bedraggled regiment was down to 400 effectives. His 254th Regiment had once been manned by the storm troopers of the *Stosstruppen*, but that was before the Marne and the Aisne and the Vesle. He had his orders, however, and to the largely middle-aged and minimally trained men who had refilled the ranks of those dynamic and disciplined young men wiped out on the banks of those French rivers, he admonished, "The attack will be pressed. The enemy must be eliminated."[48]

On the American side of the battlefield equation, Liggett, Alexander and Stacey were just as desperate to relieve Whittlesey's force as Wellmann, Quadt-Wyckradt-Hüchtenbruck and Hünicken were to destroy it. The artillery barrage at 0530 that signaled the resumption of the offensive and temporarily boosted the sagging spirits of the trapped troopers of the 308th ultimately, however, presaged just further failure. The French effort to the west of the Argonne and against La Palette was futile, and the machine-gun emplacements on the hill remained to tear into the flank of General Johnson's push toward Charlevaux Valley.

At the spearhead of the 154th's attack, were Lt. Knight's two companies—D and F of the 308th—reduced to just fifty-four unwounded men from the 100 effectives that had tried without success to punch through to the Pocket the day before. Knight was supported by the brigade reserve, the 3/308th (Detroit Blue), under Colonel Stacey's personal command, and by the battalion of the 307th which had constituted the division reserve. The remainder of the 307th, along with the 305th and 306th Regiments of the 153rd Brigade, were to strike the enemy on the east side of Charlevaux Valley.

Alexander visualized a massive artillery bombardment and a full-bore French effort paving the way for his assault units. He anticipated his troops surging through the soft tissue of the overextended German lines and reaching Whittlesey by noon. The men actually leading the relief effort carried no such optimism along with their maps and compasses. Receiving his orders from Stacey, Lt. Knight fatalistically intoned, "We'll do the best we can."[49]

Colonel Houghton, commander of the 307th, phoned Alexander, after he had consulted with his junior officers and made a personal recon of the terrain to be tackled. He objected to the inevitable waste of his men along an assault route where the enemy would most obviously expect a relief effort. Alexander was in no debatable mood and refused to brook any consideration of changes in the operational plan. Houghton could not directly disobey orders, but he could not bring himself to needlessly sacrifice his men either. Assembling his officers, Houghton declared the attack to be a forlorn hope and directed them—unless they found a gap in the enemy lines—to halt their advance as soon as they made contact with the enemy and report that they were held up by rifle and machine-gun fire. "I don't want any lives wasted in the German wire."[50]

Between reluctant leaders, tangled lines of communication and twisted chains of command, poor coordination, luke-warm support from the French, and insufficient and inaccurate artillery fire, the 77th Division attack seemed preordained to fail. The artillery spewed a lot of sound and fury that signified little. Few of the German machine-gun nests were knocked out and little of the enemy wire was cut. La Palette held out as it had all week, whether the attacker was French or American. Hill 198 was unsuccessfully assaulted three times. Stacey personally led one attack, but his charge was snagged on the wire just like the others. The colonel was lucky, unlike many of his 250 men, in that only his greatcoat was ripped to shreds by machine-gun bullets.

Companies D and F, only remnants to start with, were nearly wiped out in their vanguard position in the assault. Knight, bleeding from two wounds and numerous barbed-wire gashes, returned with the survivors to be informed that Alexander had messaged that only by successfully penetrating the wire could they escape court-martial. Knight would later be awarded a DSC for his actions in the Argonne, but now, as he limped to the aid station, his words were nearly mutinous. "Tell the Old Man to do it himself!"[51]

The "Old Man's" roller-coaster temperament, chugging toward a peak early in the morning, was descending into a precipitous plunge by noon. The 77th's onslaught was grinding to a halt all along the line. Progress on the right was as pitiful as that on the left, with the 305th stuck where it had started and the 306th winning a few yards at disproportionate cost. Alexander knew that Liggett, his corps commander, would not be happy at the 77th's failure. But Liggett possessed a stoic steadiness that would prevent him from thrashing out blindly against his subordinates before all the facts were in. It was the man at the top, the general at AEF headquarters at Chaumont, that Alexander feared. Pershing might very well take away from him both his division and one of his lapel stars for this latest setback.

Alexander's fate was inextricably tied to that of the 308th. The morale of the 77th Division, and quite possibly that of the entire First Army as well, might plummet should Whittlesey's command go under. Resentment was building against Alexander's leadership and his failure to rescue Whittlesey, both within the ranks of the division and among the generals at higher headquarters. With the infantry relief effort checked, Alexander looked for alternatives toward at least saving Whittlesey's force for one more day. Though aerial supply was still in its infancy in 1918, he ordered the 50th Aero Squadron to use the first opportunity the weather presented to drop ammunition, rations and other supplies into Whittlesey's perimeter. He also directed "divarty" (division artillery) to intensify concentrations on La Palette and around the Pocket to forestall more German assaults on the 308th's position.

Neither air nor artillery, however, would provide much aid and comfort for the men strung out on the slope above Charlevaux Creek. The U.S. artillery, indeed, would prove a greater ally to the Germans that day than to the encircled Americans. A new FO, Lt. Putnam, had been sent by the 305th Field Artillery to establish an OP with Stacey's regiment and to ascertain the exact location of the trapped battalion. Reaching the forward HQ of the 308th near the Binarville Road, Putnam found a discouraged staff, shaking their heads at the failure of the morning relief attempts. A captain there pulled out a map and pointed to a spur of Hill 198 behind Charlevaux Mill as the site of Whittlesey's force. The FO made a tracing of the map on toilet paper, jotted down the coordinates, and summoned his runner to take back to the artillery his plotting of Whittlesey's position. But the coordinates were no more accurate than those delivered by homing pigeon the day before. The staff captain's estimate was off by a half a mile.

By now the plight of the composite force pinned below the Roman road in the Argonne Forest was stirring concern, speculation and admiration, not just within the 77th Division and the U.S. First Army, but among the home front populace as well. Rumors were rampant within the division. The khaki grapevine communicated stories of dunder-headed leaders blundering Whittlesey and his command into the jaws of disaster, of staff officers giving the wrong orders to the wrong units, of brainless brass orchestrating a doughboy version of the Charge of the Light Brigade.

Such soldiers' scuttlebutt was to be expected in every such situation, but by now the American public was getting the first news of the events along Charlevaux Brook in this Lorraine forest, and the news was both intriguing and worrisome. And it was in the conveying of that news that the term "Lost Battalion" was coined, inaccurately and inappropriately, but forever indelibly. The credit for the origin of that romantic characterization is uncertain. Some chroniclers point to Lt. Kidder Mead, I Corps press officer, who had reported pre-war for the *New York World*. Working at press headquarters at Bar-le-Duc, Mead fastened on the "human interest" of the story and supposedly came up with the moniker for the wire services feeding the news-hungry stateside public. Others lay the credit (or the blame) for the misnomer on the ink-stained fingertips of United Press correspondent Fred S. Ferguson, who reported the story on October 3 to his cable editor, Harold D. Jacobs, in New York City. Jacobs wired back, "Send more on Lost Battalion."[52] The title caught the public's fancy. Within a day, newspapers across the country were headlining with "Lost Battalion" stories that crowded all other current Great War events to sidebars.

The drama in the Argonne rapidly took front and center in the papers and among the public. One editor likened it to "Custer and the Sioux on the Little Bighorn"; another reporter dubbed it the "Alamo of the Argonne." It made little difference that Whittlesey's force was not lost. As one veteran of the siege observed, "We knew exactly where we were. So did the Germans."[53] The high command was also perfectly and painfully aware of where Whittlesey was (though not precisely so, as the Allied artillery would so tragically demonstrate on October 4). And it did not matter that the force in Charlevaux Valley was a mixed unit from three infantry and machine-gun battalions, not one. The popular press and the popular imagination made it "lost" and made it a single "battalion," and so it would be stamped in both myth and memory.

Jacobs himself, in later years, tried to clear away the fog that became a fact. He claimed he employed "lost" in the sense of "doomed," rather than in the sense of "disappeared," and names such as "Surrounded Battalion" or Beleaguered Battalion" simply did not play as well in print as "Lost Battalion." He defended his title by asserting that, "I think any other newspaperman would automatically have labeled Whittlesey's outfit as I did."[54]

The objects of all this concern, notoriety and—for the men trying to rescue them— sacrifice, were having a bad day on October 4 that progressively got worse. The gray dawn had given way to a full sun that chased the chill from the air, but also lit the targeted stage for the weapons of the enemy. The *Minenwerfer* had cranked into action, and it continued to cough out shells for an hour across the American oval. Two more mortars had been emplaced by the Germans that morning, one to the right front and one to the left, to add to the torment of the besieged. A burial party, scratching at the ground in a state of semi-consciousness from lack of food and rest, had to bend double, then lie flat, as they dug away at the earth a few inches at a time. The mortar rounds, mostly landing fifty yards away from the American funk holes at the foot of the slope, or in the churned-up stream, did little further damage to human bone and tissue, but did inflict more trauma to nerves already raw and ravaged.

The German machine guns chimed in to add their counterpoint to the mortars, stitching X-shaped patterns across the perimeter and scything tree bark and limestone splinters against the "tin derbies" of doughboys, lying prone with their faces buried in the dirt. The discordant three-part harmony of the enemy's firepower attack was completed when potato mashers came cartwheeling from the cliff abutting Holderman's holes. By 1000, the *Minenwerfer* had trailed off, but then came a cloudburst of grenades from the ridge frowning above the road. A California private named Arthur Shepard watched in horror as one of those grenades met Mother Earth, its fuse sputtering sparks just inches from his feet. His brain functioning faster than his panic button, Shepard bounded feet-first onto the grenade to sink it into the mud, where it fizzled away to an unexplosive finish.

Fearing that all the incoming was merely the curtain raiser for another full-dress assault, Whittlesey stepped over to C Company's holes and asked Lt. Schenck to gather volunteers to establish an OP beyond the perimeter, in order to break up any enemy infantry attack before it could hit the Pocket. Schenck, a mild-mannered man whose face was etched with the contours of stress, assembled ten men and a Chauchat, and weaved his way up higher ground to a good fire-support position. The next upsurge of enemy fire and ballista volleys of grenades was matched by a nova burst of Chauchat and Springfield fire from Schenck's outpost, which quickly deterred the German probe.

At 1035, Whittlesey conscripted one of the three remaining homing pigeons to send off another message to Delaware One. The situation seemed to be reaching a crisis spike, and the murmurings among his red-eyed men included disgruntled calls for wholesale flight. Whittlesey informed his CO that effective strength in the Pocket was down to about 235, including forty-five in K/307th and seventeen machine gunners. He ticked off the lengthening list of wounded officers, and pointed out that neither advance nor retreat was a practical option because of the burden of moving all the wounded.

He concluded with: "Situation is cutting into our strength rapidly. Men are suffering from hunger and exposure; the wounded are in very bad condition. Cannot support be sent at once?"[55]

A lull in the enemy cannonade allowed the men of the newly dubbed (although unknown to them) "Lost Battalion" the opportunity to raise, Lazarus-like, from their funk holes to momentarily savor the warming sun and search for crumbs to appease stomachs cramping with hunger. A medic, distraught at the sight of festering and gangrenous wounds, appealed to his CO, "Those boys need a doctor, sir." Whittlesey could only respond with, "We'll soon be relieved. Do all you can."[56] But by now all the medic could do, as he pointed out to Whittlesey, was pray for the wounded and watch them die.

Whittlesey still held out hope, however. He understood that his men's endurance was not infinite, but he remained at least outwardly confident that their ordeal would end before the day was done. He had sent two pleas for help aloft, and the first hint of that help seemed to arrive also from above, during the lull. General Alexander had directed the 50th Aero Squadron to scout for the exact location of Whittlesey's force and then, once ascertained, to drop rations, ammunition and medical supplies. Marked with a tricolor cockade, the first plane in that aerial-aid mission fluttered back and forth over the Pocket shortly after noon, firing a signal rocket and lifting the eyes and the spirits of the besieged men below.

Alexander also tried to buck up his New York boys with a message dropped by a later aircraft. It read: "Defend yourself in your present position. Help is coming to you."[57] But airborne precision was decades distant in 1918. The message was recovered, not by the Lost Battalion, but by a supply company, seven miles behind the lines, south even of the division HQ from which Alexander had composed the note.

The sight of that first aircraft had lifted the morale of the men cut off in the Pocket. But fortifying their determination to hold on and to hold out more than anything was the conduct and example of their leader. The largely lumpen-proletariat privates of the 308th were, by nature and by nurture, contemptuous of an officer corps drawn almost exclusively from a social and economic class far above their stations in life. Officers had to earn the respect of the 77th's enlisted men, and few ever made the grade. Captain McMurtry, with his egalitarian, good-old-boy manner, had won the privates over early on, back in training camp. Cullen commanded respect with his sheer physicality and red-haired pugnacity. Peabody was liked by many for his cheerful demeanor and compassionate nature. Schenck was given the thumbs up because of his quiet courage and his refusal to demand more of any man than he did of himself. Holderman had soldierly qualities in abundance, but his unflagging energy drew as many scoffing comments as it did admiring remarks. The rest of the officers of the 1st and 2nd Battalions of the 308th were, in general, simply tolerated, at best.

Whittlesey, of course, had started from way behind in the estimations of most of his men. He had looked and spoken and carried himself like the perfect image of the snooty, effete upper classes carried about in the consciousnesses of these working-stiff privates. But, steadily, since the Vesle, he had impressed these men, showing a dedication to duty that never—or rarely—got in the way of his concern for the well-being of his men. The rising tide of the enlisted ranks' admiration for "Galloping Charlie" probably reached its high water mark on October 3. On that day of near constant artillery, *Minenwerfer* and machine-gun volleys, while officers and men tried desperately to escape the descending death, Major Whittlesey had calmly stepped out on his stilt-like legs to move from hole to hole along the crescent of the perimeter, seemingly serene in the shrapneled storm, to reassure his men with, "Remember, there are two million Americans pushing up to relieve us."[58]

The admiration was mutual. Charles Whittlesey was a man who had rarely brushed shoulders with the laboring legions in his life. As a Williams College student, however, he had become attracted to the egalitarian principles of socialism, and he had retained a great deal of empathy for the lesser blessed. Empathy had elevated to esteem over the months since the Battle of the Vesle, as these simple men had displayed their defiant hearts. As the noontime recess in the deadly drumbeat of fire continued on October 4, Whittlesey sat on the edge of his funk hole and exclaimed to McMurtry, "George, no matter what comes to us in later years, you and I will never meet finer and truer men than these boys."[59]

McMurtry's response was drowned out by the detonation of a single shellburst, rapidly followed by the next five explosions of a battery volley, erecting transitory towers of brown water, ribbed with a framework of stumps and stones, along the south bank of Charlevaux Creek.

A soldier in the Pocket cheered, "It's ours! It's ours! Our artillery!"[60] He was right; the incoming was obviously arcing in from the southeast (and probably from the 75 mm guns of the 305th Field Artillery and the 155 mm howitzers of the 306th Field Artillery, as well as from French artillery—Holderman, in his monograph, would specifically blame the French). Momentarily, hope popped into place in almost every heart in the Pocket; even the wounded struggled to smile through their pain.

At least one veteran noncom refused, however, to join in the cheers croaking out from thirsty throats. He could read the cuneiform of the artillery arc and quickly perceived that the rounds were falling short. "That stuff will be landing on our heads in a minute!"[61]

The sergeant was also correct. Back at regimental headquarters they knew the shells were off target as well. The operations officer of the 308th, Captain Bradley Delehanty, a New York City architect in his previous life, was discussing Whittlesey's dilemma at about 1545 with Colonel Stacey, looking haggard in his field jacket ripped by wire and riddled by bullets from this morning's failed relief attempt. When Lt. Hattemer from division artillery joined the conclave to coordinate howitzer harassing fire with infantry movements for the afternoon, Delehanty inquired as to the intended line of fire. Hattemer traced his finger across the map where he assumed the German positions to be.

Delehanty and Stacey recoiled in alarm. Stacey, aghast, said, "Those are the coordinates of Whittlesey's position."

Hattemer, who would not survive the Battle of the Argonne, asked, "Are you sure?"

"So sure," responded Delehanty, "that I'm going to call brigade about it."[62]

But it was way too late. The shells had started slicing through the sky on their way to the Pocket about an hour before. Men, whose hearts had lifted toward the penthouse at the first detonations, felt their stomachs drop to the bottom floor, as the ranging volleys came in a cacophonous parade formation directly toward their positions. The barrage, like a rapidly moving thunderstorm, advanced up to the Pocket and then seemed to remain there for the long haul.

Two men were killed and another seriously wounded with the first salvo exploding in the center of the 308th perimeter. Trees came down under the lumberjack hack of 75 mm and 155 mm howitzer rounds. Whining shrapnel stripped leaves, sent tufts of turf flying, and blew the camouflaging brush from doughboy rifle pits. With their fields of fire and the concealment over the U.S. positions cleared by the Americans' own artillery, German machine gunners and snipers opened up with their Spandaus and Mausers on the exposed doughboys.

The Pocket descended from purgatory for the ensnared Americans to pure flaming hell. The men tried to burrow more deeply into the Argonne mud, screaming and cursing more at their own artillery than they ever had at the enemy. For the first time since the siege of the Pocket had begun, the men trapped there slipped toward the edge of panic. Two and three decades later, most of the survivors of the Lost Battalion would remember those minutes as the nadir of the ordeal.

The stalwart officers of the battalion tried to restore calm in the midst of the storm. "Red" Cullen arose from his hole to shout encouragement. "Hold tight boys! It'll soon be over!"[63] Holderman dashed from bush to bush to steady each of his posts on the right wing. Schenck scurried about his C Company area to tamp down his men's tremors.

But the two most inspiring men in this bull's eye on the banks of Charlevaux Creek were the two men commanding the 1st and 2nd Battalions of the 308th. McMurtry wigged and wagged his way from the CP to the left of the line. A veteran of the Lost Battalion remembered his actions that day:

He was like a broken field runner, dodging this way and that, bullets whanging all around, shells going off, and shrapnel whizzing. I was hunched down in my funk hole when McMurtry came past. He winked at me and said, "Just like the Fourth of July, isn't it soldier?" Then he was gone. Maybe some of the grit rubbed off on me. After that, I wasn't afraid. Instead I got mad at those dumb gunners who couldn't tell us from the Krauts![64]

Even more stirring was the example Whittlesey set. He bestrode the perimeter from end to end like some form of immortal wraith, invulnerable to the steel sleet assaulting the air, steadying the men with his calming drone. "Take it easy there; take it easy. We're all right. This won't last long."[65]

Whittlesey's confident poise and his reassuring words steadied the men's nerves, but could not save their bodies from the continuing onslaught of fratricidal fire. The major returned to the CP to summon Private Richards. Richards carried his pigeon coop, containing the command's last two birds, both of which were squawking in alarm at the cascading barrage. Whittlesey directed his pigeon handler to a more protected spot among the trees. There the major, swiping at a bleeding shrapnel-slash across his nose, scribbled out an emergency message to Delaware One. It read:

We are along the road parallel [to coordinates] 276.4.
Our own artillery is dropping a barrage directly on us.
For heaven's sake, stop it.—Whittlesey.[66]

Unnerved by the weight of falling shells and life-or-death responsibility, Richards mishandled the first pigeon and it fluttered away messageless. "Sorry sir!" said Richards.

"Sorry!" replied Whittlesey. "Don't apologize man. Get off that message!"[67]

The birdman refocused, reached into the crate with sweating brow and trembling fingers, and pulled out the last pigeon. This was Cher Ami (Dear Friend), destined to be the most famous homing pigeon in military history. Clipping the message capsule to Cher Ami's leg, Richards tossed the bird and the last hope for the Lost Battalion into the air.

Cher Ami, upon whose pewter-colored wings rested possibly the very survival of Whittlesey's command, spiraled into the air, circled in shell-shocked confusion twice, then fluttered down to a tree limb, still within the perimeter, to splay his feathers as if checking for shrapnel damage. Whittlesey and Richards, blanching at shellbursts, hopped up and down with helmets waving, tossing curses, sticks and stones at the bird to reinduce flight. The pigeon simply fluttered to a higher branch to perch again in beady-eyed contemplation of the frantic men trying to force him aloft into a perilous sky.

Shouting, "Go, damn you, go!" Richards scampered up the tree, Mauser bullets splintering the bark, to vigorously shake the branch on which perched the hopes of the 308th for deliverance. Cher Ami finally lifted off, but only to wing in wide circles over the Pocket. German snipers spotted the pigeon and opened fire on it with their Mausers. Evidently deciding that no safe place remained, Cher Ami finally took off on the flight path towards the HQ coop.

The shells continued to fall while Cher Ami winged his way south. Ignoring their descent and the curses of his men upon the "redlegs" of the artillery, Whittlesey prowled the perimeter, helping to collect the wounded and move them to a less vulnerable place, where fallen trees offered some protection. Hearing a plane puttering above, Whittlesey asked signalman Private Larney to spread white cotton signal panels on the ground to mark their position. The major had just returned to his HQ hole when another "friendly" shell smashed into the parapet.

McMurtry suggested it might be best to move the unit to escape the bombardment, but Whittlesey demurred, "No, that would be out of the frying pan into the fire. At least the German artillery can't get us here, nor their trench mortars very much, and our guns can't keep this up forever."[68]

He also explained that, with no pigeons left to send further information, any relocation move might very well place the battalion under friendly fire again, once the artillery became aware of the unit's true coordinates and readjusted their guns elsewhere. Whittlesey did agree, however, to at least move the CP nearer to the base of the hillside where the wounded had been gathered.

The barrage finally lifted from the Pocket to its intended target—the enemy lines above the road—shortly after 1600, and then stopped about 1615. Cher Ami had gotten through with the twelfth message of his military career. He had been hit during his thirty minute flight by a bullet that had ripped away one leg and shattered his breastbone (although other accounts claim he sustained his wounds on a later mission). But the bird had completed his homing mission, reaching the roof of the division loft at Rampont, twenty-five miles distant from Charlevaux Brook.

There, Corporal George Gault, the duty NCO, found him, minus a leg, minus an eye, but still bearing the vital rice paper message hanging from a torn leg tendon. Gault telephoned the message in code to divisional HQ. The major who answered, to be certain he understood what he had heard, ordered Gault to repeat the message in the clear, regardless of who might be listening in. Appalled, he in turn phoned the artillery brigade to silence the guns.

The carrier pigeon Cher Ami, in his coop, balancing on his remaining leg after the friendly fire barrage of October 4, 1918. National Archives, 111-SC-47558.

The carrier pigeon that had saved the Lost Battalion was honored for his brave, if initially reluctant, service beyond the call of duty. The division veterinarian treated Cher Ami's wounds and even whittled a prosthetic wooden leg to replace the limb lost in battle. While the CO and the second-in-command of the Lost Battalion would receive the Medal of Honor and many other men of the unit were awarded Distinguished Service Crosses and Silver Stars, Cher Ami, qualifying in courage, but not, unfortunately, in species, received no American medal. The French, however, more receptive to displays of valor, no matter what the life form, did award Cher Ami the Croix de Guerre with Palm.

If not a medal, Pershing did grant this most celebrated pigeon in history a pension and saluted him and fellow wounded pigeon President Wilson—injured on the Verdun front—when they embarked for home on the transport *Ohioan*. The British bird with the French name who saved an American battalion died in 1919. He was stuffed and mounted and displayed as a museum piece in the Smithsonian Institution to serve as a feathered memorial to the courage and endurance displayed by the soldiers of the Lost Battalion.*

One of the last shells to fall, before the pigeon plea shut down the guns, struck in the middle of a group struggling its way to the new CP. Corporal Joseph Baldwin of the battalion HQ, helping a wounded comrade to cover, saw a flash, heard a roar, and in the next moment felt the injured man collapse in his arms, his chest ripped asunder. Hurled into the air by the shell's concussive force, deafened and dazed, Baldwin glanced at the spot that Sergeant-Major Ben Gaedeke had occupied seconds ago and saw only a pistol and helmet. Another man in the group, battalion interpreter Bob Manson, would later recall, "He was blotted out. Nothing remained—not even a shoelace."[70]

When the barrage finally ceased, Whittlesey sent Baldwin up and down the line to count the cost of a minor map error. The tragic toll for miscalculated coordinates came to eighty men killed or wounded (according to Baldwin's census; a later, calmer count reduced the number to thirty killed or seriously injured), including two captains—Holderman, bleeding from four shrapnel slashes, and Stromee, wounded for a second time during the siege.

The Germans were as delighted with the Allied bombardment as the Americans were distressed. Major Hünicken provided ironic praise with, "I'm glad we are not being subjected to such a bombardment."[71]

The Hun major saw his main chance here, directing his Spandau gunners and Mauser snipers to maintain a steady fire on the Pocket, while requesting reinforcements from division to exploit the effects of the accidental barrage by undertaking another infantry assault on the cornered Americans. General Quadt-Wykradt-Hüchtenbruck denied the request, however. The chance to rub out the American salient along Charlevaux Brook had to take second seat to dealing with the new threat posited by the U.S. 1st Division, which, as part of the renewed Allied offensive that day of October 4, had stormed up the Aire Valley and had made substantial gains around Exermont.

The German divisional commander told the regimental CO that he should be able to make do with what he had. After all, the Amerikaners had been most obliging with their misdirected fire. "You may attack whenever ready, Hünicken. Good luck."

---

*Historian Robert Ferrell, in his 2005 book, *Five Days in October*, doubted that Cher Ami had much to do with stopping the shelling. Because the barrage continued for an hour or more after the pigeon was released, Ferrell suggests that the gunners ended the bombardment only at the pre-scheduled time for its cessation.[69] This assumption would seem to ignore the flight time required for Cher Ami to reach the division loft twenty-five miles from the Pocket and the time required to relay his message to the artillery.

The major responded with the obligatory elan. " I will destroy the *Amerikanernest* today!"[72]

While machine guns kept the Yanks' noses in the dirt with unrelenting grazing fire, the Boche infantry of the 254th Regiment scrambled into attack position. As the Spandau fire slackened and the assault troops moved forward, Whittlesey's men popped their helmeted heads above their funk holes to lay down heavy defensive fires with their Springfields, Brownings, Chauchats and hand grenades. Company C, on the west wing of the perimeter, took the brunt of the enemy surge this time. Soft-spoken, but rock-steady Lt. Schenck commanded there. He strode the line to calm his jittery janissaries, rendering requests rather than orders in his Brooklyn gentleman tones.

"Please put a couple bursts in those bushes yonder," he politely asked of the Chauchat gunners. "I'm sure you'll find a mark. Thank you."[73]

Though fairly new to the regiment, his men had, nonetheless, grown to adore him. A beacon of quiet courage in this cauldron, Schenck would, sadly, not survive to walk out of the Pocket. On the last day of the siege—October 7—a *Minenwerfer* shell splinter smashed into his face.

A Company C rifleman later memorialized him. "The guys in 'C' were a tough bunch. But we bawled like babies over the Looey. We'd have followed him through hell!"[74]

The Germans probed on the right wing of the perimeter, as well. There, Captain Holderman ignored his four bleeding shrapnel wounds to stagger among his men and exhort them to feats of derring-do few would have thought themselves capable of. Under a bower of potato mashers hurled from the cliff, German squads maneuvered against the American line, but failed to penetrate the Pocket.

A 306th machine gunner remembered the plucky Holderman propping himself up by using two rifles as crutches and blasting away with a .45 in each hand, while "hooting and whooping like a Comanche."[75] The Germans tried again—with their first night attack—scrambling under flare light toward the American perimeter at around 2100. And again, the Yanks, with their carefully aimed fire, validated Pershing's faith in American marksmanship by repelling the attack with deadly volleys of rifle and Chauchat fire.

The lunges at the Yankee line were repelled for the time being, but it was beginning to seem, for those involved on both sides, like simply delaying the inevitable. As the day waned in gathering grayness and gloom, taunts and threats from the surrounding Germans increased. Most of the men of the Lost Battalion were too tired or too hurt to respond, but some borough boys from the German Yorkville section of New York City spit back curses in Teutonic slang at their tormentors and called them "windbetreben" (wind-bags, or, more literally, horse farts).[76]

One sardonic soldier of the German Empire employed a supercilious English accent to inquire, "I say, you chaps! You haven't a chance! Why not surrender while there's still time?"

A couple of the "chaps" maintained enough moxie to fire back, "Who's that? The Prince of Wales?" and "I thought the Limeys were on our side!"[77]

To another suggestion of "Kamerad, vil you?," a surly American voice answered, "Try and make us, you Dutch bastards!"[78]

A more reflective enemy soldier, a Bavarian officer dug in on the limestone cliff, recorded in his diary that evening his thoughts about the American soldiers and their situation:

No wonder the Americans are such stubborn fighters ... they have good Teutonic blood in their veins.... It hurts to think that we must shoot descendants of our own people, but the fortunes of war are not kind.... We shall destroy them ... if not today, then tomorrow or the day after.... The Americans are cut off, without food, medicine, and hope of escape.[79]

As the forest fell into a darkness periodically illuminated by German flares, and a cold rain began to fall, many of the miserable and hungry doughboys, hunched in their muddy funk holes, might very well have agreed with the diarist's assessment of their predicament. Their situation, by every criteria, called out desperation. Their packs carried only a few emergency rations; the soothing narcotic of tobacco was as rare as hope. Clips of rifle cartridges were down to a few per rifleman; machine-gun ammo stocks were diminishing and grenades were in desperately short supply.

As many men were dead or wounded now as were—physically—uninjured. The "lucky" ones shivered under the icy insults of the rain, breathing air thick with cordite fumes and befouled by the odors of excrement and festering wounds. They stared into the darkness with their zombie faces, listening to the whimpers of the wounded and the growls of their empty guts.

The wounded, of course, were in even worse shape. There was no salve nor shots left to ease their pain. The three vastly overburdened medics were reduced to removing the soiled bandages of those who had expired to reuse them on the more recently mutilated. No one had the strength left to bury the dead. Their graves for now could be nothing but brush and handfuls of loose earth to cover the corpses.

The commander of the AEF was as anxious to relieve the Lost Battalion as anyone. It was not so much that he was in extreme distress over the fate of 600 of his men and a single composite battalion, when he had already, in the nine days of this battle, sent ten times that number to their deaths before the enemy wire and had wrecked whole divisions, like the 35th, in his sputtering offensive. Pershing's primary concern for the Lost Battalion was because of its sudden celebrity. It was certainly important to him that any penetration of the enemy line, no matter how small scale, be secured and exploited. But even more vital was avoiding the public embarrassment, even humiliation, of a failure by the U.S. First Army to save this American Leonidas and his brave band of Bowery Boy Spartans. This would be reflected in a Saturday, October 5, order he sent to General Alexander: "I direct that a vigorous effort be made this afternoon to relieve the companies on the left of the 77th Division that are cut off."[80]

For Pershing, however, the fate of the Lost Battalion on October 4 was rather small potatoes in the larger scheme of things. That Friday, after all, was the day the Meuse-Argonne Offensive was to get going again in massive manner. The infantrymen of the 1st and 2nd Battalions of the 308th, under extreme duress and in danger of annihilation that day—by their own side, as well as by the enemy—were aware of the attempts to relieve them, but could not have known that their fight for survival was just one small segment of a renewed full-scale battle along much of the First Army front.

The divisions—new to the front or old, veteran or untested—that Black Jack aligned, west to east, for his next big push were: the 77th, anchoring the army as always on the forested west, the 28th, and the 1st, new to the Meuse-Argonne, but old (in American terms) to the war—all making up I Corps; then the 32nd and 3rd, both fresh to the battle and now composing V Corps; finally, the 80th, 4th and 33rd of III Corps, all three divisions having been on the line since the beginning. In reserve behind I Corps, were the 82nd (All

American) Division, the African American 92nd Division (less its 183rd Brigade), and the French 5th Cavalry Division. Backing up V Corps in the center was the 91st Division, still licking its wounds from round one. The III Corps, still burdened with the least demanding tasks and all three of its divisions relatively undamaged from the first phase, was given no corps reserve. Further back, in army reserve, were the still reorganizing 35th, the 29th, the 42nd (Rainbow) and the 183rd Brigade of the 92nd.

The attack had gone forward at 0530. There was no artillery preparation this time to alert the napping enemy. The troops, rested, and their leaders, wiser, moved into a hazy hash of fog and rain that helped conceal them from the enemy, but confounded their formations. For phrase two, Pershing had stressed the importance of infantry-artillery cooperation and coordination. He had told his corps commanders to advance on their objectives independently, regardless of the progress of the corps on their flanks, to go for broke and hold nothing back. Bullard's three divisions—33rd, 4th, 80th—were to seize the Cunel Heights. The Romagne Heights and the Côte Dame Marie were the targets of Cameron's V Corps. Liggett's goal was to continue the assault on the Argonne bluffs and to conquer the ridge-line north of Exermont. All those objectives were key strong points in the Kriemhilde Stellung, the outpost zone of the Hindenburg Line.

The American corps would be attacking some of the enemy's stoutest defenses, skillfully making maximum use of the naturally defensive nature of the terrain and groomed with interlocking fields of fire. The attackers would be under observed artillery fire from the Argonne promontories and the high ground east of the Meuse. To avoid the worst of the galling fire from the Meuse Heights, the III and V Corps, acting in concert, were directed to concentrate their efforts against the Cunel Heights by approaching predominantly from the west. U.S. artillery was to counter the enemy artillery in the Argonne with heavy doses of smoke and counter-battery fire. Huge stockpiles of HE and gas shells had been accumulated to support the push.

The enemy artillery, however, was not suppressed. Though the Germans were rushing their best remaining field troops into the Meuse-Argonne front, it was their artillery that remained the most effective element in resisting the American onslaught. Everywhere along the line, enemy resistance was immediate and ferocious, and the guns above the Meuse rained down an accurate shellfall that inhibited even the highest spirits. "Jack Johnsons"— Boche artillery shells, so tagged by doughboys in honor of the African American heavyweight champion, with his explosive punch—pounded down all hope. Results were minimal and gained at maximum cost, and by day's end Pershing knew that there would be no breakthrough.

On the east end of the line, the German guns mounted on the Meuse Heights pulverized Bullard's assault columns. American counter-battery fire seemed to make no dent in the volume of fire arcing over the river. The 4th Division, in the center of III Corps, clubbed its way through the Bois du Fays, southeast of Cunel, but then was driven back by vigorous enemy counterattacks when it tried to press on into the Bois de Peut de faux. The 4th wound up, after three days of grueling combat, just one mile beyond the line of departure it had left at 0530 on October 4. The 80th Division, on the west flank of the 4th, snagged a few acres in the Bois des Ogons, south of Cunel, in the face of machine-gun gales. But the III Corps made no further progress against the Kraut emplacements honeycombed across the Cunel Heights.

In the center of the battlefront, V Corps also accomplished little. The corps' right hand division—General Preston Brown's 3rd—tried again and again to win a foothold in the forest of Cunel, but was each time bludgeoned back with heavy loss. The 32nd, to the left, achieved more success, but again, at excessive cost. With tanks leading the way, the riflemen of the 32nd braved heavy fire from Hill 269 and the Romagne Heights to capture the town of Gesnes on October 5.

It was I Corps, and in particuarly Maj. General Charles Summerall's 1st Division, that conquered the most ground as it thrust down the Aire Valley behind a rolling barrage. The veteran division had taken high casualties at Cantigny and Soissons (over 8,000), and about 500 casualties each day from the Argonne-sited enemy artillery—which soaked with gas the ravines in which the 1st Division concentrated while preparing for the offensive. But morale remained at a peak, the leaders were professionals, the division was fully equipped with Stokes mortars, 37 mm guns and rifle grenades, and artillery-infantry coordination was top notch. With a frontage of four kilometers (two and a half miles), across the killing ground that had so shattered the 35th Division, the 1st had to pass under the raking fire of the enemy guns on the Argonne bluffs and go up against two fresh divisions—the 5th Guards and the 52nd—both of them first-class fighting units. The 1st had to initially occupy the Chaudron Farm and the Montrebeau hill mass, then struggle another mile up the valley, cross the intersecting Exermont Ravine, and storm a formidable height called Montrefagne. It was an assignment only Pershing's best division could hope to handle.

The combat was ruthless. Dashing through the morning mists with bayonets fixed and spearheaded by forty-seven tanks, the men of the 1st Division overran German units in a flurry of hand-to-hand fighting featuring rifle-butts, knives, bayonets and pistols. As the 1st Division riflemen passed through the old killing ground of the 35th Division, they witnessed the stomach-churning sight of hundreds of corpses from the Kansas-Missouri division, with field dressings glued to wounds by men who had tried to patch themselves and had died vainly waiting for help.

With his troops retreating more than a mile to Exermont, von Kleist, fearful that the 1st Division surge might cut off the German units in the Argonne, called for reinforcement. Elements of the elite Prussian 1st Guards Division were rushed in to help von Kleist's Group Argonnen. Gas shells saturated the 1st Division columns. The fight around Exermont and near the crest of Montrefagne raged for hours before the 1st Division assault finally lost steam.

At horrendous cost, the 1st Division had advanced as much as three miles to take the town of Fléville and the Beauregard Farm on the north side of the Exermont Ravine. Their tanks had rolled over many a machine-gun nest, but forty-four of them were out of action by day's end and 84 percent of the tank crews were dead or wounded. Gas and HE shells, machine-gun rounds and Mauser bullets had decimated 1st Division battalions. The 3/16th Infantry had marched into the mist at 0530 with twenty officers and 800 enlisted men. By 1300, the battalion's ranks were thinned to two officers and 240 privates and NCOs.

Lt. Maury Maverick of the 28th Infantry would later describe the horrible shellfall. "We were simply in a big black spot with streaks of screaming red and yellow, with roaring giants in the sky tearing and whirling and roaring. There is a great swishing scream, a smashbang, and it seems to tear everything loose from you. The intensity of it simply enters your heart and brain and tears every nerve to pieces."[81]

One of those shellbursts sent shrapnel whirling to rip apart Maverick's shoulder blade and collarbone. The three runners standing beside him when the shell struck were reduced to slabs of bloody meat unrecognizable as human forms. Fortunately, Maverick survived his wounds to become a prominent U.S. congressman from Texas in the 1930s.

To the left of the 1st and closest to the Argonne was the 28th Division. Unlike the 1st, its story on October 4 carried a theme similar to most of the American divisions—one of failure and frustration. The brigade on the right did make progress toward the Châtel Chéhéry, where sixteen German batteries were concentrated, but the west-flank brigade went nowhere at all in the melancholy forest.

On October 5, as the Meuse-Argonne Offensive's second phase sputtered into a familiar *mise-en-scène* of minimum gain and maximum carnage, the siege of the Lost Battalion began its third full day. A morose, gray dawn greeted the battalion survivors. There was just a smear of crimson on the eastern horizon, like rouge on a courtesan's cheek. Shivering soldiers, each of their funk holes turned into a gluey morass from a night of rain, stared from bloodshot eyes at a sky as dreary as their prospects. Haggard, grimy and unshaven, they looked like the most hopeless of the homeless.

Hunger, by now, seemed a more heinous enemy than the Hun. Remaining slivers of hardtack and bacon rind were as revered as the wealth of nations. Though sniper rounds were pinging through the now largely leafless trees, starving doughboys crawled into the bushes to pilfer the pockets of decomposing German bodies in search of hunks of black bread, stale and even blood-soaked, but still edible to the desperate men. When one of the scavengers offered some of the black bread to Whittlesey, he demurred, saying, "No, you deserve it all."[82]

McMurtry, his wounded knee swollen grotesquely, hobbled from the CP to inspect the line and offer encouragement, the only ration he could pass out. He agreed with one team of riflemen that a bellyful of coffee and sinkers (doughnuts) could cushion the final steps they might soon have to take toward oblivion.

Holderman too walked the line, trying to spread cheer, even though he bled from four shrapnel wounds. While his officers tried to distribute hope to the men, Whittlesey sent an orderly to count the soldiers who were still capable of more than just hope. The total of those who could still effectively bear arms (including the lightly wounded) came to 375.

Whittlesey was everywhere, trying to keep things together. Wandering a perimeter reeking with the stench of the decaying dead and the gangrenous wounded, the major had to scold a man or two for adding to the foulness because they were too exhausted to struggle over to a trench latrine. When another soldier took a bullet during a free-lance attempt to reach the water hole, Whittlesey had to post sentries along the route to water, with orders to shoot any man who tried to make the deadly passage without authorization. The water detail was reserved for those agile chameleons like Zip Cepeglia, who could complete the trip without presenting an easy target to the enemy marksmen.

Meanwhile, higher command was scrambling for ways to help Whittlesey's men. After an urgent appeal from Alexander, Hunter Liggett authorized an aerial effort to ameliorate the desperate condition of the Lost Battalion by dropping ammunition, food and medical supplies into the Pocket. Two two-seater DH-4s (called "flaming coffins") from the 50th Aero Squadron, each lifting baskets piled with provisions and attached to parachutes rerigged from flares, were sent to locate Whittlesey's position. One of the planes took "archie" (anti-aircraft fire), which ripped into its cloth fabric and damaged its struts, forcing the aircraft to turn back without delivering its parcels. The second airplane circled over Charlevaux Brook, diving to just above the treetops in search of the white signal panels Whittlesey had laid out, but the morning mist swirling through the trees masked the American position. Dropping their baskets from 200 feet into a likely-looking ravine, nonetheless, the DH-4 headed home, but then sighted three soldiers emerging from a dugout in a forest clearing, uniformed in feld grau and wearing coal-scuttle helmets. Their identity was confirmed when they opened fire on the aircraft. The pilot fired his flare pistol to mark the position for the artillery and scooted back to base.

The major's men on the ground had tried everything to attract the attention of the aircraft, but their shouts and gesticulations, even the tracer rounds they fired skyward, failed to get them noticed. An even more disheartening sight than the plane banking away without signaling that it had spotted the 308th, was the vision of parachuted parcels oscillating down into Heine lines, where the Germans, some of them yelping in delight, retrieved those gifts from above. A disappointed Yank cursed the airmen. "They dump the stuff and scoot away. What do those fucking birdmen care?"[83]

But the "birdmen" did care. Though the target zone was small—only seventy yards deep—and obscured by foilage, they kept coming back that day and the next. On Sunday—October 6—alone, in the first significant combat airdrop in U.S. aerial history, thirteen planes from the 50th Aero Squadron, carrying a total of forty packets amounting to 1,000 pounds of supplies (plus two pigeon crates), dared intense archie, machine-gun and small-arms fire to try to provision the Pocket. One DH-4, piloted by Lt. Harold E. Goettler, with artillery lieutenant Erwin R. Bleckley as his backseat observer, attempted two missions on October 6. Already hit on the wings and fuselage during their first flight, Goettler and Bleckley swooped in at 250 feet to make their pass over the 308th's position. Their DH-4 was the deadly focus of hundreds of German machine gunners and riflemen. Both airmen were mortally wounded by the tsunami of fire directed at their flying machine. The pilot clung to life and to the controls long enough to crash-land his craft behind French lines. Both birdmen were posthumously awarded the Medal of Honor.

One other DH-4 was downed that day, but sadly, the sacrifice was for naught. Almost all of the air-dropped manna ended up in enemy hands. The supremely frustrating sight of ammunition, blankets and, most precious of all, rations, falling to earth just out of reach was too much to bear for some starving Yanks. Driven to desperation by days without food, they dashed from their holes toward the beckoning bundles. Out in the ominous open, they were easily picked off by German sharpshooters.

The early efforts by the U.S. command to help Whittlesey's force from the air coincided with the German staff's preparations to complete the destruction of the Lost Battalion on the ground. Confident now that the French on the western flank had shot their wad and were now a minimal threat, Wellmann had ordered a further slide eastward by his corps to enable the 76th Reserve Division to concentrate on the *Amerikanernest*. Von Sybel had interrogated the captured American lieutenants, Harrington and Leak (taken prisoner during the German assault following the October 4 friendly fire shelling of the Pocket), and had largely accepted their inflated claims of American strength in the Pocket. According to the tall-talking Leak, there were 1,200 fire-breathing Yanks from two battalions, plentifully provisioned with cartridges and chow, in the Pocket. Consequently, the Boche commander narrowed the 76th's front to a sector stretching from La Palette east to the junction with von Kleist's group. The 252nd Regiment was posted on La Palette; the 253rd was in reserve; and the 254th, with the support of the pioneer companies brought in on October 2 and elements of the 122nd Landwehr Regiment from von Kleist's group, was focused entirely on the smashing of the American salient above Charlevaux Brook.

At approximately 0930, not long after the DH-4 pilot had fired off his signal flare to mark the U.S. position for the 305th Field Artillery, Hünicken's monster trench mortar took advantage of the clearing haze to belch out the first *Minenwerfer* rounds of the day. The teeth-rattling detonations of the mortar shells, throwing up swirls of gray mud and orange flame, were soon bracketed by flurries of machine-gun volleys and the single-shot song of small arms fire. The American mud-men, in their malodorous foxholes, assumed this ring of fire to be the prelude to another assault and braced for the inevitable. A soldier on the left flank spotted Krauts massing on the crest of the hill to the north and reported his discovery to the CP. All waited for the blow to fall.

It came at 1000, not from the north, but from the south, and in the form of exploding artillery shells instead of charging infantrymen. As a daisy-chain of fountaining eruptions thunderstepped along the loops of the streambed, panicked doughboys damned the artillery and braced for another cascade of friendly fire.

Whittlesey fearing the same, turned to McMurtry in horror. "In heaven's sake, George! That message never got through."[84]

His soldiers clawed deeper into their holes and tried to keep their panicking hearts from bursting before the fratricidal shells burst their bodies. The second volley roared in, the hammer of Thor pounding the earth. But the storm line had lifted. The column of heavy howitzer detonations marched straight up the hill on the opposite side of the Pocket, into the trees where the enemy was forming up.

The doughboys lifted their steel-potted heads, their faces grimy and gaunt but their red-rimmed eyes now aglow with hope, as American shrapnel ripped into trees to sever limbs and separate bark and send their wooden splinters slicing through the air and into German flesh. Cries of pain chased the echoes of the explosions and lifted Yankee hearts. The crest of the hill shuddered under the impact of the bursting metal, and some Americans regained enough energy to cheer as the Germans broke formation to flee the fury. Enemy machine-gun dugouts disappeared in paroxysms of flame and smoke, and even the dreaded *Minenwerfer* fell silent. With the final howitzer detonation, an uncanny quiet fell like a cleansing snowfall over the battlefield. After more than three days trapped in a killing zone, the survivors of the Lost Battalion had reason to smile.

Friday's curses of the artillery morphed on Saturday to praise. As one ground-pounder observed, "Only the day before I'd have murdered any artilleryman who crossed my path. But right then, those redlegs could've had anything I owned."[85]

Spirits rose even higher, when the sounds of the renewed Allied offensive and a report of relief forces sighted to the southwest seemed to indicate that the siege of the Pocket might end that day. When McMurtry limped over to the CP with these rumors of rescue, several of the wounded roused up weak cheers and even Whittlesey cracked a smile. But the balloon of optimism burst by midday, after patrols sent out by Whittlesey returned to report no sign of approaching friendly forces. This numbing news coincided with a renewal of mortar and sniper fire.

Morale was being viciously yanked up and down by the events of the day, and Whittlesey feared that it would soon take such a plummet that the will to carry on would vanish. Both he and McMurtry could see demoralization fossilizing the ashen faces of their men. But at 1500, when machine-gun ranging bursts forecast another attack, courage again welled up from humble holes and the men of the 308th somehow summoned the strength to fight back.

Lt. Peabody convinced Whittlesey and McMurtry to move their CP to a more protected position, just as a spasm of Maxim rounds tore into their former funk hole. The main enemy effort came twenty minutes later, near the center and right, where the Germans catapulted bundles of five or six potato mashers bound together with barbed wire to detonate explosions as big as that of the *Minenwerfer*. One of those super-grenades blew both legs off one soldier. Screaming for his mother, until shock brought anesthesia and eventually oblivion, his last faint words were, "Good-bye everybody. I forgive all."[86]

McMurtry, hobbled though he was by his painful knee wound, took charge to direct Chauchat teams to reinforce the pressure point. Firing hip-high up the slope, the auto-riflemen broke up the enemy probe, but Lt. Pool, Holderman's XO, went down with a sniper bullet smashing into his back.

The rest of the 77th Division did not just stand by idly on October 5, while the Lost Battalion teetered on the brink of annihilation. In the morning, Alexander had called for a fresh effort by the 154th Brigade to strike the Germans on Hill 198, while Whittlesey attempted to break out south from his confinement, thus squeezing the besieging Germans from both sides. Unfortunately, the new plans, to be air delivered to Whittlesey, were dropped instead on an artillery unit four miles from Whittlesey's hill. (A second attempt to reach Whittlesey with this message—overland by a ten-man patrol from Lt. Knight's battered company—was unsuccessful, with four of the soldiers failing to return from the mission.)

The 308th CO, Colonel Stacey, begged off any further role for his ransacked regiment. Stacey, on the brink of a breakdown, informed brigade commander General Johnson by telephone that, although he was making every effort, he believed it "impossible to push through with these tired, disorganized men. I must have reinforcements. Unless I get fresh troops, I request to be relieved."[87]

He complained that Alexander did not comprehend the calamity that had befallen his regiment. (Exclusive of Whittlesey's units, the 308th took 766 casualties, October 2–7), Stacey praised the raw material of his regiment, claiming that his men were plucky and always willing to try. But they lacked proper training and equipment, and his remaining officers lacked the leadership skills to fight in the forest. He mournfully informed Johnson that, "I can no longer assume the responsibility for sending my brave and loyal men to their deaths. You cannot ask me to do this!"

When Johnson passed on Stacey's refusal to Alexander, the boiler burst. "Damn it! Relieve him of command at once. The responsibility for the success or failure of the attack is mine and mine alone! I'm the commander, not Stacey!"[88]

When Johnson pointed out that, with Whittlesey snagged in the Pocket, there was no one remaining above the rank of captain to take over the regiment, the stack blew again. The one and a half miles of telephone cable between Johnson and Alexander almost seemed superfluous, as the division commander exploded. "I don't care if it leaves the regiment in command of a corporal, as long as he'll fight. Relieve that man at once and send him back to headquarters and relieve any other officer who talks in that way. You will take personal command of the attack."[89]

Stacey's twenty-year Regular Army career was effectively ended. He carried his corroded confidence straight from the front line to a field hospital, where he was diagnosed as a casualty of nervous exhaustion. It would require of him four years and a court of inquiry to clear his name of the calumny of Alexander's charges.

The command of the 308th devolved to Captain Lucien Breckinridge, young and bright and eager to take on the task. Though he might have been in over his head, it did not really matter. Alexander had made it clear that Johnson would be personally in charge of the forthcoming attack. Because of the delay in switching commanders of the 308th, the 154th

Brigade was unable to mount the morning attack ordered by Alexander. This confusion in the American command structure was fatal to the French assault that went in as the sun rose on La Palette. The dismounted cavalrymen finally took the hill, but with the American sector quiet, the Germans were able to shift reinforcements to the west and stage a successful counterattack. Driven off the crest of La Palette, the French had to fall back to Binarville, leaving twelve of their machine guns behind as trophies for the Germans.

Incensed at this new failure, Alexander's black temper was further darkened when Pershing anted in with his two cents—that carried the weight of all the gold in Fort Knox. Pershing wanted the embarrassing episode to end, and made clear his disappointment with the 77th Division's feeble rescue effort thus far.

His Celtic fury aroused, Alexander ordered Johnson to "crack the Heine line, no matter what. We've been messing around here too damn long. Now, let's have action! Get in there and slug, if you have to lead the attack yourself!"[90]

And that is what Johnson did. The fifty-seven-year-old, one-star general took personal charge of the lead company of eighty-five riflemen, and led them into the ravine at the foot of Hill 198 at 1330. The advance platoon was armed with Chauchats, but the green replacements who largely made up the platoon were not practiced in handling automatic rifles and rapidly burned up their supply of ammunition, as they ratcheted out whole twenty-round clips at a single burst. The attackers got to within ten yards of the German emplacements before their ammunition gave out, and the brigadier caught a machine-gun bullet that pierced his leather puttee

Brig. General Evan M. Johnson. National Archives, 111-SC-51866.

and creased his calf. Johnson ignored the wound and tried to rally his troops, but after ninety minutes he had to pull back, as the Germans began to fold in his flanks and threaten to put him in the same position as the unit he was trying to rescue. By 1500, Johnson had disengaged, having lost twenty killed or wounded and having earned a DSC.

Johnson's failure to reach the Pocket corroborated Stacey's evaluation of the men under his command. Johnson's after-action report affirmed that: "All the time I was within 75 to 300 yards of the actual firing line ... so when I say that these men are not fit to be sent against the enemy, I speak not at any distance.... They went without complaint and willingly, but their physical condition was such that it precluded the possibility of success."[91]

Over to the right, Colonel Houghton's 307th also attacked. The lead company got 100 yards closer to Whittlesey, but the commander, Captain Crawford Blagden, was wounded, and his XO, Captain Eddie Grant—who had covered third base for the New York Giants before the war—was killed. After his regiment absorbed nearly 100 casualties, Houghton suspended the assault.

"We can't afford the price," he pointed out. "My men deserve a better break than being sent to a slaughter."[92] Unfortunately, it was not a principle universally shared by all commanders on the Western Front.

For a third straight day the Germans had beaten back every attempt to rescue or reinforce Whittlesey. Of 450 men of the U.S. 154th Brigade engaged in the relief efforts of October 5, thirty were killed, sixty were wounded, and twenty-three were captured or missing. But the corps commander responsible for the German success was not celebrating. Wellmann, at his I Reserve Korps HQ, was, late in the day, arguing with Army *Oberkommando* (High Command) over the next move to make. Though the 77th Division was making no progress in the forest, *Ober* HQ was alarmed at the gains won by the 1st Division in the Aire Valley, gains that threatened to unpinion the Giselher Stellung and force a general German pull-back, including a withdrawal by I Reserve Korps from the Argonne.

The 1st Division had expanded on its success on October 4 by launching both its brigades up the valley. U.S. artillery fired some of the largest concentrations of HE and gas of the American military effort in the Great War. The U.S. 7th Field Artillery Regiment, for example, spiraled as many as ten shots per tube per minute for extended periods, before the gun barrels grew too hot to continue. The division's 1st Brigade (16th and 18th Infantry Regiments) grappled with the elite, but debilitated, 1st Prussian Guards Division for control of Montrefagne and Hill 272 from daybreak to mid-afternoon. Prussian Guards units resisted stoutly, sometimes to the last man, and few prisoners were taken, but eventually they gave way. The magnitude of the fighting for the 1st Division's 2nd Brigade (26th and 28th Infantry Regiments) was just as intense against the enemy defenses around the village of Ariétal. Casualties soared; fifty American infantrymen fell under the hatcheting fire of a single German machine-gun nest. The 2/26th, after a day of fighting on hill and dale, counted six officers and 285 enlisted men still standing out of the thirty officers and 1,000 enlisted men who had entered battle as the sun rose. Total casualties for the 1st Division on October 4–5 neared 3,500. But by 1700 on October 5, Group Argonnen buckled and abandoned the line to retreat to the Kriemhilde Stellung.

Wellmann was in no mood or mind, however, to have his corps accompany von Kleist's group in its waltz to the rear. He instead appealed to *Ober* HQ for more men to help reduce the Pocket. His 254th Regiment was trying hard, but it was not a shock unit, and the pioneer and 122nd Landwehr elements were basically fit only for defensive duties. What he needed was *Stosstruppen*. The 254th could not both repel Allied efforts at relief and overrun the American salient. The Yankee tumor in his lines prevented him from reinforcing more vital points in the defense works, and continued to provide the Allies with a lever that might crack the whole foundation of the I Reserve Korps fortifications in the forest. Wellmann argued that, "It will be a disgrace to the *Reichswehr* if these impudent Yankees are permitted to survive."[93] To insure their destruction, he needed at least one battalion of storm troopers.

The corps commander managed to convince *Ober* HQ. He was promised a battalion of *Stosstruppen* (though somewhat understrength, as were almost all German units by now), which would reach I Reserve Korps by the morning of October 6. Some of those storm troopers would be carrying *Flammenwerfer* (flamethrowers), with which, *Ober* pointed out, "You'll be able to give the Amerikaner a foretaste of hell."[94]

Though theirs were the most dramatic stories, the 77th and 1st Divisions were not, of course, the only AEF units engaged that Saturday. Except in the Aire, however, progress was minimal or non-existent. Though low-lying areas were still vales of mud, the weather was better, the roads were firmer, and more supplies were getting to the front. But the Germans were committing more reserves and more aircraft, and were launching localized counterattacks all along the line. Fighting was furious, often hand-to-hand, and losses mounted. By evening, Pershing realized that his hopes for a phase two breakthrough within two days were fatally unrealistic. After two all-out efforts, the AEF commander finally realized that pounding his poorly used divisions straight up the middle was not going to work.

Of course, for the men of the Lost Battalion, trapped in their tiny universe of dread and desperation, these events in the greater battle, for all their impact on the 308th's ultimate fate, might as well have been taking place on the dark side of the moon. At twilight, Whittlesey's soldiers prepared for their fourth night in the purgatory of the Pocket. The night outposts were set out to watch for German snipers, largely quiet now, but still taking occasional pot shots at any American movement toward the water hole. Whittlesey sent his battalion messenger, George Botell, and a runner, Joe Friel, out into the gathering darkness in a forlorn hope of reaching the rear and then guiding back relief.

As the rain resumed, descending Very lights flickered through the curtaining downpour, rendering a phosphorescent glow to the blood-basted corpses of the dead. Monumentally weary men tried to bring some little comfort to the wounded. Whatever could serve as a field dressing was appropriated; old dressings off the dead, even unwrapped woolen puttees. Whittlesey circulated among the suffering, giving an encouraging word here, a sliver of chocolate there. The night air was heavy with rain and the sad songs of the dying.

"I'm going boys, I'm going. Write to my mother—please—please!"[95]

October 6 struggled toward the light with rain, interminable rain, falling again. Lt. Maurice Griffin, who maintained a diary during the siege, wrote of the downpour: "It rained almost constantly and we wallowed in mud, but the mud made our bed softer."[96]

On this fourth dawn in the Pocket, the men had passed beyond the outskirts of hunger into starvation's suburbs. Food deprivation was so acute that some soldiers were now grazing on grass. The pains in their empty stomachs spiked up into their hearts, when Whittlesey's men had to endure the sight of their joyous adversaries pouncing on 1,000 pounds of supplies misdropped by thirteen DH-4s. The Germans so enjoyed those delicacies—rare treats in the past two years—that the word was soon passed to avoid firing at the "delicatessen-flyers."

While the grateful men of the German 254th Infantry Regiment smoked cigarettes and greedily consumed packets of chocolate, smoked meats, bread, butter and jam—all intended for the men of the U.S. 308th Infantry Regiment—the routine of dodging death and dealing with adversity en extremis continued for the Lost Battalion. There were those, among these walking dead, who were by now ready to take their chances at infiltrating individually by night through enemy lines to reach the rear, but their requests to do so were all denied. Overall, though, the general attitude among most of the men was one of resolute resignation to what now seemed an unalterable fate.

Some of the men felt a sense of complicity in their own entrapment. And some continued to place their fate in God's hands. But for many of the desperate doughboys, God no longer lived with them in their funk holes or on this hillside where no bird sang—or, if he was present in this brambled hellhole, he had to be a cosmic sadist. For others in the Pocket, excommunicated from hope and exiled from salvation, there was neither a merciful nor a merciless god, but only a supremely indifferent god.

The men's physical strength was ebbing rapidly. Many were even too weary to continue popping the six-legged cooties between their thumbs—and allowed them to feed unmolested up to twelve times a day on their human hosts. Whittlesey feared that a determined Heine assault would sweep over his enfeebled men. If the defenders of the Pocket had to grapple hand to hand with attacking troops, they would be easy prey for the bayonet-wielding Germans. If they retained the reserves of energy to work their weapons, they lacked the ammunition to keep those weapons working, and if they could somehow conserve enough rounds to fire their guns, those guns were breaking down. Already three of the 306th Battalion's machine guns were no longer functioning, and the Chauchats were wearing out too.

Every necessary detail—gathering water, attending to the wounded, burying the dead—was exhausting and dangerous. Enemy marksmen had every open space zeroed in, and cover was diminishing as the steady sleet of shrapnel and bullets stripped more of the Pocket bare. The dead were a particular burden. The survivors had no strength to bury them, but the sight of their comrades sprawled in their death postures was further damaging to a descending morale. Whittlesey compromised by ordering them covered with branches and brush.

Spiraling spirits further downward was the return at dawn of Private Botelle. While carrying out his "routine" sunrise stroll around the embattled perimeter, Whittlesey encountered the messenger at the dressing station, where medics were binding up his Mauser-scalped head with a jury-rigged dressing consisting of a puttee and a bandage recycled from a soldier who had died from his wounds. The blood streaming into his eyes, Botelle responded to Whittlesey's inquiry about runner Friel with a sadly familiar story of a machine-gun burst and a quick death.

There seemed to be no way through the German cordon, and this discouraging news was soon followed by the resumption of the mortars' familiar attentions and the fall of potato mashers from the escarpment above Holderman's company.

The incoming, however, was simply more routine harassing fire, not a curtain raiser or a scene setter to another ground assault. That was being planned by Wellmann for later in the day, but his plans were careening off obstacles and threatening to crash. The same rain—both from the turning of the sky and the passage of events—that was falling on the Americans was also coming down on the Germans. Both sides were enduring a cavalcade of misery, bad news nipping at the heels of exhaustion, dire options descending to desperate alternatives.

Wellmann had earlier wheedled from *Ober* HQ a promise of two extra machine-gun battalions pulled from the 1st Guards Division, but toward noon he received the telephone news that the fresh units von Kleist had thrown into counterattacks at Hill 272 and Montrefagne against the 1st Division had been mauled by heavy doses of Allied artillery and were now in full retreat. The dam across the Aire Valley had collapsed and the surging stream of American infantry was pouring through. With the German flank turned, the Le Chêne Tondu sector was compromised and had to be abandoned.

A general withdrawal from the Giselher Stellung back to the Kriemhilde Stellung was now unavoidable. The pull-back would begin in the Aire and spread by orderly stages west through the Argonne to the Aisne River. The stronghold of La Palette would finally be conceded to the French and Americans. The I Reserve Korps was given thirty-six hours to begin its retreat, with its left wing aiming for the Grandpré gap.

Wellmann was furious. He could not abide the thought of a handful of amateurish Yankee troops successfully holding out for days behind his lines and flaunting their lack of professionalism in the face of his corps. He took the insult personally, and was determined to wipe this stain from the bright banners of his command before pulling out of the Argonne. He asked for two more days and claimed the Americans "are practically prisoners now ... with [the *Stosstruppen* battalion's] help I will guarantee the crushing of this group."[97]

Ober HQ gave in partially to his pleas; the *Stosstruppen* battalion was his (although Wellmann, in turn, had to give up his pioneer battalions which were fighting as infantry, so that they could revert to their proper function and help engineer the withdrawal). But the thirty-six-hour time limit stood, and if the *Amerikanernest* was not eradicated by then, the I Reserve Korps would have to tip its hat to the tenacious American battalion commander—who lacked the proper military training and education to know when he was beaten.

Soon after winning this concession, Wellmann was notified of the arrival into the forest of the 2nd *Stosstruppen* Battalion. The reinforcements—hollow-eyed from battle fatigue—were weary and worn-down, but still the best remaining fighters in the Imperial German Army. They were, however, far too few of them, numbering only sixteen—less than a full regulation-size platoon in strength—all that could be spared or all that had survived the melee in the Aire. For all their slender numbers, they did carry six *Flammenwerfers* with them and, with attached provisional units, Wellmann hoped that they would be enough to tip the scales in favor of the 254th Regiment for the "annihilating attack" he had planned against the Pocket for that afternoon.

Both opposing higher commands were now working against the clock, with relief or annihilation for the Lost Battalion lying at the midnight hour. General Alexander had taken an early morning tour of the forest, gathering facts and looking for possibilities. The 306th Regiment, on the right, had the strength remaining to mount an attack, but was probably too far removed from the Lost Battalion's position to have much impact on its ultimate fate. The parent regiment of the Lost Battalion—the 308th—was too mangled and weak to attempt any further rescue mission. The best hope for achieving a breakthrough rested with Houghton and the 307th. That bard of battle, Colonel Houghton—many times wounded on the Western Front, starting with the First Battle of Ypres—was yellow with jaundice and nearing exhaustion. But he had turned down offers of a comfortable and safe staff job, sneering at the idea of donning a "brass hat" and standing by his boys. Houghton had clashed with his division CO before, when Alexander had demanded more from his men than he thought humanly possible, but now, as sniper rounds zipped and zinged around them, he gave the surly Scot a possible strategy for saving Whittlesey's force.

Houghton noted that, though the Germans facing them were good troops, they were not the best the enemy had to offer, and that they were no less downtrodden by the battle and the elements than the Americans. But German pioneers had constructed formidable defenses, and nature, allied with artifice, had cleverly concealed them. The greatest obstacle between Whittlesey and the rest of the division, however, was not the enemy soldiers and their bunkers, but the ubiquitous and diabolical belts of barbed wire. It was the wire more than anything else that had tripped up all the attempts at relief. Artillery had barreled in barrage after barrage in an effort to blow holes through the spiked barricades, but the irregular pattern of the steel strands, the even more irregular terrain, and the sheer density of the barbed barriers had defeated their efforts. Houghton had asked for Bangalore torpedoes to blast a path through the aprons of wire, but their arrival was delayed, like so much else, by the enduring supply snafus along the serpents of anarchy that were the transportation arteries.

Houghton, nonetheless, had reason for hope. He reported to the general that the wired moat was not totally unfordable. Lt. Richard Tillman of the 307th, on recon, had discovered a gap, and was presently leading a small force of men to cut and expand that gap. Houghton planned to filter fire teams forward through the gap after dark, and build up a concentration with which to strike the flank of the Germans besieging Whittlesey. The effort would require patience and finesse, however. Should the enemy discover the operation, they would quickly slam shut the door. Houghton estimated it would take forty-eight hours to secretly infiltrate an assault force. The brigade commander, General Johnson, had already refined and approved the plan. Though Alexander was skeptical that Whittlesey could dangle over the edge of disaster another two days, it seemed the only option remaining and he gave Houghton the go ahead.

Meanwhile, the object of all this attention, malevolent and redemptive, continued to cling to ever-unraveling threads of hope, faith and resolution. Galloping Charlie continued to lope across the Pocket on his long legs in his never-ending and almost superhuman effort to patch across the ever-opening holes in the ragged coat of his men's morale. Despite his efforts, spirits were becoming as exhausted as bodies. Tempers were being worn down to a nub, and the men were beginning to snap at one another. The gnawing hunger was the worst aspect of their benighted condition. The sight of the DH-4s, unable to spot their signal panels or even their waving towels as they gifted the enemy with those precious packages of rations, was particularly unbearable.

One H/2/308th private, eighteen-year-old Lowell R. Hollingshead, a conscript from Mount Sterling, Ohio, later recalled his near hallucinations of mammoth steaks and mashed potato mountains floating in a lake of gravy. "I only know that I had one driving thought, and that was the desire for food."[98]

Hollingshead and others like him were dozing in their foxholes, half comatose with hunger, when, at 1500, the German mortars started burping rounds. The rattle of machine guns soon joined in, and bone-weary warriors summoned remaining reserves of energy to face the inevitable assault.

One of the machine-gun rounds tore into the already gravely wounded machine-gun officer, Lt. Peabody. Given the one overcoat left in the battalion, in gratitude for his stalwart service even while nursing a shattered leg, the lieutenant was lifted out of his hole by the bullet's impact and sent sprawling downhill onto the signal man attached to the HQ group. Three men there at the battalion CP ignored the warning that it was bad luck to take a dead man's coat, and decided to wear it each in turn.

On the vulnerable right flank, still held by Holderman's Company K, came grenades, as they came so often, from the dominating limestone tower. One of the potato mashers landed in the middle of a Hotchkiss position, taking out both the gun and the machine-gun officer, Lt. Alfred Noon.

McMurtry, consulting with Holderman when the attack came, shouted above the clamor to steady the men. "You've been through this before!"[99]

McMurtry continued to rally the defenders, while Holderman dashed through heavy fire to drag two wounded men to safety. After the attack was successfully resisted, McMurtry returned to the CP, where Whittlesey pointed out to his second in command the presence of a sliver of the handle of a potato masher lodged in his back. In the frenzy of battle, McMurtry had found no time to notice another wound.

If there were cracks forming in the armor of Whittlesey's resolve, they were not visible to the men he commanded. He seemed determined to hold this position as long as necessary or die trying. But he was aware that his men were losing heart. They had fought off another fierce German attack, but how many more such tableaus of tenacity that the men were capable of producing was questionable.

A glimpse of the widening fault line in the battalion's ability to continue resistance appeared when Lt. Revnes, the last remaining 306th Machine-Gun Battalion officer, stalwartly carrying on in spite of a grievous ankle wound, had sent a message to Whittlesey suggesting, if not surrender, at least an appeal to the enemy to permit evacuation of the wounded.

Whittlesey, after bucking up the fading fortitude of Revnes, called McMurtry over for his council. The battalion's effectives were down to little more than 200 in number, and the Pocket had to be contracted in order to hold an unbroken line. Whittlesey was shouldering the burden of command almost single-handedly now. McMurtry, a caliph of courage, regardless of his battered body, was still the rock to which Whittlesey tied his anchor. But Peabody was gone and Rogers had also been killed; Holderman still pluckily tried to carry on though his injuries were gangrenous; and most of the other officers were hors de combat.

There was still, nonetheless, a glimmer of hope to hold onto in the gloom. The airplanes above, the stutter of Chauchats and zing of Springfields in the distance, telegraphed a persistent promise that the division was still trying to reclaim the battalion into its fold. Maybe, Whittlesey suggested, a messenger could still weave a route through the German lines across Hill 198 and guide their rescuers back. McMurtry agreed and left the CP in search of such a savior.

Eight men answered the call, proceeding in a crabbed crouch off to the right along the creek and into the rainy darkness. The sudden nova of a Very light plummeted the men to the ground, but not before two of them were hatcheted by a machine-gun burst. Two others, seeking to crawl to safety, found themselves instead, for several interminable seconds, right beneath the barrel of a Maxim belching out a stream of lead. Surviving this steel-jacketed outburst, the pair inched their way across the sodden forest floor from shell hole to shell hole and finally back to the Pocket's perimeter. No one made it through the enemy lines.

There would be no relief for the soldiers of the Lost Battalion on this fifth night above Charlevaux Creek. At First Army HQ, however, plans were being hatched to aid the 77th Division in its work of rescue. The 1st Division had dug in to consolidate its gains, fighting off all counterattacks by two German Guards divisions. Linking with the 1st's west flank near Fléville was the 28th Division, astride the Haupt-Widerstands-Linie, but its tattered ranks stalled before the burley butte of Le Chêne Tondu. What was needed to storm the enemy flank in the Argonne was a fresh unit, and it was on its way. From corps reserve, the 82nd All American Division (more than two decades away from its enshrinement as the elite airborne division of the U.S. Army) was in march-order, headed eight miles up the roads to tie into the line at the 28th–1st divisional boundary outside Fléville ("Fleaville" to the sardonic Yanks). Liggett's daring plan was to employ—following a fifteen-hour preparatory bombardment by I Corps artillery—the 164th Brigade from the full-of-fight 82nd to deliver a right hook blow across the German lines of communication, force an enemy withdrawal from the Argonne to protect its rear, and, in the process, help break the siege of the Lost Battalion.

The aiming points of the 82nd's attack were the town of Cornay, tucked between hills across the Aire from Fléville, and, further south, Châtel Chéhéry. Between the two was the fortified Hill 180, and around Châtel Chéhéry, north and south, were two more defended peaks, Hills 223 and 244. All the targets of the Georgia, Alabama and Tennessee men of the All American Division were north of Apremont and Le Chêne Tondu and well behind the German defenses in the Argonne. Fording the river under fire from the hilltop defenses and the ever awesome German artillery in the forest—all with their right flank dangerously unprotected—was a daunting task for Maj. General George Duncan's 82nd. But nighttime recons had found passable fords and good avenues of approach. Much of the 82nd's artillery was still in transit on the front's notoriously clotted roads (already thick with the transport of the 1st and 28th Divisions), but Summerall ordered the guns of his 1st Division shifted ninety degrees to cover the 82nd's morning assault.

The southern boys from the 327th and 328th Regiments of the 82nd waded the icy waters of the Aire early on October 7, as the 1st Division artillery pounded the German trenches with a rolling barrage. The men of the 82nd had fought at St. Mihiel, but had never faced such desperate resistance against which they now contended and overcame. Only six companies got into action and machine-gun fire cut down many of the 82nd infantrymen, but Hill 180 was taken before 0700 and 223 by noon. The 28th Division, to the south, joined in to capture the tiny one-lane village of Châtel Chéhéry and Hill 244 to the south. By late afternoon, the 82nd was at the outskirts of Cornay, with the vital north-south railroad and road servicing the German second (Giselher) line of resistance just beyond. The enemy's main position in the Argonne, some three miles to the south, was now in vital danger. Though the men of the Lost Battalion had no way of knowing of this reversal of fortune, they had only to hold out for a few hours more before the Germans surrounding them would have no choice but to retreat.

Whittlesey and his misbegotten battalion were unaware of the big picture that inevitably projected an end to their ordeal by the end of October 7. But they did expect their own brigade to renew efforts at rescue that Monday. And Colonel Houghton of the 307th was intent on finally breaking the siege. At dawn, Lt. Tillman of Company B had returned from his nocturnal patrols to report to his regimental commander that another unguarded gap in the enemy wire offered an infiltration route to maneuver west against the Huns surrounding Whittlesey.

"Go to it, Tillman" Houghton ordered from his deep CP hole.[100]

The lieutenant complied, shu· ing his men through the breach and into the Heine rear. The 306th, to the east, got moving, as well. With the sun barely peeking above the tree line, the regiment humped its way nearly one-half mile against minimal enemy resistance. The 305th Regiment, on the extreme right flank, where the 77th tied into the left wing of the 28th Division, also began to gain ground.

For the first time in nearly a week light permeated the 77th Division HQ, where General Alexander's molten rages had confined his staff emotionally to a darkened cellar. The general had already received the reports of the enemy evacuation of Le Chêne Tondu and the whole German line "folding like an accordian." Now, when Houghton telephoned Alexander to give an opinion that, "the Krauts are getting ready to skedaddle," the general was adamant that the Lost Battalion be finally and firmly "found."

To Houghton he insisted, "You've got to reach Whittlesey. He's not off the hook yet."[101]

When Houghton suggested that his 307th might slide leftward to bottle up the Germans on Hill 198 and La Palette, and thus trap the men who had trapped Whittlesey, Alexander indignantly insisted, "Your job is to get Whittlesey out. We simply can't spare the men for any other operation."[102]

Rescue, indeed, might be a matter of only several hours for the men in the Pocket, but their ever weakening condition made those hours too long and, possibly, too late. Whittlesey, during his morning circuit of the perimeter, found many of his dispirited men scribbling out what amounted to abbreviated last wills and testaments. With little paper and ink remaining, soldiers were employing shreds of bandages and strips of shirttail to scrawl out last messages to loved ones. In some cases, the pigment of communication was not black ink but red blood. Disturbed by this general attitude of impending doom, the major was further unsettled when Lt. Cullen conveyed the news that eight of his Company H men "went over the hill" at daybreak, in desperate search for the food packets misdropped into the enemy-held woods.

The famished doughboys had crawled only several meters into the fog-wrapped trees before a German patrol ambushed them. Four of the scavengers were killed outright, and all four survivors were wounded and taken prisoner. One of the injured captives was Private Hollingshead, whose dozing dream of a banquet fit for kings had been interrupted by the German assault of the day before. Staring into the barrel of a Luger pistol, Hollingshead had raised his hands and muttered "Kamerad." Hit in the right knee, fear, pain and hunger allied in a coalition of misery to sap the spirits of the teenage soldier. But his captors treated Hollingshead well. A bearded doctor dressed his wound, and a *Feldwebel* (corporal) fed him a mess-kit full of cabbage stew.

Taken to a deep dugout with bunk-space for a company of troops and a primus stove to take the chill from the October air, Hollingshead was introduced to Lt. Fritz Prinz, a blond, aristocratic-looking thirty-five-year-old Prussian, who was the intelligence officer of the 254th. Prinz spoke fluent English, having spent six years as a tungsten salesman in Seattle, Washington. He had already interrogated the captive lieutenants, Leak and Harrington, and, consequently knew much of the original details of Whittlesey's surrounded force. He proceeded to awe the young American POW with those details. After having Hollingshead take a seat and offering him a smoke, Prinz praised the bravery of his isolated unit, but warned him that a *Stosstruppen* attack was in the offing and, "this time with enough *Flammenwerfer* to make an inferno of the hillside and everyone on it."[103]

Hollingshead (who would forever insist that he had been captured not on an unauthorized food-foraging foray, but during an attempt to bring back a relief force), was offered the chance to carry a surrender request to Whittlesey. Disoriented, his knee throbbing, Hollingshead ask for time to consider the offering. Prinz ordered a *Feldweber* to escort him to the sleeping section in the cavernous dugout, where he collapsed in exhaustion onto a cot.

While Hollingshead slept with the enemy, Whittlesey searched for solutions to stave off the Hobbesian choices of annihilation or surrender. The major ambled over to Holderman's hole and found the multi-wounded captain—"bloody, battered, but unbowed"—puffing on a hand-rolled cigarette made of message paper and dried leaves, which the captain graded as "awful, just awful."

When Whittlesey asked Holderman to find a volunteer to try and get through to the 307th, the captain called for Abraham Krotoshinsky. The man who answered Holderman's summons hardly fit the standard image of the dauntless hero. An immigrant from a Jewish ghetto in Poland, the beaked-nosed, stoop-shouldered private seemed swallowed by his ragged uniform, several sizes too big for his featherweight form. His eyes projected melancholy, and his general doleful demeanor inspired little confidence. But "Krot," as his platoonmates called him, was wiry and rapid—"like a streak of greased lightning on his feet," and the weight of his courage was in inverse proportion to the size of his frame.[104]

Whittlesey, from his spindly height, looked down on the disheveled soldier, and glanced at Holderman for confirmation that this was the man best-suited for the mission on which all their fates might depend. Holderman nodded in affirmation, and the major explained the mission. Krotoshinsky was to locate the 307th and guide it back to the Pocket.

"I must caution you that the chances of success are slim. I am not ordering you to do this," Whittlesey explained.

Krotoshinsky shrugged off the warning. "I know. I know. You need a volunteer. I'm a volunteer."[105]

Two other men threw in their lot with Krotoshinsky, and about 0800, the three crept downhill through the bushes and past the water hole. The stirring of the ground foliage alerted the Heine machine-gun team covering the creek to the American movement, and soon the tacka-tacka of the machine gun broke the momentary quiet that had briefly visited the battlefield.

Holderman, with pessimism prickling his voice, said, "I hope they make it."

A little over two hours later the two men who had accompanied Krotoshinsky staggered back to the 308th's perimeter. "Couldn't get through. Too many machine guns," was their testimony, and the evidence was in the shoulder of one of the volunteers, struck by a machine-gun bullet. They had lost track of Krotoshinsky and assumed other machine-gun bullets had ended his efforts.[106]

The major saw no alternative but to continue sending runners out to guide in the 307th. He turned to Schenck's company for volunteers. The lieutenant came up with two men willing to make the attempt: Private Stanislaw Kozikowski, another Polish immigrant and, despite his small size, one of the best Chauchat gunners in the company; and Private Cliff Brown, a fair-haired man of deep religious convictions. Schenck handed the volunteers his compass, and advised them to cross the stream further up from the water hole and follow the south stretch of the valley to the lines of the 307th.

After Whittlesey prepped them on their mission, another officer added, "And tell them not to stop dropping us food from airplanes."[107] The airborne resupply efforts had continued that morning, although the pallets always seemed to end up in German hands. Prussian Lt. Prinz had cleverly assisted in this aerial misdropping by ordering the black-and-white signal panels used by the Americans to be laid out within the German lines.

At 1100, after sending the runners on their way, Schenck headed back to his funk hole. It was then that one of the most beloved officers in the regiment encountered the *Minenwerfer* splinter that ended his life. For years after the Armistice, Schenck's father would answer the door to his Brooklyn home to the knocking of countless men who had served with and so admired his son.

The lieutenant's death was devastating to the men he commanded and dispiriting even to McMurtry and Whittlesey. Their best officers were going down, just when their courage and dynamic leadership was so vitally required as the enlisted ranks' morale crumbled further. There seemed to be no end to the persecution visited upon these men for their heresy of penetrating the enemy line. In the morning, a "pirate gun" (so-called because they were disposable pieces that the Germans abandoned after they had served their purpose) had been manhandled into position where it could enfilade the Pocket with several harassing rounds. Then at noon, one more infantry assault—the seventh of the siege—had to be faced down and fought back.

The major and the captain were, at 1545, pondering the puzzle of how their men could possibly hold out against another attack, when Private Hollingshead limped, cane in one hand and a white flag in the other, into the perimeter, with a proposal from the enemy to end the battalion's dilemma.

Hollingshead had stirred from his fitful sleep about an hour before and, having decided that carrying the surrender demand would at least get him back to the battalion and out of German hands, he had accepted Prinz's proposal.

The German lieutenant had handed Hollingshead the cane and a white flag attached to a stick, stuffed his breast pocket full of gold-tipped cigarettes, and sent him blindfolded, with an escorting corporal, toward the leprous citadel of the 308th. One hundred yards from the Pocket, the German guide removed the blindfold, smiled at and shook hands with Hollingshead, and sent him on his way. Challenged by an American sentry, Hollingshead held out his white flag and asked for the major. Taken to the battalion CP, Hollingshead saluted Whittlesey and McMurtry and presented the message to the captain.

Before reading the note, McMurtry drilled Hollingshead on how and why he had fallen into the hands of the enemy. He was about to deliver a stern rebuke to the private for leaving his position simply because his stomach called louder than his duty. But Whittlesey restrained him, saying, "George, let's look at the letter."

Prinz's message politely demanded Whittlesey's surrender and praised Hollingshead as "quite an honorable fellow." It ended with: "The suffering of your wounded can be heard over here in the German lines and we are appealing to your human sentiments. A white flag shown by one of your men will tell us that you agree with these conditions. Please treat Lowell R. Hollingshead as an honorable man. He is quite a soldier; we envy you."[108]

McMurtry scanned the message and passed it on to Holderman, who had struggled over to the CP. Holderman snickered at the line appealing to human sentiments; this from an enemy that had tried to destroy them for five days. McMurtry scoffed, "We've got 'em licked. They're begging us to quit. They're more worried than we are."[109]

Whittlesey peremptorily ordered Hollingshead back to his funk hole, after scolding him for leaving it. The private did return to his company's position, where he began talking of the considerate treatment he had received at the hands of his captives, until Lt. Cullen shut him up with a threatening reproach. Hollingshead, later, after the war, while on the Lost Battalion lecture circuit, would characterize his misadventures as a volunteer mission—led by a full-blooded Indian scout—in search of rescuers, conveniently forgetting his officers' harsh condemnation of his actions.

Whittlesey's only response to the message carried by Hollingshead was to order the white aircraft signal panels taken in, so that the enemy could not mistake them for symbols of surrender. A central part of the Lost Battalion mythology is the major's scornful shout of, "Go to hell!" (or "That Kraut can go to hell!" in a more colorful version), in response to the surrender demand. But the only cursing replies to the enemy were those spit out from the funk holes of the enlisted men. Mightily offended by this call for capitulation, wounded and mortally weary soldiers were re-energized with rage. Shouts of, "You Heine bastards, come and get us," and "Just let me get near one of those Dutch bastards!" sounded a clarion call of renewed resistance.[110] Whittlesey, in his low-key, laconic style, would later recall that, "The men swore a great deal."[111]

If "Go-to-hell Whittlesey" never uttered the words—just like his surrounded force was not a "battalion" and it was never "lost"—the media and the masses made it so, nonetheless. Though Whittlesey told journalist and author Thomas M. Johnson that, "We told them nothing," and the official report written by the major and McMurtry stated, "No reply seemed necessary," others were anxious to embellish the prosaic. General Alexander, afterwards, pugnaciously proclaimed, "He told 'em to go to hell," and men on the perimeter were stirred into action when the word was passed down that, "The Major told them to go to hell."[112]

The seeds and the sprouting of the myth may have originated, however, at 77th Division HQ. From there a report reached Lt. Mead at I Corps HQ that, "The reply to the above [the surrender letter] was 'go to hell'."[113] Mead was the former *New York World* reporter, who, as press officer for I Corps, relayed reports from the front to Field Press headquarters at Bar-le-Duc, from whence the correspondents of stateside newspapers cabled the news across France and the Atlantic. Thus, Mead may have been the chief mythmaker of the siege at Charlevaux Creek, for he is also credited by many with coining the misnomer "Lost Battalion."

Whatever or whoever the source, this brilliant piece of propaganda was as inspiring and as essential to the story of the siege as would be General McAuliffe's "Nuts," in response to another surrender demand at another siege—Bastogne—during the world's next global conflict.

With no reply to their surrender summons other than scornful silence, Major Hünicken, fully aware that time was running out, launched his final afternoon assault. He threw everything he had into this last lunge at the *Amerikanernest—Minenwerfer*, machine guns, grenades, sharpshooters—and his handful of storm troopers with their *Flammenwerfers*. Those few elite soldiers made up the point of the lance Hünicken thrust into the Pocket.

The doughboys in the Pocket, jaded by five days of close combat, had thought they had seen it all before. But then came an image and an event beyond their experience.

"Oh my God! They have flame throwers!" a terrified rifleman screamed.[114]

Down the hill came five figures in gray bearing nozzles and tanks that further introduced the Yankees of the 308th to the new horrors of the young century. Flaming serpents of fire sizzled up to one hundred feet to blacken trees and two of the Americans. The OP line shuddered under this new savagery and broke. Panicked soldiers, weeping and wailing at the red beasts pursuing them, fled downhill, screaming, "Liquid fire!"

Whittlesey would have none of it. "Liquid fire, hell!" he shouted back. "Get back there where you belong."[115]

From the north and northeast, behind the gray dragons and the grenadiers of the 2nd Storm Battalion, charged two companies from the German 252nd and 254th Regiments. Terror reached a zenith as red tongues ignited the brush and oily black smoke coalesced among the trees.

But some men were beginning to rally and fight back. Sgt. Jim Carroll, a drapery salesmen back in the sane world, fired his Springfield from a kneeling position at a flame operator. The bullet pierced his tank and the man went down, consumed in the holocaust strapped to his back. Captain Holderman rallied his Company K, ignoring his four wounds. Using wounded men's rifles as crutches, he hobbled about, blasting away with his .45, shouting commands, and directing the fire of his Chauchat gunners at the flame teams. Only slightly less heroic was Alfred Summers, a sprightly English Cockney in the American ranks, whose audacity carried him from one part of the embattled field to rescue a wounded comrade, and then to the sniper-bullet-swept creek to fetch water for the parched defenders.

While Holderman's company stood fast on the right, Cullen's Company H on the left held off the enemy thrust and Company C firmed up the center. The auto-rifles and Springfields mowed down the remaining *Flammenwerfer* operators, and the German forays petered out by 1730.

Four more doughboys had died in the attack and several more were wounded. Surprisingly, however, after incinerating the two men on the outpost line, the satanic instruments that had caused such initial panic seemed not to have inflicted any of the other casualties. A few men had also been taken prisoner and two machine guns lost. The Pocket was still intact, but its defenders and defenses were fewer now, and many more such attacks would inevitably breach the leaking dam.

The attackers, striking from front and flank, had been met with incandescent ferocity. Defenders, on their last legs of resistance, somehow seemed to collectively and simultaneously draw from a reservoir of rage filled to overflowing by the surrender note. The soul of the defense had been Holderman, anchoring the right flank as always. Ignoring his four wounds, he absorbed a fifth while blasting away with his pistol like a Western gunfighter, knocking down as many as five of the storming Heines while chanting a mantra of bloodletting delight. He and his company sergeant made up the dike upon which the German wave against the right flank broke. Holderman's exploits on the 7th provided the polish on the diamond of a week's worth of heroic display, for which he would be awarded the Medal of Honor.

This surge of defiance steadied the wraith-like defenders the length of the perimeter. On the west wing, the Yanks of the 308th were even able to mount a miniature counterattack that rolled over a German platoon, killing their leader and dispersing his men.

The repulse of this last enemy assault was probably the single most remarkable achievement by the men of the 308th in the course of the five-day siege. Men, whose physical and emotional wells had run all but dry, somehow conjured up the spiritual fire to fight back and to hold on. The wellspring of their resistance may have fountained from the last lashings of a dying animal, clawing back against onrushing oblivion. Perhaps their collective pride had been pricked by what these doughboys interpreted as intolerable Prussian arrogance in the letter carried by Hollingshead. Almost certainly, they were motivated in great part by their determination, in what could be their last hours, not to disappoint their leaders—Whittlesey, McMurtry, Holderman and the others—men of sterling caliber and courage, without whom this unit, like a hundred or a thousand others in similar jeopardy and facing comparable long odds, would have long since surrendered or been overrun. Whatever the convergence of battle-craze and fatalism that powered their final fury, these men, more ghosts than creatures of flesh and substance in the morning, had fought like titans in the afternoon. Now they grimly awaited the end of their story.

That denouement most assumed would be doom. An entry in Lt. Griffin's diary reflected this sense of fatalism: "Every man expected to die, but did not flinch—nor surrender."[116]

Only two machine guns were still operable and just five boxes of ammunition remained. There were no grenades left and there were few cartridges remaining for their rifles. The last reserves of willpower and defiance had been tapped out, and another German attack on the scale of the last one would surely sink their listing ship. The pull of panic during the brief stampede induced by the canistered lightning of the flame throwers had lasted only minutes, before the men's to-the-death doggedness had reclaimed their will. But the introduction of death by fire, added to the already myriad methods of destruction levied on the men of the Lost Battalion, accelerated the slide downhill toward despair for many of the survivors. They could only sit and wait, and construct scenarios in their minds, in which one of the volunteers sent to guide in relief forces accomplished that mission of mercy before the enemy completed their mission of annihilation.

While the men of the 308th waited for the day to deliver its final judgment, the two sets of runners Whittlesey had set out in the morning tried to puzzle their way through the enemy labyrinth. Kozikowski and Brown had crossed the Charlevaux Brook, and were working their way uphill when they almost ran into a German five-man, water-gathering patrol. Flattening themselves into the brush, the Americans evaded this group only to stumble across more enemy soldiers as they worked their way south by Schenck's compass. At one point they had to lay in cramped, fear-struck motionlessness for two hours while the enemy meandered past, before the two Yanks could move on. Then, as darkness and rain arrived, like twin messengers of misery, long range machine-gun fire, probably from American units to the south, forced Kozikowski and Brown to hug the boggy ground for what seemed a millennium. Finally, Brown discovered they were on the right track when he tumbled into a funk hole that he recognized was his own handiwork, dug during the October 2 advance to the Pocket. Soon afterward, a 308th patrol sent out by Breckinridge ran across the forlorn pair, and escorted them to a restful bivouac and a can of beans. Their perilous crossing over into Jordan earned Kozikowski and Brown the DSC.

It was Abe Krotoshinsky, however, who reached the rescuers and led them back to the relief of the Pocket. The machine-gun burst near the water hole that had wounded one of his two companions and had convinced both that the whole effort was fruitless, had not killed the scrawny but agile Polish American, as the other two runners reported to Whittlesey. Ducking behind a stump, Krotoshinsky had wiggled inches at a time for several hundred yards away from the killing arc of the machine gun. Then he dashed in heart-pounding sprints from bush to bush in the general direction of his objective. This ended when Krotoshinsky almost fell into a machine-gun post in a five-foot deep camouflaged dugout. Luckily, the inattentive crew did not spot him, and he was able to slither, again by agonizing inches, away from the gun. The drizzle and the darkness had both descended before Krotoshinsky could resume his rat-scampers from cover to cover. He had just scooted to the hoped-for beneficence of another tree, when he detected voices to his left—English-speaking voices!

Krotoshinsky stood up and shouted in a joyful delirium. Instantly surrounded by American soldiers, he was recognized by a fellow Brooklynite in the 307th, and given a canteen cup of coffee and a can of corned willy. As he gulped and chomped at this finest feast of his life, Krotoshinsky sputtered out between swallows the location and condition of the battalion and urged, "You should come right away."

"Can you lead us back?" asked the lieutenant.

Undaunted by his just completed odyssey, for which he would be presented the DSC, Krotoshinsky responded, "Sure, I feel good now."[117]*

Krotoshinsky's welcoming party was from Major McKinney's 1/307th. The major had spent the day working his battalion through the gaps in the German wire cut by Tillman's team. By last light, he had slipped his battalion CP through the wire and was deploying his companies left and right behind the enemy trench system. Tillman, with Company B, was furthest forward and just east of the Pocket, yelling at his subordinates, "Put the whip on them," when the men seem to be tiring and slowing down as the dark and the downpour deepened.[119] When a Boche machine gun opened up, Tillman sent teams left and right to flank it and eliminate it with sheets of Springfield fire.

Moving on through the brush, Tillman suddenly tumbled into a shellhole and onto a wounded man, who cried out in distinct Brooklynese. The wounded man's companion in the crater lunged at Tillman with his bayonet, which the lieutenant just managed to evade.

After Tillman identified himself and his mission, the bayonet-wielder apologized and then lifted up his wounded buddy to proclaim, "See? We're relieved. You're going to be all right."[120]

The bleeding doughboy cheered feebly, and in this manner, in another incident of near fratricide, was the Lost Battalion finally freed from their five-day ordeal—at approximately 1900 on the evening of October 7.

The almost anticlimactic ending to this most dramatic episode in the AEF's adventure in Europe came for Whittlesey as he talked over the darkening prospects for his unit with McMurtry, while artillery Lieutenant Teichmoeller and Holderman nursed their wounds nearby. A private appeared, saluted lackadaisically, and reported the arrival of Lieutenant Tillman.

Not grasping the significance of the soldier's message, Whittlesey told McMurtry to stay at the CP funk hole, wearily rose to his feet, and collected his runner, Cepeglia, to investigate the report. As the two faded into the rainy eveningtide, McMurtry was suddenly struck by a bolt of comprehension and, unable to contain himself, he lurched, with as much speed as his wounded knee would allow, east toward the road in pursuit of the major. There in the road, so long swept by German machine-gun and sniper fire, McMurtry spotted Whittlesey with a cluster of men around him, including a lieutenant in a uniform that, though soiled from battle, was not a grimy collection of deteriorating rags, as were their own. When McMurtry further comprehended that the object being conveyed by Whittlesey from hand to mouth was a sandwich, McMurtry burst out, "For God's sake. Give me a bite of that!"[121]

The officers were not the only ones sharing the wealth. A 307th private sauntered into the perimeter with tins of willy suspended from his bayonet. Krotoshinsky, completing his round trip back to the Pocket, sought out his old buddy, Art Fein, who was almost as happy to see his comrade as he was the can of corned beef in his hand. "Oh God, Abe. I thought I'd never see you again."

---

*Robert Ferrell points out that, for all his valor, Krotoshinsky and his message was not all that vital, for the 307th was already close to the Pocket, was aware of its coordinates, and would have reached the Lost Battalion that evening regardless.[118]

Major Whittlesey with relieving officer from the 307th Infantry, October 8, 1918. Williams College Archives and Special Collections.

Bearing a wide grin, as well as the willy, Krotoshinsky remarked, "Believe me Artie. I wasn't too sure of it myself."[122]

Tillman posted his Company B of the 1/307th around the perimeter. Holderman's Company K had reported sounds of an enemy withdrawal from the crest of the hill just minutes before the relief, but hard experience had taught the Yanks to beware of German deception. Tillman then dispatched a runner to inform McKinney of the 1/307th that he had reached Whittlesey, and that more rations and—more desperately—medical supplies and personnel were required in the Pocket, post-haste. Realizing that a strong chain of runner posts had to be reestablished to the creek to guard against the many Germans still lurking in the woods south of Whittlesey's position, McKinney sent his intelligence officer, Captain Stone, and a formidable force to man and secure the route. Though the rain was intensifying and the splintered woods were dangerous and dark, Tillman's runner, a Western timberjack, negotiated his way back through the valley.

As they began to move up the slope of the Pocket, the men of the 307th could discern the location of the Lost Battalion by the noxious odors of death and corruption, considerably before they sighted the survivors. Still before sight came sound—of bayonets popping open corned willy tins, of men jabbering in joy at their rescue, of other men moaning in wounded pain, and of one man in particular, who, over and over, loudly pleaded for

Lieutenant Pool to bring him a drink. Lt. Pool, a bullet in his back, was too badly wounded to bring anybody water.

In the rain and the dark, light flooded the Pocket. At first, most of the soldiers of the Lost Battalion were too paralyzed by the possibilities of an end to their ordeal to celebrate this resurrection. They sat and stared at the new arrivals, as if they were phantoms from their shell-shocked dreams. But the taste of food on their tongues from the sixty cans of rations brought in by the 307th was real, and furtive sips of whiskey from the rescuers confirmed life.

Then men began moving about all over, men who had hardly stirred from their miserable holes for days. Smiles were the common currency and even jokes reentered the lexicon. There were still sounds of warfare in the distance, but they were largely Stokes mortar fire and Chauchats chugging away, not *Minenwerfers* or Mausers. Whittlesey would later recall that the sounds of American-wielded weapons was for him like the squeal of the relief force's bagpipes to the besieged of Lucknow during the Sepoy Rebellion.[123] But most of the men of the "Lost," now "found," battalion, gave those echoes of combat little attention. Their focus was on the food being distributed. Captain Stone presented Whittlesey and McMurtry with the special treat pulled from his musette bag of steak sandwiches and chocolate. For these men, for now at least, the end of the world would not be located in the Argonne Forest.

H Company's Lt. Maurice Griffin, the diarist, wrote to his wife of his pride in surviving. "The picture I have of you has a hole in it from a piece of shell. I have four bullet holes in my coat, and my trousers were torn to pieces by a grenade, but I only had my knees cut besides the bullet in my shoulder. The strap to my field glasses was cut by a bullet, my gas mask was cut in half by shrapnel, and my helmet has a dent from a bullet. But they did not get me."[124]

That the Germans did not get Griffin and more of Whittlesey's force than they did seemed all the more remarkable following the discovery on the morning of October 8, by Lt. John Taylor's Company K from the 308th, of evidence of the firepower the Germans had concentrated on the Lost Battalion. On Hill 198, Company K found heaps of empty machine-gun cartridges every ten yards on the now deserted trench line. With a Maxim emplacement every thirty feet, whatever the enemy lacked in manpower at this stage of the battle, they certainly had no deficit in firepower.

Early on the morning of October 8, the Charlevaux road was thick with ambulances ferrying the wounded directly to the rear, or to narrow-gauge railroad flatbed cars, where Knights of Columbus workers soothed them with bites of chocolate. Ration bearers were depositing bags of canned meat, jam and molasses, prunes and tomatoes. The iron rations brought up by McKinney's men the night before had seemed a Roman emperor's repast to the emaciated men of the 308th. Now some of them had to be restrained by arriving Army doctors to keep them from gorging themselves sick on the orgy of food.

Just after dawn, Corporal Baldwin spotted an officer, bearing two stars on his cap, sauntering down the Roman road with a Malacca cane in one hand and a cigarette in the other. He paid no heed to the sporadic German machine-gun fire still coming from La Palette. When the general barked out, "Major!" and then gru·y inquired, "Where's Whittlesey?" the orderly recognized Dreadnaught One (the divisional commander) and informed Alexander, "Down at the foot of the hill, sir."

Baldwin pointed out the major, standing like a soup-line server, personally distributing rations to his hobo heroes. "Shall I get him for you?" Baldwin asked.

Alexander shrugged off the offer. "By no means. I'll go to him."

The general bounced up to the major, an attenuated Atlas in a ripped and ragged uniform, still seeming to bear a planetary weight on his sloping shoulders. Summoning as much warmth as his chill Celtic soul was capable of, Alexander intoned, "How do you do? From now on, you're Lieutenant Colonel Whittlesey."[125]

The newly promoted Whittlesey mumbled his appreciation, but could corral little enthusiasm in this place where so many men of three battalions had died. Trying to bridge the awkward silence that followed, Alexander pointed his cane at the surrounding leafy canopy, much ravaged but far from stripped away by a week's worth of exploding ordnance, and commented, "Well, I can see why the airplanes couldn't find this place."

Whittlesey did not respond, but runner Cepeglia, no more intimidated by a general's stars than by German machine-gun fire, popped off with, "General, the artillery certainly found it."

The division commander, already cutting and editing the story of the Lost Battalion to suit his purposes, did not let that indictment go unchallenged. "Oh no, that was French artillery," he insisted.[126]

The battle just ended was, indeed, being already refought in the mind of General Alexander and others up the chain of command, and, most certainly, in the mind and heart of the freshly minted Lieutenant Colonel Whittlesey. Alexander would soon be insisting to the press that they had overcooked the whole story, that: "This command was neither 'lost' nor 'rescued'. Major Whittlesey and his command held the position to which they had proceeded under my order and were found by one, when I visited them on the early morning of October 8, an organized command, in good order, and in excellent spirits."[127]

Below the din of the popular press, breathlessly engaged in their work of lionization and legend-making, other officers, at division HQ and corps HQ, were already whispering opinions that questioned Whittlesey's decisions—choices which might have brought about an unnecessary ordeal and unjustified sacrifices. And perhaps the loudest whispers of doubt clamored in the mind of the Lost Battalion commander himself.

For most of the survivors of the siege, however, a rehashing of their five days in hell was beyond their benumbed minds and spirits. As one observer recalled, the men of the 1st and 2nd Battalions of the 308th, Holderman's Company K of the 307th, and the 306th Machine-Gun Battalion, those still alive and those not hauled away in ambulances, looked, "like figures in some immemorial pagent of suffering," as they formed up at 1500 on the afternoon of October 8 to march out of the ravine.[128]

Of the 554 men who had entered the Pocket on the night of October 2 or had reinforced the perimeter on October 3 (K/3/307th), 194 assembled in a ragged formation behind Whittlesey and McMurtry to walk out. One hundred and seven of Whittlesey's men had died in the Pocket, or in trying to get into or out of the Pocket. Another sixty-three were missing in action, either captured or lying dead in some unnoticed corner of the hellish woods. One hundred and ninety doughboys were wounded too badly or were too sick to walk out of the position. Of twenty officers in the composite battalion, four had died and fourteen had suffered wounds. The unit carried just one still functioning machine gun out of the perimeter, out of the nine carried in (seven from D/306th and two from C/306th).

4. The Battalion

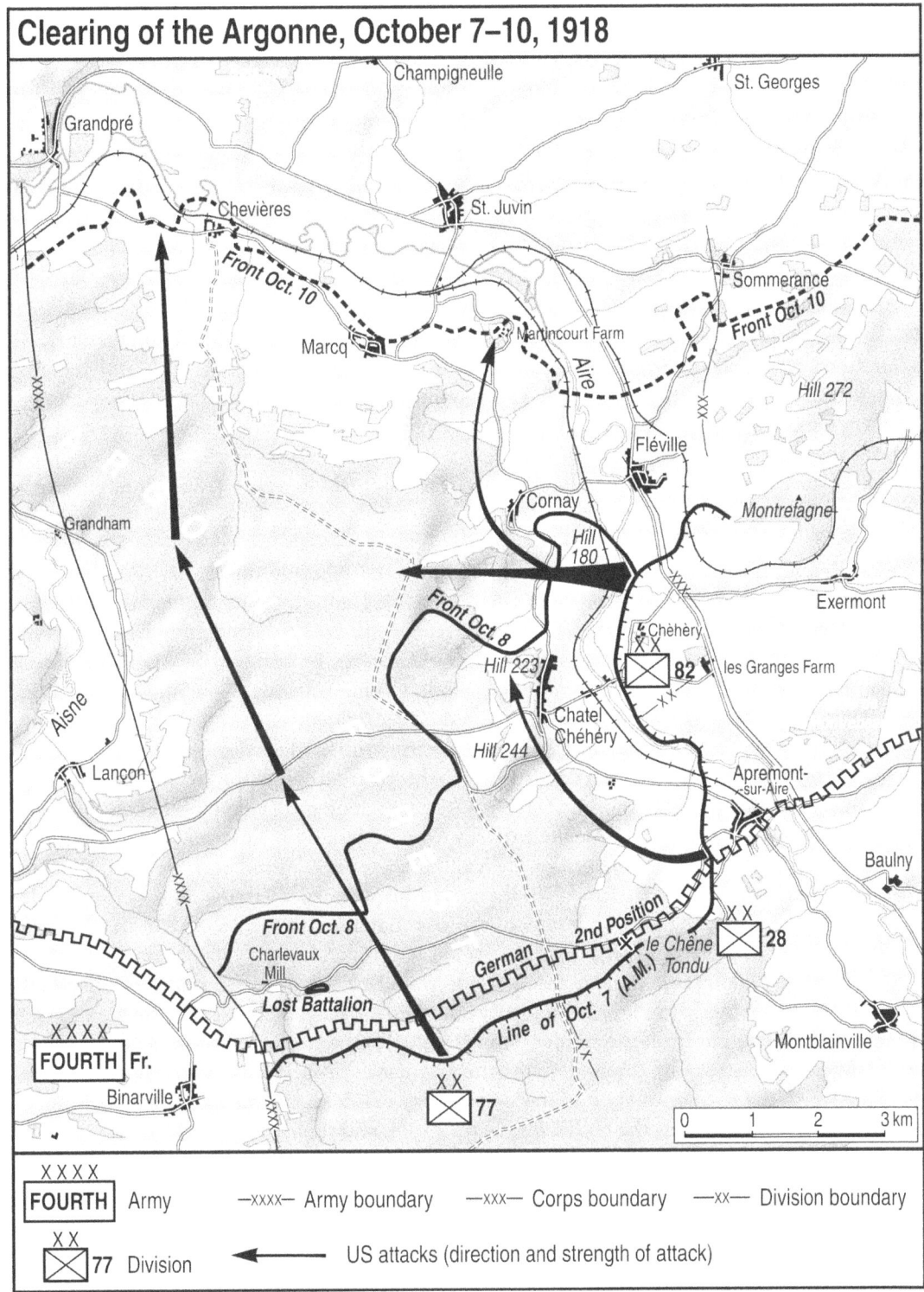

Except for the occasional scavenged scrap, the famished survivors of the Lost Battalion had gone for 104 hours with no food whatsoever—from noon on October 3 to 2000 on October 7.*

Tramping across Charlevaux Valley to the mouth of the ravine, the toilworn and wartorn soldiers of the Lost Battalion, wizened and shivering in the raw wind, ignored the few spent rounds zinging over their heads from the enemy hold-outs on La Palette. The snapping of those machine-gun bullets above their helmets was as inconsequential to them as the buzzing of bees. Their facial expressions spoke volumes. A soldier who witnessed the solemn parade remembered, "When I looked into those eyes, there was nothing I could say to them. It made your heart lump up into your throat just to look at them. Their faces told the whole story of their fight."[130]

Incredibly, some of those men who had entered this cathedral of blood on October 2 and had come out whole volunteered to reenter the line after the briefest of rests, rejoining the division as it pursued Wellmann's withdrawing corps toward Grandpré. Among them was Sgt. James Carroll of K/3/307th. Though most of the dauntless volunteers found that their exhausted bodies could not keep up with their stalwart spirits and had to drop out of the pursuit, Carroll hung in until the 77th reached Grandpré. "We skinny guys are the tough ones," he later explained.[131]

Behind this last march of the Lost Battalion, the relieving units were gathering up the dead and clearing the debris from the pockmarked hillside. Among the men policing the Pocket was Lt. Paul Knight. Though his tiny force had tried mightily to reach the Pocket on the night of October 3, Knight would forever be haunted by his inability to complete the link. "We didn't do our job—didn't come up with them," he would later lament.[132]

On the afternoon of October 8, he was scouring the battlefield to ensure that all the living had marched out or been carried out of the position. Near the stream, Knight discerned a whispered plea, "Take me. Take me." There, among the fallen in khaki heaps, lay Private Lionel Bendheim, a Yorkville native, whose leg had been smashed by the "friendly fire" of the October 4 artillery barrage. He had somehow been missed by the medics. Knight rounded up a stretcher party, and Bendheim and his crushed, festering limb were carried out of the position, the last living man of the Lost Battalion to leave the Pocket.

For the fallen, their tour in the Argonne would be extended for some considerable time. Men from the 53rd Pioneer Infantry would harvest the dead, collecting them not just from the Pocket, but from the runner posts as well. The bodies of the runners were found in inexplicable stacks of three (perhaps the Germans' cultural obsession with neatness extended to the corpses of their enemy), their rifles beside them and their shoes expropriated. They were added to the bodies beside the brook and their dog tags removed. One ID disc from each pair would be sent home, along with other personal items, to the families

---

*Just as there were varying counts of the men trapped in the Pocket (or posted in the runner chains), ranging from a 77th Division April 1919 estimate of just 419 to Holderman's calculation of 700, so too were there differences in casualty estimates. General Drum wrote that there were 438 survivors—128 from 1/308th, 256 from 2/308th, 33 from K/3/307th, and 21 from the 306th Machine-Gun Battalion. A hospital list carried the names of 202 members of those units carried out of the Pocket with wounds, sickness or exhaustion. A 1919 estimate counts only sixty-nine men killed or missing, but a Lost Battalion roster compiled by Robert Ferrell lists ninety killed, eight missing and 164 wounded.[129]

of the individual soldiers. The other was affixed to a crude wooden cross erected at the head of a single wide and deep trench in Charlevaux Valley, bearing the remains of the men who did not march out of the valley with their comrades.

The mass grave would later be submerged by the damming of the creek further downstream, but by then the fallen of the Lost Battalion had passed on to another stage of their journey. The bodies had been exhumed to complete the process of identification as much as possible. Then, according to the wishes of their families, the dead of the Lost Battalion were either shipped home to family plots, or re-interred with over 14,000 of their fellow doughboys in the American cemetery at Romagne-sous-Montfaucon.

5

The Offensive II

The siege of the Lost Battalion was history, but the legend was just in its infancy. The greater battle, the Battle of the Meuse-Argonne, of which the stand on Charlevaux Brook had been just a small-tent sideshow, went on in full roar and savage fury. On the day that the remnant of Whittlesey's Spartan band marched away from that Argonne creek, the Meuse-Argonne campaign was just thirteen days old. It would rage on for thirty-four more days, almost five weeks.

The great contest was in full swing again on October 8. The nagging complication of the Lost Battalion removed, Alexander continued to drive his men hard as they approached Grandpré, just above the north edge of the Argonne. His 77th Division was a weary outfit, but its commander permitted no straggling and insisted on an unyielding advance.

On the front of the 82nd—the division that had been so instrumental, along with the 1st, in breaking the Boche blockade of Whittlesey's command—another feat of martial renown, destined (due mainly to Hollywood) to become even more legendary and iconic in American military history than that of the Lost Battalion, took place the very day that Whittlesey's and McMurtry's men walked out of the Argonne and into myth.

It is hardly a surprise that the two most remembered and celebrated events of the American participation in the Great War took place within the span of and upon the ground of the AEF's greatest battle of the conflict. It is rather startling, however, to comprehend, that—on a battlefield nearly twenty miles in length and, ultimately, nearly as many miles in depth, and in the course of a campaign of forty-seven days in duration—the collective courage of the Lost Battalion and the singular heroism of Sergeant York were displayed under history's light within one day and little more than a mile of each other.

Near Hill 223, on the east edge of the Argonne on the foggy morning of October 8, occurred what Marshal Foch described as, "The greatest thing accomplished by any private soldier of all the armies of Europe."[1] The architect of this "greatest thing," (then) Corporal Alvin York, was a rangy, raw-boned, red-haired Appalachian from Pall Mall in the Cumberland Mountains of east Tennessee. Born in a one-room log cabin in 1887, York had been a corn-whiskey-swigging hellraiser in his youth, a devout Christian in his maturity, and always a crack shot with the traditional cap-and-ball, black powder-burning long rifles carried by the mountain boys of the region since the days of Daniel Boone. The man who would become one of the most prolific killers of the Germans had to overcome a crisis of his Christian conscience about heeding his draft call in the summer of 1917 and possibly breaking the sixth commandment. Assigned to Company G, 2/328th Infantry of the 82nd Division, York landed in France in May 1918. The 82nd had served in quiet sectors until St. Mihiel,

Sgt. Alvin C. York on the slope of the hill near Cornay in the Argonne where he won the Medal of Honor. U.S. Army Military History Institute.

where York first went over the top on September 12, 1918. On October 7, York's battalion entered the Battle of the Meuse-Argonne, deploying into the line on Hill 223 against units of the 2nd Württemberg Landwehr Division.

After a sodden night spent in a drainage ditch, the shivering, groggy-eyed men of the 328th began their movement northwest down the reverse slope of 223 into the fog-shrouded valley to the west. Their objective, one mile away, was the Decauville railroad, a north-south field railroad that served as the logistical lifeline for the enemy forces in the forest. The ridges and treeline of the Argonne lay about 600 yards to their front. From that swarm of vegetation and elevation came a sudden storm of tripod-mounted Maxim 08 and bipod-mounted Maxim 08/15 machine-gun fire, mowing down Americans who stood frozen in shock at the abrupt and awful violence, and pinning the rest to the ground. Unsupported by a planned artillery barrage that never materialized, the regiment was stalled, unable to go forward or backward under the methodical raking of the thirty or more German machine guns. Seeing that the only solution was a flanking maneuver to the south (and left), where the woods projected out and curved around the south edge of the valley, a platoon sergeant in Company G organized a patrol of seventeen soldiers from three squads—led by Sergeant Bernard Early and including Corporal York—to work their way around and behind the Boche gunners and silence them.

Dashing from stump to bush in the thick vegetation, the patrol made it behind the German positions. Bursting through the undergrowth, across a stream, and into an open ravine, Early's patrol surprised a German major, the commander of the machine-gun battalion facing the 328th, and at least twenty members of his HQ staff. The Germans, mostly runners and stretcher bearers, put up little resistance before raising their hands and shouting "Kamerad!" As Early ordered the POWs rounded up, the German machine-gun teams on the hill above their battalion CP turned their guns around toward the ravine and opened fire from just thirty yards away. Sergeant Early went down, shredded with six wounds; two other Americans were wounded, and six were killed in that first volley. The unwounded Yanks flattened themselves to the ground, with the exception of Corporal York—who now commenced his turkey shoot.

Armed with the model 1917 Enfield (not the 1903 Springfield in the common Sergeant York mythology), the pious, eagle-eyed mountaineer took deadly aim at the fifty-some Germans on the semi-circular hill above. Realizing that most of the German fire was whizzing over his head—because the enemy gunners could not depress their barrels enough without exposing themselves—York fired clip after clip at the Boche helmets, first from the kneeling position, then from a standing pose. Finally, a German lieutenant and five soldiers sprang from a trench twenty-five yards away with bayonets fixed. York drew his 1911 .45 caliber pistol and shot down all six of the attackers, hitting the last man first and the first man last—in accordance to his turkey hunting philosophy of, "we don't want the front ones to know that we're getting the back ones."[2]

This demonstration of steel-nerved sharpshooting was enough for the Germans to call it quits. The major called out to his men to surrender. Collecting the American survivors—seven doughboys from the patrol were dead—and his POWs, York led his column back the way they had come, with the corporal prodding the German major into demanding the surrender of other enemy machine-gun nests as they marched back to American lines. Twenty-eight Germans had been killed by the patrol, most of them by York, but undoubtedly several accounted for by other members of the unit (Sergeant Early and a corporal would be awarded the DSC for their valor in the ravine). The POWs numbered 132. Though the legend claims thirty-five machine guns captured, the official records (according to Lieutenant Colonel Taylor Beattie) mentioned no Boche machine guns brought back in by the patrol.[3]

York's exploit broke the deadlock on Hill 223 and sent a jolt of panic through the German lines. Convinced that their flank had been rolled up, the demoralized enemy pulled out of his positions as 82nd Division soldiers swarmed into the forest to capture the Decauville railroad. The corporal immediately became a sergeant, and was subsequently pinned with the DSC, the French Croix de Guerre and, on April 18, 1919, the Medal of Honor. When asked by 82nd Division commander General Duncan how he had plinked so many of the enemy, Alvin York explained, "General, I would hate to think I missed any of them shots; they were all at pretty close range—fifty or sixty yards. It weren't no trouble nohow for me to hit them big army targets. They were so much bigger than turkeys' heads."

York was surprised, however, at the generally dismal aim of his comrades. "They missed everything but the sky."[4]

But later, when interviewed by Brig. General Julian Lindsey, the Tennessee marksman consigned his success to, "A higher power than man power guided me and told me what to do."[5]

York was a much different man from Whittlesey in background, social class and education, but was very similar in backbone and stoic devotion to duty. They were also alike in their disdain for the spotlight and their discomfort for the encompassing celebrityhood that enveloped them after their heroic days in the Argonne. But the sergeant, unlike the major, was eventually able to come to terms with the cult of hero-worshiping that at times seemed more terrifying than German Maxims, and was even able to use it in later years for beneficial purposes. Few doubts and fewer ghosts from that dark wet forest haunted York. Whittlesey was overwhelmed by them and, ultimately, defeated by them.

Of course, nine out of ten Americans who register an awareness of Sergeant York conjure up a mental picture of Gary Cooper above the title, thus both immortalizing (as only Hollywood can do) and distorting the image of the man. Major Whittlesey, as great a hero as Sergeant York in almost everyone's eyes but his own, never received a cinematic canonization, never was stamped by the Hollywood mint into iconic coin. Less than a quarter of a century after the fact, Gary Cooper, in a motion picture classic, inherited and inhabited the legend, if not the life, of Alvin York. More than three-fourths of a century beyond the reality, Rick Schroeder pretended to be Charles Whittlesey in a made-for-television movie, and few in its small audience pretended to care. When York died on September 2, 1964, he was a much venerated, even idolized man, with statues built and schools constructed to honor him. He was seventy-six when he died, having survived forty-five years as a legend. On the day of his death, York was more than twice as old as Whittlesey was when he ended the intolerable burden of his own fame.

The monster that was the Meuse-Argonne had, in the meantime, stomped on along its ravening way, indifferent to these moments of human drama that could not distract the beast from its charnelhouse intensity. The monster was not only chewing up and spitting out American lives at an unprecedented rate, it was also threatening to consume the career and reputation of John J. Pershing, who had unleashed this hobgoblin of Mars and had tried to ride it to victory.

At the height of the battle and the depth of his frustration, Black Jack drove everyone around him hard and himself hardest of all. Pershing demanded unceasing effort by all his subordinate commanders, and brooked no excuse for any failure to meet his expectations. He was ruthless in replacing any leader who could not maintain his proclaimed pace of progress toward the finish line. Liddel Hart pointed out: "Commanders of all grades fell beneath Pershing's sickle almost as fast as their men beneath the scythe of the German machine guns"[6]

Pershing's relentlessness pushed him near the brink, over which he had already shoved so many of his subordinates. Pershing testified that the first half of October placed "the heaviest strain on the army and me." A HQ staff officer recalled, "The strain was too great; this last battle overburdened him."[7]

While riding in his command "Locomobile" limousine (with double rear wheels and four-star license plates) one day in early October, the AEF commander suddenly buried his stricken face in his hands and sobbed to his wife—killed more than three years earlier in the Presidio fire—"Frankie, Frankie ... my God, sometimes I don't know how I can go on."[8]

But the steel in his soul and the sweetness in his French mistress's embraces helped him navigate this darkest passage in his voyage into history. In the valley of despair, Pershing looked to the highest hill, telling 90th Division commander Maj. General Henry T. Allen, "Things are going badly ... but, by God! Allen, I was never so much in earnest in my life. We are going to get through."[9]

However, even John J. Pershing, this avatar of the attack, began, by the third or fourth day of the renewed offensive, to see the futility of pressing on with unrelenting head-on mass assaults that were piling up corpses for little gain. For all the valor of the individual American soldier, the straight-up frontal charge into a maelstrom of artillery, mortar and automatic weapons fire from heavily fortified defensive positions was not working. As a German assessment of the Meuse-Argonne Offensive observed: "The American infantry is very unskillful in the attack. It attacks in thick columns, in numerous waves echeloned in depth, preceded by tanks. This sort of attack offers excellent objects for the fire of our artillery, infantry and machine guns."[10]

AEF casualties on the Meuse-Argonne front, September 26–October 6, were estimated at 75,000 (although official records put losses there, September 26–October 20, at 54,158). In the first week of October (officially, September 29–October 5), American battle deaths on the Western Front totaled 6,589, the highest weekly toll of the war for the United States. Most of those deaths occurred along the twenty-some miles from the Meuse Heights through the Argonne Forest. In the week of October 6–13, another 6,019 Americans were killed in combat in France and Belgium, the war's second deadliest seven-day compilation. And in the following reporting period—October 14–21—another 5,019 battle deaths were recorded, the third highest sacrifice for the U.S. in a single week. All told, more than 21,000 American servicemen died in battle in October 1918, the highest thirty-day toll in our nation's history. (World War II's record month was March 1945, when 20,325 Americans died in combat.)

This ostentatious sacrifice of lives for so relatively little gain cried out for a change both in tactics and strategy. Pershing's original formula for success had failed; mass could not overcome energy—a moving wall of massed troops could not penetrate the enemy's energy field of colossal firepower. Pershing had gambled on the spirit and momentum of his fresh, untried, but enthusiastic troops, closing with and prevailing over the vastly outnumbered defenders. But a hellish terrain and an even more diabolical design of long-range machine gun, mortar, aerial and, particularly, artillery fire, had kept the relatively few German infantrymen, for the most part, safely distanced from the tips of the American bayonets.

If the high command was having trouble adjusting their strategic conceptions, at least at the tactical level—down on the ground, away from HQ's maps and sandbox models, where men actually fought and died—junior officers and noncoms were learning lessons. American infantrymen were beginning to understand the defense-in-depth philosophy of the enemy, and to grasp the fact that almost all German positions were mutually supported. Doughboy units were employing more fire-and-maneuver tactics, particularly in ravines and defiles, to silence enemy dugouts. The Yanks were learning that grenades tossed into machine-gun nest apertures was the most effective way to knock out the emplacements.

They were also getting used to the enemy's tricks and the enemy's diehard determination. The attackers were encountering booby traps, wired to houses that offered the enticement of shelter and even attached to dead bodies. Machine-gun nests that were silent and appeared to be knocked out of action were checked out more thoroughly, after several incidents of "dead" Boches turning a "resurrected" fire onto the rear of American columns after they had passed by. The Yanks had also encountered many automatic weapons emplacements forward of the main German lines manned by "sacrifice" gunners, sometimes reportedly chained to their machine guns (although, in several cases, this turned out to be a misperception of dead gunners who had become entangled in the chain used to keep the water-cooled tank from becoming lost when the gun was shifted).

If innovative methods to deal with the enemy's infantry defenses were being discovered—mostly by a trial-and-error process that exacted a heavy human cost—solving the deadly dilemma posed by the Germans' long-range artillery still eluded the U.S. First Army. The flank attack and breakthrough by the 28th and 82nd Divisions on October 7–8 had—besides liberating the Lost Battalion—forced a withdrawal by the Boche big guns from the Argonne ridges. But the heavy howitzers on the heights east of the Meuse still plagued the American assault columns and made it all but impossible for V and III Corps to conquer the Cunel-Romagne heights, which were the key to the Kriemhilde Stellung, west of the river.

According to Pershing's memoirs, the original operational plan for the offensive had included an infantry attack on the Meuse Heights. This, however, had been vetoed in favor of the less ambitious option of employing the 33rd and 80th Divisions of the III Corps to remain west of the Meuse to protect the First Army's eastern flank, and substituting heavy counter-battery fire at the enemy emplacements on the heights in place of infantry assault. Pershing, by the end of October's first week, recognized the utter failure of this strategy, and finally ordered a major infantry attack on the Meuse Heights. Undertaking the mission was the French XVII Corps, made up of—from the east bank of the Meuse on farther east—the French 18th and 26th Divisions, plus six Senegalese battalions from the 10th Colonial Infantry Division. Supporting the French on their river flank was the 58th Brigade of the 29th Blue and Gray Division—a Guard unit from Delaware, Maryland, New Jersey, Virginia and the District of Columbia. Three battalions from the U.S. 33rd Division, on the west bank, would, at the same time, cross the Meuse on two pontoon footbridges—erected by engineers the night before—to strike the defenders of the heights on their flank.

The early morning attack on October 8 was at first successful. The town of Consenvoye was seized, and the Allies stormed up the slopes of Richene Hill, capturing over 3,000 POWs. German resistance quickly hardened, however. The German command knew that to lose the heights was to lose the battle. Reinforcing the Austrian and Württemberg defenders with another two divisions, the Germans counterattacked on October 9. Though the 33rd sent six more battalions across the river and advanced a total of five kilometers in the first two days of the attack, they and the other Allied units could not push the Germans and their fiendish firepower off the Borne de Cornouiller (or Corned Willy Hill, in the doughboys' dialect), the highest ground on the Consenvoye Heights.

To retain the vital Meuse Heights, the Germans made promiscuous use of their artillery stockpiles, hammering the French and American troops in this eastward extension of the Battle of the Meuse-Argonne with falling skies of high explosive and gas shells. The 33rd Division endured the worst gas shellings of any American division during the war as it fought for the heights. Over 2,000 men of the 33rd suffered death or disability from the poison clouds detonated within their ranks. By the time Pershing pulled the 33rd from the line on October 21, the clothes of the survivors were rotting off their backs and the flesh was peeling from their feet.

Though the 113th and 114th Regiments of the 29th took the Bois de Ormont on October 12 at a cost of 118 killed and 812 wounded, they were then deluged by German HE and mustard gas shells for thirty-four hours, with the 114th alone taking 706 gas casualties. The agony was unrelenting. The gas soaked into the wet ground on one day, then rose to contaminate and kill a second time the next day, as the rising sun warmed the ground to rerelease the poison. In three weeks east of the Meuse, the 29th would suffer 4,965 casualties, until relieved by the 79th Division on October 30.

The 4th Division, on the left of the 33rd, was also heavily gassed as it struggled forward at a rate of 500 yards a day. The analogy was later made that the Ivy Division soldiers were, in those dire days, as used to donning their masks as were catchers readying for opposing batters to come to the plate.

All this sacrifice was largely in vain. Though the press of the Allied attacks east of the Meuse and along the western bank had pushed the enemy back as much as four miles, and had lessened the volume of flanking fire hitting the U.S. III and V Corps as they tackled the Kriemhilde Stellung, the German guns never stopped firing, and the enemy clung to those artillery emplacements until the final week of the war.

The horrible punishment taken by the 29th and 33rd Divisions on the Meuse Heights did pay off to a certain extent in diminishing the observed fire from German artillery east of the river, thus making the task of the rest of III Corps and of V Corps easier. V Corps barreled into the Bois de Romagne on October 9 and, as the day waned, it had seized a swath of the woods and the corps' 91st Division was clawing its way up Hill 255. To the right, III Corps' 80th and 4th Divisions advanced against the usual stubborn German opposition on October 10. The Bois de Romagne was essentially secured that day, but by nightfall the momentum of the attack had sputtered out. Though the 4th was able to slash out a salient in the Bois de Forêt on October 11, the Meuse-Argonne's second phase had shot its bolt, and another pause was required for the First Army to once again rehabilitate.

As in the offensive's first week, some American units were so used up in this cavalcade of combat that they were knocked out of the ring. The 181st Brigade of the 91st had been bled dry in successful assaults on Hill 255 and unsuccessful attacks on Côte Dame Marie. It was pulled from the line on October 11. The 80th Division, having taken 2,767 casualties, October 4–12, had to be relieved by the 5th Division. Most sorely hurt of all the American divisions was the 1st—whose success on the Argonne flank had probably saved Pershing's career. It was king of the mountain on Hill 272 and had reached the first barbed strands of the Kriemhilde line. But "Pershing's Best" had absorbed 8,231 casualties, October 1–12—including about 1,800 battle deaths—the heaviest losses of any U.S. division in the Meuse-Argonne campaign, and was beginning to show the stress. Summerall's supermen, worn down now to human dimensions in this vale of vipers, were relieved by the 42nd Rainbow Division on the night of October 11.

It was not only the men of the front-line divisions that needed rest and refitting. The minds and emotions of the commanders required at least a few days free from the oppressive press of events to rejuvenate their spirits and restructure their strategy. Division and corps commanders, as well as the First Army commander, were learning some hard lessons in tackling the honeycomb of defenses on the Meuse-Argonne front. The exorbitant price for that harshly acquired wisdom was paid for in the currency of the blood of their privates and corporals. There was no lack of fire-eaters and head-butters, such as Alexander and Summerall at the division level, Bullard at corps altitude, and J.J. Pershing himself at the top—commanders who were determined that nothing would stop them in their once-more-into-the-breach ardor. Tactically innovative and strategically adept minds like that of Hunter Liggett—the most nimble in brain power and the most ponderous in physicality of all the U.S. commanders—were rare in an army of over-zealous under-achievers. But even the most arrogantly mule-headed of the zealots were beginning to realize what British and French commanders had understood for years. That without new tactics, new weapons, and new ideas, the breaking of the formidable enemy, particularly when ensconced in strong defensive positions, was a nearly impossible challenge. Elan alone, whether Gallic or Yankee, whether in the Battles of the Frontiers in 1914 or in the Battle of the Meuse-Argonne in 1918, was not the answer.

Renovation and restoration were prerequisites to any hope for further or expanded success by the U.S. First Army. Very little was going according to plan; very few units were functioning according to expectations. The Meuse-Argonne Offensive had been designed to be a terrible swift sword, forged of Damascus steel, wielded to slash and stab until the enemy died a quick death of a thousand cuts. But the campaign had turned out to be a rough cudgel, a knobby primitive club, swung exhaustively in a battle of attrition, that pounded and pummeled against an enemy seemingly able to absorb the most punishing blows.

By mid–October, the U.S. First Army was short of everything—men, weapons, equipment and hope. Horses were dying, trucks were breaking down, and the supply system was foundering. With infantry and machine-gun units a priority since spring 1918, little space remained aboard the trans-Atlantic transports for horses and motor vehicles. Pershing unsuccessfully pleaded with Foch for 25,000 French horses because the AEF was short 43 percent of the 100,000 horses and mules needed. The motor transport section had less than one-fifth of the equipment it required. When trucks and other mechanical equipment gave out there was nothing to replace them with and no spare parts to repair them. Supplies were pyramiding at ports and railroad sidings with no way to transport them to the front. At least two divisions were literally unable to move into the line in late September for lack of transport. Artillery ammunition was also in short supply. Division artillery was even ordered to restrict its shell expenditure at critical moments in the battle.

The troops themselves in the front-line divisions were miserable paupers in mud-heavy, cootie-ridden khaki. The weather was turning colder and the rain seemed unceasing. They existed in a smashed landscape, fraught with filth and awash in a sewer stench. The air they tried to breathe was a malign atmosphere of smoke, gas and shrapnel.

Besides the crippling combat casualties, sickness was further thinning the ranks. Potable water rarely reached the front lines and thirsty troopers filled their canteens from streams and shell holes polluted with the decaying flesh of men and horses. Dysentery and diarrhea were rampant and the cheese ration that helped staunch the flow was, as with all supplies, inadequate. Some of the dysentery was caused by the bread rations, often arriving with a crust of mold and a soggy center. Stories were frequent of railroad cars filled with bread shoveled out onto the dirt at forage dumps and left overnight under filthy tarps.

Worse than dysentery was the Spanish flu, conducting its early campaigns in a global catastrophe that would kill more of mankind than did the Great War—up to twenty-one million in eighteen months, including nearly 600,000 Americans (five times the Great War toll). Still outfitted in summer uniforms, with few blankets and overcoats, the hungry, exhausted men of the AEF were easy prey to the infectious predator. In September, 11,910 cases of the flu were recorded in the AEF; in October the number tripled to 37,904 American casualties inflicted by virus instead of violence. If the war had continued past November 11, 1918, the flu might have accomplished what the Imperial German Army could not—halting the grinding, bloody, but inexorable American advance.

The flu plague was just as out of control at stateside bases. At one point, President Wilson was ready to plug the replacement flow to Europe altogether, rather than continue exporting the conquering microbe. The transport *Leviathan* was typical of many trans-Atlantic plague ships in autumn 1918. On one crossing alone, the vessel consigned to the sea each day fifty-five men who had fallen victim to the flu.

In the end, however, Wilson reconciled himself to the terrible toll taken by the flu on the troopships. The voracious appetite of the Meuse-Argonne demanded a constant flow of reinforcements and a hardening of every heart.

Further sapping the strength of the U.S. First Army was a second epidemic. Behind the front-line divisions was a second army of stragglers, approaching 100,000 in number. Command and control was breaking down as more and more officers and NCOs became casualties. Most of the wayward men were simply lost, separated from their units by the fortunes of war. A good number had been temporarily tasked to rearward duties—such as to stretcher detail to carry the wounded to the rear—and, with the fluid situation on the front, had been subsequently unable to relocate their units in the confusing terrain and demoralizing wreckage of the 115-square-mile battlefield. Large numbers of the unattached men were shell-shocked or starving. But a good proportion of them were outright deserters (although only 4,316 American servicemen were ever court-martialed for desertion, and just 3,362 were convicted). The temptation to flee from this anteroom to hell was powerful and, for many, irresistible. The woods, the ravines, the thousands of abandoned dugouts, bunkers and foxholes offered a plethora of places to hide. The presence of YMCA canteens brought close to the front, with their offerings of coffee, cigarettes and sandwiches, sometimes provided these desperate men with just enough sustenance to maintain their unauthorized absences from the trenches.

The drain of desertion, disease and battle created a manpower crisis for the AEF. Only 45,000 replacements were available for the combat divisions in October, and those divisions were in the hole by a total of 80,000 personnel. GHQ had to demobilize seven divisions in training or in transit to provide replacements for the divisions already under the gun. Company strengths were reduced from an authorized 250 to 175, but by mid-month few could even tally that number on their morning reports. Chief of staff Hugh Drum estimated combat effectives in the 3rd, 5th and 82nd Divisions at less than 5,000 each.

Pershing authorized strict, even Draconian, measures to deal with these uniformed refugees. MPs and special units (including French colonial troops) patrolled the rear areas, rounding up the strays. Punishment usually consisted of returning the wanderers directly to the front, often with placards hung from their necks branding them as "Stragglers from the Front Line." Pershing told his corps and division commanders that officers must take summary action against deserters, "even to the point of shooting men down who are caught in such disgraceful conduct."[11]

Pershing would have driven his officers and men with a whip hand even if everything had been going strictly according to plan. It was in his genes. But adding to Black Jack's impatience and frustrations was his own case of the flu, nagging and constant dental problems, and an even more debilitating case of Allied—particularly French—criticism. The chorus of Gallic complaints had revved up during the offensive's first phase and had hardly ever diminished. Foch and Clemenceau were urging Wilson to replace Pershing with General Tasker Bliss. Pétain was among the harshest critics of the American performance. Rather than credit the skill and ferocity of the German defenders for the inability of the U.S. First Army to punch through to the Kriemhilde Stellung, he blamed the failure on "the problems which the American general staff had experienced in transporting and supplying their troops."[12] Pétain's proposed solution was to have French staff officers take over the role of managing U.S. divisions. He also suggested that the unwieldy First Army be disbanded, and that American command be limited to division or, at most, corps level. Pétain also petitioned for more U.S. divisions to be distributed "among the French armies," claiming that the American logistical staff could not master the job of supplying all the Yankee divisions. Ten of the twenty-nine combat-ready American divisions were already parceled out among Allied armies under French or British command.

Foch was hardly more complementary. He suggested that the French Second Army take over Liggett's I Corps in operations both west and east of the Argonne, and proposed limiting Pershing's responsibility solely to the Meuse. Clemenceau wanted Pershing relieved of his command entirely. Pershing, of course, had fought tooth and nail to retain his position at the head of the AEF and, in the end, Foch had agreed to leave First Army's command structure intact provided "your attacks start without delay and that, once begun, they are continued without any interruptions such as those which have just arisen."[13]

Bullied into another round of improperly prepared attacks, Pershing's second round of offensive thrusts had also stalled out, endangering Foch's and Haig's grand strategy of remorseless coordinated attacks from the Channel to the Meuse which were to finally crack the German line. The AEF commander retained the support of Secretary of War Newton Baker, who stated: "It will be a long time before any American commander would be removed by any European premier."[14] But the French continued their drumbeat of disapprobation.

Pétain's staff officers, for example, postulated the theory that the initial American failure was due to employing too many assault divisions in the first attack. Their French commanders, they claimed, facing similar terrain and similar defenses, would have used only half as many troops. The close-packed infantry on the front lines was impossible to supply, and the gargantuan traffic jams were the result. They also faulted the Americans for slack liaison and communication between units, insufficient reconnaissance, and, as always, sloppy staff work.

On October 13, Foch and Pershing conferred at French headquarters at Bombon. The French marshal carped about the American inability to maintain the same offensive pace as the other Allied armies. When Pershing blamed the terrain for the slow U.S. progress, Foch demurred and said, "I judge only by the results."[15] Foch further pointed out that Pershing had chosen the field of battle for the American army and was consequently responsible for the results.

Unlike Clemenceau, however, who wanted Pershing's head on a platter, Foch did concede that the difficulties faced by the inexperienced Americans were great, and was willing to work with the U.S. high command to find a way out of the impasse. One path leading at least part of the way out, and long since obvious to most of Pershing's staff, required a reorganization of the First Army. With Foch's endorsement, Pershing stepped aside from his direct combat command of the First Army and, effective October 12, created a U.S. Second Army.

The First Army had grown both unwieldy and overextended. Its units were deployed over eighty-three miles of front from Port-sur-Seille, east of the Moselle River, to the Argonne. Its strength had reached 1,031,000 soldiers, including 135,000 French troops. The new Second Army was to take over thirty-four miles of front from Fresnes-en-Woevre, east of the Meuse, to Port-sur-Seille. The sector would witness little action until the war's final week. General Bullard was named commander of the new army, which, by October 31, numbered 176,000 men in three corps, with five divisions in total.

Given command of the First Army, effective October 16—in Pershing's place (who now ascended to army group commander, as well as overall AEF chief)—was General Liggett, generally recognized as the best of the corps commanders. Replacing Liggett at I Corps was Maj. General Joseph Dickman and taking Bullard's slot at III Corps was Maj. General John

Hines. Before October ended, V Corps command would also change hands. Pershing, crowning heads and lopping them off with wild abandon to find the right winning combination, decided that George Cameron lacked the win-at-all costs drive necessary to prevail and replaced him with the 1st Division's hard-charging Charles Summerall. Pershing, who had already in the campaign's first week relieved four brigade commanders of their duties, also cashiered three division commanders after the mid-October attacks had misfired.

If Pershing was unhesitant about changing lead horses in the middle of the operational stream, he did often muster the perspicacity to recognize military skill when he saw it. He demonstrated that acute judgment when he picked Liggett as First Army commander. Liget, at first glance, did not present a Caesarian image of a natural-born leader of warriors. A self-effacing man, little skilled in the manipulative charms and gamesmanship required for self-promotion, Liggett, at sixty-one, was, in theory, too old and too fat—forty pounds overweight—to be the man on horseback best suited for such exalted command. He did not blend well with Pershing's "Chaumont crowd," but he had excelled at every step up the military ladder.

Secretary of the Navy Josephus Daniels judged Liggett "one of the ablest, broadest and wisest military men I have ever talked to."[16] But Liggett was not just a man of intellect and profound understanding of the art of war. He was also a man of action, a fighting general who combined a strategic vision with a finely honed tactical sense that enabled him to adjust, stay flexible, and stay patient. Liggett had demonstrated a strong measure of that sense and sensitivity when he insisted on delaying his transition to army commander, until he could supervise and see through—at his original corps level command—Pershing's next round of frontal attacks planned for October 14. Liggett, in truth, held out little hope for yet another headlong lunge at the German line, but he wanted his old corps as prepared as possible for it before he moved upstairs.

It was not, however, only the American high command that was beset with doubt and confusion about the right next step to take on the Meuse-Argonne front. Had the U.S. Army staff been aware of the discouragement a·icting the very top of the enemy command structure, some of the rain clouds that seemed to permanently canopy the Argonne might have parted.

Many German generals, in the face of non-stop pressure from eight Allied armies advancing from the Channel to the Moselle, were beginning to accept the inevitability of defeat. In their judgment, the Americans, in particular, seemed to be unrelenting, showing their inexperience with their continuing costly massed frontal attacks, but still eager to press on regardless of heavy casualties. General Wellmann observed that, unlike the French, whose attacks seemed half-hearted and whose poilus appeared exhausted, the Americans were still, "fresh, eager for fighting, and brave."[17] Though still slow to exploit success, Americans seemed confident of ultimate victory and, no matter the attrition rate from battle and disease, there seemed an unending stream of them pouring onto the battlefield. The impression was correct. Regardless of the flu, regardless of the cataclysmic casualties in the Argonne, by October 31 the AEF numbered 1,867,623.

The Germans, on the other hand, were literally running out of men. Understanding that to lose the Meuse-Argonne was to lose the war, Ludendorff had ordered von Gallwitz, on October 10, to reinforce the front with every unit available. Von Gallwitz had to press into service worn-out reserve elements, division fragments, and logistical troops ill-trained for the battlefield. Units due for relief remained stuck in the trenches, exhausted, sick with the flu, and vastly understrength, because there were no troops to replace them. German losses were far fewer than American, but the well was running dry for the defenders, while the attackers were refreshed by a constantly renewable spring. In the second and third weeks of October, the German Fifth Army alone suffered 24,928 killed or wounded and 7,887 missing on the Meuse-Argonne. From September 26–October 20, the U.S. First Army claimed capture of 18,591 POWs from elements of thirty-six German and three Austrian divisions, Altogether, forty-four Central Powers divisions were employed on the Meuse-Argonne—although many were just fragments of divisions—seventeen of them moved over from French zones and one from the British sector. If the Americans were not breaking through on the Meuse-Argonne front, they were certainly wearing the Germans out.

Even the top leaders of Kaiser Bill's army had, by now, realized the hopelessness of the situation. First Quartermaster General Erich Ludendorff, always of mercurial temperament, had reached a near breaking point on September 28, the day after Montfaucon had fallen. The failure of his last great offensive on July 15 and the Black Day of August 8 had started him on the spiral down to despondency. As his armies' progress came under ever increasing battery, so did his nerves. A doctor at Ludendorff's HQ at the Hotel Britannique in Spa reported the general's "erratic ways, marked by vicious outbursts of temper, restless nights broken by angry telephone calls to individual commanding generals, on occasion too much drinking, and crying spells." On September 28, he had hit bottom. Witnesses had him in "a genuine fit, foaming at the mouth and collapsing on his office floor."[18]

Still in tears, Ludendorff carried his despair to Hindenburg, who agreed that Germany must seek an immediate armistice, based on the generous terms of Wilson's beneficent Fourteen Points. There would be no lenient peace, however. The Allies demanded punishment for the Germans, revenge for 1871, and rewards for their four years of sacrifice. And Pershing, on this point, was fully in agreement. Influenced by his ambition and perhaps, by his French mistress, Michette, Pershing favored, not his President's Fourteen Points, but unconditional surrender. To achieve this, to prevent Wilson from negotiating a soft peace, he accepted Foch's demands for more attacks on the Kriemhilde Stellung.

He was also motivated by the desire to make Haig eat his words, when the British field marshal complained about the ineptness of the American soldiers and their leaders. Pershing may have lacked sufficient artillery, enough time to prepare, and, most of all, compassion for his own men, but he did not lack for an abiding lust for his own star in the historical firmament, achievable only with an overwhelming American victory that would break the back of the German army.

There were American officers, other than Liggett, who sought alternatives to the costly strategy of head-butting against the formidable German wall, a strategy that so much of the U.S. high command seemed locked into. Among them were men whose vision focused upon a different dimension in the ancient art of death-dealing. Aerial power pioneers like Colonel Billy Mitchell insisted that the key to cracking the Kriemhilde Stellung lay, not in punching through or swinging around the wall, but in pounding the enemy ramparts from above.

Though the tank, the other major Great War innovation in modern warfare, was ill-suited to make much of an impact on the craggy carpet of the Meuse-Argonne, Colonel Mitchell and other airpower advocates were convinced that their warbirds could play a vital, if not decisive, role in American's most massive military undertaking.

Some 324 tanks (all of French or British manufacture) operated on the Meuse-Argonne front, and they often proved effective against the often otherwise impregnable German machine-gun bunkers. But they broke down too easily and were too vulnerable to enemy artillery. By November 1, I Corps' original tank strength of 189 had been reduced to sixteen. Fortunately, American forces did not suffer from this armor shortfall in the region, for the enemy deployed no tanks at all on the battleground.

American and Allied air units, on the other hand, did make a difference in the final outcome, even if Pershing insisted on a far more limited role for his aerial wing than that desired by the ambitious and often abrasive Colonel Mitchell. Pershing demanded direct tactical support for his ground troops as the air force's primary mission, and overruled Mitchell's more sweeping vision that encompassed interdiction, reconnaissance, intelligence gathering, and an all-out effort against Germany's aerial resources.

The Meuse-Argonne was not the budding U.S. air service's greatest Great War campaign in terms of warplanes committed to action. St. Mihiel holds that distinction, with 1,481 aircraft (872 piloted by French or British airmen)—701 pursuit planes, 366 observation craft, 323 day bombers and 91 night bombers, all of Allied make—providing air support. Mitchell had six weeks to prepare for that campaign and, although the rain and wind limited air operations for the first two days of the offensive, complete air supremacy was won over the battlefield by September 14. The Germans were able to counter the American air assault with only 243 warplanes, and most of them had to be reserved for defense of the lines of communication and rear area depots.

The air aspect of the last great American operation of the war was, like that on the ground, a much tougher experience. The weather did not break after two days, as at St. Mihiel, but remained, with brief intervals, miserable throughout, with highly unfavorable flying conditions. Mitchell again commanded more planes than the enemy, but did not enjoy overwhelming superiority in numbers. On the first day of the battle—September 26—the French and Americans could pit 842 aircraft against 302 German birds. By October 15, the odds had narrowed, with Mitchell mustering 756 planes to 504 German. When the battle's final phase began on November 1, the opposing line-ups had closed to 697 Allied versus 486 German.

In the course of the campaign, the Germans' original pursuit plane squadron on the front, the Stenay-based Jagdgeschwader II, had been reinforced by Jagdgeschwader I—von Richthofen's famous Flying Circus. The "Red Baron"—who, as an uhlan cavalry officer, lost ten of a fifteen-man patrol in an Argonne ambush in the fall of 1914—had been killed on April 21, 1918. The squadron had been commanded since July by Ober-lieutenant Herman Göring. The long, zeppelin-shaped sweep of the Argonne gave German planes the option of attacking from three sides. They could buzz along the forest's defiles to suddenly pop up over Argonne ridges and strafe the U.S. rear. A favorite target of the Fokkers were American logistical troops clustered at mess tents.

Given the adverse weather and Pershing's demand for close air support for his infantry columns, Mitchell had to rein in his maverick instincts and grander goals for his aerial regiments. Most air sorties were flown either to collect information for the infantry, to counter the effectiveness of the enemy artillery—particularly in busting the observation balloons of the German artillery corps—and in strafing the opposing infantry. Mitchell saw the air arm not as a supporting weapon for the infantry in the ground war, but as a war winner all its own. He conceded the necessity of tactical air in the overall effort, but leaped at every opportunity to carry out bombing missions against the enemy rear. On October 19, for example, he convinced the French to fly 322 of their Breguet bombers over a massive German troop concentration five miles behind the lines at Damvillers, on the east side of the Meuse.

Escorted by nearly 200 single-seat pursuit planes, the huge procession, flying in V-shaped formations, dropped thirty-two tons of bombs (another forty-nine tons were dropped by the British nearby) to break up the developing German counterattack. Some sixty German fighter planes swarmed toward the Allied bombers, but managed to down only a single plane, while losing twelve aircraft in the fracas.

For Mitchell, the bombing raid was a thunderous portent. "Think what it will be in the future when we attack with one, two, or three thousand airplanes at one time; the effect will be decisive."[19]

And the far-sighted colonel saw far beyond mass bombing of enemy formations. Had the war lasted into 1919, Mitchell planned U.S. strategic bombing attacks, the employment of parachute infantry regiments, and even an unmanned aerial rocket—called the "Bug"—similar to the Nazi V-rockets of the next world war. But the Armistice cut short Mitchell's grand schemes. General "Hap" Arnold later observed: "For Billy, the Armistice was an untimely interruption—as if the whistle had ended the game just as he was about to go over the goal line."[20]

Mitchell, of course, would never cease his apostolic advocacy of airpower. When his impassioned public criticisms of the armed services—for their "criminal, almost treasonable" neglect of the aviation arm—reached a petulant crescendo in September 1925, he was court-martialed, found guilty of, among other things, "conduct prejudicial to good order and military discipline," and forced to resign his commission in 1926.[21]

If Mitchell's "canvas falcons" were not the decisive actors who finally tipped the scales toward victory, his "winged cavalry" was invaluable in scouting and interdicting the enemy lines, in boosting morale for the tired troops on the ground, and, most vitally, in drawing a veil over the sky-eye view of the German aerial observers. In the first five days of the Meuse-Argonne, American and French pilots destroyed 100 German planes and twenty-one observation balloons.

The balloon-busting missions of the AEF's air arm were particularly important and no easy task, regardless of the size of the target. The inflated observation platforms were superior in many respects to reconnaissance airplanes. From the typical altitude of 1,500–2,000 feet, and relatively safe from enemy ground fire, the observers in their wicker baskets could scan many miles of terrain with their binoculars and report within seconds by the telephone line that connected them to the ground. Aircraft, on the other hand, had to often make dangerous multiple passes over enemy-held ground to confirm a sighting, and then had to fly back and land at a friendly airstrip to report.

The *Drachen* (barrage balloons), anchored by steel cables and usually winched down by night, were protected by anti-aircraft artillery batteries. The AA gunners could fix their sights on a single stairstep of the sky, because attacking aircraft had to maintain an exact altitude for several seconds to fire off the long machine-gun burst required to ignite the gas in the balloons. In addition to the archie fire, the attacking planes often had to fight off flights of Fokkers circling in wait in the clouds or behind the sun's glare, above the flight paths of the attackers. Should the Allied biplanes survive these hazards, they then had to negotiate a perilous path through more AA fire after coming out of their assault approach.

Regardless of the risks to his pilots, Colonel Mitchell made the destruction of the *Drachen* a top priority. He later stated: "The safety of thousands of our attacking soldiers depended upon our success in eliminating these eyes of the enemy."[22]

On October 10, he canopied the Argonne with three squadrons to take out the barrage balloons. The Germans, in turn, put up flights of Fokkers to defend the *Drachen*.

In the resulting swirl of dogfights, four German and three American pursuit planes flamed earthward, but the balloons maintained their lofty perch.

The ace of Mitchell's *Drachen* hunters was the 27th Aero Squadron's Lt. Frank Luke, the "Arizona balloon buster." Irrepressible and insubordinate, but an aerial predator who could shoot as well as he could fly, Luke downed eleven balloons and four planes in seventeen days in September. Together with his tailman and only friend, Lt. Joseph Wehner, they accounted for nine enemy aircraft in two days at St. Mihiel, with Luke alone accounting for two balloons and three planes on September 18. His total September bag was eighteen German aircraft (second only to Eddie Rickenbacker). Five times he returned to base in planes so shot up they had to be scrapped.

Frank Luke's string ran out on September 29 over the Meuse-Argonne. Driven to a kill-crazy frenzy by the dogfight death of Wehner on September 16, Luke, though grounded for unauthorized flights and for being AWOL, took off for the German lines in his Spad. Badly wounded in the course of blasting out two *Drachen*, the man who Rickenbacker considered the best pilot in the AEF drilled a third balloon and then strafed German troops near the village of Murvaux, before finally being forced down by ground fire. Even then the fearless flyer refused to surrender, firing at surrounding German troops with his pistol until enemy bullets ended his exploits. Luke was posthumously awarded the Medal of Honor.

Eddie Rickenbacker was the most famous American fighting above the Argonne treetops, rivaling in renown those U.S. heroes such as York and Whittlesey battling down in the squalor beneath the trees. Leader of the 94th Hat-in-the-Ring Aero Squadron, flying Spad 13 pursuit planes, Rickenbacker was a former race car driver who was tethered to Nineteenth Century values and attitudes on the ground, but a wild-eyed radical once airborne. He demanded the best from the men he commanded, but demanded the most from their commander. With tailman Reed Chambers, Rickenbacker would lead the daily patrol, return to base for a cup of coffee, then join Chambers in an additional hunt for the iron cross-branded prey. He was also a stone-cold killer, puttering in his predatory loops at near-stalling speed, then diving in a r.p.m. scream down on the almost always surprised victim. Chambers testified that, "Most of the pilots he killed never knew what hit them. Out of the sun, a quick burst and gone. That was Rickenbacker."[23]

Rickenbacker was aloft immediately after the initial artillery bombardment ceased on September 26. He recorded his first kill of the Meuse-Argonne campaign that morning, while other 94th Squadron pilots exploded a *Drachen*. He rang up two more victories by the end of the battle's first week. By the last week of October he had shot down twenty-four enemy aircraft. On October 30, Rickenbacker scored his twenty-fifth and twenty-sixth points in the deadly game, making him the top U.S. air ace of the war. On the next day he dropped, not bombs, but 100 bundled newspapers to cheer the advancing doughboys with the news of the Ottoman Turk surrender that brought the war closer to its conclusion. By the Armistice, Rickenbacker's 94th Squadron had accounted for sixty-nine enemy aircraft, the top tally for any U.S. squadron.

Rickenbacker was in his element in the skies over northern France. With every day of battle, he wrote, "comes renewal and recementing of ties that bind together these brothers-in-arms. No closer fraternity exists in the world."[24] With the inevitable crumbling of that camaraderie as the selfish pursuits of peace reasserted themselves post-Armistice, Rickenbacker became, in many respects, a bitter and disillusioned man.

For all of the oracles of the warplane and the tank like Mitchell and Patton, airpower and armor were destined to be the arbiters of the century's second global convulsion, not the first. In the near run of autumn 1918 they could only supplement the infantry and artillery in deciding the outcome of the Battle of the Meuse-Argonne and of the Great War.

As the new First Army commander, General Hunter Liggett, and his newly appointed operations officer, George Marshall, prepared for the October 14 resumption of the offensive, the situation looked depressingly familiar. The Germans were expertly dug in on the high ground of their "crowning" defenses, the Kriemhilde Stellung. As with each prior phase of the offensive, the Americans faced terrible terrain, terrible weather and terrible odds as they went up against the intricately interlaced network of wire, machine-gun nests, and forward observer posts, from which the uncannily accurate artillery cascade could be called down to devastate the creeping columns of U.S. troops. There were some rested and experienced divisions in the line and, with the Argonne emplacements captured, the artillery fire this time would arc over only from the Meuse Heights flank (as well as from the front). But most of the other American divisions were so battered they could render only limited support for the fresh troops, and the enemy, understanding the utter necessity of holding on here, had continued to reinforce their crown jewel of the Kriemhilde.

Liggett—whose fat cells had never infiltrated above the collar—had delayed accepting First Army command to complete his tactical and organizational reforms for the I Corps in time for the new attacks. These reforms, which Liggett fully intended to institute army-wide once he assumed control, included more German storm trooper-type fire-and-maneuver attacks and fewer straight-up-the-middle assaults, and the bypassing and isolating of machine-gun dugouts and fortified bunkers holding up the advance. The "no trespass signs" delineating boundary lines between units would go down. Battalions and regiments would advance where they could and strike out on their flanks, regardless of whose terrain they trespassed on. There would be no more reining in of advancing forces to allow their sister units time to catch up and secure an unbroken line. Drive and determination would still be stressed, but initiative and flexibility would become the new hallmarks of the First Army's tactical doctrine.

Round three, set for October 14, was to be launched by nine U.S. and three French divisions in four corps, from the north rim of the Argonne to the east bank of the Meuse. The French Fourth Army, on the left flank of First Army's I Corps, was to launch a simultaneous offensive, so that the dense northern extension of the Argonne, called the Bois de Bourgogne, would come under assault from both sides. Assaulting this Kriemhilde section of the Hindenburg Line were, from left to right: I Corps' 77th and 82nd Divisions, V Corps' 42nd and 32nd Divisions, III Corps' 5th, 3rd and 4th Divisions, and—east of the Meuse—the French XVII Corps' 33rd U.S. and 29th U.S. Divisions, along with the French 18th, 26th and 10th Colonial Divisions. In immediate reserve were four divisions: the U.S. 78th and French 5th Cavalry Divisions behind I Corps, the U.S. 89th behind V Corps, and the U.S. 26th Yankee Division backing up the French XVII Corps. Four more U.S. divisions were in First Army reserve: the 1st, 80th, 90th and 91st. Defending the Kriemhilde were seventeen battle-weary Central Powers divisions, still resolute but with thinned ranks and thinner hopes. Six more German divisions were in reserve.

While the I Corps secured the western flank of the offensive and the French XVII Corps continued its drive east of the Meuse, the V and III Corps in the center were to carve out deep salients in the Hindenburg Line and then squeeze the enemy from the terrain between. Should the Americans take the Kriemhilde, they would then only have to overrun the final and less formidable positions in the Barricourt Heights farther north. Once through those

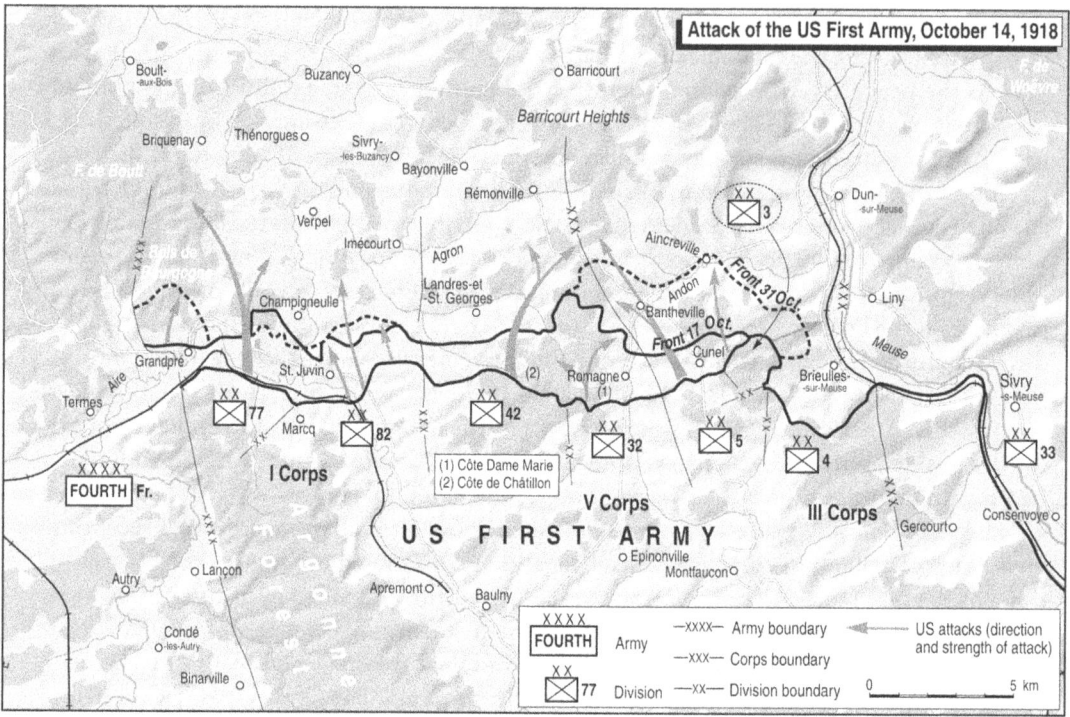

redoubts, open country beckoned and the crucial prize of the Sedan-Mézières railroad, the supply spine of the German army on the Western Front, would be within the Allies' grasp. General von Gallwitz had told his troops on October 13, "There is no question of volunteer withdrawal."[25] Without the railroad lifeline, the German occupation of northern France was unsustainable.

The left (western) anchor of the renewed push was, as it had been from the first day of the Meuse-Argonne Offensive, Alexander's 77th Division. The Statue of Liberty Division had been on the firing line for nineteen straight days and, unlike every other American division in the U.S. inventory, had never stopped attacking as it made its grueling way through and beyond the Argonne. The division's greatest leap forward had come October 10–11, when, despite a prolixity of rear-guard snipers and die-hard machine-gun nests, it had advanced six and a quarter miles to a line just 600 yards south of the western curve of the Aire River. Pershing now asked one more task of the hard-used division. The target was the Bourgogne Woods, the northern resumption of the Argonne on the escarpment above the Aire and the cornerpost of the Kriemhilde. To reach those woods, however, the 77th would have to attack across the open valley formed by the western loop of the Aire, cross the rain-swollen river, and seize the fortress town of Grandpré, atop a thirty-foot-high cliff.

A second target for the 77th on October 14 was the village of St. Juvin, three miles to the east of Grandpré, near where the Aire bent westward from its hitherto northern course. The lead battalion of the 306th Regiment was stopped dead in its tracks in the opening frontal assault across swampy ground south of the river. However, the regimental commander maneuvered a second battalion of the 306th around to the east of the town and surprised the defenders. St. Juvin and several hundred POWs were captured before nightfall. The 82nd, on the right, secured a vital hill and ridge line east of the village and fought off a fierce German counterattack by the evening of October 15.

The thrust at Grandpré achieved more limited success. The stronghold (which Liggett was convinced would have fallen on October 7 if the 82nd could have committed a full brigade to their left hook into the north Argonne) was an impossible target in the daylight. The approaches to the Grandpré Heights were under full observation from the high ground above town, and every avenue was precisely calibrated by machine guns, trench mortars and artillery. Consequently, Johnson's 154th Brigade, supported by the division's artillery brigade, rushed the position after nightfall on October 14. The main ford was attacked by a full battalion, while smaller detachments crossed the Aire by boat-bridges and even by swimming across.

Under heavy plunging fire, the men of 1/307th struggled upslope all night long before finally clawing out a foothold in the southern section of Grandpré. The close combat was street by street and sometimes hand to hand. Solitary 75 mm field guns—the so-called pirate guns—from the 303rd Field Artillery were manhandled through the narrow cobbled lanes to place direct fire on German machine-gun burrows.

On the evening of October 15, Maj. General James H. McRae (a West Point classmate of Pershing) directed the New Jersey, New York and Pennsylvania draftees of the 78th Lightning Division on a cold slog through the rainy night to the relief of the 77th. While the 78th continued the Herculean task of clearing Grandpré on October 16, the 77th was finally pointed to the rear, instead of at the enemy. The "New York ghetto" troops of the 77th had been in the line since September 21, and had been in battle for twenty straight days. The division had advanced eleven miles since the jump-off on September 26, most of it through the satanic whimsy of the Argonne. Those eleven excruciating miles and twenty endless days had cost the 77th a total of 4,061 casualties.

As the men of Alexander's division re-entered the Argonne, this time from the north instead of the south, and this time expecting Rest and Relaxation instead of Hell and Damnation, they were directed towards the craftily constructed rest camps and spa-like dugouts originally engineered for the rehabilitation of battle-worn German army units. Along with such luxuries as pianos, wine and champagne cellars, and comfortable chairs and beds, some of the dugouts indicated the former presence of female company. General Alexander and his staff appropriated the almost palatial HQ facilities of von Kleist. But the holiday away from hell would last only fifteen days. On October 31, the 77th was moved back into the line at Hill 182, north of St. Juvin, in time to take part in the campaign's final offensive.

Left behind by the Metropolitan Division to complete the job of taking Grandpré, was McRae's untested Lightning Division, just three months removed from disembarkation in France. The task proved to be one of the most difficult, costly and lengthy missions of the entire campaign. The German command equated the importance of retaining Grandpré with that of the Meuse Heights, the two positions representing the anchors for the whole German line. Consequently, they concentrated some of their best troops at Grandpré and in the Bois de Loges, a mile-square forested hill to the northeast of the Grandpré Heights.

McRae was, personally, almost recklessly courageous, a man who, "feared neither God, man, nor the Devil or General Pershing either."[26] But for all his fearlessness and his men's valor, they could not crack Grandpré for day after day. The heights above the town were dominated by the ruins of a medieval castle called the Citadel, and the only approach to its stone walls was by way of a narrow causeway. In the Bois de Loges, the Germans concentrated their machine guns on the hilltop center of the woods to enable them to fire over the tree-studded slopes and into the open fields the Americans must traverse to reach the forest.

The town of Grandpré was taken after two days of house-to-house combat, but the Swabian Territorials of the 2nd Landwehr Division fell back only to the Citadel and to a hilly rampart at the south edge of the Bourgogne Woods. On October 19, a brigade of the 78th attempted to storm the Citadel, but deeply dug-in German batteries in the Bourgogne and waves of machine-gun fire from the old fortress kept the New Jersey draftees at bay. The other brigade of the 78th crossed the Aire on the 16th and advanced through knee-deep mud against the Loges Woods. Machine-gun nests, sited at forty-yard intervals, pinned down the attackers and, after four days of murderous machine-gun and sniper fire, as well as cascades of gas and HE artillery shells, the brigade was withdrawn from its toehold in the Loges.

Following three days of reorganization, McRae sent his men against the Citadel and the south rim of the Bourgogne again. With help from the 82nd Division on the right and the French on the left, the Grandpré Heights were finally conquered by October 27, though the Loges Woods still bristled with enemy machine guns. The ghastly battle for Grandpré had cost the 78th over 4,000 casualties (total 78th losses, October 16–November 5, were 4,876).

The 82nd, the division to the right of the 78th and the farthest east of the I Corps units, persisted in its attacks on the ridge and plateau northeast of St. Juvin, pushing forward another 500 yards on October 21 to the area of Ravine aux Pierres. With total effective rifle strength in its regiments reduced to 4,700, General Duncan's division held the line to the end of the month. Finally relieved by the 80th and 77th Divisions on October 31, the 82nd—the division that had broken the Argonne deadlock on October 7–8—counted 6,377 casualties in its time in the tempest, October 7–31, 1918.

On the 82nd's eastern flank on October 14, the V Corps, in the center of the line, stormed the heart of the Kriemhilde Stellung. Summerall's corps occupied the rolling plateau between Montfaucon and the Romagne Heights. The hilly sector to be stormed, from Romagne on Andon Creek west to Fléville on the Aire, was about eight miles wide and dominated by the roads that merged through the Landres gap and thence to von Kleist's new headquaters at Buzancy, farther northwest. V Corps would have the advantage in being safely distant from the batteries on the Meuse Heights, and in no longer having to worry about those eliminated in the Argonne. But the corps was going up against what was considered by many as the strongest redoubt in the Kriemhilde—the Côte Dame Marie—a scimitar-shaped ridge five-eighths of a mile long, with two promontories at either end, and overlooking the town of Romagne to the east. The second major target of the V Corps assault was the Côte de Châtillon, farther west, just short of Landres and just north of the Romagne Woods.

Taking on the Côte de Châtillon was the fresh 42nd Division. The Rainbow Division, commanded by Maj. General Charles T. Menoher, had gained its appellation after it was mobilized, August 1, 1917, by combining National Guard units from twenty-six states and the District of Columbia. After entering the line on February 21, 1918, it gained its reputation for spirited, aggressive action in the Aisne-Marne Counteroffensive and at St. Mihiel. The division also became known for absorbing disproportionately heavy casualties, in large part due to its propensity to charge headlong into phalanxes of enemy machine guns. In the Battle of Soissons (Aisne-Marne) alone, the 42nd recorded 6,451 casualties in just ten days, July 25–August 3.

The two brigades of the 42nd—the 83rd on the left and the 84th on the right—burst, side by side, out of the northern cusp of the Romagne Woods on October 14. The 83rd, composed of Ohioans of the 164th Infantry and of the Fighting Irish of William "Wild Bill" Donovan's 165th Infantry (which also included the famous Father Duffy), aimed for the twin villages of Landres-et-Saint-Georges. Donovan—the future leader of the Second World War's OSS (predecessor to the CIA) and the most bemedaled soldier in the division—led his men up against three solid lines of trenches protected by a five-foot high belt of wire twenty feet deep. The 83rd had been promised tanks to back their assault, but their failure to put in an appearance, plus anemic artillery support, did not stop the infantry attack. Enemy troops from the 15th Bavarian and 37th Divisions threw the 83rd Brigade back with terrible losses on October 14–15. Lt. Colonel Donovan, though badly wounded in the leg by a machine-gun bullet, refused evacuation and remained the rock upon which his men rallied.

Donovan would get the Medal of Honor, but other 83rd Brigade officers got the boot, by an irate, morale-mashing Summerall. Visiting the brigade line on the evening of October 15, the sulfurous corps commander demanded "results, no matter how many men were killed."[27] He relieved the brigade commander, Brig. General Michael Lenehan, as well as a slew of colonels, captains and lieutenants, all for questioning why doughboys were the only soldiers on the Western Front still required to go up unsupported against wired-in machine-gun and artillery positions.

The 84th Brigade's target on October 14 was the Côte de Châtillon. Though not as formidable as the Côte Dame Marie—the 32nd Division's objective, farther east—it was yet another of those natural fortresses in the twenty miles between the Argonne and the Meuse that exacted so much heartache and bloodshed from the U.S. First Army. The 1,000-foot high ridge was steep, replete with trees, and rife with wire, pillboxes and machine-gun nests.

Private John Taber of the 84th Brigade's 168th Infantry would later describe the ground facing his regiment: "The terrain was as forbidding as any the 168th had ever seen. Thick woods, tangled underbrush, scarred trees, gaping shellholes, deep ravines, and lofty ridges united to make a country already desolate and difficult still more forbidding. Dead bodies, some of them in a bad state of decomposition, littered the woods and slopes."[28]

Leading the 84th was Colonel Douglas MacArthur. An Alexandrian figure—at least by his own estimation—MacArthur had flair as well as substance and always leaped toward the limelight. It had been he—in the summer of 1917—who had suggested the concept of the all-encompassing 42nd Division to Secretary Baker. As chief of staff of the division initially, MacArthur in World War I was no "Dugout Doug," as he was scornfully called by many of his men in World War II. Often tramping about the battlefield, gathering and giving impressions, he was wounded twice and harvested two DSCs and seven Silver Stars, all before he led his men up the slippery slope of the Châtillon. Resplendent in a blazer and scarf, but without bothering with the accoutrements of rank, MacArthur roamed about so frequently that he was once mistaken for a German spy and briefly detained.

Pershing, perhaps sensing a rival for fortune's favor, did not appreciate MacArthur's self-promoting stunts, and tried unsuccessfully to block his promotion by the War Department to brigadier general in July 1918. Leading the 84th Brigade at St Mihiel, MacArthur again pulled off another Achillian exploit, sneaking, with only his adjutant, through the enemy lines to within sight of Metz. Finding this hinge to the German line of communication only lightly defended, MacArthur wanted to push his brigade on to seize the vital target. In spite of his personal distaste for the man, Pershing might have agreed to MacArthur's proposal a few weeks earlier, when the AEF chief had wanted to expand the St. Mihiel

Offensive on into the Woevre Plain. But he had capitulated to Foch's concept of converging offensives, and had committed the U.S. First Army to the Meuse-Argonne Offensive. MacArthur would later claim that, had Pershing made the right decision and given him the go-ahead against Metz, the war could have been greatly shortened and the tragic losses of the Meuse-Argonne would have been unnecessary.

Summerall had a better opinion of MacArthur than did Pershing, but he was no less demanding of the Civil War general's son than he was of the commander of the 83rd Brigade. On the soggy evening of October 11, the corps commander popped in on MacArthur's HQ and demanded, "Give me Châtillon or a list of 5,000 casualties."

MacArthur was, as always, up for the challenge. "If this brigade does not capture Châtillon, you can publish a casualty list of the entire brigade, with the brigade commander's name at the top."[29]

According to MacArthur's recollection, "Tears sprang into General Summerall's eyes. He was evidently so moved that he could say nothing. He looked at me for a few seconds and then left without a word."[30]

The conquest of the Côte de Châtillon did not require a casualty count of 5,000, with MacArthur at the top of the list, but it was a difficult and costly enterprise. MacArthur lost

Brig. General Douglas MacArthur, C.O. of the 84th Brigade, 42nd "Rainbow" Division. National Archives, 111-SC-18904.

no blood on the rain-slicked slopes of the Châtillon, but did win further fame to burnish his reputation. Congenitally unable to fight a battle from his CP bunker (at least not at this stage of his career), MacArthur took personal charge of the attack and even carried out his own reconnaissance, during which he discovered a weakening of the enemy defenses on the flanks. MacArthur later boasted that the patrol he led to scout the Châtillon was deluged by a sudden artillery shower that killed everyone but himself—"God led me by the hand, the way he did Joshua."[31] There were, however, many doubting Thomases who questioned the authenticity of his Old Testament exploit.

The East Prussians of the 41st Division stoutly resisted MacArthur's 84th Brigade for three days. The attack on the hill was preceded by a six-hour barrage pumped out by all of the 42nd and 1st Division artillery, as well as by eighteen U.S. and French corps artillery batteries and three 8-inch battalions from the 59th Coastal Artillery Regiment. The first two assault battalions were, nonetheless, ripped to pieces 500 yards from their start line, with 70 percent casualties. One of the battalions had seventy men fit for duty by midday out of 500 who carried out the attack in the morning.

Despite all, on the first night Hill 288, at the southeast approach to Châtillon, fell to the Rainbow men. The next day Hill 282 and La Tuilerie Farm fell. On October 16, while MacArthur personally led a diversionary frontal attack, Major Lloyd Ross guided his battalion around to the vulnerable section of the German earthworks discovered by MacArthur on his patrol, cut the wire, and won the hill. After beating back the usual German counterattacks—with the help of an artillery barrage on the massing enemy forces—Ross's battalion was reduced to six officers and 300 men still standing out of twenty-five officers and 1,450 men who went into action three days before. But the Côte de Châtillon was now an American possession. Almost 200 German machine guns were counted amongst the blossoms of blood flowering the hillside after the battle. Total Rainbow casualties for October 14–16 were 2,895.

MacArthur was recommended for the Medal of Honor, but Pershing's staff at Chaumont—under their boss's resentful eye—downgraded the award to a Distinguished Service Cross. The citation read in part: "On a field where courage was the rule, his courage was the dominant factor."[32] Though MacArthur would later write that he was satisfied with the DSC, it was obvious to many that he desired and expected the nation's highest medal, won by his father, General Arthur MacArthur, in the Civil War. He would have to wait for Bataan and World War II for his Medal of Honor.

For all of MacArthur's grandiloquent claims and actions, and the undeniably lethal fact that the Côte de Châtillon was a tough nut to crack, the capture of the Côte Dame Marie was both the key to unlocking the Kriemhilde and a more arduous and costly undertaking. Maj. General William Haan's 32nd Iron Jaws Division had been in the line since September 30, and had absorbed 5,000 raw recruits—"a gun was about as much use to them as a broom," observed one company commander—to make up for 6,800 casualties suffered at Aisne-Marne in July and Juvigny in August.[29] Consequently, it was expected only to pin the Germans in place on the côte, while the fresh 42nd and 5th Divisions enveloped the ridge from the flanks. Haan, however, went for broke on October 14, smashing his Arrows (named for their red arrow patch) against the ridge line. The Michigan and Wisconsin Guardsmen lost heavily to intense machine-gun fire and pre-registered artillery barrages. Fortunately, a patrol of eight men found a gap in the German wire, rushed it, and eliminated a Maxim nest with rifle grenades, thus opening a path to the top of the ridge. By the end of the day, the Côte Dame Marie—the keystone of the Kriemhilde—as well as the town of Romagne, were in American hands.

Pershing wrote in recognition of the Arrows' success: "Unstinted praise must be given the 32nd Division" in taking "perhaps the most important strong point of the Hindenburg Line on the Western Front."[33] Fighting off several German counterattacks and enduring a nighttime gas artillery bombardment, the 32nd punched one and a half miles through the Kriemhilde on the 14th. Their glorious day and those that came before and after, until relieved by the 89th Division on October 20, were dearly bought. The division counted casualties of 5,518 from September 30–October 20, 1918.

Hines's III Corps, on the right, consisting of three Regular Army divisions—5th, 3rd and 4th, from left to right—was also heavily engaged in this third offensive phase on October 14. The 5th had been pushing at the critical Cunel Heights, east of the Côte Dame Marie, since entering the line of October 12.

In the Bois de Pultiére, north of the town of Cunel, the 5th Division's Lt. Samuel Woodfill, an old Regular Army sergeant and veteran of the Filipino Insurrection, performed feats of heroism on October 12 that won him the Medal of Honor and the selection by Pershing—along with York and Whittlesey—as one of the outstanding heroes of the AEF. Born in Kentucky, Woodfill had worked as a woodchopper in Indiana before enlisting. He had learned musketry with an old muzzle-loader, like Alvin York, and was a crack shot, also like the Tennessee woodsman. During four hitches of duty in Alaska, Woodfill had hunted with Eskimos and outshot Canadian Mounties in championship matches.

Before the day of October 12 was done, Woodfill, firing at the dark shapes made by the blankets that the Germans erected around their machine guns to mask the muzzle flashes, silenced at least three machine-gun nests and killed eleven Germans with his Springfield, with his .45 pistol, and—when his pistol jammed after he had to crawl through foot-deep mud—with a pickax. Disabled by poison gas—probably U.S.-released—he inhaled while ducking from shell hole to shell hole, he was evacuated at the end of the day. After recovery, Sam Woodfill returned to his Wabash country home and married his boyhood sweetheart.

The 5th Division, despite heavy losses from a two-hour shelling before it jumped off on October 14, fought its way through the Pultiére Woods and on north to the edge of the Bois de Rappes, by the end of the second day of the push. Unfortunately, the overwrought division commander, Maj. General John McMahon, panicked after hearing reports of heavy casualties, and ordered his forward units to give up their hard-won gains in the Rappes Woods. Pershing and new III Corps commander General Hines motored to McMahon's HQ and immediately relieved the rattled division leader, replacing him with General Hanson Ely, the victor of Cantigny, America's first Great War battle.

Because of McMahon's nervousness and timidity, the 5th had to fight for another week before it could clear the Bois de Rappes of the enemy. By October 17, its rifle strength had declined to 3,316. By the time the 5th was relieved on October 22 by the 90th Division, the Red Diamond Division had taken 4,343 casualties in its eleven days on the Cunel front. In addition, as many as 2,500 men had wandered off. A good number of those stragglers had been among the 3,044 recently arrived and barely trained replacements for the division.

To the east of the 5th Division, the 3rd and 4th Divisions struggled to secure the broad Bois de Forêt, stretching almost to the Meuse. The forest was finally swept clear of the foe by October 22. The 3rd was finally pulled from the line on October 27, after losing 7,873 killed in action, wounded in action and missing in action, September 30–October 27, most of the casualties coming in the Bois de Forêt and the earlier contest for the Madeleine Farm (secured October 9). The "Bulldogs" of the 4th ended their time on the Meuse-Argonne front on October 19, having captured 2,731 prisoners and forty-four guns, but also having lost since opening day—September 26—6,216 in total casualties in places such as Septsarges and Bois de Fays. Included in that toll was 200 4th Division doughboys killed or wounded by a sudden barrage of friendly artillery fire from the southwest on the evening of October 12. Far surpassing the Lost Battalion's experience on October 4, it was the worst friendly fire incident of the Battle of the Meuse-Argonne.

The end was now truly in sight. The Kriemhilde Stellung was pierced; the heart of the Hindenburg was broken. The morale of the German defenders was starting to crack; the will to resist of the nation for which they fought was beginning to falter.

But logistics, the weather, and the inexorable demands of sustained combat forced Liggett to ease off the accelerator of the general offensive, though never entirely applying full brakes. While rifle regiments continued to drive ahead at several points to secure higher ground or seize a vital crossroads, the First Army commander enlisted the two weeks between October 17–31 in preparing the groundwork for the fourth and final—and hopefully decisive—phase of the Meuse-Argonne offensive.

Liggett resisted all of Black Jack's blandishments to continue the offensive. When Pershing continued to hector Liggett about persisting with the offensive, Liggett told his supreme commander to "go away and forget it."[34] Possibly only Liggett could have been so brutally honest with J.J. Pershing. The man, who wrecked careers as easily as he did divisions, meekly complied.

Though the final strong points of the Kriemhilde were taken by late October, the First Army commander insisted that the army needed to be "tightened up" before it could continue the attack. He knew the Germans had to be hurting, but could not know just how desperate their situation was by now. Ludendorff observed that, "Our best men lay on the bloody battlefield" of the Kriemhilde.[35] All that remained between the Americans and Sedan were the relatively frail defenses of the last-gasp Freya Stellung, and no major reserve units remained to back up those defenses.

But Liggett's own army was suffering. By October 19 one staff officer characterized the First Army as "a disorganized and wrecked army." The 32nd Division, for example, was down to 2,000 combat effectives. Overall casualties were so massive that Pershing reduced the authorized strength of U.S. divisions by 4,000 men each. Two newly arrived divisions were broken up to fill the decimated ranks of units in the field. Straggling and malingering were still massive problems.

Liggett wanted the ill-used infantry to be not only rested, but also retrained. Fire-and-maneuver was stressed and small unit combat emphasized. Special assault squads were formed to attack fortified positions with grenades and submachine guns. Most importantly, the troops were re-indoctrinated in dealing with the deluges of poison gas that the Germans had poured down on them (30 percent of the casualties of the attacking divisions were from phosgene, mustard and chlorine gas). The artillery also needed to be revamped. Once again it had failed to keep pace with the advancing infantry, because of bad weather, bad roads and a scarcity of draft horses. To replace the animals, soldiers of the 6th Division (which was never committed to combat) were employed to pull and push the artillery forward along the abysmal roads, and to haul up the vast stockpiles of ammunition required for the renewed push. The American cannoneers—like Harry Truman—were becoming more efficient and professional, but were still far behind their German counterparts in such redleg arts as screening smoke barrages and poison gas bombardments.

Granted the unprecedented luxury of sufficient time to properly prepare, Liggett and Hugh Drum, his chief of staff, took full advantage. Also unprecedented was the extended break in the enduring rain. The weather actually cleared for five of six days in late October, as the First Army geared up for the final push (in the forty-seven days of the Meuse-Argonne, the rains fell for a biblical forty of those days).

Under those amazingly blue skies, Liggett worked his tireless and methodical magic. He made sure the staff work at all levels was precise and well-coordinated. He rotated in revived or fresh divisions to replace those, like the 4th and 32nd, that were too damaged to continue. He plumped up the ranks of divisions staying in the line, not only with replacements, but also with returned stragglers. To get a handle on this "second" army roaming about the rear, Liggett established "straggler posts" on all roads and dispatched patrols to scout the woods, depots and dugouts for the malingerers. In this way thousands of soldiers were returned to their units. By the time the attack was ready to roll forward, the First Army totaled over one million men, including 135,000 French soldiers. About 500,000 of that number were infantrymen.

The ordnance and supply situation also greatly improved. Pioneer troops pushed forward roads and narrow gauge railroads to enable the stockpiling of vast quantities of ammunition and other supplies. Though still deficient in tanks—only fifteen were available—and heavy trucks, the First Army was, by November 1, at last back up to the same logistical standards it had possessed on September 26. The First Army was particularly rich in artillery, with "cannon enough to conquer hell." In the center, Summerall's V Corps alone was allotted 608 guns and howitzers to shatter the German dugouts on the Barricourt Heights. Intense counter-battery fire was prescribed for enemy artillery and infantry reserve positions. U.S. batteries were to lay down heavy interdictory fires on the German-held heights, plastering reverse slopes and rearward approaches to isolate the defenders and prevent their reinforcement. Toxic gas shells, including mustard gas, would be prolifically employed. Even before the final-phase offensive began, U.S. artillery, using detailed maps provided by aerial reconnaissance, was softening up the enemy. Three batteries of 14-inch naval guns, mounted on railroad cars, spiraled 1,400-pound projectiles as far as twenty-five miles into the German rear all through the last week of October. On October 30–31, forty-one and a half tons of gas (36,000 rounds) drenched the four weak German divisions in the Bois de Bourgogne, eliminating nine of the twelve enemy batteries in the woods.

Billy Mitchell's air squadrons also carried out repeated bombing raids on the German rear. Forty-five DH-4s, for example, dropped five tons of bombs on Montmedy. U.S. pursuit planes were also establishing air superiority. In just two days, American pilots shot down forty-seven German airplanes and five balloons, while losing only fourteen aircraft of their own.

With the front four miles shorter than it had been on September 26, Liggett deployed seven divisions for the final thrust, instead of the nine committed on September 26. All seven attack divisions were battle-hardened. The lineup from the Meuse on west was: Hines's III Corps, with the 5th and 90th Divisions on the line and the 3rd in reserve; Summerall's V Corps, made up of the 89th and 2nd Divisions in line and the 1st and 42nd in reserve; and Dickman's I Corps, composed of the 80th, 77th and 78th Divisions attacking and the

82nd in reserve. Farther back, in army reserve, was the 32nd Division. The offensive would swing forward in coordination with the French Fourth Army on the western side of the Bois de Bourgogne and with Bullard's U.S. Second Army, which would undertake only limited local attacks south and east of the Meuse to pin the Hun forces in that area.

The original operational plan called for the offensive to kick off on October 28. French general Gouraud, however, informed Pershing that his Fourth Army would not be ready until November 1. Liggett, the prince of preparedness, was not unhappy to be granted four more days to fine tune the assault. The emphasis of the attack was also redirected from a Franco-American pincer movement on the western and eastern sides of the Bourgogne Woods to a straight punch at the Teutonic jaw on the Barricourt Heights. Taking this center linchpin of the Freya Stellung might force a total German evacuation of the Meuse-Argonne sector, rather than just a limited pullback from the Bourgogne, on the German right.

Liggett's ultimate objective remained as it had at the battle's beginning on September 26—the breaching of the Sedan-Mézières railroad line. He hoped to realize that goal with a three-stage assault. Round one would encompass the capture of the Barricourt Heights by V Corps' 2nd Division, backed by the 89th Division on the right flank and by the First Army's fifteen remaining tanks. The two corps on Summerall's flanks would support his primary effort. The III Corps, on the right, would thrust toward Brieulles-sur-Meuse; the I Corps on the left would strike toward Boult-aux-Bois on the northeastern edge of the Bois de Bourgogne. In order to bypass the woods and cut off the Germans posted there, stage two would feature an exploitation drive by the 1st and 42nd Divisions toward the Meuse above Sedan. Phase three, launched hopefully on November 4, was to attain a crossing of the Meuse at Dun-sur-Meuse in order to overrun the last German artillery emplacements on the Meuse Heights.

The November 1 plan was similar in many respects to the original attack on September 26—a frontal attack, with the main effort in the center against enemy-occupied commanding heights. This time, however, the enemy was much weaker and Liggett expected quick success. Liggett knew, largely from aerial scouting, that von Marwitz had been shu· ing his few remaining intact units to the western side of the German line, in anticipation of the main Allied thrust occurring there. The long two-week struggle by the 78th Division to take Grandpré and push into the Bourgogne had convinced the German commander that the Bourgogne was to be the primary focus of the upcoming U.S. offensive. Taking full advantage of the enemy's distraction and debilitated condition, Liggett was ready to apply overwhelming force, moving as rapidly as possible against the critical nexus of the enemy line.

And finally, after five weeks of bloody frustration, it worked. Everything came together on November 1. The weather cooperated; the enemy was at the end of his tether; the First Army—for really the first time—operated like a well-oiled, professional fighting force, intent on its mission and intent on victory.

The final massive barrage of the greatest artillery war in history split open the night sky at 0330 on November 1. "Like a million hammers," Allied howitzers and field guns pounded down on the enemy's front line and reserve positions alike, smashed German batteries, and ranged rearward to pummel HQs, bridges, crossroads and depots.[36] The intense fire, accurate and coordinated, lasted a mere two hours—an eye blink by Western Front artillery standards—but it devastated the German positions. On the hammering heels of

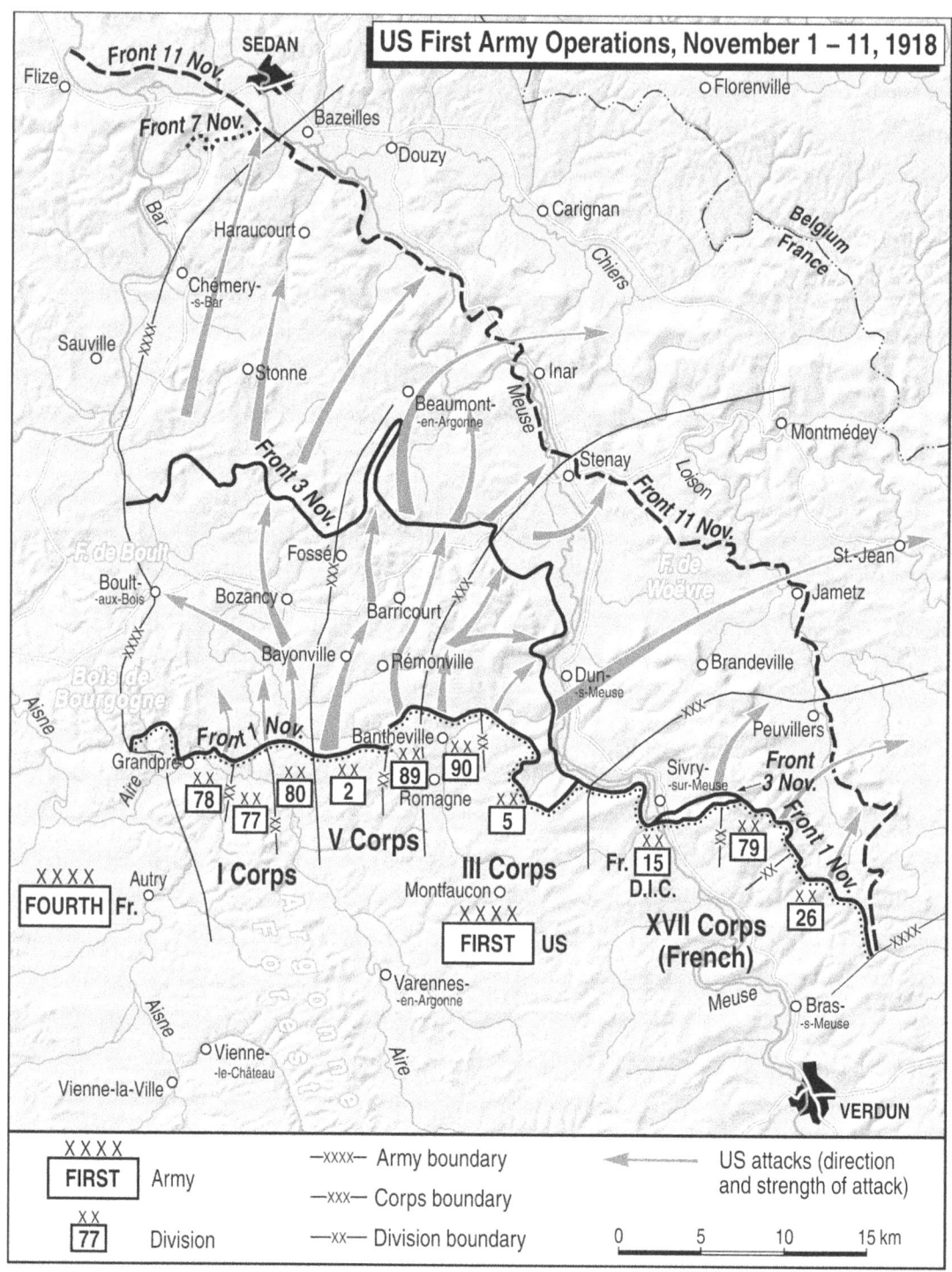

the barrage, treetop-skimming pursuit planes strafed German trenches and artillery emplacements, while high-flying bombers dropped their wrath on enemy troop concentrations, ammo depots and lines of communication.

The infantry leaped forward at 0530. As on September 26, the early morning was cold and foggy, but unlike that first day of the Battle of the Meuse-Argonne, the advancing riflemen took most of their objectives with relative ease. Summerall had been exhorting the soldiers of his corps for days with such burley slogans as: "There is no excuse for failure!" "The best way to take machine guns is to go and take 'em!" and "Press forward!"[37] Inspired by these rah-rah exhortations, the doughboy infantry of V Corps rushed the Barricourt Heights with the alacrity of conquerors.

USMC Maj. General John Lejeune's 2nd Division, veterans of Château Thierry, Belleau Wood, Soisson and Blanc Mont, moved forward behind both the fifteen surviving Whippet tanks and the densest rolling barrage ever laid down by U.S. artillery in the Great War. The first target of the 5th and 6th Marine Regiments and the 23rd Infantry Regiment was Landres-et-Saint-Georges, the charnel house for Wild Bill Donovan's 83rd Brigade two weeks before. This time, the Marines swept through the village with ease. There and elsewhere, demoralized German POWs explained, "the reason they were taken was that artillery concentrations were so effective as to confine them to shelters and to isolate them in small groups. Artillery POWs stated that they were unable to leave their shelters to serve their guns."[38]

The 2nd went on to storm the Barricourt Heights, with 37 mm teams blasting machine-gun bunkers as the infantry simply bypassed them in their surge toward the heights. The V Corps divisions swarmed over the high ground and pushed beyond the enemy's last defensive barrier for a total of five and a half miles by nightfall. On the right, III Corps protected V Corps' flank by securing Cléry-le-Grand and Andevanne. Only on the left was progress limited, with Dickman's I Corps advancing only one-half mile. Though 16,000 HE and phosphorus rounds were deposited on the defenders of the Bois de Loges, the Germans there held firm against a brigade of McRae's 78th Division. Alexander's 77th Division—in the center of the corps this time, instead of at its usual post as the corps' left anchor—was stymied before the town of Champigneulle.

I Corps' mission on November 1 had been restricted to "threaten furiously" von Marwitz's best remaining divisions facing the Americans, in order to keep the Germans occupied, and to gird V Corps' flank. But this holding action evolved into an all-out assault, as Liggett later recalled: "Our men were so eager that part of the corps got out of hand and the demonstration developed into a real attack. It was magnificent, but it was not war, for it played into the enemy's hands and led to a deplorable loss of life."[39]

Nevertheless, V Corps' overwhelming success forced all along the line a general German withdrawal to the Meuse. The Bois de Loges and Champigneulle were evacuated that night, and in the next few days I Corps, though advancing with its infantrymen in trucks, could not catch up with the rapidly fleeing foe.

November 1 was the red-letter day for the AEF in the Great War. As Pershing commented: "For the first time the enemy lines were completely broken through."[40] Even Foch and Clemenceau stooped from their Gallic heights to praise the American success. Four divisions of the German Fifth Army had been smashed, including two first-class units. The U.S. First Army had rounded up 3,602 POWs, 63 guns and hundreds of machine guns.

Many German regiments were reduced to 200 effectives without machine guns, and many of their artillery pieces had to be abandoned because they lacked the draft animals to move them. The German rear was in chaos. Supply lines were constantly cut, not only by Allied air and artillery, but also by roving gangs of German deserters scavenging for survival. Little food was reaching the front and German soldiers were beginning to starve. The advancing Americans encountered dead horses carved up and consumed by hungry enemy soldiers.

Success for the Americans was contagious and demoralization for the Germans epidemic. The pursuit was on, as the Germans began a general pullback all along the Western

Front. Called Kriegsmarsch, the plan was to break contact with the Allied forces and withdraw to a new defense line east of the Meuse. But the American advance was so rapid now, regardless of a cornucopea of booby traps and some fierce rear-guard resistance by several still intact enemy units, that the Germans were never able to re-flex their muscles.

On November 2–3, III Corps drove forward six miles and chased the enemy across the Meuse. V Corps forged ahead seven miles, with the 2nd Division capturing La Tuilerie Farm, just two miles from the Meuse. I Corps galloped forward ten miles. Flying above the collapsing German front, Eddie Rickenbacker witnessed an enemy retreat degenerating into a rout. "Every road was filled with retreating Heines. They were going while the going was good and their very gestures seemed to indicate that for them it was indeed the finis de la guerre."[41]

With the 5th Division as the pivot on the Meuse, the other six U.S. divisions reoriented their axes of advance toward the northeast to close in on the northwest-running curve of the river. The rains resumed and the mud returned, bringing back the molasses-slow flow of supplies and the overall clogging of the roads reminiscent of the late September days at the beginning of the battle. The congestion was intensified by the debris of defeat. A private in the 80th Division reported: "As we advanced, the roads and fields were strewn with dead Germans, horses, masses of artillery, transports, ammo limbers, helmets, guns and bayonets."[42]

The surging infantry regiments ranged far ahead of their logistical lines. For two or three days, soldiers in I Corps, on the fastest track of the three corps, had to make do with canned salmon—derisively referred to as "goldfish" by the doughboys—before more palatable rations could reach them. But poor rations were but an easily shrugged-off inconvenience for men who were racing to victory after weeks of crawling through hell.

At the head of the I Corps race to the Meuse was Whittlesey's and Alexander's 77th Division. Of course, the hero of the Pocket was no longer with the Statue of Liberty Division to see its agonies in the Argonne vindicated by final victory on the Meuse. When the Armistice ended fifty-two months of mayhem, Whittlesey was surrounded by the blue-gray of the Atlantic in place of the gray-green of the Argonne, as he headed for home aboard a transport ship. He had embarked on October 31, as his old division prepared to finish its time on the Meuse-Argonne front by being in on the finish. The 77th, after occupying abandoned Champigneulle, swept up to Haraucourt by the evening of November 2. Four days later, the Metro Division had completed a twenty-five mile advance since November 1 that put its regiments in and around Remilly-sur-Meuse, just four miles southeast of the ultimate target of Sedan. The 77th commenced bridging of the river and patrols scouted east of the Meuse, but the Armistice intervened before the 77th could renew its chase of the Hun.

When the guns fell silent on the Western Front, the 77th Division was finally withdrawn from active duty after 119 days in the line and sixty-three days in active combat—the most of any division (the 3rd Division, with fifty days in battle, was in second place). In those 119 days at the front, the men of the 77th had suffered 2,110 battle deaths and 8,084 wounds. Of those 10,194 total casualties, 4,958 had come during the Battle of the Meuse-Argonne—4,061 during the division's first tour in the rainy woods, September 26–October 16, and 897 in the breakout offensive of November 1–11.

The first elements of the New York division would embark for home at Brest on February 9, 1919, and most of the 77th would board homeward-bound ships on April 17, 1919. The final transport bearing the division entered New York Harbor on May 6, 1919, and the citizens of the city welcomed home their very own heroes with unbridled enthusiasm as they paraded up Fifth Avenue. Just three days later, the division that had provided history and the world with the saga of the Lost Battalion was demobilized at the same Camp Upton that had witnessed its genesis just two years before.

The 77th Division would again be called to the colors for a second global conflict in 1942. It would fight—from July 1944 to June 1945—in the Central Pacific, from Guam to Leyte to Chocolate Drop Hill and other stations of hell on Okinawa, never seeing a German during this second tour of combat duty. Though in battle far longer in World War II, the division never fought a tougher or more costly battle than that of the Argonne Forest. The Second World War cost the 77th Division 1,850 killed in battle and 5,935 wounded— a loss rate 20 percent lighter than it incurred in little more than two months of major combat in the Great War.

The other six U.S. divisions in the line and the five more following in their wake also continued to make giant strides forward in the first week of November. Liggett, who liked to play solitaire in order to decompress during periods of high stress, could now confidently set aside his cards as his soldiers surged toward now certain victory.

On the army's river flank, the 5th Red Diamond Division used improvised rafts to put two companies across the eighty-two-foot-wide Meuse at Dun-sur-Meuse before dawn on November 3. This force from the 6th Infantry Regiment was led by Lt. Colonel Courtney Hodges (who would command the U.S. First Army in World War II). The companies were pinned down for forty hours by heavy German fire, in an open plain between the river and a sixty-five-foot wide canal, before they could fight their way to the other side in the evening darkness of November 4. Three more 5th Division regiments pushed across the canal on November 5 to capture Milly and push south to the Bois de Châtillon. In the course of the 5th's leap over the Meuse, Captain Edward Allworth of Company M of the 60th Regiment won the Medal of Honor, as he rallied two stalled platoons by bounding into the frigid river, swimming across, and leading his men to the capture of Hill 260.

The Germans were helpless to stop the expansion of the bridgeheads. Supreme HQ, on November 5, had ordered von Gallwitz to stop the Americans "at all costs" and drive them back over the Meuse. But the German general had no further resources in men or firepower to carry out the mission. On November 6, he despairingly observed through his field glasses as Red Diamond infantrymen burst through the woods between Murvaux and Fontaines, more than two miles east of the river. The 32nd Division was also crossing the Meuse, at Brieulles, a mile south.

As victory hoved into view, Pershing, Foch and, quite naturally, all of France set their sights on the glittering prize of Sedan. The strategic value of this railroad hub aside, the city carried even greater symbolic heft from the heavy load of history. The opportunity to efface the scars of 1870 was there for the taking. The French assumed that they would have the honor of reversing Napoleon III's historic shame, but Pershing roused their Gallic ire by announcing, on November 6, that he intended to liberate Sedan with his own AEF.

While the French fumed, the situation became even more confused and more a political game between high commanders with big egos, as Summerall picked his former, and still favorite, division—the 1st—to pluck this brightest feather from a triumphal air. This required the 1st to hook left, across the 42nd's divisional boundary and even into the French Fourth Army's sector. Five columns of 1st Division infantry (filled out now with 8,000 replacements), including the 26th Regiment, commanded by Colonel Theodore Roosevelt

Jr., were soon tearing across the Rainbow Division's rear, disrupting their supply lines and threatening a massive entanglement of the two divisions. MacArthur was even "arrested" by 1st Division troops, who burst into his CP and mistook him for an enemy leader. Roosevelt's 26th Infantry penetrated four miles against minimal resistance and reached a forest several miles northwest of Chéhéry, deep into French Fourth Army territory, before a furious Liggett and a violently outraged General Gouraud halted their progress and ordered them to pull back into the I Corps zone.

The 42nd, meanwhile, had managed to put patrols into the villages of Torcy and Wadelincourt, across the Meuse from Sedan, though they were soon slapped back by German artillery and machine-gun fire. An investigation into this "Sedan Affair" would ensue. But, because the Germans were too weak and disorganized to take advantage of the embroglio and because the whole dust-up had been initiated by Pershing's lust for history's limelight, the incident was brushed away in the backwash of victory.

The endgame was indeed at hand. All along the front, not just in the Meuse-Argonne sector, but from the North Sea to the Vosges Mountains, the Belgians, the British, the French, as well as the Americans, were smashing through the Hindenburg Line, attempting to exploit and expand the scope of the victory before politicians and their peace could intervene. Pershing had always advocated total war and total victory and he, on November 9, unleashed Bullard's Second Army—the 33rd, 28th, 7th and 92nd Divisions—east across the Woevre Plain to Marchéville and Lachausee. The U.S. divisions attached to the French XVII and II Colonial Corps—the 79th, 26th and 81st—were also on the move, sweeping over the east rim of the Meuse Heights to take the Borne de Cornoueller on November 7 and Ville-devant-Chaumont on November 8.

Aware that peace could break out at any moment, Pershing urged his divisions on, anxious to inflict the maximum damage on a German army that he wanted not just defeated, but smashed to smithereens. He had called for "unconditional surrender" right before meeting with Colonel House—the bearer of Wilson's soft peace of Fourteen Points—at a Supreme War Council.

At 0510 on November 11, the Armistice was signed in Foch's railroad car at Compiègne. The supreme American commander was planning more extensive pursuits of the broken foe further north and east toward Briey and Metz, when First and Second Army HQ's received news of the signing of the Armistice at 0630. The guns were to fall silent at the eleventh hour, and no useful purpose but further carnage could be served by continuing hostilities. But Pershing and Summerall had ordered the advance to continue to the maximum moment. Foch, who had lost a son and a son-in-law on the same day of the Great War and hated the Hun with an abiding fervor, concurred. Liggett tried to put a brake to further action, but he was too late.

And so men continued to fight and die, and the roar of the cannon persisted to that last minute of madness. Historian Donald Smythe, in his book, *Pershing, General of the Armies*, wrote: "The men who died or were maimed in those last few hours suffered needlessly and their mishandling provoked a Congressional investigation after the war."[43]

East of Verdun, near the village of Hermèville, Harry Truman's Battery D fired some of the last American artillery rounds of the war. He reported: "I fired the battery on orders until 1045, when I fired my last shot," spiraling new shells with a range of 11,000 meters—a 2,200 meter increase over the old 75 mm shell.[44] His 129th Field Artillery Regiment had suffered 129 casualties during the battle, but the men under Truman's direct command had suffered not a scratch in America's bloodiest battle of all time.

George Patton noted in his diary: "Got rid of my bandage. Wrote a poem to peace."[45] Pershing, his dream of invading and conquering the kaiser's empire, of occupying Berlin, dashed, paced his Chaumont HQ before a huge map tracing his never-to-be unleashed arrows into Germany and complained, "I suppose our campaigns are ended, but what an enormous difference a few more days would have made. We would have rounded up the entire German army. What I dread is that Germany doesn't know that she was licked. Had they given us another week, we'd have taught them."[46]

Black Jack was prescient to a degree he could not have fathomed at the time. Among those convinced that Germany was not "licked" and that not a military defeat, but a "stab in the back" by internal enemies, had cost Germany victory in the Great War, was an Austrian-born corporal. Hospitalized on Armistice Day with temporary blindness caused by mustard gas, his four years in the trenches had earned him an Iron Cross and deepened the darkness of his black dreams.

At that famous triple eleven—eleventh hour of the eleventh day of the eleventh month—the murderous air of the Western Front, saturated with the cacophony of combat, cleared to the sounds of silence. Men had continued to fight and kill one another with all the malevolent methods and anonymity of mass slaughter through the last hours and up to the last minutes of the 1,569-day war.

The 2nd, 89th and 90th Divisions, in a race to bite off more territory and win more points for their commanders, fought their way over the Meuse in the hours before 1100, at a cost of 1,130 casualties, including 127 killed. Had their vain-glorious leaders not pushed them senselessly into the face of enemy fire, they could have—according to the terms of the Armistice—occupied the same ground without loss after 1100. The commander of the 89th Division, hearing there were bathing facilities intact at Stenay and anxious to claim the honor of liberating the last German-held city to be retaken by American units, ordered his men to storm the town in the war's last hours. The honor cost the 89th 365 casualties.

On the entire Western Front, as many as 10,944 casualties—including 2,738 killed—were added in those last eleven hours. At least 3,240 of those casualties were American, including 320 dead (although officially, the under-reported count was 268 killed and 2,769 wounded).

George Marshall, now operations officer of the 1st Division, very nearly became one of those final casualties. One-half hour before the Armistice, a bomb fell out of the bomb bay of a French Nieuport. The bomb destroyed the division headquarters at Souilly. Marshall was draped in debris, but escaped without harm. Not as fortunate was Private Henry Gunther of the 79th Division's 313th Regiment. He was killed near Damvillers at 1059, the last doughboy to die in battle in World War I. He posthumously received the DSC for the distinction.

The crew of one of the naval 14-inch guns hurled a 1,400-pound shell twenty-five miles deep into German lines, its arc timed to end explosively exactly at 1100. It may have been the last shot of the Battle of the Meuse-Argonne.

The sudden silence of the battlefield after that eleventh hour was astounding to many of the combatants. For almost seven weeks, hundreds of thousands of soldiers on both sides had existed in a cosmos of chaos and almost uninterrupted explosive tumult. Now the quiet that enveloped the heights and woods and villages of the Meuse-Argonne sector seemed uncanny and unreal. After recovering from the stunning silence, doughboys began to crack smiles and jokes, and marvel that it was really over and they were still alive. Cheering among the exhausted infantrymen was subdued; the riotous celebration was reserved for the folks back home. Fraternity with the former enemy was forbidden, but some soldiers approached the German trenches with hands out instead of bayonets poised. "A few Germans came to shake hands; they gave our men coins, and even pulled buttons off their clothes to give them."[47] The doughboys reciprocated with cigarettes and chocolate.

Jubilation was more overt in the rear, at aerodromes and supply depots, and had started early, with the rumors of impending peace the night before. At Rickenbacker's 94th Squadron HQ, an AA battery opened up the fanfare, followed by machine guns, rifles, Very pistols, .45s, captured Lugers, horns, sirens, gleeful shouts and laughter. Fuel barrels were overturned and ignited, and revelers joined hands to dance around the bonfire. Pilots emptied flasks into the mess kettles, and soon drunken airmen, including Rickenbacker, were wrestling in the mud.

Rickenbacker recovered from his celebratory spree on November 11 to take an unauthorized flight over the lines, just minutes before the Armistice went into effect. His plane was holed by bullets fired by some disgruntled Germans unwilling, even at this late hour, to accept defeat. But at the moment the Armistice began, Rickenbacker observed clusters of khaki and gray-green figures emerging from their positions to embrace. Skirting the French lines, Rickenbacker saw poilus hugging Huns and planting Gallic kisses on both cheeks.

Harry Truman joined in the celebration too, but, like his commander, John Pershing, he preferred the Germans crushed, not just defeated. To his fiancé, Bess, he penned a harsh letter replete with words of revenge, wishing that his unit could occupy German towns and carry out acts of retribution, such as, "cutting off the hands of German children and scalping the old men."[48]

That night the front line infantrymen built fires to warm themselves against the falling temperatures that sheathed every blade of grass in its own scabbard of ice. They watched the artillery fire their kaleidoscopic designs of multi-colored flares to signal an end to it all. The Battle of the Meuse-Argonne was ended and the Great War was over.

The victory, that seemed out of sight and even unattainable in early October, had been achieved. But it had been won at a prodigious cost. No American army, before or since, has paid such a price to overcome its enemy as had the U.S. First Army. Only Grant's Army of the Potomac, in the spring of 1864, came close to counting as many casualties as did Pershing's army of doughboy infantrymen and artillerymen. Even the final phase of the Meuse-Argonne Offensive—November 1–11—against relatively spotty enemy resistance, was no stroll down a sunny lane. The twelve American divisions engaged in those November days—including those attached to the French east of the Meuse—lost 18,000 killed, wounded or missing (including up to 3,200 on the last day), as they stormed toward Sedan. The 79th Division accounted for 2,300 of those casualties and the 5th Division for over 2,000.

The grand total of U.S. casualties for the entire forty-seven days of the Battle of the Meuse-Argonne was computed at 26,277 battle deaths, 95,786 wounded, 5,000 missing or captured. The battle deaths represented 49 percent of all U.S. combat fatalities—53,519—suffered in the nineteen months of American participation in the Great War. The wounded of the Meuse-Argonne accounted for 47 percent of all American battle injuries incurred in the conflict. Over 173,000 American military personnel had been evacuated from the battlefield with wounds, sickness or exhaustion, and 100,000 fresh troops funneled in to replace them.

The Meuse-Argonne more than tripled the toll for the second bloodiest battle of the war for the United States—the Aisne-Marne, which piled up 40,353 American casualties, including 6,992 battle dead, in nineteen days (July 18–August 5, 1918). On average, the fighting from the Meuse to the Argonne took the lives of 558 doughboys every one of its forty-seven days.

The American toll was exacted from twenty-two U.S. divisions, including the two—the African-American 92nd and 93rd—which fought exclusively under French Second Army or French Fourth Army control. The 92nd and 93rd aside, divisional losses ranged from a high of 8,814 (including attached units) for the 1st Division to a low of 3,074 for the 37th Division—which was engaged in the battle for only five days, September 26–30. The average divisional casualty toll for the twenty directly engaged divisions was over 6,000.

Of course, it was not just American flesh and bone that was torn or obliterated under the whirling blades of German firepower in the Meuse-Argonne campaign. Including Fourth Army losses in Champagne, west of the Argonne Forest, and XVII and II Colonial Corps casualties east of the Meuse, over 50,000 French poilus joined the casualty lists of the seven-week battle.

A total of 1,256,478 American servicemen participated directly in the battle or in support of it. About 850,000 of that total were classified as combat troops. They had been backed by 842 airplanes, 324 tanks, and, most decisively, by 2,417 artillery pieces—which fired off over four million shells, exceeding the total tonnage of ammunition expended by all Union forces in all four years of the American Civil War.

All this effort and sacrifice had come against a total of 470,000 soldiers in forty-four German and Austrian divisions (according to the AEF's count), drawn to the Meuse-Argonne battlefield at one time or the other in those last seven weeks of the war. Many of those divisions had been second rate, understrength, or only the shell of a division, but they too had suffered greatly. The U.S. First Army claimed to have taken 26,000 POWs and inflicted a total of 100,000 casualties on the enemy.* The Germans also lost 874 artillery pieces and over 3,000 machine guns. In the air, they had lost 417 planes and 53 balloons (compared to U.S. losses of 192 planes and 22 balloons). By the end of the offensive, the Germans had retreated thirty-two miles from their original line west of the Meuse, and fourteen miles from their September 26 positions east of the Meuse.

The Germans had fought largely from heavily fortified defensive positions which kept their attrition rate low. But their propensity for launching immediate and often costly counterattacks and the rout of the battle's last days greatly increased their casualty rolls. Unlike for America, the Meuse-Argonne was not Germany's greatest battle or greatest sacrifice of the Great War. But it had cost the German army casualties and energy it could not afford, and it convinced the enemy, from Ludendorff down to the humblest Boche private, that they could no longer sustain a war against an Allied force revitalized by an ever increasing flood of Yankee doughboys riding the waves across the Atlantic to the shores of France.

---

*Liggett claimed that the Germans lost 100,000 killed or wounded, *in addition to* the 26,000 taken prisoner, thus bringing German casualties for the battle to a near balance with American losses. It is more likely, however, that the 100,000 figure represents *total* German losses, including POWs.

6

The Veterans

The great American army—the largest in the history of the republic—rapidly returned homeward and demobilized. Except for a quarter of a million soldiers in five divisions and supporting units slated for occupation duty in the Rhineland, the two million doughboys in France and Belgium boarded ships in the first months of 1919 to recross the Atlantic and return to the New World, hailed as saviors of the old. The men who had planned, directed and fought the Battle of the Meuse-Argonne—from the supreme commander to every doughboy private—would carry the campaign with them to the end of their days. For many, the battle was the most traumatic and defining moment in their lives. For others—like Patton, MacArthur and Marshall—the campaign was just a formative, if very formidable, episode in their long march toward military renown.

John J. Pershing, the rigid but resolute face of the American Expeditionary Forces, returned to the United States in September 1919, after the signing of the Treaty of Versailles. A grateful Congress bestowed upon him the six stars of a general of the Army—a constellation carried otherwise only by George Washington in all of American history. Appointed as Army chief of staff in 1921, he had to witness—in a disillusioned climate of isolationism and anti-militarism—a Great War Army of four million drastically decline by mid-1923 to 131,254 men under arms. After retiring on September 13, 1921, Pershing accepted the post of president of the American Battle Monuments Commission in Paris, working to memorialize the sacrifices of his soldiers and honor their final resting places.

While in Paris, Pershing resumed his relationship with Micheline Resco (Michette). He had met the then twenty-three-year-old French-Rumanian artist when he posed for her for an official portrait in 1917. Although Pershing would continue to be frequently linked to other women in society gossip, he would continue the romance with Michette for the rest of his long life. In 1946, at age eighty-four, Pershing finally took as his bride the fifty-two-year-old Michette.

Pershing's memoirs—*My Experiences in the World War*—were published in 1931. They were self-serving and highly critical of some of his superiors and subordinates—most particularly of the World War I Army chief of staff, General Peyton March—but they won him the Pulitzer Prize for history. His health declining, he was an invalided patient in Walter Reed Hospital when his former operations planner, George C. Marshall, now chief of staff, brought him the news of America's entrance into World War II. Pershing died on July 15, 1948, not quite eighty-eight years of age. Among the generals who led the funeral procession of the World War I commander from the Capitol Rotunda to Arlington National Cemetery were World War II leaders Dwight Eisenhower and Omar Bradley.

Hunter Liggett, the man who, more than anyone, was responsible for transforming the U.S. First Army from an almost ad hoc collection of enthusiastic amateurs into a tactically agile and professionally managed fighting force, remained in Europe as commander of the occupation forces in Germany until June 1919. Posted at the Presidio as commander of the IX Corps, he served there until his retirement on March 21, 1921. Enamored with the Bay area, he made San Francisco his final home, dying there on December 30, 1935.

Liggett had earned the highest esteem of the Regular Army officer corps. Maj. General Frank Baldwin—the bearer of two Medals of Honor from duty in the Civil War and the Indian wars—pronounced that Liggett "has no equal in professional ability or noble character among our American generals."[1] General Bullard recognized his perspicacity, judgment, and strategic vision: "Liggett had the valuable faculty of seeing what was important and what not; and he did not waste his time or attention on what was not going to count."[2]

Robert Bullard, post-Armistice, commanded II Corps from its headquarters at Fort Jay on Governor's Island, New York, until 1925. Contrary and cantankerous, a man who thought Black Jack Pershing was too "soft," he grew increasingly isolationist and reactionary in the 1930s. At one point in 1935, he claimed that the relief agencies established by the New Deal administration of Franklin D. Roosevelt were little better than Communist fronts dedicated toward toppling the American system. Bullard died on September 11, 1947, at Fort Jay at age eighty-six.

Charles Summerall, the firebrand of the 1st Division and then the V Corps, went on to become Army chief of staff. After retiring, he became president of the Citadel Military College in Charleston, South Carolina. Though many generals—Alexander, Johnson, even divarty commander Brig. General Manus McCloskey, whose guns nearly destroyed Whittlesey's force on October 4—tried to take credit for "saving" the Lost Battalion, it was Summerall (and his hard-charging Big Red One) who, more than anyone, was responsible for loosening the German cordon around Charlevaux Creek.

William "Wild Bill" Donovan went on to become a titan of World War II and the Cold War. The daring director of the Office of Strategic Services from 1942–45, he became the patron saint of the CIA in the twilight struggle with the Soviet Union. Donovan had been one of the most highly decorated American soldiers of the Great War. Besides the Medal of Honor he won in the Argonne, Wild Bill acquired two wound chevrons, the DSC with bronze oak leaf cluster (denoting a second award to the original), and a dozen foreign decorations. Though there were many exploits to come in Wild Bill's life and career, Donovan's October day in the Argonne was his most shining moment. He died on February 8, 1959.

Eddie Rickenbacker returned to the auto industry after November 11 and in 1938 became general manager of Eastern Airlines. During World War II Secretary of War Henry Stimson sent him and seven companions on a tour of U.S. bases abroad. After his plane crashed in shark-infested Pacific waters, Rickenbacker and his crew endured twenty-four days drifting on a rubber raft before they were rescued. After the Second World War, he visited the Heroes Veteran Cemetery in East Berlin to pay homage to his old aerial opponents, such as Oswald Boelke, Manfred von Richthofen and Ernst Udet. Rickenbacker died in 1973.

Robert Alexander, the fiery, fighting Celt and leader of the 77th Division, embarked for home in the spring of 1919. With the drastic downsizing of the post-war American military, he reverted to his previous Regular Army rank of colonel. Re-promoted to brigadier general in 1921, Alexander took command of the 3rd Field Artillery Brigade. Attaining the rank of major general, he remained at that post until his retirement in October 1927, after forty-one years in the Army. He spent his final decades in La Jolla, California. The veterans of the 77th Division—which Alexander had flogged into shape, driven unmercifully, and venerated as his highest achievement in life—made him their guest of honor at the American Legion convention in New York City in September 1937. He died in New York in August 1941.

Brigade commander Evan Johnson did not long survive the Argonne. A medical condition that afflicted him throughout the campaign required an operation following the Armistice. The surgery was unsuccessful and he died shortly afterwards, in Paris in October 1923.

Regimental commander Cromwell Stacey—who had begun his military life twenty-four years before the Argonne as a Marine drummer boy—retired to live in Port Angeles, Washington. Though he was recommended for the DSC for his courageous effort to relieve the Lost Battalion, his request to be relieved from his command, rather than continuing to waste the lives of his men in further futile rescue efforts, effectively ended his military career and squelched his chances at receiving the cross.

The commander of the 307th Infantry, Colonel Eugene Houghton, veteran of Central American conflicts as well as the Great War, tried to retire to peaceful pursuits after the eleventh day of November, working as a grain broker in Winnipeg, Canada. But in the revolutionary turmoil of the post-war era, he once again found himself in the middle of the action. Drafted as an acting chief of police during a Communist-inspired general strike, Houghton settled the dispute with his usual rapid and iron-fisted decisiveness.

For the direct participants in the saga of the Lost Battalion, the Battle of the Meuse-Argonne would lend them an even greater legacy than their other million-plus comrades who fought in the campaign. In the two decades between the world wars, the veterans of the Lost Battalion were the living symbols of the collective courage of the American doughboy. In much the same way that the survivors of the Light Brigade of Balaclava fame were for many years the objects of renown, so too were the men who had been carried out or marched with Whittlesey out of the Pocket on Charlevaux Creek on October 8, 1918. Most of those men handled their notoriety with grace and aplomb; some tried to capitalize on it financially, socially or politically. Others were uneasy with the attention and wanted only to blend back into society and forget; more than a few were incapable of forgetting—even for a moment—those five days in the dreadful forest, and were haunted and hounded to the grave by their memories.

George McMurtry, who earned in the Argonne a Medal of Honor, several wounds, and—next to Whittlesey—the most fame and acclaim accorded to any man in the Pocket, carried his sunny self-confidence back out of the deadly forest and on home to a relatively easy readjustment to peace and—for him at least—prosperity. The Argonne never left his side, but never seemed to invade his soul. He stayed in contact and remained loyal to his Lost Battalion comrades, rarely missing a reunion and never giving a cold shoulder to a friend who had shared his experience along Charlevaux Brook, but had not shared his post-war good fortune. The war would forever remain a vital part of McMurtry, but, unlike his CO, it did not consume him.

Returning to New York City after the war, McMurtry resumed his career as a stockbroker. With homes on Park Avenue and in Bar Harbor, Maine, and membership in the best clubs, his practice flourished until his retirement in 1938. In September 1958, McMurtry hosted a Lost Battalion reunion at the Shelburne Hotel in New York. In attendance were forty-six of the 114 men still surviving their time in the Argonne. Two months later, on November 22, 1958, he died at the age of eighty-two.

Nelson Holderman, the third man—after Whittlesey and McMurtry—to receive the Medal of Honor for his gallantry in the Pocket, remained in the Army after the war, even though he was permanently disabled by the multiple wounds he suffered there in the Argonne. Always immensely proud of being a member—and an essential member—of the Lost Battalion, he authored a monograph on the events of October 2–8 for the U.S. Army Infantry School. By the late 1930s, Holderman was a full colonel and in charge of a veterans hospital in California. A heart attack claimed him on September 3, 1953.

Major George G. McMurtry aboard a transport returning to the United States, 1919. National Archives, 111-SC-48170.

Other former officers of Whittlesey's command similarly devoted large segments of their post-war lives toward enriching or enshrining the legend of the Lost Battalion. Lt. Arthur McKeogh, Whittlesey's battalion adjutant and leader of the patrol sent back for help when the 1/308th was surrounded the first time in late September, wrote a lionizing article for *Collier's* magazine about his CO and his battalion almost as soon as he stepped off the ship returning them from the war. He became an authority on the Lost Battalion and went on to serve as managing editor of *Good Housekeeping* magazine before his death in New York City in 1938.

Lt. William Cullen, McMurtry's second in command and winner of the DSC, carried his command presence into the courtroom as a New York City attorney after the war. He would be a frequent speaker on the Lost Battalion lecture circuit. He became a major in the 308th Infantry, Organized Reserves—with the unit's mill-wheel emblem, symbolizing Charlevaux Mill and the Lost Battalion—and would serve again in World War II.

Among the other officers who made it out of the Pocket, Captain Leo Stromee recovered from his grave wounds inflicted by the *Minenwerfer* shell, but one side of his face remained partly paralyzed. Remaining in the Reserves after the war, Stromee also worked for the city of Los Angeles and served as a director of the Napa, California, Veterans Home at the same time that Colonel Holderman was superintendent. He was quoted as saying, "I think the Lost Battalion episode deserves a place in history with the Alamo, and I am proud to have been in it. But—never again!"[3]

Lieutenants Leak and Harrington, both captured in the Pocket, were repatriated and returned home, Harrington to Detroit, Michigan, and Leak to Longview, Texas, where he took up "lawyering." Lt. Knight, twice wounded in his determined but unsuccessful attempt to add his company to the Pocket's defenders, received the DSC for his efforts and became a major in the Regular Army. By the late 1930s, he was presiding over the La Salle Military Academy in Oakdale, New York. Lt. Pool, second in command of Holderman's Company K, recovered from the sniper's bullet wound in his back to become a deputy sheriff in Beaumont, Texas.

A good many of the enlisted men of the 308th also remained closely identified with the legend of the Lost Battalion after the Armistice. Abe Krotoshinsky, "the man who got through and the man who came back," took up Zionism and migrated to Palestine to till that biblical soil.[4] His health weakened from the toxic gas he had inhaled, Krotoshinsky had to give up his Middle Eastern farm and return to New York. Drifting from job to job, he finally got his lucky break in 1927, when a *New York World* newspaper story brought his plight to the attention of President Coolidge. With Oval Office help, Krotoshinsky was given a position in the Postal Service. He died in 1953.

Two other privates who got through the German lines with rescue appeals and won the DSC for their daring, Stanislaw Kozikowski and Clifford Brown, went different directions with their Lost Battalion experience. Brown became a frequent public dispenser of Lost Battalion lore in between his duties as head of an electrical equipment service in Jamestown, New York. Kozikowski eventually went to work in the Brooklyn Navy Yard, and bulked up to 225 pounds on the once spare frame with which he had slithered through the enemy positions. He remained generally tight-lipped about his days in the Argonne, dismissing the event rhetorically, if not emotionally, with the comment, "Well, it's only history now."[5]

George Newcom, one of the Midwestern replacements added to the 77th after its Vesle bloodbath and one of the eight unsuccessfully sent out by McMurtry to bring back help, returned to Kansas to eventually fight another war—this time exclusively against nature—on his Dust Bowl farm near Oakley.

Another lithe and agile hero of the Pocket and winner of the DSC, water-gatherer Philip Cepeglia, remained quick in mind and body in his post-war life in the Bronx. At a reunion of Lost Battalion veterans in the late 1930s, he recalled that terrifying time with a down-to-earth poise. But the mention of his CO broke his bright-eyed composure. "I don't know why he disappeared afterward, but it wasn't because he was afraid of anything. He was the bravest man in the AEF."[6]

James Larney, the signal panel carrier, who kept a diary during his days on Charlevaux Creek, also had trouble dealing with the way Whittlesey finally escaped the Argonne. A political big-wig in St. Lawrence County in upstate New York after the Great War, he was actively involved in American Legion activities, and often got together with his old 308th comrades to reminisce and read over his diary entries from the Pocket. His emotional engagement with those October days in that French forest extended to a pilgrimage cruise he took aboard the same steamer on the same course that carried Whittlesey to his final resting place in

1921. Standing by the ship's railing throughout a contemplative night, Larney stared into the sea and tried, with little revelation, to divine in those dark waters the reason for Whittlesey's timing and manner of exit.

Like Larney, most of the E.M. veterans of the battalion successfully re-integrated into society. Corporal Walter Baldwin, in charge of Whittlesey's message runners, attained the rank of sergeant-major before demobilizing and returning to New York City. In 1960, he helped pen a tribute to the Lost Battalion in an article entitled, "Alamo in the Argonne" for *True* magazine. James Carroll, acting first sergeant of the 307th's Company K, and one of the few who carried on from Charlevaux Creek to stick it out on the front line until the 77th reached Grandpré, returned to New York and resumed his job as a drapery salesman with the same company he had worked for before conscription. Twenty years later, he was still at it with the same firm, his time in the Argonne just a brief, if violently vivid, interruption in his otherwise unremarkable middle class life.

Lowell Hollingshead, the young replacement private who carried the German surrender demand to Whittlesey's CP, took advantage of his moment of fame to become for a time a popular lecturer on the war-story circuit. Eventually, however, he became jaded enough about his time in the sun to remark, in response to audience member claims that they would give a million dollars for a similar experience: "Hell, I'll take the million."[7] At the end of his celebrity run, Hollingshead settled in Mt. Sterling, Ohio, working at an oil and gas company.

For others, however, there was no easy re-emersion into America, no long-lasting resumption of lives into the relative placidness of peace. Lt. Teichmoeller, the artillery liaison man whose miscalculations may have contributed to the deadly friendly fire of October 4, suffered increasing hearing loss and headaches from that misguided shelling. As Whittlesey was sailing to the end of his story, Teichmoeller underwent an operation to halt this worsening condition, but it succeeded only in halting his heart. Other wounded survivors of the Lost Battalion also succumbed to their injuries in hospitals in the immediate years after the war. They, like their CO, died of wounds received in battle, months or even years after the shell storm had abated. But unlike the major who so gallantly led them, their wounds were of the flesh and not of the soul, and the mystery remains as to why the commander of the Lost Battalion could not, in the end, avoid becoming the battalion's final casualty.

Strictly speaking, it may be inaccurate to claim Whittlesey as the last casualty of the Lost Battalion. Though he did not die in the dark woods of the Argonne, he died in the darker depths of his soul. Though no Maxim bullet nor scimitar of shrapnel ended his life in October 1918, his psyche suffered mortal wounds and he succumbed to those wounds three years later. Other men of the brigade must have carried injuries to mind and spirit out of the Pocket that they tried to treat with alcohol or other sources of oblivion in the years or even decades ahead, only to ultimately lose the battle they had thought had ended on November 11.

But Whittlesey was certainly the most prominent post-Armistice casualty and the most tragic. His tactical mistakes may have carried his men into the trap of the Pocket and cost the lives of many, but his inspiring leadership enabled the survivors to walk out of that trap and saved the lives of more. He was publicly praised and bemedaled and made a hero for saving the remnants of his command, but privately tormented and, finally, dammed by remorse for failing the men who died. In the end, the silent voices of the dead spoke louder to Whittlesey than all the praise and all the cheers. He drowned out all those silent shouts the only way he could.

Theories abound to explain Whittlesey's decision to walk the plank of the *Toloa*. From almost the day after his disappearance to nearly the day before yesterday in the new millennium, comrades, reporters and historians have offered reasons why. There were from the onset, amongst all the hoopla and huzzahs that cascaded down on the Lost Battalion and its commander in that final fall of the Great War, contrary voices of doubt and even derision. A comedic sketch during a post-Armistice Army entertainment included this scathing sarcasm: "Gosh, I just lost my wrist watch.... That's nothing; a major over in the 77th Division just lost a whole battalion!"[8] Though this and the other caveats of the scattered skeptics were little heard in the din of praise and acclamation, their dissenting opinions persisted.

Charles Whittlesey was almost universally admired post-Argonne as a leader of nearly unrivaled moral, as well as physical, courage. Even the naysayers among his peers and among historians granted him a bedrock bravery from which he never wavered. But those less willing to swallow the legend whole questioned his tactical judgment and operational decisions.

In fact, the skeptics and outright cynics may not have been that few and far between in the immediate aftermath of the Argonne events. Thomas M. Johnson and Fletcher Pratt, in their seminal study, *The Lost Battalion*, maintained that as late as two decades after the Armistice up to 90 percent of Americans believed that, "Whittlesey's excessive zeal led him into a trap from which he later had to be rescued when he might easily have escaped."[9] This impression, the authors believed, arose mainly from the trial of Lieutenant Revnes, the former actor and machine-gun officer court-martialed in December 1918, whose note to Whittlesey on October 6 suggested negotiation with the enemy about surrender or at least about evacuating the wounded. The trial had lasted three days, and forty witnesses, including McMurtry and Holderman, testified. He was initially found guilty of "misbehavior on the field." But he was exonerated after a review of the verdict—when it was pointed out that Revnes, hobbled though he was with an ankle injury, had consistently crawled, pistol in hand, to wherever the fires were hottest. To a large extent, however, the proceedings became more of a general inquiry into the choices and conduct of the commander of the battalion, than it was an investigation into the words and actions of one junior officer.

Whittlesey could not have been unaware of the carping criticisms, both general and specific, about his decisions, October 2–7, nor of the impression held by many that the Army chose to promote him and reward him with the Medal of Honor to avoid the embarrassment of court-martialing him. But Johnson and Pratt believed that the motive for his suicide was due, not because he believed his tactical blunders had caused the unnecessary deaths of over 100 of his men, but because he was unable to deal with the consequences of fame.

In their book, Johnson and Pratt investigated the charges of misjudgment and incompetence levied against Whittlesey and found them unconvincing. Easiest of the claims and outright calumnies against Whittlesey's record and reputation for the authors to refute was the accusation that he had brought down the friendly fire barrage on his men by sending in the wrong coordinates of his position. Following the relief of the Lost Battalion, Alexander had ordered an investigation into the incident. The Army, more concerned about morale than truth, followed the path of least resistance and less embarrassment by arriving at the official verdict of enemy responsibility for that October 4th shellfall. None of the battalion survivors and no objective observer swallowed the pabulum. The enemy possessed no artillery that could arc a trajectory so high as to land shells in the Pocket. The men of the 308th had clearly heard the discharges of the artillery pieces before the shells landed among them. To veteran ears attuned to the distinct differences in the explosive reports of friendly and enemy field guns and howitzers, the incoming rounds were clearly launched, not from German 77s, but from French or American 75s. Confirming this, was the hard fact that all of the dud rounds that had failed to explode in and around the Pocket were 75 mm shells.

Some of the survivors of the shelling were so incensed at the Army's whitewash, that they approached Whittlesey about swearing out an affidavit to fix the blame where it properly

Whittlesey receiving the Congressional Medal of Honor on Boston Common, December 24, 1918. Williams College Archives and Special Collections.

belonged. But the Armistice had silenced the big guns on both sides now, and Whittlesey advised, "Forget it; the war's over."[10]

The obviousness of whence the shells had come aside, the question yet remained as to the identity of the man whose miscalculations had sent them on their way. From the remaining message traffic in the records, Johnson and Pratt concluded that the coordinates sent back by Whittlesey were accurate. Though the records are incomplete and (as is so often the case in warfare's paper trail) sometimes contradictory, the available evidence points to either artillery liaison officer Lt. Teichmoeller, or Lt. Putnam, forward observation officer for the 305th Field Artillery, as the men most likely to have originated the misinformation that sent the shells on their wrong way to the wrong target.

An exhaustive post-war study of the incident by Major Henry O. Swindler of the American Battle Monuments Commission scraped away the Army's flaking coat of whitewash and concluded that the barrage was "friendly," not German, and that the shells spiraled in from the southeast, where some hands that yanked the lanyards were French, but most were American. Given the fact that Whittlesey's command was cut off and surrounded in rugged, uncertain terrain, far in front of the main American line, with limited and, eventually, no communication with the rear—in an environment rich with the possibilities of miscalculation and misadventure—it is far less surprising that shells fell on the wrong place at the wrong time, than it is that an indomitable creature of feathers and instinct was able to end their fall.

Thus it would seem unlikely, according to Johnson and Pratt and other historians, that Whittlesey blamed himself specifically for the friendly fire barrage. On the other hand, it seems quite likely, given the stern dictates of his conscience and sense of loyalty, that he took onto himself a portion of the general responsibility for the tragedy by placing his men in a place and situation that made such mishaps almost inevitable. It is there, in the contemplation of his overall conduct of the mission, in the choices he made and the options he chose, that Whittlesey may have come to the slowly dawning conclusion that he had done too many things wrong and had made too many fatally incorrect decisions. Given his sensitive temperament and even more sensitive conscience, the weight of that realization may have been too much for him to bear.

Again, Johnson and Pratt go down the list of tactical choices made or not made, and again they absolve Whittlesey, even if, in the end, he could not absolve himself. Given the facts with which he had to work—conscript soldiers, brave but poorly trained, with limited experience; his own relative lack of professional leadership training and background; a terrain that could hardly be more difficult, and an enemy, who, though tired and outnumbered, could hardly have been more experienced and more proficient in defensive warfare; and, finally, a high command, from Alexander to Pershing to Foch, who insisted on pushing forward "without regard to flanks or losses," and on maintaining the rhythm and momentum of the offensive no matter what the enemy did or did not do—given all the limitations involved and all the imponderables imposed, Whittlesey performed magnificently and deserved both the plaudits of the public and the absolution of history.

Johnson and Pratt also show that, quite separate from Whittlesey's own decisions, it was only by way of a string of events caused by other leaders' bad luck and bad choices that the Lost Battalion became "lost." Alexander, on October 1, was not intimidated by the German tactic of pulling in Allied attacks on a limited front, allowing them to reach their limits of exhaustion, then mounting counterattacks to cut off and annihilate those overextended units. The division commander was confident that he could punch through enough units along his divisional front—small protrusions into the enemy line that would eventually link and form an unbroken bulge. But unit after unit, from company strength to battalion strength, failed, on October 2–3, to establish these salients. Only Whittlesey's force got through and beyond the German line and managed to stay put. Flanking units failed and follow-up units floundered. Only Whittlesey successfully reached his objective and accomplished his mission—not as a result of heedless enthusiasm or reckless overzealousness, but from a dedication to carrying out his orders and a combination of skill and luck in being able to do so. Whittlesey was, consequently, cut off, not because of his success, but because of others' failure. As Whittlesey himself responded to one of his so-called rescuer's claims: "Rescue, hell, if you had come up when we did, you wouldn't have put us in that fix."[11]

The blame in general overturned, Johnson and Pratt then discredited the specific complaints lodged against Whittlesey's leadership by his detractors. Some critics complained that Whittlesey should have left Holderman's Company K back to hold the German trench line on the morning of October 3, instead of calling it forward to reinforce his command. How—Johnson and Pratt perceptively inquired—a single company of ninety-eight men could have held those trenches against the 600 to 700 Germans who eventually infiltrated behind Whittlesey to reoccupy Hill 198 is not explained by those grousing voices. Whittlesey was also faulted for failing to tie in with American units right and left, but the major sent out strong patrols to both flanks. That those patrols failed to make contact was hardly their fault; there was no one to establish liaison with.

As for the charge of failure to maintain contact with the rear and to secure the rear against encirclement, Whittlesey again did his best with his limited resources. He dropped off a double-strength chain of runner-posts as he advanced, and assumed—as was professional and proper—that regiment, brigade and division would take on the responsibility of supporting his advance from the rear. Alexander's general order had clearly directed that, "Troops occupying ground must be supported against counterattack."[12] That Whittlesey's battalion was plainly not properly supported was not Whittlesey's failure.

Finally, the Monday morning quarterbacks questioned Whittlesey's failure to break out of the Pocket back to the safety of the American lines after it became obvious that he was surrounded, with little hope of reinforcement or relief. But again—as Johnson and Pratt point out—Whittlesey can hardly be faulted for adhering to Alexander's (and Stacey's) specific orders that, "he halt at the objective and await orders for a further advance," nor for his awareness of the general order that any officer authorizing a retreat was sanctioning treason.[13]

Whittlesey's superiors were certainly not among the doubters. Colonel Stacey concluded: "There is not the slightest criticism of Whittlesey's splendid conduct."[14] The new 308th regimental commander, Colonel Gordon Johnstone, a keenly intelligent officer sent down by GHQ to interrogate Whittlesey, McMurtry and other regimental officers about the events of October 2–7, ended his report by praising Whittlesey and proffering him "the thanks of General Pershing in the name of the American people" for his courageous and intelligent conduct.[15] General Alexander, in a letter to the American Battle Monuments Commission in 1930, stated: "The order for the advance was given by myself on what I believed to be good and sufficient grounds. The responsibility was mine, and was and is, accepted by me. Whittlesey's command did what it was told."[16]

But though generals and historians, comrades and friends, exonerated Whittlesey of any substantial blame for his men's Argonne pain and predicament, that did not ensure that the major himself was able to cast self-doubt aside. This was, after all, a man who Fletcher Pratt, in an *American Legion* magazine article, described as, "no conventional hero, but a sensitive highly civilized man who under fire displayed perfect self control in his waking hours ... but sometimes cried in his sleep."[17] After the war, Whittlesey was reticent about his Argonne experiences, but he told friends about waking up in a funk hole he had shared with a wounded comrade, with his cheek pressed to the cold dead face of the soldier. Pratt's conclusion was that it was not rumor nor his own "tender conscience" that lifted him over the rail of the *Toloa*. "He could and probably would have courageously lived down the accusations of being a phony hero," Pratt wrote. "What he was unable to bear was the fact of being a real hero."[18]

Lt. Colonel Beattie, on the other hand, in his *Military History* magazine article about the Lost Battalion, speculated that Whittlesey ended his life, not from some super-sensitive inability to live with the horrors of the Great War and the deaths of his men, but from an almost Samurai-like sense of honor—making sacrificial restitution for the tactical mistakes he made in the Argonne that resulted in his battalion becoming bunched up in a killing-zone cul-de-sac at the mercy of the enemy.[19] Beattie's speculations are indeed supported by the lack of any real evidence that Whittlesey's stiff and morally sturdy demeanor hid a soft, weak inner core that was unable to deal with the emotional and spiritual demands of combat and its consequences on the Western Front.

The major certainly venerated his troops. That he owed everything—body and soul—to the men he led (and to the men he may have felt he failed) was made evident by many public utterances, such as:

> We remember them as friends. When Lieutenant [Clinton L.] Whiting was shot through the lungs at the cemetery in the Argonne, and was being sent to the hospital from which he never returned, I told him how splendidly I felt he had done. Up to that time he had been smiling in spite of pain, but there were tears in his eyes and a sob in his words as he choked out his short good-bye, "Oh, Whittlesey, I don't want to leave the men."
>
> "When, on one of the last days in the Pocket, after other runners had, one by one, been killed or captured in trying to get through the enemy that surrounded our detachment, Joseph Friel was asked whether he thought he could carry a message to regimental HQ. "I know I can," he said, and he said it with a smile. He was found later, dead, not far beyond the outposts.
>
> Such men we are richer to have known.[20]

There was little doubt and little controversy about the major among the men he led. Typical of the attitude of the men of the Lost Battalion toward their CO was this elegy, written by a 308th private from Brooklyn, New York, just four days after his death. Charles Wendler of Company A wrote:

> Unlike many officers, Colonel Whittlesey talked to his men as if they were on equal footing with himself. He was loved and honored by them all. During those dark days in "the trap" where hope of rescue grew fainter and fainter, regardless of his own danger, he daily went from man to man, speaking a word of personal cheer and encouragement to each.
>
> As one man, that little company were ready to die for and with Colonel Whittlesey.[21]

Tributes would continue decades after his death. On April 21, 1948, the Whittlesey Room was dedicated in the Williams Club at 24 East 39th Street in Manhattan. The master of ceremonies for the evening was Edward R. Bartlett, Williams Class of 1912 and a lieutenant who served under Whittlesey's command. McMurtry was there to unveal a portrait of the major, painted by Walter Frankel, from contemporary photos. Speaking to the crowd, which included survivors of the Lost Battalion and members of Whittlesey's Class of 1905,

was Richard Patterson, former secretary of war and a captain in the 77th Division in the Great War. Eight years later, the Charles White Whittlesey Army Reserve Training Center was dedicated. There was no one pointing fingers or casting blame at either event.

The mystery of his motivations on the night of November 26, 1921, will, however, remain forever unanswered and forever buried with Charles Whittlesey at the bottom of the sea. It seems incredibly unlikely that anything else besides the Argonne and its consequences compelled Whittlesey to leap over the *Toloa*'s railing. As far as is known, he did not have financial difficulties; there was no shattered romance breaking his heart; he led no secret scandalous life about to be revealed. But what particular shadows from

Top: Whittlesey portrait in the Whittlesey Room at the Williams Club in New York City. Williams College Archives and Special Collections. Bottom: George McMurtry at the Whittlesey Room dedication, Williams Club, New York City, 1948. Williams College Archives and Special Collections.

that faraway forest or what poisonous fruit from those Argonne trees made life unbearable for Whittlesey, we can never fully fathom. We can only know for fairly certain that, for three years, Whittlesey tried to leave behind those men buried in the Argonne, but, in the end, chose to rejoin them.

As of Memorial Day 2005, fewer than thirty American veterans of the Great War were still among the living. As far as is known, no veteran of the Lost Battalion remains alive today. Though many soldiers of the battalion survived those hellish days in the Argonne Forest, none have survived the inching hours and the bounding years that have marched on.

7

Myth and Memory

The story of the Lost Battalion rapidly acquired mythical status. An arsenal of articles, books, poems, songs, and even a motion picture were mobilized in the weeks, months and years after the Armistice to immortalize the men and events that shined so brightly out of the mud-colored muck of the Argonne. After the first wave of Lost Battalion parades, speeches, dedications and lecture tours came 308th regimental and 77th divisional histories, a rash of narrative articles and books, and "Buck Private" L.C. McCollum's collection of odes to the men and the event, entitled *History and Rhymes of the Lost Battalion*. The booklet was so popular that its fifth printing in 1929 still amounted to 700,000 copies.

In 1938, with two decades intervening with which to take a more measured and longer view, Thomas Johnson, *a New York Sun* war correspondent, and Fletcher Pratt, a prominent military historian, combined to write the best book yet—and still to this day—about the siege of the Lost Battalion. With time to test and temper their opinions, but with the memories of participants on both sides still fresh, Johnson and Pratt wrote an in depth and almost minute-by-minute account of those five days of flame and folly and of those 554 men trapped by fate and circumstance in the Argonne Forest. Though limited in its view of the larger picture—of the great battle of which the Lost Battalion was a fragment—Johnson and Pratt's classic account cannot be surpassed in its depiction of undaunted Americans surviving the worst, with indomitable courage and grace.

Along with the traditional avenues of art and information, the cinema, still in its toddler stage, also briefly jumped aboard the Lost Battalion bandwagon in the early post-war years.

Oddly enough, for a martial drama that practically screams screen treatment, the Lost Battalion has been all but truly "lost" by Hollywood. While the Alamo and the Little Bighorn have gone through numerous big screen incarnations, and even relatively minor Korean War and Vietnam War hill fights—albeit with catchy-sounding names—like Pork Chop Hill and Hamburger Hill, have been resurrected on celluloid, the most famous incident in America's greatest battle has been all but ignored by the cinema.

All the traditional elements are there for a war film, patriotic and hawkish or revisionist and pacifist—the courage of the common man, the sterling leadership of unlikely heroes, the waste, the agony, the horror, the perfect war story of a unit cut off, surrounded by superior numbers and facing with resolute valor the imminent threat of annihilation. The self-same situation of the trapped, apparently doomed, company of comrades has, in fact, been invented and fictionalized in countless battles that existed nowhere else but on celluloid. And yet the easy pickings of the Argonne's Lost Battalion, history's offering to Hollywood that could practically write itself for the screen, was plucked from the awful arbor of the deadly Twentieth Century only once—before the television era—by the mythmakers behind the projectionist's lamp.

That one screen depiction of the Argonne epic was rushed to production within a year after the actual event. Capitalizing on the effusion of publicity surrounding the siege of Whittlesey's command, producer Edward E. MacManus and director Burton King churned out an eight-reel film that was released in September 1919, and starred Gaston Glass, Marion Coakley, and nine actual veterans of the battle and of the battalion—Whittlesey, McMurtry, Cullen, Cepeglia, Krotoshinsky, Sgt. Herman J. Bergasse, and Privates Jack Hershkowitz, John W. Rosson and John J. Munson (who died shortly thereafter of Great War gas-induced consumption and whose funeral was attended by, of course, Charles Whittlesey). This ensemble mix of acting pros and veteran survivors was not unprecedented in the cinema of war. Several other combat flicks had already employed such combinations of actors who were pretending to be soldiers, with soldiers who were attempting to be actors, to provide an ersatz verisimilitude to the motion picture re-enactment.

The film also featured other attempts at lending a semi-documentary authenticity to it. Signal Corps combat footage was intercut with Hollywood combat, and stills of some of the 77th Division's original maps and orders were used to signpost the narrative flow.

The cinematic *Lost Battalion* depicted the 77th Division units' siege and rescue, woven with flashback scenes of the home life of some of the besieged. The director and producer seemed, however, less concerned with compiling a careful reconstruction of the battle than with presenting the story of the Lost Battalion as a metaphor for America in all its "democratic diversity molding into a powerful unity in the face of war."[1]

General Alexander was given the courtesy title of superintendent of production. Along with Whittlesey, he made an inspection tour of the film's shooting location, which had been selected by the regimental engineer as conforming in almost every respect to the actual site in the Argonne. In addition to approving the terrain, Whittlesey was asked to choose men who had distinguished themselves in the siege to play in the movie.

MacManus tossed into his *Lost Battalion* practically every racial and social type—blacks and Orientals, bankers' sons to represent the rich and "second story" burglars to stand in for the lumpen-proletariat—to portray a cross-section of American manhood bridging, with the steel span of comradeship forged in battle, all the social and ethnic canyons separating them. Thus, many of the screen soldiers in *The Lost Battalion* were not so much characters as archetypes, as the producer worked to depict a battalion of cross-sectional Americans "cut out of the heart of Manhattan, including the dregs," who were able to surmount their ordinariness, and "out of this mixed, and they said 'despicable mass' was to be forged a thunderbolt to be hurled against the proudest army in Europe."[2]

The movie began by introducing the characters. In a New York ghetto a Jewish boy kisses his parents good-bye; a wealthy businessman tries to wield his influence to ensure soft duty in camp for his spoiled son; a thief, wanted by the police, poses as a conscript who failed to report.

After brief scenes of their Long Island training camp and the division's arrival in France, the film portrays the opening of the offensive, as trees are torn down to open firing lanes and doughboys go over the top. Scenes of the siege of the battalion are intercut with a sequence of girls back home watching a newsreel of the boys in France relaxing before the Big Push.

The film captured many of the highlights, real and imagined, of the battalion's battle, including the apocryphal, but instantly famous reply of, "Go to hell!" in response to the German surrender demand. After Cher Ami saves the day, a title announces: "At 9 P.M. October 7, 123 hours from the moment of entering the Pocket, the Battalion was once again in touch with the Division and another chapter of heroism was included in American history."[3] The picture concludes with a parade welcoming the division home to New York and a view of the cemetery where the dead of the Lost Battalion were buried.

MacManus conceived his film as a prestige project and aimed for critical acclaim as well as commercial success. He screened the movie at Hartford, Connecticut, to a jury of 100 VIPs—including many battalion survivors—for their endorsement, and supplemented its patriotic airs with the oratory of stage speakers. According to the *Moving Picture World*, "These veterans sometimes twitted each other on their respective appearances in the film."[4]

Some of the details were wrong. The "Germans," for example, wore helmets that bore little similarity to their coal-scuttle headgear they donned in the real trenches. But it is difficult today to judge the film's middle reels, because the surviving print (in the Library of Congress) is missing much of its close-combat footage, excised and employed as newsreel filler in the 1933 compilation *The Big Drive*. In what remains, there seems little attempt to individualize the characters during the siege, and no wide shots to contrast the position of the battalion in relation to the surrounding enemy.

White Carrara marble crosses and Stars of David mark the graves at the U.S. military cemetery at La Romagne (the trees in the background are linden). La Romagne is the largest U.S. military cemetery in Europe, with 14,246 interred there. Photograph by the author, April 2002.

Although *The Lost Battalion* opened strong, the temper of the times was already changing, and the film never really enjoyed popular success. Nineteen-nineteen was a year of reaction and gradual disillusionment, as the realization spread across America—like the blood that had coated Europe—that the Great War had been a great monstrosity, demanding unparalleled sacrifices for unconvincing causes and unintended consequences. By late 1919, the public was in little mood for a film extolling the war-time virtues of self-sacrifice, patriotism, and a noble comradeship fighting for common goals. As the decade of the 1920s would emphasize, Americans began to hunger for self-fulfillment and self-enrichment. Indifference to the greater gods of patriotism and nationhood arose, as did selfishness and bigotry. The contributions of African American soldiers and workers in World War I were ignored, and racism once again took wing as lynchings increased and some twenty race riots shamed the cities of America in 1919.

MacManus's fraternal, though inaccurate, inclusion of African American soldiers in his *Lost Battalion* was quickly seen by the distributors as a mistake. All of the black characters in the film ended up on the cutting room floor soon after the movie's initial release.

Even this concession to the racist temperaments of American audiences did little to boost ticket sales. Filmgoers either wanted light, escapist fare on the silver screen or war stories focusing on individual stories, not pseudo-documentary and reportorial films that seemed more educational than entertaining. As early as November 1919, Buffalo, New York, exhibitors, previously enthusiastic about war films, forbade patriotic stage orations following screenings of *The Lost Battalion*, or the solicitation of funds for disabled veterans in the aisles—all in response to patrons' complaints that "the war was over."

Thus, there was no second rescue of the Lost Battalion by American movie audiences. Films in the 1920s, like *All Quiet on the Western Front*, *The Big Parade*, and *What Price Glory*, that hammered home the themes of the waste and futility of the Great War, were successful. Filmland and its patrons seemed generally more interested in the world war as a calamity and a catastrophe, and not as a repository for heroic deeds by gallant men. To many, if they thought about the subject at all, the valor of the men and the drama of the moment of the Lost Battalion seemed misplaced in the madness of the Western Front's meatgrinder attrition that had wrung the last drop of romance from warfare.

Not until the Second World War era, when patriotism and sacrifice to the greater good was again in vogue, would there be receptive audiences for a heroic film about doughboys in the Argonne. And this time the subject that benefited most from the renewed martial spirit was not a battalion of heroes, but a single, soft-spoken, but sharp-eyed hero by the name of Sergeant Alvin York.

In November 2001, as part of a mini-revival of American interest in the Great War, the A&E Television Network broadcast the second motion picture—and the first talkie—to be filmed about the Lost Battalion. Produced by David Gerber, directed by Russell Mulcahy, written by Jim Carabatsos, and starring Rick Schroder as Whittlesey, supported by an international cast, the 100-minute movie was a melange of missed opportunities. Given the chance to tell the most dramatic story of the doughboy war—a tale with all the trimmings of action, suspense, tragedy, and a central character both compelling and complex—the filmmakers settled for an all too typical Hollywood war movie.

The movie was not entirely without merit. It did, by way of the popular arts, add to the American public's general fund of information about and awareness of World War I. Specifically, it reacquainted the American audience with the Battle of the Argonne and the

Lost Battalion episode. The movie was fairly accurate in its depiction of the events, uniforms, weapons and tactics, pointing out, for example, the Allied origin of many of the weapons wielded by the doughboys. The varied class and ethnic backgrounds of the soldiers of the Lost Battalion was also vividly displayed. The audience was also introduced (or reintroduced) to another American hero of World War I, other than the usual trinity of Pershing, Eddie Rickenbacker and Sergeant York. The *Lost Battalion* movie was most successful in its realistically graphic and gritty depiction of Great War combat. The flamethrower attack, the high point of the action, was, in particular, harrowing and well-filmed.

There were, however, many more things wrong with the film than right. To begin with, its 100-minute running length was far too brief to do proper credit to the characters and story. The saga required a mini-series or at least a movie of three hours' length to encompass the epic. Too many things were left out.

Most glaringly, the depicted events were displayed in a historical vacuum. There was no attempt to put the siege of the Lost Battalion in the context of the greater Meuse-Argonne battle. As large a failure was the film's portrayal of the central character of the story—Major Whittlesey. Schroder was miscast and his character underwritten. Although the wire-rimmed glasses helped, this former star of *Silver Spoon*, *Lonesome Dove* and *NYPD Blue* had still too much of the look of a Hollywood action hero, and lacked the scholarly, introspective and intellectual qualities that made Whittlesey stand out from the common crew of American officers.

The movie missed most of the growth in mutual respect and trust between Whittlesey and his men, that evolved from the original lack of communication and outright scorn due to class distinctions and appearances. With most of the film devoted to concentrating on the action, there were not minutes enough left to reveal the relationships between Whittlesey and the enlisted men, as well as between Whittlesey and his subordinate officers.

Though the action was indeed vivid, the over-emphasis on combat scenes came at the sacrifice of more intimate and quieter details of the ordeal. And the separate dramatic and unique events of the story were not highlighted to best advantage. Most things got caught up and lost in seemingly uninterrupted action sequences.

The terrain of the battle was also not accurate. In the movie, the Pocket exists in a countryside of relatively gently rolling terrain, instead of on a steep hillside thick with undergrowth. The movie was filmed—because of the typically uncooperative French—in the Ardennes of Luxembourg instead of in the Argonne of France. The Ardennes is more typical of Western Europe's park-like forests than the Argonne's tangled brush and thicker foliage.

The single most dramatic event of the siege—the friendly fire barrage and the avian heroics of Cher Ami—was unimpressive and uninspiring in the movie, compared to other recent scenes of cinematic artillery hell—the tree-burst shelling in the snow of Bastogne in one of the episodes of the mini-series *Band of Brothers*, for example.

Finally, the ending was disappointing and incomplete. The movie ended, not as it should have, in the Atlantic, but in the Argonne. No mention was made of Whittlesey's tragic destiny. This failure to show the battle's consequences for its commander cheated the audience of what was, in many ways, the most dramatic aspect of the story of the Lost Battalion.

Possibly, *Saving Private Ryan* has raised the bar too high for standard war movies. A&E's *Lost Battalion* motion picture, in comparison, failed as both near-war documentary on the level of *Private Ryan*'s first thirty minutes, and as riveting war drama, as with *Private Ryan*'s final two hours. The *Lost Battalion*'s biggest missed opportunity was its failure to portray a great central character—like Tom Hanks's captain in *Private Ryan*—though Whittlesey was intrinsically an even more conflicted and compelling personality than was Hanks's fictional character.

In April 2002, I walked in the footsteps of those young doughboys who fell prematurely and of those older doughboys who, according to the whims and dictates of time and history, lingered longer. Traveling with my sister and brother-in-law, I spent two days touring the sites of the Battle of the Meuse-Argonne. We had driven down the day before from Bastogne, in the Ardennes, another great American battlefield in an even greater war. Only about fifty miles in distance, but twenty-six years in time, separated the two forest battlefields. After studying the landscape of America's greatest battle, we motored back east some ten miles to visit the sacred soil of France's greatest battle—Verdun. In just those three days and fifty miles, from west to east, we traversed possibly the greatest killing ground in human history.

The three of us began our tour on the eastern (river) flank of the battle named for the river and the forest that bracketed it. At Dun-sur-Meuse, on the bank of the Meuse River canal, we paused before a bronze statue of a French poilu, striding forward with bayonet fixed. It had been erected to honor the U.S. 5th Division, which had liberated the city and crossed the Meuse there in the waning days of the offensive and of the war.

From this eastern border of the battlefield, we drove to Romagne and its heights, forest and cemetery. Even forewarned with the knowledge I had of the place and photos I had studied, I was stunned by the sight of the acres upon acres of white Carrara marble crosses, bordered by square-trimmed linden trees, and extending in a vast rectangle at the foot of the wooded hills. The sight of 14,246 graves in this largest U.S. military cemetery in Europe must be both surprising and perplexing to the typically ill-informed American visitor who is not a Great War buff nor a scholar and happens upon this unexpected vista while touring northern France.

Those visitors were few and far between that day, though the spring weather was beautiful and the grounds and landscaping wonderfully well-maintained by the American Battle Monuments Commission. Judging by the few entries in the sign-in book at the memorial building, that day was typical of all days at the cemetery. There was a busload of young Frenchmen, possibly on a school or university excursion, but the three of us made up the majority of American visitors at that hour. From the comments in the visitors' book, most American tourists seemed to be U.S. servicemen on day or weekend tours from their German bases.

The day before we had rubbed shoulders with swarms of American tourists at the Bastogne battlefield museum and memorial, one of the sites of the war—World War II—that really still counted in American minds and memories. For me, wandering through the endless rows of crosses and Stars of David, the contrast was both a sad commentary and a melancholy confirmation of Americans' selective memory and their carefree disrespect for so many who have died in their name. As we stood solemnly for the eveningtide playing of "Taps" and the "Battle Hymn of the Republic," I shared with all those fallen, a burden imposed by the passage of time and the fading gratitude of a nation for the sacrifices of its soldiers. Would the men who died beside me in Vietnam—after the lapse of another quarter of a century or half a century—be similarly forgotten by a country too busy rushing forward to look behind at all those fallen warriors who had not served in Civil War blue or gray or in World War II olive-drab?

7. Myth and Memory 217

Though neglected by myopic American tourists, this final resting place for so many thousands of the men who fought and died in the Meuse-Argonne was, however, rendered supreme respect and superb attention by its American and French staff. The 130.5 acres of the cemetery are on ground captured by the 32nd Division during the battle. Complete with a fountaining pool in the center and overlooked by the Romanesque beauty of the memorial and chapel, which contain the names of 954 of the missing, the eight rectangular plots include the graves of 486 "Unknowns."

Pershing had dedicated the cemetery in 1919 with these memorable words: "And now, dear comrades, farewell. Here, under the clear skies on the green hillsides and amid the

Statue of French *poilu*, erected to honor the crossing of the Meuse River canal by the U.S. 5th Division at Dun-sur-Meuse on November 5, 1918. Photograph by the author, April 2002.

flowering fields of France, in the quiet hush of peace, we leave you forever in God's keeping."[5]

Later, on Memorial Day of that year, when the living paused—however briefly—to honor the dead, I wondered how many American tourists interrupted their Parisian holidays to take the day trip to Romagne, the greatest resting place for Americans on the European continent. Their numbers would be few, just as they would be on November 11, the day that prior to its submersion into a generalized martial Day of the Dead (Veterans Day) in 1954, was the one truly recognized national memorial to the doughboys of the Great War. Only a handful of Americans laying their wreaths and floral tributes on either day would know or pause to reflect that the First World War's greatest battle for the United States put more of their countrymen into early graves than did any other contest of arms in our nation's history.

We next drove five miles south to another hill mass that figured so prominently in the Battle of the Meuse-Argonne—Montfaucon. The memorial tower, the tallest U.S. military monument in Europe, was visible—200 feet atop the butte—from a great distance. We camped for the night at the edge of the monument's parking lot, with the remains of an old trench system and numerous shell craters a few feet from our camper. Except for a maintenance man and an elderly Frenchman, who spent just a few minutes strolling about in a reflective pose, we were the only visitors for the fourteen hours we remained overnight and into the morning.

The morning of our second day in the Meuse-Argonne, my brother-in-law and I climbed the 234 steps of the circular stairway of the 180-foot Baveno granite shaft to the observation platform of the memorial. Above our heads, capping the Doric column, was the figure of a woman warrior symbolizing liberty. Below us were ruins, both of a village dating back to the Sixth Century and of a church destroyed in the Great War. Beyond us, on all sides, were sweeping views of most of the battle zone of fall 1918. On the wall enclosing the main terrace below were inscribed the divisional order of battle of the U.S. First Army, along with the names of many of the places where those divisions had struggled so hard.

From Montfaucon, we drove west to the road between Apremont and Binarville, in search of the site of the Pocket. The area was lush with grass and flowering trees in that April of 2002. I tried to imagine the ungodly contrast of the five-to-ten-mile deep Western Front moonscape in April of 1918. It must have seemed to the soldiers then like a suppurating scar across the radiant face of a pre-Raphaelite beauty.

Just beyond Apremont, a tiny village that looked literally stuck in Great War time, we passed a German military cemetery, in which were buried the dead of the 27th Landwehr Regiment. Each of the crosses, black instead of the American white, carried the names of two soldiers of the German Empire whose stories ended in the Argonne Forest. The visitors' sign-in book indicated that prior to our arrival only three visitors had bothered to view the grounds in the last seven months—two German citizens and one man from Trenton, New Jersey.

Past the cemetery, the farmed acres bordering Apremont quickly gave way to the eastern edge of the forest. The land rose rather abruptly, and a dense tree cover swept the horizon in a long band from south to north.

More than halfway to Binarville, along the 1918 road built atop the foundations of the ancient Roman road, we found the granite marker with an arrow symbol pointing downslope to the (then) eighty-four-year-old rifle pits of the Lost Battalion. Even though

7. *Myth and Memory* 219

Church ruins viewed from the tower of Montfaucon Monument. Photograph by the author, April 2002.

the original stone marker had been recently replaced by the American Battle Monuments Commission with one twice as large, containing a synopsis of the siege, it still seemed rather nondescript and low key for such a dramatic event that had once loomed so large in the mythology and memory of the American warrior.

There on the road at the marker, I chanced to encounter Edward Coffman, author of one of the preeminent books about America's role in the Great War—*The War To End All Wars*. He was accompanied by the retired head of military history at the U.S. Military History Institute at Carlyle Barracks in Pennsylvania. They were scouting locations for a World War I tour for U.S. Army officers stationed in Germany, for which they were to be tour guides. Coffman informed me of recent research at the site and a pending article about the Lost Battalion by Army Lt. Colonel Taylor Beattie, whose perceptive analysis of the siege has been incorporated into this book.

Heading downhill, I was immediately struck by the steepness of the slope and the almost claustrophobic confinement of the relatively constricted space into which almost 600 men had been crowded perilously close to hell. The funk holes of the doughboys were still clearly distinguishable, though filled with leaves and rimmed with green moss. At the foot of the hill flowed the gently rippling Charlevaux Brook. The watering hole—the favorite target of the German snipers—was, with its vegetative debris and scummy surface, identical to the old photographs.

As I walked the length of the Pocket's perimeter, I could better understand why—the

Top: German cemetery for 27th Landwehr Infantry Regiment, near Apremont in the Argonne. Photograph by the author, April 2002. *Bottom*: American Battle Monuments Commission marker on Apremont-Binarville road, pointing to the site of the Lost Battalion and the Pocket. Photograph by the author, April 2002.

difficult French aside—the recent A&E movie had been shot in the Luxembourg Ardennes instead of the French Argonne. The Ardennes location, with its open woods and better camera angles, was far less dense and tangled, and the terrain was gentle and rolling, not steep and precipitous, as at the actual site.

The Argonne seemed unchanged from the Great War descriptions I had read. Unlike other regional woods—the Ardennes, the Vosges, the Palatine, the Black—with their courtly spruce and pine and other coniferous trees, and their almost prim-and-proper forest lanes, the Argonne—just as in the contemporary literature of World War I—was still a dense, unwelcoming bramble of secondary deciduous growth and tangled brush, inhabited by the ghosts of doughboys, poilus and Landwehr soldiers. To this veteran of Vietnam, the Argonne seemed hauntingly similar to the jungles of the Central Highlands and much less like the serene bois and walds of other Western European woods.

There seemed an oppressive aura to this forest. I wondered if that sinister sensation sprang from my own Vietnam associations or perhaps from my pre-knowledge of the Argonne's history. Did other tourists—non-veterans—feel it? Other than fellow "battle-buffs" and military historians, there were no tourists there—this was not the Black Forest, these were not green glens with spas and resorts. There were memories there, but they were stark and brooding—this was not a dreamscape of golden nostalgia.

The villages at either end of the forest—Apremont, on the east, and Binarville, on the west—were quiet, insular and uninviting to the urban folk normally seeking leafy relief. Even other forests heavy with the sediment of ancient battles—the Ardennes, the Rhineland and Bavarian woods, even the forested forts around Verdun—have moved on, outgrown the old animosities, welcomed younger generations and more recent times. But the Argonne seems anchored in time, yoked firmly to a four-year era when its tangle tormented tens of thousands of young men in French pale blue, Prussian gray and American khaki. There are no bucolic meadows in the Argonne, no stately spruce.

I tried to imagine how Charles Whittlesey saw these woods. Did he compare and contrast the serene rolling glens of the Berkshires, where he went to school at Williams College, to the gory green of the Argonne—this bloodiest forest in American history, more deadly than the Wilderness, Belleau Wood, the Ardennes, the Hürtgen, the Central Highlands of Vietnam? In the three years left to him after the Argonne, was Whittlesey ever able to walk in the woods without falling through a trap door into the Pocket?

With my day in the Argonne completed, we went on to travel the northern loop of the Verdun battleground. We visited the Trench of the Bayonets, where a poilu company was buried alive by a German artillery shell—the French bayonet tips the only evidence visible above the shattered ground of their prior existence. We gasped in subdued shock at the displayed bones of 130,000 French and German soldiers in the Ossuary. As artillery and machine-gun fire from a nearby French Army firing range provided an appropriate aural background, we traipsed over the turrets of Fort Douaumont, where the enemy shrapnel hits on the steel rims were still clearly visible. Then we departed the ruins, monuments and memories of this fifty-mile-long butcher block between the Argonne Forest and the Woevre Plain, driving back into the Twenty-first Century and away from a sanguinary segment of the Western Front, where the most dreadful century in human history—the Twentieth—had its genesis.

And so the story ends, a story filled with heroes—if not really villains—filled with incident and high drama, a story with moments of pure madness and pure grace; a story, seemingly, for the ages. But, in the end, what is its legacy? What significance have we carried forward from it, on a human scale and a historical scale? Maybe, from the widest lens of history, not a great deal, and, it would seem, from the more amorphous view of public or national memory, very little at all.

It was, after all, only a battalion-size action of five days' duration, within an army group-size battle of forty-seven days length—one of the greatest battles in human history, and, without question, the most momentous in size and savagery of all American battles. And for all the brave men and brave hours in the saga of the Lost Battalion, for all the moments when unexceptional men were required to perform exceptional deeds, military history is a thick stew of stories of valor and sublime sacrifice.

The essential questions remain. Why does not the title "The Lost Battalion of the Argonne" resonate, among both those who either venerate or villainize the history of warfare, with the same mythic awe—or scorn—as does the "Charge of the Light Brigade," "Custer's Last Stand," "Pickett's Charge at Gettysburg," or the "Rough Riders' Charge up San Juan Hill?" Was it because no Tennyson immortalized the Lost Battalion? Was it because that, instead of a flamboyant Teddy Roosevelt, Major Charles Whittlesey—quiet and self-effacing, though no less a hero—commanded the Lost Battalion? Why, among those famous military units of history, is the Lost Battalion not preserved in the same amber of adulation as the Light Brigade, the 7th Cavalry, the Rough Riders?

American military history, like all warrior heritages of all nations, is overpopulated with larger than life characters, elite units of near super-soldiers, and do-or-die, to-the-last-man stands that both promote pride and augment arrogance. So often the myth is little mirrored in reality, the facts get in the way of the good story, and the truth takes off a hero's boots to reveal feet of clay.

The Alamo's defenders turn out to be, in many cases, men preserving their right to own slaves. Rather than all going down swinging their empty muskets at the onrushing Santa Ana hordes, a good many of those stalwart Texans tried to flee, only to be captured and subsequently executed. Many of the horse soldiers of the 7th Cavalry at the Little Bighorn did not so much make a last stand as attempt a panicky and fruitless final flight. Davy Crockett was probably one of those who tried to survive the thirteen days of glory at Bejar by raising, not his musket in defiance, but his hands in surrender. And the golden-haired George Armstrong Custer proved not to be a fearless Indian fighter, but a flamboyant fool and a tactical idiot.

Though the saga of the Lost Battalion has its apocryphies and exaggerations to ornament its glory, the epic in the Argonne bears up better under close scrutiny and beneath the cold eye of historical research than many of our other martial myths. Whittlesey did not defiantly tell the Huns to, "Go to hell!" in response to their surrender demands, but rendered a much more in character non-response to the German message. And of course, the Lost Battalion was neither lost nor a battalion. But so much more of the drama and detail of the ordeal of the 600 doughboys was authentic and as amazing in reality as it was in romance.

The Lost Battalion, though in the strictest sense, neither lost nor a battalion, nonetheless, earned and deserves its title. Though the exact coordinates of the location of Major Whittlesey's command were not known—as was evidenced, with near disastrous consequences, by the fall of friendly fire upon the surrounded doughboys—the general position of the cut-off units was known throughout the ordeal by higher headquarters. And the troops making up the Lost Battalion were composed of both companies from the major's own battalion and units from other battalions and other regiments.

But, if not technically a "lost battalion," those men, isolated and under siege in a corner of the Argonne, seemed for much of their five-day trial by arms lost to hope and destined to be permanently lost to German firepower. And the collection of soldiers from various companies and battalions ringed by the kaiser's army were of approximate battalion strength, and were certainly united forever—both in the moment and in memory—as a "battalion of brothers" who had passed through the fire.

Just as authentic and deserving of his fame was the primary actor in the drama. Charles Whittlesey did present an unlikely image of the military hero. But then that is true of many real heroes—as opposed to the imagined. Most men who have demonstrated courage in and out of battle have looked little like John Wayne or Arnold Schwarzenegger. Whittlesey, with his gangly form and owlish bearing, appeared more suitably in charge of a college classroom than a combat battalion.

Charles Whittlesey looked like Woodrow Wilson. He did not resemble Chesty Puller or George Patton. Americans don't necessarily demand that their real-life heroes look like celluloid action figures. In fact, the meek and the mild rising manfully to the challenge, the ninety-eight-pound weakling striking down the brutish bully, are preferred staples in tales of American heroism. Audie Murphy hardly looked the part, with his baby fat and all-American boy looks. Alvin York, though appearing able to handle himself in some Appalachian spat, little resembled an incarnation of Odin, let alone Hollywood's or pulp fiction's image of G.I. Joe or Sergeant Rock.

So Whittlesey's un-warrior-like visage hardly explains his swift disappearance from America's memory. Of course, many brave men won the Medal of Honor and flashes of notoriety for astonishing feats of courage and then were forgotten. But it is passing strange that the central figure in America's most famous single episode of armed conflict in the Great War should not only fail to win iconic status, but should slide away into near oblivion.

The commander of the Lost Battalion, the lamb who fought like a lion, emerged from the Argonne as famous as the Christian sharpshooter from Pall Mall, Tennessee. And yet today, nearly all Americans—at least those sentient enough to be aware that important things did happen before the advent of their own existences—are at least vaguely aware of Sergeant York (or—more likely—of Gary Cooper as Sergeant York), but only Great War enthusiasts can tell you about Major Whittlesey. True, Gary Cooper helped hugely in preserving the name and fame of Alvin York (Rick Schroder is hardly in the same league). But lack of a major motion picture starring a Hollywood icon cannot fully explain away Whittlesey's absence from America's awareness.

Perhaps Whittlesey failed to find a place in the national pantheon of military heroes, not because of the fickleness of fame, but because of his self-inflicted fate. Americans can accept, even relish, their heroes emerging from unheroic origins, from dead-ends or nondescript lives. But they have difficulty accepting a hero who cannot deal with the consequences of his heroism or with the price of his fame. If a hero is strong enough to overcome his fears and his enemies in wartime, he should be strong enough also to overcome his memories and nightmares in peacetime.

Americans don't understand the more Eastern concept of an honor that requires one who feels manifest regret for his actions, however praised by his peers, to follow the dictates of conscience with an act of final self-sacrifice. For Whittlesey, the promotion, the Medal of Honor, the praise and public acclaim, all fell light as feathers on scales fatefully unbalanced by a black hole of remorse.

Where those with a different sense of honor might see Whittlesey's mortal act as a courageous acceptance of ultimate responsibility, many Americans had to see the colonel's plunge into darkness as a final failure of nerve in his last campaign. Whether Whittlesey intended to join the ghosts of his men lost in the Pocket, or simply could no longer endure their silence, he may also have carried his legend in the making down with him. A hero goes out swinging, not submitting. Ironically, one of the things Whittlesey craved most of all—a return to his pre-Argonne privacy and anonymity—he ultimately achieved with his final act of desperation.

The story of the Lost Battalion was, in a sense, a microcosm of the whole stupendous Battle of the Meuse-Argonne—as it is a metaphor for a Lost Generation, a Lost Innocence, a Lost Optimism. Though surely among the most dramatic, the experiences of the Lost Battalion during their five-day siege were not manifestly more intense or more agonizing than those endured by many of the 264 infantry battalions and sixty-six machine-gun battalions engaged at one time or another along the twenty-mile front. The Meuse-Argonne was too vast and too monstrous to be absorbed wholly or in its multiple parts then or later by the American public. A few stories of heroism and endurance in this gigantic contest would stand out, helped along by the media and the military's public relations machine, but most of the myriad bloody details of so huge an event would be obscured by the amorphous nature of the killing machine that was the Battle of the Meuse-Argonne.

Most of us see historical moments—if we see them at all—as calving floes of ice birthing from the great glacier of some momentous historical event. As they flow past us in their largely indistinguishable iciness, a few will catch our eye because of their shape or size or because of the luster of the light illuminating their crystals. But the white mass that foaled the icy flotilla will get only a cursory glance or two by most, in recognition of its very massiveness. Then the typical observer will transfer his attention elsewhere, to leave the glacier frozen in the ghostly isolation of its own awesomeness. Such were the siege of the Lost Battalion, the exploits of Alvin York and Sam Woodfill, and the many other moments of explosive lucidity shining out from the colorless calamity of the Meuse-Argonne.

With the events of September 11, 2001, the calendar's ninth month should be one of remembrance and respect in American history. For generations, almost all Americans will recognize the traumatic significance of Nine-Eleven. A great many Americans will also know that September 17 marks the anniversary of the Battle of Antietam in 1862—the deadliest day in U.S. military history. But how many will recognize the importance of what should be the third of a trinity of September dates marking the ultimate in American blood sacrifice?

Who but a relative handful of historians and Great War buffs will recall that September 26 was the day in 1918 when America commenced its greatest and bloodiest battle? How many know now and how many a generation from now will know that on that date a forty-seven-day battle began that involved more American soldiers and cost more American lives than any other in our history? How many will know that the Meuse-Argonne—not Okinawa, nor the Bulge, nor Iwo Jima; not Gettysburg, nor Antietam, nor Shiloh—was our greatest battle; that along the twenty miles between the banks of the Meuse and the trees of the Argonne, more than twice as many Americans died as during each of our second and third bloodiest battles—Okinawa and the Bulge?

Size and significance, obviously, do not alone determine the wealth of remembrance for historical events. Besides its bloodshed, the Meuse-Argonne was decisive—not just another Western Front abattoir. It was one of the great battles that ended the second greatest war in history. Antietam, for all its death-dealing significance, was neither tactically nor strategically decisive. But you can find a hundred people familiar with Antietam for every one who knows of the Argonne. Almost all minimally educated Americans are cognizant of the Little Bighorn, but how many have an inkling about the Argonne (or, for that matter, General St. Clair's 1791 disaster on the Wabash River, where the red man killed more than twice as many American soldiers as at Custer's Last Stand)?

A nation's historical memory is a fickle and serendipitous entity. A concurrence of drama and timing, personality and perception, determine the longevity of a particular event in national myth and culture. The Battle of the Wabash had no Custer or Crazy Horse, nor remotely the same number of newspapers to enlarge the fame or infamy of the leaders of the Ohio battle. Nor did the 1791 battle come at the relative end of three centuries of white man-red man conflict. The Meuse-Argonne, on the other hand, was full of drama—Montfaucon, the Côte de Châtillon, the Lost Battalion, Sergeant York, to name only a few examples—and flooded with personalities—Patton, MacArthur, Rickenbacker, Woodfill, Whittlesey. And it achieved a breakthrough—at heartbreaking cost—on a static front that had been paralyzed by blood and mud for almost four years.

And for two decades the Meuse-Argonne was everything that Gettysburg has always been and that Midway, Guadalcanal and Normandy have since become—battles recognizable and recalled by many, if not most, citizens. In the 1920s and 1930s monuments, memorials, parades and other public events marked the anniversaries of the Argonne and kept the slaughter and sacrifice formidable in our collective memory.

What loosened the hold of the Argonne on America's remembrance, and ultimately nearly effaced it altogether, was the onset of World War II—a war far greater and more momentous for America than the Great War. Its battles and campaigns, though not as massive and murderous as the Meuse-Argonne, took on an importance far in excess of any Great War engagement. Though the majestic misery of the Somme and Passchendaele for Britain and the Marne and Verdun for France still sears the consciousness of their citizenry generations later, the American memory of the Argonne is obscured by the Ardennes, the Aisne-Marne by Anzio, St. Mihiel by St. Lo.

The shelf life of the Meuse-Argonne memorialization—in granite, in print, on film—lasted less than a quarter of a century. The 1941 Gary Cooper dramatization of Sergeant York probably marks the end of the Argonne's run as America's most famous battle. Had America's greatest foreign war—World War II—not occurred, America's greatest battle—the Meuse-Argonne—would still be its most recalled and its most celebrated. Timing, not time—for our Civil War battles are much further back in time than the Argonne, but much fresher in our memory—is everything in our culture and in our capacity to mourn and memorialize.

Though 117,000 Americans died in the Great War—a greater loss than America has sustained in any of its wars other than the Civil War and World War II—the toll, from a population of eighty million, was insignificant in a demographic sense compared to the 1,400,000 French dead from a population of forty-five million, the 750,000 fatalities from the United Kingdom's fifty million, the 1,700,000 from Germany's sixty million. Though there was a significant anti-war faction in the United States, the war did not divide the country along seemingly unbridgeable generational, cultural and ideological fault lines for years—and in many cases, decades—as did the Vietnam War. Though the Jazz Age Twenties caused society to loosen its Nineteenth Century Victorian constraints, America did not undergo a profound shift in its attitudes toward sex, family, authority, government and personal responsibility, as it did following the Gulf of Tonkin and the fall of Saigon.

America was not bled of the best and brightest of a generation in the trenches of the Western Front, as was Britain. America was not fatally weakened morally and militarily, as was France in Artois and Champagne and at Verdun. America was not so corrupted and coarsened by megadeath and disappointment, as was Russia, Germany and Italy, that it would succumb to the temptations of totalitarianism and genocide, as did those nations. Thus, though America had to deal with the personal tragedies of 117,000 burials of its young men, it did not have to face the shattered prospects or the nightmarish future that became the national tragedies of so many of the states of Europe.

Most wars, though weighted with thousands, if not tens of thousands of personal tragedies for the fallen and the families of the fallen, are not national or international tragedies. The long term effects on societies, cultures and governments of all but a minority of armed conflicts are usually minimal. And the tragic impact of a war, though often measured in lives lost, is just as often calculated in the costs to a nation's moral course. The Great War was, of course, a national tragedy for Britain, France, Germany, Italy and Russia, and, thereby, an international tragedy as well. The First World War was not, on the other hand, a national tragedy for the United States, as were the American Civil War and the Vietnam War.

Though the Great War took over twice as many American lives as did the Vietnam War—and most of them in just six months, May to November 1918, compared to the seven years, 1965–72, in which most U.S. casualties in Vietnam occurred—it did not have the profound and long-term impact on American culture, morality and politics as did the Southeast Asian conflict.

Wars are almost always unnecessary and fought for foolish reasons. Wars almost always bring about negative or even disastrous results. Even in the rare cases where bloodshed brings some benefit, that positive outcome could have come about through less destructive devices. Through the two century-plus sweep of U.S. history since independence, only two American wars can truly be said to have been fought for and to have brought about clearly noble purposes—the Civil War, which abolished slavery and preserved the Union, and World War II, which rid the planet of genocidal Nazism and Japanese imperialism (the jury is still out on our current conflicts). In both cases, however, a very strong argument can be made that the conflicts were avoidable had leaders and statesmen shown greater vision and made wiser decisions. It is one of the many great tragedies of the Great War that, no matter how you try to spin it, the cataclysm was unbearably unnecessary and irredeemably evil in both its course and its consequence.

Thus, it can be said that the American boys in blue and the men in olive-drab—regardless of whatever private or public motivations and coercions required them to fight—struggled and died in 1861–65 and 1941–45 to achieve a higher purpose and a greater good for mankind. But the same cannot be said for the Fritzes, Tommies, poilus, doughboys and fanti (Italian infantrymen) of World War I. For the Great War was not like the American Civil War or World War II, but like most wars—unnecessary in outbreak and unspeakable in outcome. And because it was the second bloodiest conflict in human history and because what followed directly from it was the worse century in mankind's story—with its Stalinism, Holocaust, Second World War and Cold War—the sacrifice of the nine million military dead of the First World War can only be considered as the saddest sacrifice in man's time on earth.

But the Great War sacrifices, if not made for grand purposes and productive of great goals, achieved some meaning, at least in a personal sense. Most men's lives are mundane and their deaths are just as prosaic and without significance beyond the sorrows of their families and friends. For the common man, those passed by or unengaged by the great political or historical events of his time, service in armed conflict is often the only opportunity for him to be an active participant in history. For most men who experience it, whatever the hardships and tragedies attendant, war is the great adventure in their lives. And death in warfare thus becomes, for the individual, a historical event—an almost always tiny element in the grand sweep of the story, but still a part of a greater whole. No matter how insignificant a man's prior life might have been, no matter how bereft of interest or accomplishment, a life ended in battle becomes a life weighted with some sliver of significance.

A man succumbing to heart attack or a car wreck may be recognized by a long list of accomplishments in his obituary and may be mourned by long lines at his funeral, but newsprint fades and tears dry. His name will not be preserved in granite on the Vietnam Memorial or on the Menin Gate at Ypres. He will not be granted that special honor of remembrance and memorialization given by communities and nations to warriors fallen in combat. Men whose pre-battle lives were unremarkable become heroes in memory, because their lives concluded with the whine of shrapnel or the clatter of machine-gun fire.

There is, besides, a certain amount of intellectual and emotional sophistry involved in the bemoaning of the young lives cut short by combat's claims. Along with the fact that an actuarial percentage of the war dead would have died anyway—in peacetime—from ill health or ill fortune, exists the other unpleasant truth that not all those lives lost were of—or would have been of—particular value to society or to themselves. Such a politically incorrect pronouncement may seem heavy-handed or even lacking in human feeling, but all the wailing and whining of dreams shattered and promising futures obliterated cannot conceal the downward arc or at least the flat trajectory of many of the lives snuffed out by battle.

Indeed, for those who would have died unnoticed or unmourned by all—except for a handful of family and friends—in their later decades, their premature deaths in combat grant them a kind of absolution from most previous faults and failures. It provides them a sense of a life ended honorably and for a greater purpose, that would have been lacking had they lived out their allotted years as a burden or even a bane to a planet not always—or even often—served well by the human species inhabiting it.

In almost every instance, it is the warrior, not the war, that must be honored. In ninety-nine cases out of every one hundred, war is unwise, unnecessary, and its purposes unrequited. A soldier's odds at serving in a "just war," a "good war," are so steep that whatever honor he might earn is dependent on his conduct, his loyalty to his comrades, and his stalwartness under fire, and not to any association with the bungled and benighted conflict in which he serves.

Such was the sad story for the American doughboy. The causes for which they fought and the consequences of their combat could never measure up to the sense of grandeur and noble self-sacrifice which sparked the fires of their elan. Yes, they had escaped their trite existences, their narrow self-interests, their selfish individualism, but not for something grand and sublime. Those at least who were reflective and honest—either in the flame of immediacy or in the ashes of hindsight—had to concede that, yes, they had escaped the pedestrian and had charged headlong into the monumental; that, yes, they had been a part of something vast in scale and vast in consequence—but that, ultimately, their spirit and sacrifice would pass from this earth, that their blood and bones would not nourish a better world, but only add another layer of dust.

There will, however, always be a "new romance" of war—as there was even after 1918. War's attraction will always hold sway. Even the anti-romantic depictions of war in film and prose create a new, tragic, but still irrepressibly "romantic" image of combat. All the supposedly disillusioning truths about the misery, filth and horror of war still render war a kind of solemn sublimity, still paints the face of battle with a horrible beauty. If the Great War could not kill the allure of battle, nothing can.

Only the soldier at the sharp end of combat can escape—for a time at least—the romance of war. Only he can see through the grand scope and the awesome spectacle of destruction to the reality of war as a filthy, monotonous grind, spiced with moments of terror and flavored with gore and ghastliness. But even the combat soldier, more often than not—as time tempers the truth and his grunt's eye view becomes a veteran's nostalgic hindsight—is recaptured by the romance of war. Those moments of madness and months of mud become, with time and tale, the touchstones of his past.

War, its causes, conduct and consequences, should always be painted in a palette of blood red and the murkiest of grays, and never ever in black and white. But war is so often romanticized because war *is* romantic. Truly indeed, war is the essence of evil, tempered only by tedium. But it is also the grandest game played by a human species made schizophrenic by the lure of the light and the tug of darkness. No matter how ghastly the reality in detail on the human scale, war in the abstract, in the full flight of the imagination, awakens and inspires whole societies and can even ennoble the individual, while it plunders the soul.

What other endeavor of the human mind and body calls forth such powerful emotion and colossal effort? What other toil, what other task, does man enter into with such fervent impracticality, such freedom from the proper and the prosaic, such concentrated rebellion against the conventions of civilization? Love is never more intense than in time of war because both spring from the same romantic source. Man may look toward the stars, but he sees the blackness between as well.

You walk as a tourist across the green fields of the Meuse Valley into a spring breeze and try, but fail, to imagine what it must have been like to struggle through this same terrain, churned the color and consistency of feces, into a steel gale of sound and fury. Perhaps it is best that some cosmic cloth seems to have wiped clean the slate bearing most memories of this place. Perhaps it is for the better that neither classroom nor culture cares to recall what happened here.

After all, what did the men wearing khaki and mud in that final fall of the Great War construct but another in the chain of charnel houses rendering men into meat, tossed as a red detritus on a floor slimy with the prospect of an even fouler feast twenty years hence? They had certainly not built a perfect peace or laid the foundations of a global Athens, as their president had sent them there to do.

Often the argument is made that a proper memorial to the fallen of armed conflict is not some stone obelisk, but a renewed dedication to the cause of peace. But man has rarely served any cause consistently other than that of personal power and acquisition, and the token periods of peace have been but restless truces before a new appeal to arms summons society to man's true calling. Self-centered generations ignore the sacrifices of their more selfless predecessors and lay the groundwork, with their apathy and appetites, for renewed armed conflict. No matter how horrendous the experience, no matter how staggering the statistics, the race of man—seemingly disabled by a genetic blindspot—will shake loose the shackles of history and plunge headlong into another bout of butchery. We keep singing, "Give Peace a Chance," and then shout, "Remember the Alamo" or chant, "Death to the Infidel." We insist we are going to "study war no more," then always reopen the book of war.

All our lives are measured by mortality. Life is an accumulation of losses and a thin stack of saving graces. We, all of us, as we walk toward the end, carry a great load—heavy luggage filled with remembrance, regrets, remorse—a weight that is both a burden and a ballast, weighing us down even as it allows us to stay afloat.

So it was for the men who died in the Argonne. The tens of thousands of American and German soldiers whose lives were abbreviated by shot and shell in the Battle of the Meuse-Argonne endured deaths that—in the end—were special only in their grimness and circumstance. Their deaths served no pride of purpose and were incurred for cloudy abstractions that proved either false or unattainable. They died in vast numbers in hideous ways on a tiny piece of the planet in a compressed moment in time.

And that, ultimately, is really all that can be said of their sacrifice. But if we cannot learn any lesson from their mass slaughter or avoid repeating the same sad story—and, nearly a hundred years on, we have not and, seemingly, cannot—we can at least respect and honor the resolution, the courage, the persistence in the eye of oblivion, demonstrated by so many of those mortal men, as their last hopes foundered and their futures flashed into darkness.

With fearless hearts and bloody steps, the men of the Argonne had hastened headlong into history, and with equal haste have marched away from memory. May this not be their final epitaph.

> None saw their spirits' shadow shake the grass,
> Or stood aside for the half used life to pass
> Out of those doomed nostrils and the doomed mouth,
> When the swift iron burning bee
> Drained the wild honey of their youth.
>
> *from "Dead Man's Dump"*
> Isaac Rosenberg

Chapter Notes

Prologue

1. Richard Baumgartner, "Strong Force Encircled," *Military History* (April 1988), p. 49. Taylor V. Beattie, "Ghosts of the Lost Battalion," *Military History* (August 2002), p. 28.
2. Fletcher Pratt, "To Hold It High," *American Legion Magazine* (February 1940), p. 23.
3. Thomas M. Johnson and Fletcher Pratt, *The Lost Battalion* (New York: Bobbs-Merrill, 1938), p. 281.
4. *New York Times*, December 9, 1921. Whittlesey Papers, from the Charles White Whittlesey Collection, Box 1, Folder 1.
5. *New York Times Magazine*, January 1938. Whittlesey Papers, Box 1, Folder 1.
6. John Toland, *No Man's Land: 1918—The Last Year of the Great War* (Garden City, N.Y.: Doubleday, 1980), p. 449.
7. Whittlesey Papers, Box 1, Folder 3, Whittlesey letter to John Pruyn, undated, (found aboard S.S. *Toloa*).
8. Whittlesey Papers, Box 1, Folder 3, Whittlesey letter to Max Berking, October 13, 1918.
9. Whittlesey Papers, Box 1, Folder 3, Whittlesey letter to Major Lewis M. Scott, 1/308th Infantry, August 12, 1921.
10. *New York Times*, December 1, 1921.
11. *New York Sun*, November 22, 1918, Whittlesey Papers, Box 1, Folder 1.
12. Ibid.
13. Ibid.
14. *Syracuse Post-Standard*, January 12, 1919, Whittlesey Papers, Box 1, Folder 1.
15. *New York Sun*, December 16, 1918, Whittlesey Papers, Box 1, Folder 1.
16. Ibid.
17. Ibid. Byron Farwell, *Over There: The United States in the Great War, 1917–1918* (New York: W.W. Norton, 1999), p. 314.
18. Baumgartner, p. 49.
19. *New York Times*, November 30, 1921.
20. Whittlesey Papers, Box 1, Folder 1.
21. *New York Times*, December 1, 1921.

Chapter 2

1. Pratt, p. 23.
2. Ibid, p. 54.
3. Ibid.
4. Ibid, p. 23.
5. Ibid.
6. Johnson and Pratt, p. 128.
7. Laurence Stallings, *The Doughboys: The Story of the AEF, 1917–18* (New York: Harper and Rowe, 1963), p. 199.
8. Ibid, p. 200.
9. Irving Werstein, *The Lost Battalion* (New York: W.W. Norton, 1966), p. 29.
10. Pratt, p. 54.
11. Ibid.
12. Ibid.
13. John J. Pershing, *My Experiences in the World War, Vol. 1* (New York: Frederick A. Stokes, 1931), p. 17; Henry J. Reilly, *Americans All: The Rainbow at War* (Columbus, Ohio, 1936), p. 26.
14. Maj.General James G. Harbord, *The American Army in France 1917–1919* (Boston: Little, Brown, 1936), p. 444.
15. Ibid, p. 434.
16. Maj.General Robert Lee Bullard, *Personalities and Reminiscences of the War* (Garden City, N.Y.: Doubleday, 1925), p. 251.
17. Robert H. Ferrell, *Five Days in October: The Lost Battalion of World War I* (Columbia: University of Missouri Press, 2005), p.7.
18. Ibid, p. 51.
19. Maj.General Robert Alexander, *Memoirs of the World War* (New York: Macmillan, 1931), p. 107.
20. Ibid.
21. Stallings, p. 198.
22. Bullard, p. 249.
23. Ibid, p. 250.
24. Edward Coffman, *The War to End All Wars: The American Military Experience in World War I* (Madison: University of Wisconsin Press, 1986), p. 45.
25. Gene Smith, *Until the Last Trumpet Sounds: The Life of General of the Armies John J. Pershing* (New York: John Wiley & Sons, 1998), p. 208
26. Ibid.
27. Record Group 200, Pershing Papers, Box 380.
28. Donald Smythe, *Pershing: General of the Armies* (Bloomington: Indiana University Press, 1988), p. 55.
29. Paul F. Braim, *The Test of Battle: The AEF in the Meuse-Argonne Campaign* (Newark: University of Delaware Press, 1987), p. 66.
30. Frank E. Vandiver, *Black Jack: The Life and Times of John J. Pershing, Vol. 2* (Fort Worth: Texas Christian University Press, 1977), p. 950.
31. Rod Paschall, *The Defeat of Imperial Germany 1917–*

1918 (Chapel Hill, N.C.: Algonquin Books of Chapel Hill, 1989), p. 180.
32. Braim, p. 50.
33. Record Group 120, AEF GHQ, G-3 Reports, Box 3152, File 1033/1085, "Notes on the Operation, by Fox Connor."
34. Merion and Susie Harries, *The Last Days of Innocence: America at War 1917-1918* (New York: Random House, 1997), p. 345.
35. Ibid, p. 347.

Chapter 3

1. Harries, p. 352–353.
2. Ibid, p. 353.
3. Record Group 120, IEF GHQ, G-3, Box 3241, I Corps: The Battle of the Argonne.
4. Coffman, p. 300.
5. Harries and Harries p. 349.
6. Coffman, p. 301.
7. Martin Gilbert, *The First World War: A Complete History* (New York: Henry Holt, 1994), pp. 126–127.
8. Barry Gregory, *Argonne 1918: The AEF in France* (New York: Ballantine Books, 1972), p. 86.
9. Gilbert, pp. 465–466. 77th Division Association, *History of the 77th Division* (New York: Crawford, 1919), p. 101.
10. Braim, p. 76.
11. Harries and Harries, p. 351.
12. Private Vernon Nicholls, *Infantry Journal* (September 1919), p. 183.
13. Harries and Harries, p. 354.
14. Ibid.
15. Toland, p. 402
16. Alexander, pp. 175–176.
17. Maj.General Hunter Liggett, *AEF: Ten Years Ago in France* (New York: Dodd, Mead, 1928), pp. 167–168.
18. H. Holger Herwig and Neil M. Heyman, *Biographical Dictionary of World War I* (Westport, Conn.: Greenwood Press, 1982), p. 225.
19. Ibid, p. 226.
20. Ibid.
21. Toland, p. 409.
22. Braim, p. 86.
23. Harries and Harries, p. 356.
24. Stallings, p. 245.
25. Record Group 120, IGO Inspections (5), V Corps, 91st Division, W.H. Johnston statement, September 29, 1918.
26. David McCullough, *Truman* (New York: Simon & Schuster, 1992), p. 129.
27. Gilbert, p. 465.
28. Omar Bradley, *A Soldier's Story* (New York: Henry Holt, 1951), p. 98.
29. Martin Blumenson, ed., *The Patton Papers 1885–1940, Vol. 1* (Boston: Houghton-Mi in, 1972), p. 613.
30. Ibid.
31. Record Group 120, 77th Division, Box 16.
32. W. Kerr Rainsford, *From Upton to the Meuse: With the 307th Infantry* (New York: Appleton, 1920) p. 166.
33. Gilbert, p. 468.
34. John S. D. Eisenhower, *Yanks: The Epic Story of the American Army in World War I* (New York: The Free Press, 2001), p. 221.

35. Robert Bullard, *American Soldiers Also Fought* (New York: Longsmans, Green, 1936), p. 92.
36. Hubert Essame, *The Battle for Europe 1918* (London: Batsford, 1972), p. 169.
37. E.V. Rickenbacker, *Fighting the Flying Circus* (New York: Frederick Stokes, 1919), p. 303.
38. Werstein, p. 44.
39. R.T. Ward, "Study of First Army Situation," (September 29, 1918), in *The U.S. Army in the World War, Vol. 9, General Missions* (Washington, D.C.: Government Printing Office, 1948).
40. Record Group 120, 77th Division, Box 3, Captain N.H. Holderman Monograph, "Operation of the Force Known as the Lost Battalion," 1925, p. 13.
41. Record Group 117, American Battle Monuments Commission, "Epic of the Lost Battalion," Box 237.
42. Record Group 120, 77th Division, Box 15, "Conversation with 'Dakota,'" September 27, 1918.
43. Ibid.
44. Harries and Harries, p. 365.
45. Record Group 120, 79th Division, Box 18, "Report of Operations for 314th Infantry and 158th Infantry Brigade."
46. Harries and Harries, p. 366.
47. Toland, p. 415.
48. Ibid.
49. Record Group 120, First Army, Box 30, W. Howell, "Memo for Chief of Staff,," September 29, 1918.
50. Record Group 120, First Army, Box 3240.
51. Holderman Monograph.
52. Joe McCarthy, "The Lost Battalion," *American Heritage* (October 1977), p. 89. Robert Maddox, "Ordeal of the Lost Battalion," *American History Illustrated* (December 1975), p. 45.

Chapter 4

1. Werstein, p. 57.
2. Record Group 120, 77th Division, Box 16.
3. Alexander, p. 218.
4. Holderman Monograph.
5. Record Group 117, American Battle Monuments Commission, "Epic of the Lost Battalion," Box 237.
6. Holderman Monograph.
7. Werstein, p. 64.
8. W. Kerr Rainsford, *From Utopia to the Meuse with the 307th Infantry* (New York: Appleton, 1920), p.155.
9. Richard Wellmann, *Das I Reserve Korps in der Letzten Schlacht* (Hanover: Edler and Krissche, 1924), p. 150.
10. Lt.Colonel Taylor Beattie, "Ghosts of the Lost Battalion" *Military History* (August 2002), p. 28.
11. Werstein p. 76.
12. Holderman Monograph.
13. Beattie, p. 32.
14. Ibid, p. 31.
15. Wellmann, p. 151.
16. Werstein, p. 83.
17. Holderman Monograph.
18. Ibid. 77th Division Association.
19. Holderman Monograph.
20. Ibid.
21. Johnson and Pratt, p. 56.
22. Holderman Monograph.
23. Johnson and Pratt, p. 62.

24. Record Group 117, American Battle Monuments Commission File, Box 237, "Epic of the Lost Battalion."
25. Johnson and Pratt, p. 78.
26. Ibid, p. 79.
27. Werstein, p. 101.
28. Ibid, p. 104.
29. Johnson and Pratt, p. 89.
30. Werstein, p. 106.
31. Record Group 120, 77th Division, Box 22.
32. Ibid.
33. Stallings, p. 278.
34. Werstein, p. 107.
35. Record Group 120, 77th Division, Box 27, Whittlesey Report.
36. Johnson and Pratt, p. 86.
37. 77th Division Association.
38. Record Group 117, Box 237.
39. Record Group 120, Whittlesey Report.
40. Werstein, p. 119.
41. Ibid.
42. 77th Division Association.
43. McCarthy, p. 90.
44. Record Group 120, 77th Division, Box 22.
45. Ibid.
46. Record Group 120, Whittlesey Report.
47. Werstein, p. 123.
48. Ibid, p. 124.
49. Ibid, p. 126.
50. Johnson and Pratt, p. 115.
51. Werstein, p. 128.
52. Baumgartner, p. 45.
53. McCarthy, p. 88.
54. Johnson and Pratt, p. 309.
55. Record Group 120, 77th Division, Box 9.
56. Werstein, p. 135.
57. Record Group 120, 77th Division, Box 22.
58. Toland, p. 445.
59. 77th Division Association.
60. McCarthy, p. 90.
61. Werstein, p. 138.
62. Johnson and Pratt, p. 133.
63. Record Group 120, 77th Division, Whittlesey Report.
64. William Matthews and Dixon Wector, *Our Soldiers Speak* (Boston: Little, Brown, 1943), p. 306.
65. Record Group 120, Box 9.
66. Record Group 117, Box 237.
67. Werstein, p. 140.
68. James M. Merrill, *Uncommon Valor* (New York: Rand McNally, 1964), p. 330.
69. Ferrell, p. 36.
70. Werstein, p. 145.
71. Ibid.
72. Ibid.
73. Johnson and Pratt, p. 124.
74. Werstein, p.148.
75. Ibid, pp. 148–149.
76. Baumgartner, p. 46.
77. McCarthy, p. 91.
78. Toland, p. 445.
79. Holderman Monograph.
80. Record Group 120, 77th Division, Box 22.
81. Coffman, pp. 321–322.
82. Braim, p. 112.
83. Werstein, p. 79.
84. Ibid, p. 156.
85. Ibid, p. 158.
86. Toland, p. 446.
87. Holderman Monograph; Ferrell p. 91–93.
88. Record Group 120, 77th Division, Box 3.
89. Ibid; Holderman Monograph.
90. Ibid.
91. Ferrell, p. 92.
92. 77th Division Association.
93. Wellmann, p. 171.
94. Ibid, p. 174.
95. Johnson and Pratt, p. 188.
96. James Halles, *Doughboy War: The AEF in World War I* (Boulder, Colorado: Lynne Reiner, 2000), p.260.
97. Wellmann, p. 176.
98. L.C. McCollum, *History and Rhymes of the Lost Battalion* (Columbus, Ohio: L.C. McCollum Co., 1929), p. 66.
99. Stallings, p. 272.
100. Werstein, p. 178.
101. Ibid, p. 179.
102. Record Group 120, Whittlesey Report.
103. Werstein, p. 179.
104. Johnson and Pratt, p. 223.
105. Werstein, p. 179.
106. Record Group 120, Whittlesey Report.
107. Johnson and Pratt, p. 232.
108. Record Group 120, Whittlesey Report.
109. Stallings. p. 274.
110. McCarthy, p. 93.
111. Halles, p. 263.
112. Baumgartner, p. 47.
113. Johnson and Pratt, p. 306.
114. Werstein, p. 186.
115. Toland, p. 447.
116. Hallas, p. 263.
117. Johnson and Pratt, p. 252.
118. Ferrell, p. 66–67.
119. Johnson and Pratt, p. 252.
120. Ibid, p. 253.
121. Ibid, p. 255.
122. Werstein, p. 190.
123. Ferrell, p. vii.
124. Hallas, p. 263.
125. McCarthy, p. 93; Baumgartner, p. 49.
126. Johnson and Pratt, p. 263.
127. Alexander, p. 222.
128. Baumgartner, p. 49.
129. Ferrell, pp. 94–115.
130. L. Wardlaw Miles, *History of the 308th Infantry: 1917–1918* (New York: Putnam, 1927), p. 60.
131. Johnson and Pratt, p. 307.
132. Ibid, p. 308.

Chapter 5

1. John Perry, *Sgt. York: His Life; Legend and Legacy* (Nashville, Tenn.: Broadman and Holman), p. 97.
2. George Larrabee, "Sharpshooter From the Hills," *Military History* (June 1987), p. 57.
3. Taylor Beattie, "In Search of Sgt. York: The Man, the Myth, and the Legend," *Military Heritage* (June 2001), p. 33.
4. Coffman, p. 324.
5. Herwig and Heyman, p. 277.

6. David F. Trask, *The AEF and Coalition Warmaking, 1917–1918* (Lawrence: University of Kansas Press, 1993), p. 130.
7. Ibid; Herwig and Heyman, p. 388.
8. Smythe, p. 208; Thomas Fleming, "Argonne, Paying the Price," *America's Great Battles 1775–2002* (Military History and Military History Quarterly, 2002).
9. Smythe, p. 209.
10. Ibid, p. 204.
11. Coffman, p. 333.
12. Harries and Harries, p. 380.
13. Smythe, p. 204.
14. Braim, p. 122.
15. Ibid.
16. Harries and Harries, p. 390.
17. Coffman, p. 336.
18. Eisenhower, p. 241.
19. Ibid, p. 253.
20. Coffman, p. 211.
21. Harries and Harries, p. 460.
22. Rickenbacker, p. 212.
23. Ezra Brown, *Knights of the Air: The Epic of Flight* (Alexandria, Va.: Time-Life Books, 1980), p. 175.
24. Stephen Longstreet, *The Canvas Falcons: The Story of the Men and Planes of World War I* (New York: World Publishing Co., 1970), p. 256.
25. Harries and Harries, p. 395.
26. Coffman, p. 334.
27. Francis P. Duffy, *Father Duffy's Story* (Garden City, N.Y.: Garden City Publishing Co., 1919), p. 276.
28. John H. Taber, *The Story of the 168th Infantry* (Iowa City: State Historical Society of Iowa, 1925), p. 101.
29. Eisenhower, p. 256.
30. Harries and Harries, p. 397.
31. Ibid, p. 398.
32. Ibid.
33. Smythe, p. 218.
34. Pershing, *My Experiences*, vol. 2, p. 352.
35. Braim, p. 128.
36. Fairfax Downey, *Sound of the Guns: The Story of American Artillery* (New York: David McKay, 1955), p. 233.
37. Coffman, pp. 344–345.
38. Harries and Harries, p. 401.
39. Liggett, *AEF: Ten Years Ago in France*, p. 222.
40. Gilbert, p. 490.
41. Rickenbacker, p. 352.
42. Coffman, p. 346.
43. Smythe, p. 232.
44. Gilbert, p. 501.
45. Braim, p. 137.
46. Smythe, p. 232.
47. Braim, p. 137.
48. Joseph E. Persico, *Eleventh Month, Eleventh Day, Eleventh Hour: Armistice Day 1918* (New York: Random House, 2004), p. 158.

Chapter 6

1. Coffman, p. 249.
2. Ibid.
3. Johnson and Pratt, p. 313.
4. McCollum, p. 85.
5. Johnson and Pratt, p. 305.
6. Ibid, pp. 301–302.
7. Ibid, p. 285.
8. *Stars and Stripes*, November 1918.
9. Johnson and Pratt, pp. 268.
10. Ibid, pp. 277.
11. E. Wardlaw Miles, *History of the 308th Infantry* (New York: Putnam, 1927), p. 243.
12. Record Group 120, 77th Division, Box 3.
13. Ibid.
14. Record Group 120, Whittlesey Report.
15. Record Group 120, 77th Division, Box 3.
16. Record Group 117, American Battle Monuments Commission File, Box 237.
17. Pratt, p. 23.
18. Ibid.
19. Beattie, "Ghosts of the Lost Battalion,," p. 32.
20. Joseph P. Demaree, *History of Company A (308th Infantry) of the Lost Battalion* (New York: George U. Harvey, 1920), pp. 7–8.
21. Charles Wendler, Company A, 308th Infantry, eulogy, Whittlesey Papers.

Chapter 7

1. Michael T. Isenberg, *War on Film: The American Cinema and World War I, 1914–20* (East Brunswick, N.J.: Associated University Presses, 1981), p. 78.
2. Ibid, p. 89.
3. Kevin Brownlow, *The War, the West and the Wilderness* (New York: Alfred Knopf, 1978), p. 178.
4. *Moving Picture World* (November 1919).
5. Smythe, p. 259.

Bibliography

Books

Adamson, Hans C. *Eddie Rickenbacker*. New York: Macmillan, 1996.

Addison, James T. *The Story of the First Gas Regiment*. New York: Houghton-Mi·in, 1919.

Adler, Major Julius Ochs, ed. *History of the 77th Division*. New York: Winthrop, Hollenbeck and Crawford, 1919.

Alexander, Maj. General Robert. *Memories of the World War*. New York: Macmillan, 1931.

Anonymous. *The Cannoneers Have Hairy Ears: A Diary of the Front Lines*. New York: J.H. Sears and Co., 1917.

Arminius (translated by Gerald Griffin). *From Sarajevo to the Rhine: Generals of the Great War*. London: Hutchinson and Co., 1933.

Barbeau, Arthur E., and Florette Henri. *The Unknown Soldiers: Black American Troops in World War I*. Philadelphia: Temple University Press, 1974.

Berry, Henry. *Make the Kaiser Dance*. Garden City, N.Y.: Doubleday, 1978.

Blumenson, Martin, ed. *The Patton Papers 1885-1940. Vol. 1*. Boston: Houghton Mi·in, 1972.

Bowen, Ezra. *Knights of the Air, Epic of Flight*. Alexandria, Va: Time-Life Books, 1980.

Bradley, Omar. *A Soldier's Story*. New York: Henry Holt, 1951.

Braim, Paul F. "Meuse-Argonne Campaign." In Anne C. Venzon, ed., *The United States in the First World War: An Encyclopedia*, pp. 380–86.

____. *The Test of Battle: The AEF in the Meuse-Argonne Campaign*. Newark: University of Delaware, 1987.

____. "U.S. Army: American Expeditionary Force." In Anne C. Venzon, ed., *The United States in the First World War: An Encyclopedia*, pp. 607–16.

Brown, Anthony Cave. *The Last American Hero: Wild Bill Donovan*. New York: Times Books, 1982.

Brown, Ezra, and eds. of Time-Life Books. *Knights of the Air: The Epic of Flight*. Alexandria, VA: Time-Life Books, 1980.

Brownlow, Kevin. *The War, the West and the Wilderness*. New York: Knopf, 1978.

Buchan, John. *A History of the Great War, Vol. IV*. Boston: Houghton Mi·in, 1922.

Bullard, Maj. General Robert Lee. *American Soldiers Also Fought*. New York: Longmans, Green, 1936.

____. *Personalities and Reminiscences of the War*. Garden City, N.Y.: Doubleday, 1925.

Campbell, Craig W. *Reel America and World War I: A Complete Filmography and History of Motion Pictures in the United States, 1914-1920*. Jefferson, N.C.: McFarland, 1985.

Carver, Michael, ed. *The War Lords*. London: Weidenfeld and Nicolson, 1976.

Catlin, Brig. General A.W. *With the Help of a Few Good Marines*. Garden City, N.Y.: Doubleday, 1919.

Coffman, Edward. *The War to End All Wars: The American Military Experience in World War I*. Madison, Wisconsin: University of Wisconsin Press, 1986.

Cooke, James J. *Pershing and His Generals*. Westport, Conn.: Praeger, 1997.

____. *The Rainbow Division in the Great War, 1917-1919*. Westport, Conn.: Praeger, 1994.

Cornebise, Alfred E. *The Stars and Stripes: Doughboy Journalism in World War I*. Westport, Conn.: Greenwood Press, 1984.

Dallas, Gregor. *1918: War and Peace*. New York: Overlook Press, 2000.

Demaree, Joseph P. *History of Company A (308th Infantry) of the Lost Battalion*. New York: George U. Harvey, 1920.

D'Este, Carlo. *Patton: A Genius for War*. New York: Harper Collins, 1995.

Downey, Fairfax. *Sound of the Guns: The Story of American Artillery*. New York: David McKay, 1955.

Duffy, Francis P. *Father Duffy's Story*. New York: George H. Doran Co., 1919.

Eisenhower, John S.D. *Yanks: The Epic Story of the American Army in World War I*. New York: The Free Press, 2001.

Endress, Charles A. "U.S. Army: 77th Division." In Anne C. Venzon, ed., *The United States in the First World War: An Encyclopedia*, pp. 664–67.

Essame, H. *The Battle for Europe 1918*. New York: Charles Scribner's Sons, 1972.

Ettinger, Albert M., and A. Churchill Ettinger. *A Doughboy with the Fighting Sixty-Ninth: A Remembrance of World War I*. New York: White Mane Publishing Co., 1992.

Falls, Cyril. *The Great War 1914–1918*. New York: G.P. Putnam's Sons, 1959.

Ferrell, Robert H. *Five Days in October: The Lost Battalion in World War I*. Colombia, Missouri: University of Missouri Press, 2005.

———. *Woodrow Wilson and World War I 1917–21*. New York: Harper and Row, 1985.

Fleming, Thomas. *The Illusion of Victory: America in World War I*. New York: Basic Books, 2003.

Foss, Michael, ed. *Poetry of the World Wars*. New York: Peter Bedrick Books, 1990.

Franks, Norman L.R., and Russell Guest and Frank W. Bailey. *Bloody April, Black September*. London: Grub Street, 1995.

Freidel, Frank. *Over Here: The Story of American's First Great Overseas Crusade*. Boston: Little Brown, 1964.

Gilbert, Adrian. *World War I in Photos*. London: Orbis Book Pub., 1986.

Gilbert, Martin. *The First World War: A Complete History*. New York: Henry Holt, 1994.

Hallas, James H. *Doughboy War: The AEF in World War I*. Boulder, Colo.: Lynne Reiner, 2000.

———. *Squandered Victory: The American First Army at St. Mihiel*. Westport, Conn.: Praeger, 1995.

Halsey, Francis W. *The Literary Digest History of the World War, Vol. VI*. New York: Funk and Wagnalls, 1919.

Hamby, Alonzo L. *Man of the People: A Life of Harry S. Truman*. New York: Oxford University Press, 1995.

Harbord, Major General James G. *The American Army in France 1917–1919*. Boston: Little, Brown, 1936.

Harries, Merion, and Susan Harries. *The Last Days of Innocence: America at War 1917–1918*. New York: Random House, 1997.

Haythornthwaite, Philip J. *The World War I Sourcebook*. London: Arms and Armour Press, 1992.

Herwig, Holger H., and Neil M. Heyman. *Biographical Dictionary of World War I*. Westport, Conn.: Greenwood Press, 1982.

Heywood, Chester D. *Negro Combat Troops in the World War: The Story of the 371st Infantry*. Worcester, Mass.: Commonwealth Press, 1928.

Hillman, Rolfe. "Blanc Mont Ridge." In Anne C. Venzon, ed., *The United States in the First World War: An Encyclopedia*, pp. 90–4.

Hoffman, Robert C. *I Remember the Last War*. York, Penn.: Strength and Health Publishing Co., 1940.

Holden, Frank A. *War Memoires*. Athens, Ga.: Athens Book Co., 1922.

Hopper, James. *Medals of Honor*. New York: John Day Co., 1929.

Howland, Colonel Harry S. *America in Battle*. Paris: Herbert Clarke, 1920.

Huidekoper, Frederic L. *The History of the 33rd Division AEF, Vol. 2*. Springfield: Illinois State Historical Library, 1921.

Isenberg, Michael T. *War on Film: The American Cinema and World War I, 1914–1941*. East Brunswick, N.J.: Associated University Presses, 1981.

Jackson, Edgar B. *Fall Out to the Right Side of the Road*. Verona, Va.: McClure Press. 1973.

James, D.C. *The Years of MacArthur. Vol. 1*. Boston: Houghton Mi· in, 1970.

Johnson, Hubert C. *Breakthrough! Tactics, Technology, and the Search for Victory on the Western Front in World War I*. Novato, Calif.: Presidio Press, 1994.

Johnson, Thomas M., and Fletcher Pratt. *The Lost Battalion*. Indianapolis and New York: Bobbs-Merrill, 1938.

Jones, Nigel H. *The War Walk: A Journey Along the Western Front*. London: Robert Hale, 1983.

Knapp, Michael J. "Lost Battalion." In Anne C. Venzon, ed., *The United States in the First World War: An Encyclopedia*, pp. 353–54.

Kennedy, David M. *Over Here: The First World War and American Society*. New York: Oxford Press, 1980.

Kurtz, Leonard P. *Beyond No Man's Land*. Buffalo, N.Y.: Foster and Stewart, 1939.

Langer, William L. *Gas and Flame in World War I*. New York: Alfred A. Knopf, 1965.

Lawrence, Joseph. *Fighting Soldier: The AEF in 1918*. Boulder: Colorado Associated University Press, 1985.

Liddell Hart, Captain B.H. *The Real War: 1914–1918*. Boston: Little, Brown, 1930.

———. *Through the Fog of War*. New York: Random House, 1938.

Liggett, Major General Hunter. *AEF: Ten Years Ago in France*. New York: Dodd Mead, 1928.

———. *Commanding an American Army*. Cambridge, Mass.: Riverside Press, 1925.

Little, Arthur W. *From Harlem to the Rhine: The Story of New York's Colored Volunteers*. New York: Covice Friede Pub., 1936.

Longstreet, Stephen. *The Canvas Falcons: The Story of the Men and Planes of World War I*. New York: The World Publishing Co., 1970.

MacArthur, Charles. *War Bugs*. Garden City, N.Y.: Doubleday, 1929.

Mackin, Elton E. *Suddenly We Didn't Want to Die: Memoirs of a World War I Marine*. Novato, Calif.: Presidio Press, 1993.

Manchester, William. *American Caesar: Douglas MacArthur 1880–1964*. Boston: Little, Brown, 1978.

Marshall, George C. *Memoirs of my Services in the World War 1917–18*. Boston: Houghton-Mi· in, 1976.

Marshall, Brig. General S.L.A. *The American Heritage History of World War I.* New York: American Heritage Publishing Company/Bonanza Books, 1982.

Matthews, William, and Dixon Wector. *Our Soldiers Speak.* Boston: Little, Brown, 1943.

McCollum, L.C. "Buck Private." *History and Rhymes of the Lost Battalion.* Columbus, Ohio: L.C. McCollum Co., 1929.

McCullough, David. *Truman.* New York: Simon and Schuster, 1992.

McElroy, John Lee. *War Diary of John Lee McElroy.* University of Kansas Collections, 1919.

McKeogh, Lt. Arthur. *The Victorious 77th Division.* New York: John H. Eggers, 1919.

Mead, Gary. *The Doughboys: America and the First World War.* Woodstock, N.Y.: Overlook Press, 2002.

Merrill, James M. *Uncommon Valor.* Chicago: Rand-McNally, 1964.

Miles, L. Wardlaw. *History of the 308th Infantry, 1917-1919.* New York: Putnam, 1927.

Mitchell, Brig. General William. *Memoirs of World War I.* New York: Random House, 1960.

Morrow, John H. Jr. *The Great War in the Air: Military Aviation from 1909-1921.* Washington: Smithsonian Institute Press, 1993.

Mosier, John. *The Myth of the Great War: A New Military History of World War I.* New York: Harper Collins, 2001.

Mudd, Thomas B.R., comp. *The Yanks Were There: A Chronological and Documentary Review of World War I.* New York: Vantange Press, 1958.

Murrin, James A. *With the 112th in France: A Doughboy's Story of the War.* Philadelphia: J.B. Lippincott, 1919.

Nofi, Albert A. *The Spanish-American War 1898.* Pennsylvania: Combined Books, 1996.

O'Shea, Stephen. *Back to the Front: An Accidental Historian Walks the Trenches of World War I.* New York: Walker and Co., 1997.

Page, Arthur W. *Our 110 Days' Fighting.* Garden City, N.Y.: Doubleday, 1920.

Palmer, Frederick. *Our Greatest Battle.* New York: Dodd, Mead, 1919.

Paschall, Rod. *The Defeat of Imperial Germany 1917-18.* Chapel Hill, N.C: Algonquin Books, 1989.

Peixotte, Ernest. *The American Front.* New York: Charles Scribner's Sons, 1919.

Perisco, Joseph E. *Eleventh Month, Eleventh Day, Eleventh Hour: Armistice Day 1918, World War I and its Violent Climax.* New York: Random House, 2004.

Perret, Geoffrey. *Old Soldiers Never Die: The Life and Legend of Douglas MacArthur.* New York: Random House, 1996.

Perry, John. *Sgt. York: His Life, Legend and Legacy.* Nashville, Tenn.: Broadman and Holdman, 1997.

Pershing, General John J. *My Experiences in the World War.* New York: Fredrick A. Stokes Company, 1931.

Pitt, Barrie. *1918: The Last Act.* New York: W.W. Norton, 1962.

Proctor, H.G. *The Iron Division—National Guard of Pennsylvania—in World War I.* Philadelphia: John C. Winston Co., 1919.

Rainsford, W. Kerr. *From Utopia to the Meuse with the 307th Infantry.* New York: D. Appleton, 1920.

Ranlett, Louis F. *Let's Go: The Story of Army Serial No. 2448602.* Boston: Houghton-Mi· in, 1927.

Reilly, Henry J. *Americans All—The Rainbow at War.* Columbus, Ohio: F.J. Heer Printing Co., 1936.

Rickenbacker, E.V. *Fighting the Flying Circus.* New York: Frederick Stokes, 1919.

Rizzi, Joseph N. *Joe's War: Memoirs of a Doughboy.* Huntington, W. VA: Der Angriff Publishing, 1983.

Rogers, Horatio. *World War I Through My Sights.* San Rafael, Calif.: Presidio Press, 1976.

Rollins, Peter, and John E. O'Connor. *Hollywood's World War I Motion Picture Image.* Bowling Green, Ohio: Bowling Green University Press, 1997.

Roze, Anne. *Fields of Memory: A Testimony to the Great War.* London: Seven Dials, 2000.

Schmitt, Bernadotte E., and Harold C. Vedler. *The World in the Crucible 1914-1919.* New York: Harper and Row, 1984.

Seldes, George. *Witness to a Century.* New York: Ballatine, 1987.

Sheffield, Gary. *Forgotten Victory: The First World War: Myths and Realities.* London: Headline Book Publishing, 2001.

Sherman, Malcom C. *Shock Troops.* New York: Vantage Press, 1961.

Sherwood, Elmer W. *Diary of a Rainbow Veteran.* Terre Haute, Ind.: Moore-Langen Co., 1929.

Sibley, Frank P. *With the Yankee Division in France.* Boston: Little Brown, 1919.

Simonds, Frank H. *History of the World War.* Garden City, N.Y.: Doubleday, 1920.

Smith, Gene. *Until the Last Trumpet Sounds: The Life of General of the Armies John J. Pershing.* New York: John Wiley and Sons, 1998.

Smith, Page. *America Enters the World: A People's History of the Progressive Era and World War I.* New York: McGraw Hill, 1985.

Smith, Robert Barr. *Men at War: True Stories of Heroism and Honor.* New York: Avon Books, 1997.

Smythe, Donald. *Pershing: General of the Armies.* Bloomington: Indiana University Press, 1986.

Stallings, Lawrence. *The Doughboys: The Story of the AEF 1917-18.* New York: Harper and Row, 1963.

Taber, John H. *The Story of the 168th Infantry.* Iowa City: State Historical Society of Iowa, 1925.

Terraine, John. *To Win a War: 1918, the Year of Victory.* Garden City, N.Y.: Doubleday, 1981.

Thomas, Lowell. *Woodfill of the Regulars: A True Story of Adventure, From the Artic to the Argonne.* London: William Heineman, LTD, 1930.

Tiebout, Frank B. *A History of the 305th Infantry.* New York: The 305th Auxiliary, 1919.

The Times History of the War. London: Printing House Square, 1919.
Toland, John. *No Man's Land: 1918–the Last Year of the Great War*. Garden City, N.Y.: Doubleday, 1980.
Tompkin, Raymond. *The Story of the Rainbow Division*. New York: Boni and Liveright, 1919.
Trask, David. *AEF and Coalition Warmaking 1917–18*. Lawrence: University of Kansas Press, 1993.
Truman, Margaret. *Harry S. Truman*. New York: W. Morrow, 1973.
Vandiver, Frank. *Black Jack: The Life and Times of J.J. Pershing*. College Station: Texas A&M Press, 1977.
Van Every, Dale. *The AEF in Battle*. New York: D. Appleton, 1928.
Venzon, Anne C., ed. *The United States in the First World War: An Encyclopedia*. New York: Garland Publishing, 1995.
Viereck, George S., ed. *As They Saw Us*. Garden City, N.Y.: Doubleday, 1929.
Walton, Robert C. *Over There: European Reaction to Americans in World War I*. Itasica, Ill.: F.E. Peacock Pub., 1971.
Weigley, Russell. *The American Way of Warfare: A History of U.S. Military Strategy and Policy*. New York: MacMillan, 1973.
Weintraub, Stanley. *A Stillness Heard Round the World: The End of the Great War: November 1918*. New York: E.P. Dutton, 1985.
Wellmann, Richard. *Das 1. Reserve-Korps in der Letzten Schlact*. Hanover, Germany: Edler and Krasche, 1924.
Westbrook, Stillman F. *Those Eighteen Months: Oct. 9, 1917-Apr. 18, 1919*. Hartford, Conn.: Case, Lockwood and Brainard Co., 1934.
Wilson, Bryant, and Lamar Tooze. *With the 364th Infantry in America, France and Belgium*. New York: Knickerbocker Press, 1919.
Young, Rush S. *Over the Top With the 80th, 1917–1919*. New York: 1933.
Zander, Harry W. *Thirteen Years in Hell*. Boston: Meador Publishing Co., 1933.

Articles

Baldwin, Walter, and Rich Hanser and Hy Stockton. "Alamo of the Argonne." *True Magazine* (December 1960).
Baumgartner, Richard. "Strong Force Encircled." *Military History* (April 1988).
Beattie, Lt. Colonel Taylor. "Ghosts of the Lost Battalion." *Military History* (August 2002).
———. "In Search of Sergeant York: The Man, the Myth, and the Legend." *Military Heritage* (June 2001).
Desch, John. "The Meuse-Argonne Campaign." *Command: Military History, Strategy and Analysis*, Issue 51.
Fleming, Thomas. "Argonne: Paying the Price." *America's Great Battles 1775-2002*, eds. of *Military History* and *Military History Quarterly* (2000).
Fuller, Hurley E. " 'Lost Battalion' of the 77th Division." *Infantry Journal*, No. 28, (June 1926)
Hayes, Richard. "Intelligence." *Military Heritage* (December 2002).
Holman, John. "Lt. Colonel Charles W. Whittlesey: Something About the Leader of the Intrepid 'Lost Battalion.'" *International Military Digest*, Vol. 5, (January 1919)
Huston, James A. "Artilleryman of Destiny." *Military History* (December 1988).
James, Edwin L. "The Battle of the Argonne Forest." *N.Y. Times Current History*, Vol. 9, Part 1, 1918.
Johnson, Thomas M. "The Lost Battalion." *American Magazine*, No. 108, (November 1929).
Kolb, Richard K., and Joe Moran. "Great War Vets Shaped Decades to Come." *VFW* (May 2001).
Larrabee, George. "Sharpshooter From the Hills." *Military History* (June 1987).
Maddox, Robert. "Ordeal of the Lost Battalion." *American History Illustrated* (December 1975).
Martin, Gregory. "German Strategy and Military Assessment of the AEF, 1917–18." *War in History*, Vol. 1 (1994).
McCarthy, Joe. "The Lost Battalion." *American Heritage* (October 1977).
Nenninger, Timothy K. "American Military Effectiveness in the First World War." *Military Effectiveness, Vol. 1: The First World War*, eds. Millett, Alan, and Williamson Murray. Boston: Allen and Unwin, 1988.
Nichols, V.R. "The Lost Battalion." *Infantry Journal* (September 1919).
Schuessler, Raymond. "Cool under Fire." *Military History* (April 1986).
Snow, Richard F. "A Friend in Need." *American Heritage* (October 1977).
Warner, Philip. "America's Offensive: The Argonne." *The Marshall Cavendish Illustrated Encyclopedia of World War I*, Vol. 10, 1918–19. Young, Brigadier Peter, editor-in-chief, London: Marshall Cavendish 1984.
"Whittlesey Death." *New York Times*, November 30 and December 1, 1921.
Williamson, Samuel T. "The Lost Battalion." *New York Times* (September 25, 1938).
Wukovits, John F. "Best-Case Scenario Exceeded." *Military History* (December 1992).

Documents

American Battle Monuments Commission. *Summary of Operations of the 77th Division in the World War*. Washington, D.C.: Government Printing Office, 1944.

Black, Christian, and Henry Hall. *The Fourth Division* (published by the division, 1920).

Center of Military History, U.S. Army. *Order of Battle of the U.S. Land Forces in the World War, Vol. 2: American Expeditionary Forces Divisions*. Washington, D.C.: Government Printing Office, 1988.

_____. *U.S. Army in the World War 1917–1919: Military Operations of the AEF, Vol. 9: Meuse Argonne*. Washington, D.C.: Government Printing Office, 1990.

_____. *U.S. Army in the World War 1917–1919: Military Operations of the AEF, Vol. 12: Pershing's Final Report*. Washington, D.C.: Government Printing Office, 1990.

_____. *U.S. Army in the World War 1917–1919: Military Operations of the AEF, Vol. 19*. Washington, D.C.: Government Printing Office, 1990.

Edmonds, Brig. General Sir James E., and Lt. General R. Maxwell-Hyslop. *Official History of the Great War: Military Operations, France and Belgium, 1918, Vol. 5: The Advance to Victory*. London: His Majesty's Stationary Office, 1947.

Joint War History Commissions of Michigan and Wisconsin. *The 32nd Division in the World War*. 1920.

Ninety-first Division Publishing Committee. *The Story of the 91st Division*. San Mateo, California, 1919.

Official History of the 82nd Division, AEF. Indianapolis: Bobs-Merrill, 1919.

77th Division Association. *History of the 77th Division*. New York: Crawford, 1919.

Society of the First Division. *The History of the First Division*. 1919.

Archives and Manuscripts

Record Group 117—American Battle Monuments Commission File, Box 237, "Epic of the Lost Battalion."

Record Group 120—Records of the American Expeditionary Forces, 1917–1923. National Archives, Washington D.C.

Williams College—Archives and Special Collections. *Charles White Whittlesey (1884–1921) Collection, 1905–1948*.

Holdermann, Captain Nelson. "Operations of the Force Known as 'The Lost Battalion.'" monograph, The Infantry School, Fort Benning, GA., 1925.

John J. Pershing Papers, Record Group 200. Library of Congress, Washington, D.C.

Newspapers and Periodicals
Motion Picture World, 1919
New York Sun, 1918
New York Times, 1918, 1919, 1921
New York Times Magazine, 1928, 1938
Stars and Stripes, 1918
Syracuse Post-Standard, 1919.

Index

Numbers with (p) are pages with photographs. Numbers with (n) shows footnotes on indicated pages

Aire River Valley 52, 54, 59–60, 63, 67–70, 77, 82, 122, 125, 134, 138, 144, 147, 150, 181–182
Aisne-Marne, Battle of the 16, 39–40, 56, 60, 126, 182, 185, 197, 225
Aisne Offensive 40
Aisne River 52, 59, 77, 88, 113, 147
Alamo, Battle of the 3, 21, 128, 211, 229
Alexander, Maj. General Robert 33–35, 57–61, 70–71, 71 (p), 81, 86, 93–94, 105–106, 115–118, 122–123, 126–127, 130, 136, 139, 142–143, 147–148, 151, 154, 159–160, 170, 180–181, 191–192, 199–200, 206–207, 212
Allen, Maj. General Henry T. 47 (p), 167
Allworth, Captain Edward 193
Alris der Kronprinz 55
American Battle Monuments Commission 22, 198, 206–207, 216
American Civil War 1, 3, 19, 61, 197, 216, 225–226
American Expeditionary Forces (AEF) 2, 4, 6, 33, 37, 39, 70, 85–86, 99, 164, 168, 171–174, 198; Allied plans for 39–40, 172–173; American plans for 39–40, 172–173; early battles of 31, 37, 40, 44; in the Meuse-Argonne Campaign 56, 193, 197; Spanish flu in 171–172, 174
American Revolutionary War 1
Amerikanernest 104, 116–117, 119, 125, 135, 140, 147, 154
Amiens, Battle of (Black Day) 39, 42, 57, 175
Anderson, Sergeant Herman 80
Angelo, Private Joseph 69
Antietam, Battle of 1, 224
Anzio, Battle of 1, 225
Apremont 150, 218, 220 (p), 221
Ardennes (the Bulge), Battle of the 1, 22, 216, 221, 224–225
Argonne Forest 14, 85, 128, 162–163, 174, 181, 199–200, 210–212, 214, 222–225, 229; campaigns in 1914–17 17–18, 53; description of 52, 59, 215, 219, 221; German defenses in 60; Lost Battalion in 90–136, 139–159; 77th Division in 57, 70–72, 77–81, 87–89; U.S. capture of the 161, 164–167, 182; visit (author's) to 216–221, 220 (p)
Ariétal 144
Armistice Day 153, 177–178, 192, 194–196, 199, 206, 211, 218
Army Group von Gallwitz 56
Army of the Potomac 196
Arnold, General Henry "Hap" 177
Autry 89, 93, 104–105, 109, 116, 125
Averill, Colonel Nathan K. 31, 35

Baccarat Defensive Sector 30
Bagatelle Pavilion 71–72
Baker, Secretary of War Newton 40, 173, 183
Baldwin, Maj. General Frank 199
Baldwin, Corporal Joseph 134
Baldwin, Sergeant-Major Walter J. 79, 103, 107, 113, 159–160, 203
Bar-le-Duc 48, 128, 154
Barricourt Heights 53–54, 179, 188–189, 191
Bastogne, Battle of 3, 154, 215–216
Bathelemont 30
Baulny 82
Bazoches 32, 36
Beattie, Lt. Colonel Taylor 98–100, 166, 208, 219
Beauregard Farm 138
Bell, Maj. General J. Franklin 28
Bell, Maj. General George 33, 66
Belleau Wood, Battle of 2, 16, 40, 87, 191, 221
Bendheim, Private Lionel 162
Bergasse, Sergeant Herman J. 212
Bethincourt 54, 66
Binarville 79, 87, 106, 118, 127, 143, 218, 221
Blagden, Major Crawford 96, 115, 144
Blanc Mont Ridge, Battle of 87, 191
Bleckley, Lieutenant Erwin R. 140

Bliss, General Tasker 172
Bois de Bourgogne 54, 58, 179–180, 182, 188–189
Bois de Chauvignon 86
Bois de Cusy 65
Bois de Fays 137, 187
Bois de Forêt 170, 186–187
Bois de la Grurie 77
Bois de Loges 181–182, 191
Bois de Peut de faux 137
Bois de Pultière 186
Bois de Rappes 186
Bois des Ogons 137
Bonus Army 69
Borne de Cornouiller (Hill 378) 66, 169, 194
Botell, George 145–146
Bradley, General Omar 68, 198
Breckinridge, Captain Lucien 142, 156
Brieulles 66, 189, 193
Briquenay 92, 125
Brooks, Captain Belvidere 9
Brown, Private Cliff 152, 156, 202
Brown, General Preston 137
Buck, Maj. General Beaumont 86
Bud Bagsak, Battle of 38
Buhler, Lieutenant Fred 99, 125
Bulge, Battle of the 1
Bullard, General Robert 32, 34, 36, 58, 61–62, 66, 74, 86, 137, 170, 173, 189, 194, 199
Bunker Hill, Battle of 2
Buzancy 58, 182

Cameron, General George 43, 58, 65, 86, 137, 174
Camp Upton 26–28, 193
Cantigny, Battle of 2, 37, 138, 186
carrier pigeon *see* Cher Ami
Carroll, Sergeant James 114, 155, 162, 203
Cavello, Private Tomasso 112
Cepeglia, Private Philip 120, 139, 157, 160, 202, 212
Chambers, Lieutenant Reed 178
Champ Mahaut 68
Champagne-Marne Offensive 31, 60
Champagne Offensive 87
Champigneulle 191–192

241

Charge of the Light Brigade (Battle of Balaklava) 128, 200, 222
Charlevaux Brook 6–7, 14, 88, 92–93, 95, 98–99, 104–106, 111–112, 114, 116, 122–123, 127–128, 131, 133, 139, 149, 154, 156, 162–164, 199–200, 202–203, 219
Charlevaux Mill 8, 92, 104, 115–116, 128, 201
Charpentry 67, 82
Château de Diable 32
Château Thierry, Battle of 60, 191
Châtel Chéhéry 139, 150, 194
Chauchat auto-rifle 96, 99, 109, 112, 129, 135, 142–143, 146, 149, 152, 155, 159
Chaudron Farm 138
Chaumont HQ 127, 174, 195
Chemin des Dames, Battle of the 57
Chêne Tondu 68, 72, 147, 150–151
Cheppy Wood 66, 68
Cher Ami 3, 132–134, 133 (p), 213, 215
Cierges Ridge 82–83
Citadel, Battle of the 181–182
Clemenceau, Georges 37, 83–84, 86, 122, 172–173, 191
Coffman, Edward 219
Collins, Private Shano 113
Compiègne 194
Conner, Lt. Colonel Fox 44
Consenvoye 169
Cooper, Gary 167, 223, 225
Cornay 150
Côte Dame Marie 53, 86, 137, 170, 182–186
Côte de Châtillon, Battle of 3, 53–54, 86, 182–185, 225
Crockett, Davy 3, 222
Cronkhite, Maj. General Adelbert 66
Cullen, Lieutenant William 99, 108, 115, 118, 125, 130–131, 151, 153, 155, 201, 212
Cunel 53, 86, 137–138, 169, 186
Custer, Lt. Colonel George Armstrong 3, 128, 222, 225

Damvillers 176–177, 195
Daniels, Secretary of the Navy Josephus 174
Dannevoux 66
Decauville Railroad 165–166
Degoutte, General Jean 32
Delehanty, Captain Bradley 131
DH-4 airplane 139–140, 145, 148, 188
Dickman, General Joseph 43, 173, 188, 191
Donovan, Colonel William "Wild Bill" 183, 191, 199
The Doughboys (book) 27
Drachen (barrage balloons) 177–178
Drum, General Hugh 51–52, 172, 188

Duncan, Maj. General George B. 33, 86, 150, 166, 182
Dun-sur-Meuse 54, 189, 193, 216, 217 (p)

Eager, Lieutenant Sherman 99
Early, Sergeant Bernard 165–166
Eastman, Max 24
18th Colonial Division (French) 58, 169, 179
80th "Blue Ridge" Division 58, 66, 86, 136–137, 170, 179, 182, 188, 192
81st "Stonewall" Division 194
82nd "All American" Division 19–20, 86, 122, 136–137, 150, 164–166, 169, 179–183, 189
83rd "Ohio" Division 182–183
84th "Lincoln" Division 182–183
89th "Middle West" Division 179, 186, 188–189, 195
11th Grenadier Regiment (German) 52, 74
Ely, General Hanson 186
Epinonville 66
Esne 73 (p)
Esparges 43
Essame, Hubert 74
Etzel Line 54–55
Etzel Stellung 54–55, 77
Exermont 82–83, 134, 137–138

Farncomb, Private Harvey 113
Farnsworth, Maj. General Charles 66, 82
Fein, Private Arthur 114, 157–158
Ferguson, Fred S. 128
Ferme de la Madaleine 83
Ferrell, Robert 134 (n), 157 (n), 162 (n)
Fifth Army (German) 56, 175, 191
5th Bavarian Reserve Division (German) 62, 66
5th Cavalry Division (French) 86, 137, 179
V Corps 42–43, 58–60, 65–66, 74, 84–86, 136–138, 169–170, 174, 179, 182, 188–189, 191–192
5th Guards Division (German) 49, 138
5th Marine "Devil Dogs" Regiment 87, 191
5th "Red Diamond" Division 170, 179, 185–186, 188, 192–193, 216, 217 (p)
15th Bavarian Division (German) 183
15th Colonial Division (French) 58
50th Aero Squadron 127, 130, 139
52nd Division (German) 138
59th Coastal Artillery Regiment 185
First Army (French) 53
First Army (U.S.) 40, 168–169, 171–172, 187–188, 199, 218; casualties of 43, 45, 168, 182–187, 192–193, 195–197; command structure of 40, 172–174; early battles of 31, 40; in Meuse-Argonne Campaign 16, 46, 56, 58, 63, 65–66, 68, 72–73, 81–86, 122, 127, 179–180, 184, 189, 191–194; organization of 42, 173–174; in St. Mihiel Campaign 42–45
1st "Big Red One" Division 19, 56, 82–83, 122, 134, 136–138, 144–145, 147, 149–150, 170, 179, 185, 188–189, 193–195, 197, 199
I Corps 42–43, 58–60, 63, 66, 74–76, 84–86, 122, 136–138, 150, 154, 173, 176, 179, 189, 191–194
1st Gas Regiment 43
1st Guards Division (German) 55, 73, 138, 147
1st Prussian Guards Division (German) 70, 144
I Reserve Korps (German) 92, 104–105, 126, 144–145, 147
First Tank Brigade 3, 43, 49, 68–69
Fismes 32
Fismette 32
Five Days in October (book) 134 (n)
Flammenwerfer (flame thower) 145, 147, 151, 154–155
Fléville 138, 150, 182
Foch, Marshal Ferdinand 11, 37, 42, 57–58, 84, 94, 122, 164, 171–173, 184, 191, 193–194, 206
Forges Wood 66
40th "Sunshine" Division 36
41st Division (German) 185
41st "Sunset" Division 34, 60
42nd "Rainbow" Division 3, 56, 86, 137, 170, 182–185, 188–189, 193–194
45th Reserve Division (German) 125
IV Corps 42–43
Fourteen Points 175, 194
Fourth Army (French) 46, 51, 57–58, 70, 72, 77, 86–88, 93, 113, 179, 189, 193–194, 197
4th "Ivy" Division 30, 32, 58, 66, 86, 136–137, 169–170, 179, 186–188
4th Marine Brigade 87
Franz Ferdinand, Archduke, assassination of 13–14
Freya Stellung 54, 187, 189
Friel, Joe 145–146, 208
Frontiers, Battles of the 2, 30
Fuchs, Lt. General Klaus 40

Gaedeke, Sergeant-Major Ben 80, 134
Gallipoli, Campaign 15
Gallwitz, General Max von 42, 49, 56, 62, 72–73, 174, 180, 193
Gault, Corporal George 133
George, David Lloyd 37
Gettysburg, Battle of 1, 3, 21, 31, 81, 222, 224–225
Giselher Stellung 54, 66, 73, 88, 90, 93, 98, 104, 106, 117, 144, 147, 150

Index

Goettler, Lieutenant Harold E. 140
Göring, Lieutenant Herman 176
Gourard, General Henri 88, 189, 194
Graham, Sergeant Robert 119
Grandpré 59, 147, 162, 189, 203
Grandpré, Battle of 180–182
Grant, Captain Eddie 144
Grant, Captain Farquah H. 5–6
Griffin, Lieutenant Maurice 99, 119, 125, 145, 156, 159
Griffiths, Colonel William 44
Group Argonnen 92, 95, 125, 138, 144
Gunther, Private Henry 195

Haan, Maj. General William 86, 185
Haig, Douglas 37, 86, 122, 173
Harazeé, La 59, 63, 70
Harbord, General James 31, 34
Harrington, Lieutenant Victor 99, 112, 125, 140, 151, 202
Hat-in-the-Ring Squadron 61
Haupt-Widerstands-Linie 98, 104–105, 109–110, 116–117, 150
Hershkowitz, Private Jack 80, 212
Hill 180 150
Hill 182 181
Hill 198 92, 94–98, 103, 109–110, 112–114, 117, 123, 127–128, 142–143, 149, 151, 159, 207
Hill 210 87
Hill 223 150, 165–166
Hill 244 150
Hill 255 170
Hill 272 144, 147
Hindenburg Line 54–55, 137, 179, 194
Hines, Maj. General John 21 (p), 66, 173–174, 186, 188
Hirschkovitz, Private Abraham 34
History and Rymes of the Lost Battalion (book) 211
Hitler, Adolf 13–15, 195
Hodges, Lt. Colonel Courtney 193
Holderman, Captain Nelson 10; in the Pocket 106–108, 111, 113–114, 118, 125, 129–131, 135, 139, 142, 146, 149, 152–156, 160, 207; post–Armistice career of 201–202, 204
Hollingshead, Private Lowell R. 148, 151–154, 203
Hotchkiss machine gun 88, 96, 107–109
Houghton, Colonel Eugene 106, 122, 126–127, 147–148, 150–151, 200
Howell, Colonel Willey 85
Hüchtenbruck, General Freiherr Quadt-Wykradt- 92–93, 104–105, 125–126, 134
Hünicken, Major Manfred 92, 109–110, 116–119, 125–126, 134–135, 141, 154
Hutt, Private 105

Iwo Jima, Battle of 1, 224

Jacobs, Harold D. 128
Jagdgeschwader I "Flying Circus" 176
Joffre, Marshal Joseph 57
Johnson, Brig. General Evan 28, 79, 88–89, 93–94, 106, 115–116, 119, 122–123, 126, 142–144, 143 (p), 148, 181, 199–200
Johnson, Thomas M. 154, 204, 206–207, 211
Johnston, Maj. General William 66, 92
Judd, Private Roland 120
Juvigny 185

Kee, Sergeant Sing 34
Kleist, General Heinrich von 92, 95, 104, 108–109, 125, 138, 140, 144, 181
Knight, Lieutenant Paul 110, 112, 117, 126–127, 162, 202
Korean War 1, 20, 211
Kozikowski, Private Stanislaw 152, 156, 202
Kriegsmarsch plan 192
Kriemhilde Stellung 54–56, 73, 137, 144, 147, 169–170, 175, 179–180, 182, 187
Krotoshinsky, Private Abraham 152, 156–158, 157 (n), 202, 212
Kuhn, Maj. General Joseph E. 64–65, 75

Landres-et-Saint-Georges 182–183, 191
La Palette Hill 72, 93–99, 104–109, 111, 114, 116–117, 122, 125–127, 140, 143, 147, 151, 159, 162
Larney, Private James 98, 132–133, 202–203
Lawrence, T. E. 26
Leak, Lieutenant James 99, 112, 125, 140, 151, 202
Lejeune, Brig. General John 87, 191
Lenehan, Brig. General Michael 183
Leviathan 171
Liddell Hart, Captain B. H. 60, 167
Liggett, Lt. General Hunter 34, 50, 58–61, 61 (p), 63, 66, 74–76, 86, 118, 122, 126, 137, 139, 150, 170, 173–174, 179, 181, 187–189, 194, 199
Little Bighorn, Battle of the 3, 21, 128, 211, 222, 225
Lost Battalion 1, 4, 36–37, 77, 94, 129, 132–134, 136, 204–208, 211; books and movies about 167, 211–216; legacy of 160, 200–203, 210, 222–225; losses of 160, 162, 162 (n); magazine and newspaper stories about 6, 128, 201–203; myths of 128, 154, 164, 202–203, 222–223; in the Pocket 90–123, 125–136, 139–142, 145–159, 218; reunions of 201–202
The Lost Battalion (1938 book) 204, 211
The Lost Battalion (1919 movie) 4, 212–214
The Lost Battalion (2001 movie) 4, 214–216
Ludendorff, General Erich 42, 57, 72, 109, 174–175, 187, 197
Luke, Lieutenant Frank 178
Luneville 49
Lusitania, Sinking of the 26

MacArthur, General Arthur 185
MacArthur, Brig. General Douglas 30, 183, 184 (p), 225; in the Meuse-Argonne 3, 183–185, 194; in St. Mihiel Campaign 50, 183–184
MacManus, Edward E. 212–213
Madeleine Farm 187
Manson, Private Bob 134
March, General Peyton 198
Marne, Second Battle of the 40, 126, 225
Marshall, Colonel George C. 3, 41, 46–48, 47 (p), 59, 62, 179, 195, 198
Marwitz, General Georg von der 56, 189
Maverick, Lieutenant Maury 138
Maxim 08 machine gun 64, 165
Maxim 08/15 machine gun 64, 165
McCloskey, Brig. General Manus 199
McCollum, Lee "Buck Private" 211
McKeogh, Lieutenant Arthur 80, 201
McKinney, Major 157–159
McMahon, Maj. General John 186
McMurtry, Major George 7, 10–11, 88, 164; in the Pocket 90, 95, 103, 105, 108, 115–116, 118, 120, 123, 130–131, 139, 141–142, 149, 153–156, 157, 160; post–Armistice career 200–201, 201 (p), 204, 207–209, 209 (p), 212; pre–Great War career 95
McRae, Maj. General James H. 181, 191
Mead, Lieutenant Kidder 128, 154
Menoher, Maj. General Charles T. 182
Metz 40, 49–50, 56, 183, 194
Meuse-Argonne, Battle of the 1–4, 15–22, 37, 52, 164–165, 170–175, 180, 184, 187–188, 195–198, 216–218, 224–226; air operations in the 175–179, 188, 197; casualties of 2, 6, 15–22, 45, 168–170, 175, 181–182, 185–187, 196–197, 197 (n), 216; German defenses in 53–56; phase one 61–86; phase two 86, 122–123, 136–139, 167–170; phase three 179–187; phase four 189–196; preparation for 46–50, 56–59, 179–180, 187–189
Meuse, Heights of the 40, 43, 51–52, 54, 63, 73, 137, 169–170, 181–182, 194
Meuse Valley 193–196, 216–218,

228; memorials in 17 (p), 22, 217, 217 (p); terrain of 51–53
Mexican War 1
Mézières 58
Michel Line 40, 42
Miles, Captain Wardlaw 35
Miller, Private Henry 112
Minenwerfer mortar 109, 111–113, 117–119, 130, 135, 141–142, 154, 159, 201
Mitchell, Colonel Billy 21 (p), 43, 63, 175–178, 188
Montfaucon 52–54, 58–59, 64–66, 72, 74–75, 75 (p), 78, 83–84, 86, 175, 182, 218
Montfaucon Memorial 17 (p), 22, 218, 219 (p)
Montmedy 62, 188
Montrebeau Wood 82, 138
Montrefagne 138, 144, 147
Morte Homme 66, 79
Moselle River 40, 49, 51, 173–174
Moulin de l'Homme Mort 79
Mudra, General Bruno von 53
Muir, Maj. General Charles H. 59, 68
Mulcahy, Russell 214
Munson, Private John J. 212
Murvaux 178, 193
My Experiences in the World War (memoirs) 169, 198

Newcom, Private George 202
Nicholls, Private Vernon 56
90th "Alamo" Division 167, 179, 186, 188, 195
91st "Wild West" Division 56, 58, 66, 86, 92, 137, 179
92nd "Buffalo" Division 58, 70, 87, 137, 194, 197
93rd Division 87, 197
94th "Hat-in-the-Ring" Aero Squadron 178, 196
Nivelle, General Robert 50, 57
Noon, Lieutenant Alfred R. 99, 149

Oise-Aisne Offensive 32–33, 37
Okinawa, Battle of 1, 16, 21, 193, 224
101st "Screaming Eagles" Airborne Division 20
110 Engineer Regiment 82
117th Reserve Division (German) 62, 81
122nd Regiment (German) 92, 95–96, 116, 140, 144
129th Field Artillery 67, 194
132nd Infantry Regiment 66
152nd Field Artillery Brigade 29
153rd Infantry Brigade 29, 33, 77, 88, 94, 116, 123, 126
154th Infantry Brigade 29, 33, 77, 88–89, 94, 106, 116, 122–123, 126, 142–143, 181
165th Infantry Regiment ("Fighting 69th") 30, 183
Operation Desert Storm 45
Ossuary, the (Verdun) 221

Passchendaele, Battle of 15, 81, 225
Patton, Colonel George S. 3, 43, 63, 68–69, 178, 195, 223, 225
Peabody, Lieutenant Marshall 99, 119–120, 125, 130, 141, 148–149
Pershing, General John J. 2, 6, 16, 21 (p), 33, 94, 134–135, 183–184, 195, 198, 207, 215, 217–218; "Black Jack" 39; character of 38–39, 167, 172, 175, 196, 198–199; early career of 37–39; family of 38–39, 167; in Meuse-Argonne Offensive 46–49, 51, 54–58, 61–63, 72–75, 83–86, 122, 127, 136–138, 143, 168–176, 180, 186–187, 191, 194, 206; in St. Mihiel Offensive 40–45
Pershing, General of the Armies (book) 194
Pétain, Marshal Henri 50, 54, 172–173
pirate gun 153, 181
Plattsburg Movement 26–27
Pocket, the (Argonne Forest) 6, 8, 10, 14, 100 (p), 101 (p), 102 (p), 160, 162–163, 200–202, 204–208, 215–216; day one 90–109; day two 109–122; day three 122–136; day four 139–145; day five 145–149; day six 150–159; visit to 218–221, 220 (p)
Pool, Lieutenant Thomas 107, 113–114, 142, 159, 202
Powers, Private William 108
Pratt, Fletcher 26, 204–208, 211
Prescott, Colonel Austin F. 35
Princip, Gavrilo 13
Prinz, Lieutenant Fritz 151–153
Probst, Private Max 112
Pruyn, J. Bayard 7–8
Pullen, Lt. Colonel Daniel T. 43
Punitive Expedition (Pancho Villa Campaign) 29, 39, 68
Putnam, Lieutenant 127–128, 206

Rainsford, Captain Kerr 71, 96, 115
Ravine aux Pierres 182
Renault tank 43, 68
Resco, Micheline "Michette" 39, 175, 198
Revnes, Lieutenant Maurice 99, 119, 125, 149, 204
Richards, Private Omer 98, 111, 125, 132
Richene Hill 169
Richthofen, Baron Manfred von 176, 199
Rickenbacker, Captain Eddie 3, 61, 76, 76 (p), 178, 192, 196, 199, 215, 225
Rockenbach, Brig. General Samuel 68
Rogers, Lieutenant Harry 97, 99, 149
Romagne 182–183, 186
Romagne Cemetery 163, 213, 213 (p), 216–218

Romagne Heights 53–54, 86, 137–138, 169–170, 182–183
Rommel, Lieutenant Erwin 53
Roosevelt, Theodore 3, 26, 38, 95, 222
Roosevelt, Colonel Theodore, Jr. 193–194
Ross, Major Lloyd 185
Rosson, Private John W. 212
Rough Riders 3, 95, 222

St. Chaumont tank 43
St. Etienne-a-Arnes 87
St. Hubert Pavilion 71
St. Juvin 180–181
St. Mihiel, Battle of 16, 18, 37, 39–47, 50, 55–57, 60, 63, 68–69, 176, 182–184, 225; casualties of 2, 18, 43, 45; preparation for 40–42
St. Quentin, Battle of 56
San Juan Hill, Battle of 3, 38, 95, 222
Sarajevo, Bosnia 13–14, 24
Sarrail, General Maurice 53
Saving Private Ryan (movie) 215–216
Schenck, Lieutenant Gordon 99, 113–114, 129, 130, 135, 152–153, 156
Schneider tank 43, 68
Schroeder, Rick 167, 214–215, 223
Schwetter Line 40
Second Army (French) 51, 72, 197
Second Army (U.S.) 173, 189, 194
2nd "Arrowhead" Division 40, 56, 87, 188–189, 191–192, 195
II Colonial Corps (French) 42, 51, 194, 197
2nd Landwehr Division (German) 60, 69, 92, 165
Sedan 40, 58, 192–194, 196
Sedan-Metz Railroad 54–55, 189
Seicheprey, Battle of 2
Septsarges 187
7th Division 194
7th Field Artillery Regiment 144
7th Reserve Division (German) 62, 73, 81
XVII Corps (French) 51, 58, 63, 66, 169, 179, 194, 197
76th Division 56
76th Reserve Division (German) 92–93, 97, 104, 109, 116, 140
77th "Statue of Liberty" Division 8, 14, 136, 154, 211–212; casualties of 35–36, 160, 162–163, 181, 192–193; in the Meuse-Argonne 6, 52, 57–61, 69–72, 70 (p), 77–81, 86–89, 108, 114–116, 122, 128, 142–145, 149, 151, 179–180, 188, 191–193, 203–204; organization and training 26–30; return to U.S. 192–193; on the Vesle 30–37, 202; WWII service of 193
78th "Lighting" Division 179, 181–182, 188–189, 191

79th "Liberty" Division 49, 58–59, 64–66, 75, 83, 86, 169, 194–195
Shepard, Private Arthur 129
6th Division 187–188
XVI Corps (German) 53
16th Infantry Regiment 138
Smith, Lt. Colonel Frederick E. 35, 79–80
Smythe, Donald 194
Soissons, Battle of 2, 16, 31, 138, 182, 191
Somme, Battle of the 2, 15, 18, 50, 81, 225
Sommepy 87
Souilly 65, 195
Spanish American War 20
Spanish flu 171–172, 174
square division (U.S.) 19, 28–29
Stacy, Colonel Cromwell 28, 88–89, 93–95, 103, 111, 115, 122, 126–127, 131, 142, 200, 207
Stadie, Captain Herman 34
Stalingrad, Battle of 50
Stallings, Lawrence 27
Stenay 176, 195
Stokes and Stokes-Newton mortar 28, 63, 65, 71, 88, 108, 138
Stonne 58
Stosstruppen (shock troops) 125–126, 145, 147, 151
Stowers, Private Freddie 87
Stromee, Captain Leo 99, 119, 125, 201–202
Summerall, Maj. General Charles 21 (p), 138, 170, 174, 184, 188, 194
Summers, Private Alfred 155
Swindler, Major Henry O. 206
Sybel, Hauptmann von 104, 109, 116, 140

Taber, Private John 183
Taylor, Lieutenant John 159
Teichmoeller, Lieutenant J. 111, 157, 203, 206
10th Colonial Division (French) 58, 169
10th (Negro) Cavalry Regiment 38–39
Third Army (French) 53
Third Army (German) 56
III Corps 58, 66, 74–75, 136–137, 169–170, 173–174
3rd "Rock of the Marne" Division 19, 31–32, 40, 56, 86, 136–138, 186–187
30th "Old Hickory" Division 56
32nd "Iron Jaws" Division 86, 136–138, 179, 183, 185–187, 189, 193, 217
33rd "Prairie" Division 66, 86, 136, 169–170, 194
35th "Santa Fe" Division 58–59, 66–68, 82–83, 86, 122, 137–138
36th "Lone Star" Division 87
37th "Buckeye" Division 56, 58, 66, 82–83, 86, 197

37th Division (German) 183
XXXVIII Corps (French) 77, 87
305th Field Artillery 29, 127, 131, 141, 206
305th Infantry Regiment 29, 36, 60–61, 72, 90, 122–123, 126–127
306th Infantry Regiment 29, 60–61, 90, 106, 116, 122–123, 126–127, 147
306th Machine Gun Battalion 29, 88, 92, 96, 99, 107–108, 123, 135, 146, 149, 160, 162 (n)
307th Infantry Regiment 29, 36, 60–61, 70 (p), 90, 92–93, 95–96, 103, 105–108, 114–115, 122–123, 126–127, 129, 147–148, 150–152, 156–160, 162, 203
308th Infantry Regiment 10, 23, 26–27, 29, 36, 60–61, 72, 88–89, 92–100, 97 (p), 106–108, 110–118, 126–127, 130–132, 142, 146–148, 154–156, 202, 204, 211; 1st Battalion 27, 78–81, 88, 90, 92–100, 103, 107, 110–112, 116, 123, 130–131, 136, 160, 162 (n); 2nd Battalion 88, 90, 92–100, 107, 110–112, 116, 123, 130–131, 136, 148, 160, 162 (n); 3rd Battalion 8, 88, 90, 106, 118, 123, 126
313th Infantry Regiment 65, 195
314th Infantry Regiment 65
315th Infantry Regiment 83
327th Infantry Regiment 150
328th Infantry Regiment 150, 164–165
368th Infantry Regiment 58, 70, 87
369th Infantry Regiment 87
371st Infantry Regiment 87
372nd Infantry Regiment 87
Tillman, Lieutenant Richard 148, 150, 157–158
Tollefson, Private Theodore 98
Toloa, S.S. 5–7, 11, 98, 204, 207–209
Trainor, Lieutenant Leo 99
Traub, Maj. General Peter E. 59, 66, 82
Trench of the Bayonets (Verdun) 221
Truman, Captain Harry S. 3, 67–68, 188, 194, 196
Tuilerie Farm 185, 192
26th Infantry Regiment 144, 193–194
26th "Yankee" Division 169, 179, 194
27th Landwehr Regiment (German) 218, 220 (p)
27th "New York" Division 56
28th Infantry Regiment 138, 144
28th "Keystone" Division 31–33, 58–60, 68, 70, 77, 86, 88, 122, 136–139, 150, 169, 194
29th "Blue and Grey" Division 169–170, 179
252nd Infantry Regiment (German) 105, 109, 140, 155

253rd Infantry Regiment (German) 104, 109, 140
254th Infantry Regiment (German) 92–93, 95, 104–105, 109–110, 116–119, 126, 135, 140, 144–147, 151, 155

Unknown Soldier, entombment (1921) 10
Upton, General Emory 28

Varennes 68–69
Vauquois Butte 53, 67
Vaux 40
Verdun, Battle of 15, 40, 50–51, 53, 55, 79, 134, 194, 216, 221, 225–226; casualties of 2, 17–18, 53; visit to sites of 221
Versailles, Treaty of 198
Véry 66
Vesle River, Battle of the 30–37, 70, 126, 130, 202
Vietnam War 1, 20, 211, 216, 221, 225, 227
Vigneulles 43
Vosges Mountains 30, 194, 221

Wabash River, Battle of the 225
Warren, Helen Francis 38–39, 167
Wehner, Lieutenant Joseph 178
Wellmann, General Richard 92–93, 108–109, 125–126, 144–147, 162, 174
Wendler, Private Charles 208
Whiting, Lieutenant [Clinton L.] 208
Whittlesey, Annie 23
Whittlesey, Colonel Charles W. 4, 14, 128, 159–160, 164, 178, 186; character of 27–28, 130, 215–216; death of 5–11, 202–204, 209–210, 223–224; early interest in Socialism 24–25; early life of 23–24, 221; early military career of 26–28; early months in France of 30–31; family of 23; first days in the Argonne 77–81, 87–89; legacy of 167, 209 (p), 222–224; motion picture depiction of 167, 212, 214–216; in the Pocket 90, 92–103, 106–108, 110–120, 123, 125–135, 139–140, 144–146, 148–160, 158 (p); post-Armistice career of 166–167, 200–201, 205 (p), 212; tactical decisions of 98–100, 204–209; on the Vesle 30–31, 35–37
Whittlesey, Elisha 7, 23
Whittlesey, Frank R. 23
Whittlesey, Melzar 7, 23
Whittlesey, Russell 23
Whizz-Bang 30
Wilderness, Battle of the 59, 221
Wilhelm, Lieutenant Karl 99, 107, 110–113, 115–116, 125
Wilhelm Line 40, 42–43
Williams Club 9–10, 208–209, 209 (p)

Williams College 7–9, 23–24, 95, 130, 221
Williamson, Lieutenant Henry 99
Wilson, Woodrow 39, 134, 171–172, 194, 223
Wittenmeyer, Brig. General Edmund C. 88
Woevre Plain 50, 184, 194, 221
Wood, General Leonard 26
Woodfill, Lieutenant Samuel 186, 224–225
World War I 13–15, 20, 195, 214–215, 221, 225–228; statistics of 2, 195, 197, 210, 225–226
World War II 2, 4, 20, 168, 198–199, 214, 216, 225–226

York, Sergeant Alvin 3, 6, 164–167, 165 (p), 178, 186, 215, 223–225
Ypres, Battles of 18, 147, 227